UNDER THREE

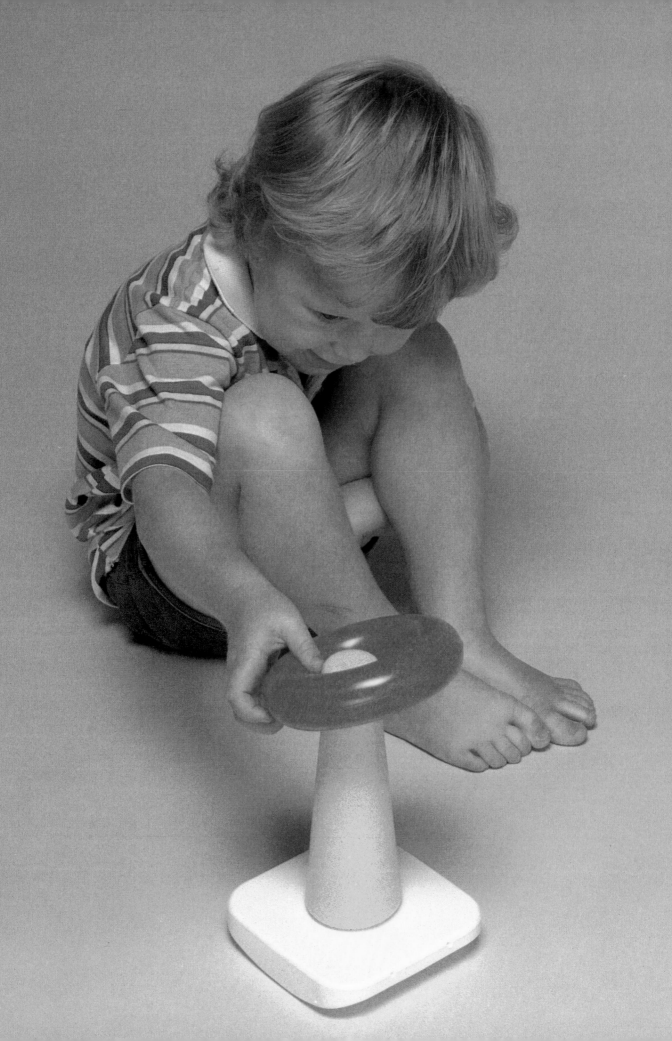

UNDER THREE

A Comprehensive Guide to Caring for Your Baby and Toddler

Edited by
John S. O'Shea, M.D.

VNR Van Nostrand Reinhold Company
_____ New York

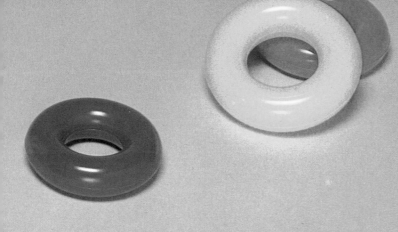

Printed in the United States of America

Designed and illustrated by Eddison/Sadd Editions, 2 Kendall Place, London W1H 3AH

Van Nostrand Reinhold Company Inc.
115 Fifth Avenue
New York, New York 10003

Macmillan of Canada
Division of Canada Publishing Corporation
164 Commander Boulevard
Agincourt, Ontario M1S 3C7, Canada

16 15 14 13 12 11 10 9 8 7 6 5 4 3 2 1

Library of Congress Cataloging in Publication Data
Main entry under title:

Under three.

  Bibliography: p.
  Includes index.
  1. Infants–Care and hygiene. 2. Children–Care and
hygiene. I. O'Shea, John S. [DNLM: 1. Infant Care–
popular works. WS 113 U55]
RJ61.U53 1985 648′.122 84–27023
ISBN 0–442–27247–2

Phototypeset by Bookworm Typesetting, Manchester, England
Origination by Columbia Offset, Singapore
Printed and bound by Kingsport Press, Kingsport, Tennessee

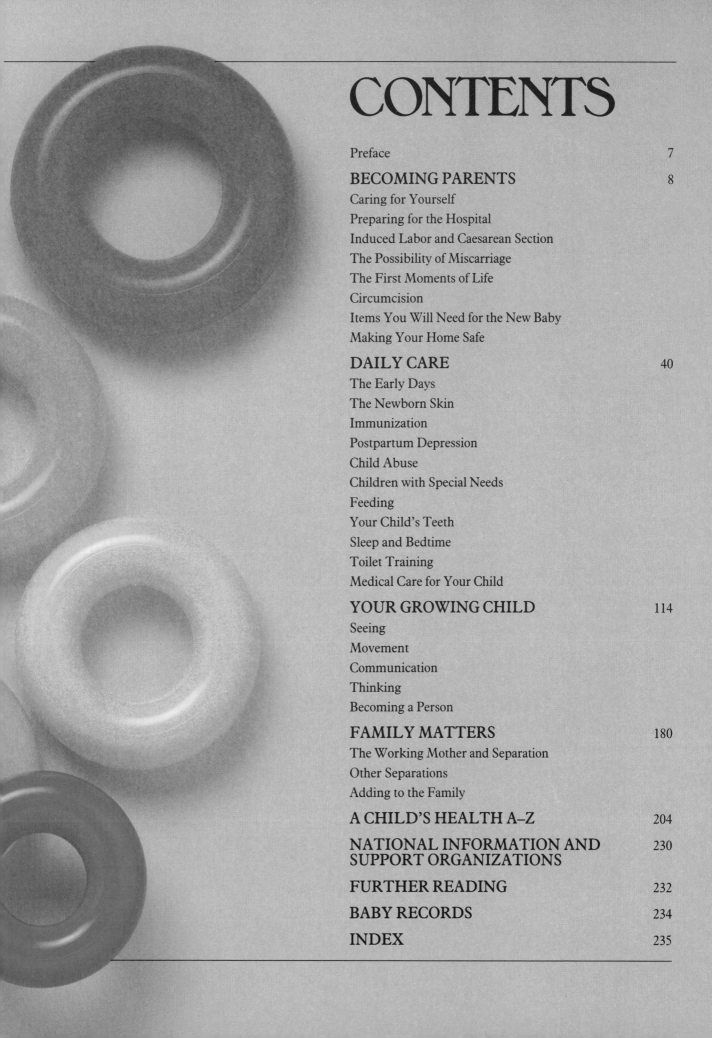

CONTENTS

CONTRIBUTORS

Edward W. Collins, M.D.
Director, Department for Children and Their Families, State of Rhode Island.

Daniel L. Coury, M.D.
Assistant Professor of Pediatrics, College of Medicine, The Ohio State University, Columbus.

Eric Denhoff, M.D.
Late Clinical Professor of Pediatrics, Brown University, and Director, Meeting Street School, Providence.

Penelope Dennehy, M.D.
Division of Infectious Diseases, Rhode Island Hospital; Assistant Professor of Pediatrics, Brown University, Providence.

Louise S. Kiessling, M.D., M.A.
Director of Pediatric Education, The Memorial Hospital, Pawtucket, Rhode Island; Assistant Professor of Pediatrics, Brown University, Providence.

Gary Leske, D.D.S., M.S., M.P.H.
Professor, Department of Children's Dentistry, School of Dental Medicine, State University of New York at Stony Brook.

Daniel Marwil, M.D.
Developmental Pediatrician; Clinical Instructor in Pediatrics, Brown University, Providence.

Lorraine G. McCleary, M.S., R.P.T.
Senior Physical Therapist, Stanford University Hospital, California.

Beverly A. Myers, M.D.
Child Psychiatrist, Psychiatric Specialists, Inc., Providence; Clinical Assistant Professor of Psychiatry and Pediatrics, Brown University, Providence.

John S. O'Shea, M.D.
Director, Division of Ambulatory Pediatrics, Rhode Island Hospital, Providence; Associate Professor of Pediatrics, Brown University, Providence.

Siegfried M. Pueschel, M.D., M.P.H.
Director, Child Development Center, Rhode Island Hospital, Providence; Associate Professor of Pediatrics, Brown University, Providence.

J. Barry Regan, Ed. D.
Director, Hearing and Speech Center, Rhode Island Hospital, Providence; State Consultant in Audiology, Rhode Island Department of Health; Adjunct Professor in Audiology, University of Rhode Island, Kingston; Clinical Assistant Professor of Otolaryngology, Brown University, Providence.

Louis S. Ripa, D.D.S., M.S.
Chairman, Department of Children's Dentistry, School of Dental Medicine, State University of New York at Stony Brook.

Edward Sassaman, M.D.
Director of Developmental Services, Medical West Community Health Group, Inc., Springfield, MA.

Wendy Sue Sassaman
Mother of twins.

Monica J. Schaberg, M.D.
Director, Ambulatory Pediatrics, Roger Williams General Hospital, Providence; Assistant Professor of Pediatrics, Brown University, Providence.

Edwin A. Sumpter, M.D.
Practicing Pediatrician, Roanoke Amaranth Community Health Group, Inc., Weldon, North Carolina; Clinical Professor of Pediatrics, University of North Carolina, Chapel Hill.

Wilson F. Utter, M.D.
Practicing Pediatrician, Providence; Clinical Associate Professor of Pediatrics, Brown University, Providence.

PREFACE

This book is a practical guide to parents of children less than three years old. But unlike most other similar works, it covers both medical and psychosocial topics, each written by a pediatric health care provider with special expertise in that particular area.

Besides the expected discussions of feeding, elimination, sleeping, immunizations, and other medical subjects, attention is given to such important considerations as the interaction between parents and their child, factors to weigh when choosing daycare, and coping with such disruptions in parenting as divorce, serious illness, and death. The last part of the book is devoted to an alphabetical examination of medical concerns selected on the basis of the questions most frequently asked by parents of infants and toddlers.

The editor wishes to thank the contributors for their patience and productivity, and Barbara Ravage and Ruth Wreschner for their help in coordinating the book.

BECOMING PARENTS

Having a baby can be one of the best things that ever happens to you. If you already have children, you know about the work, rewards, and changes a baby brings. If this is your first child, you may be feeling excited but apprehensive about your ability to cope with parenthood. Man and woman, husband and wife become father and mother; couple becomes family, with new responsibilities and fundamental shifts in priorities.

Most parents feel a degree of uncertainty about the new arrival. Parents of several children may wonder if they will be able to give the baby enough care and attention without neglecting the needs of the older children, whose demands may intensify when the baby intrudes on their established routine. But most also find the concerns, worries, and stresses far outweighed by their love for the newborn, pride in their family, and their sense of accomplishment; and most of the changes they encounter are positive, presenting opportunities for sharing, strengthening, and broadening relationships. Indeed, it would be difficult to imagine anything more positive than the reason for these changes—a new life.

Although we all, to varying degrees, have parental instincts, more than instinct is needed to handle the innumerable aspects of child care. At first the task may seem overwhelming, but fathering and mothering are simply skills that must and can be learned.

Pregnancy engages the mother-to-be in a uniquely intimate way, but the father-to-be plays a vital role too—that of providing support and understanding. After the baby arrives, the father can and should take part in her care. It is unreasonable to think that raising a baby is exclusively the mother's job and that the father should enter the picture only when the child is old enough to ride a bicycle or play sports. A father who does not involve himself in his child's upbringing will not only miss out on a great deal of pleasure and discovery, he may never develop quite so close a relationship with his child in later life. Our advice to fathers is this: Hold your baby, cuddle her, carry her around, feed her, change her diapers. You will be surprised at how much fun it is, and you and your partner will share in adjusting to what at first may seem endless unfamiliar tasks and unpredictable interruptions.

In previous generations, families were usually large, and family members tended to stay in one locality. There were few only children. Cousins, aunts, uncles, grandparents, parents, brothers, and sisters formed a family support system that new parents could call upon for advice and help. Parenting skills and knowledge were thus passed from one generation to the next. Today, families tend to be smaller, and family members frequently move away from each other, leaving no comforting relative within reach. To a large extent, their place has been taken by experts—by books, magazines, radio and television programs, and governmental health and advisory services. But research into child care and development has been so intensive in recent years that a parent might well be daunted by the resulting flood of advice and might begin to doubt his or her own ability to cope. If even experts disagree, you may think to yourself, what hope is there for an untried amateur?

Take heart: You will not be an untried amateur for long. Parenting skills can be learned, not only from books and medical advisors, but from friends and from your own observation. Even before your baby's birth, you may be aware that at times she is active and at others she seems to be

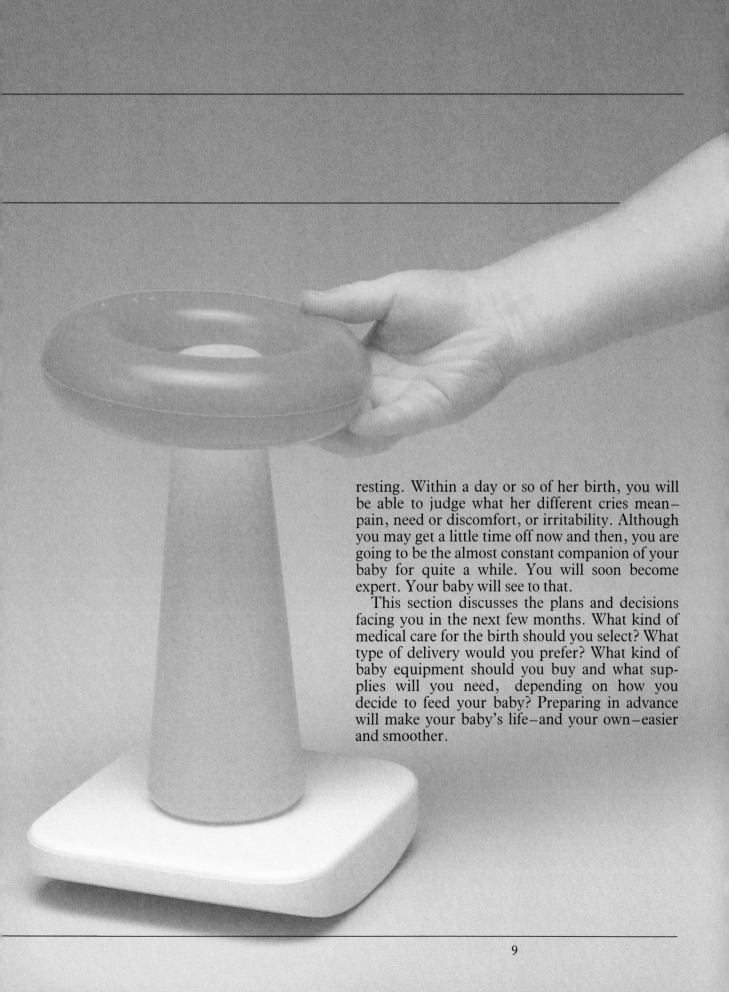

resting. Within a day or so of her birth, you will be able to judge what her different cries mean—pain, need or discomfort, or irritability. Although you may get a little time off now and then, you are going to be the almost constant companion of your baby for quite a while. You will soon become expert. Your baby will see to that.

This section discusses the plans and decisions facing you in the next few months. What kind of medical care for the birth should you select? What type of delivery would you prefer? What kind of baby equipment should you buy and what supplies will you need, depending on how you decide to feed your baby? Preparing in advance will make your baby's life—and your own—easier and smoother.

CARING FOR YOURSELF

The first baby in a family obviously causes the most dramatic changes in his parents' lives. To some extent he bears the brunt of being brought up by novices, but he also benefits from undivided attention and from the sense of novelty he inspires, which more than compensates for the occasional inexpert handling.

A mother learns very quickly what her new status means. Even if you intend to return to work outside the home eventually, you will have several uninterrupted weeks (at least) of daylong physical intimacy with your baby–feeding, cuddling, talking. In today's most usual pattern of employment, this experience is not so certain for the father.

One child development specialist has found a novel way of showing his male students what it is like to care for a baby. With string, he ties a raw egg in its shell to each man's wrist. For a week the student must take the egg everywhere he goes–to meals, to bed, to lectures, to the movies. At the end of the week, the professor asks to see the unbroken egg.

In many respects, fathers-to-be are better off now than in the past. Today's climate of childbearing and child-rearing is geared toward the father's involvement. No longer is it his role–as in the movies and in his father's generation–to pace the floor during labor, endlessly smoking cigarettes. Many expectant fathers now attend childbirth education classes, and a growing number of men, informed and participating, are present at the birth of their children.

Before the baby arrives, you should look realistically at your present life habits and at yourselves–as individuals, as a couple, and as a family. Assess what changes will be necessary, and try to prepare for them in advance. Here are a few suggestions.

If the mother is going to give up work outside the home, have you considered:
whether you can manage living on one income?
taking up a new occupation that could be carried on at home?
making local friends?
finding out what support systems, such as play groups and parent resource networks, are available in your area?

If you share a hobby outside the home at present, have you discussed:
whether you will continue going to it together, leaving your child with a babysitter?
whether the father will go on his own?

Gentle exercise your body is already used to is beneficial in pregnancy. Swimming is a good choice because the buoyancy of the water counteracts the mother-to-be's increased weight.

whether the mother will go on her own?
whether each is reconciled to the decision if you go separately?

If you share domestic jobs at the moment, have you thought about:
whether you will continue to do so?
whether one or both of you will take on fresh responsibilities?
whether the present system needs reorganizing in view of the extra work that will soon be involved?

If vacations have been important in your life together, have you determined:
whether some types of holidays you like may not be possible with a baby?
whether one or both of you might want the same sort of vacation anyway?
how you would feel if one of you went alone?

Anticipating with realism some of these possible changes will make your transition to parenthood a great deal easier.

PREPARING FOR PREGNANCY
Many parents-to-be like to equip their homes before they embark on a family, and this practice is generally applauded as sensible. Until recently, however, parents did not receive very strong urging to prepare themselves for pregnancy by making sure of their own good health before conception.

The baby develops most rapidly in the early stages of pregnancy, and yet a mother-to-be does not usually have her pregnancy confirmed until shortly after she has missed one or even two menstrual periods. By that time, she could be five to ten weeks pregnant; and by twelve weeks, all the organs and parts of her baby's body will have formed. The nourishment the baby receives during those first weeks is thus vital.

An unborn baby receives the nourishment she needs from her mother. It passes from the mother's bloodstream through the umbilical cord, which is attached to the placenta. If the mother is not eating adequately, the baby must draw on the stores already in her mother's body. In some cases these stores are inadequate to keep both mother and baby healthy. The baby will nevertheless continue to draw the full nourishment she needs, even though it leaves the mother depleted. It is not uncommon, for example, for a baby to be born with an adequate level of iron in her blood–drawn from her mother's stores of iron – while her mother has become anemic.

Even among pregnant women who are not economically disadvantaged, instances of malnutrition are surprisingly frequent. Rarely is this due to the high cost of food; more common contributing factors are misguided attempts to diet, rushed and strenuous lives, the habit of snatching junk-food meals of little nutritional value, and inadequate preparation of the food itself.

Women who are seriously undernourished run the risk of giving birth prematurely or to low-weight babies or to babies prone to infection.

EATING ADEQUATELY
The United States Department of Agriculture publishes a recommended daily allowance of nutrients for pregnant women. Many health care providers feel a level even higher than this is needed for an optimal pregnancy. Ask about adequate diet at your first and subsequent prenatal visits. Remember that economics are frequently not the cause of faulty eating habits. In addition to the factors detailed above, the lethargy or nausea many women experience during the early weeks of pregnancy may interfere with a healthy diet. The father-to-be can help enormously by seeing to it that his partner eats a balanced variety of foods each day.

It is not uncommon in the first trimester of pregnancy to experience morning sickness– nausea and even vomiting upon arising. If the nausea is severe, discuss it with your health care provider. Medication may be prescribed to relieve the symptoms, although birth abnormalities have been associated with some antinausea drugs no longer available. A satisfactory alternative for some women is to eat something starchy–a few crackers or a piece of dry toast–before they get out of bed. In any event, the nausea usually passes before the third month is out, and despite the unpleasantness it causes, morning vomiting does not seem to interfere with maternal or fetal nutrition. Frequent small meals will ensure that the daily intake is sufficient.

Three maxims to remember are:
buy fresh foods and use them as soon as possible
do not ruin them by inadequate preparation or (with vegetables) by overcooking in too much water
eat whole-grain breads and cereals

Ask your health care provider about a multivitamin and mineral supplement designed specifically for pregnant and lactating women.

Many women, during pregnancy, have cravings for unusual food. The tendency has never been fully explained, although one theory is that the body is automatically making up for some deficiency. The cravings are not likely to last for the entire pregnancy nor to harm the baby. All the same, mention

The most dramatic changes in a human fetus occur in early pregnancy. By the end of twelve or thirteen weeks, the baby is fully formed. Eight weeks after conception, the baby is about 1¼ inches (30 mm) long but clearly has a human shape. Almost all the major internal organs have formed. During the first thirteen weeks of pregnancy the baby is referred to as an embryo; for the last two trimesters (periods of thirteen weeks), it is called a fetus.

By the end of eight weeks, almost all the internal organs have formed. Hands, fingers, feet, and toes are emerging. The primitive heart has been beating since the twenty-eighth day after fertilization. A rudimentary nervous system is developing and will form the brain and the spinal cord. At five weeks, the embryo measures about 0.08 inches (2 mm). By the sixth week it will have doubled in length. Here it is shown about two and a half times actual size. A face can be discerned on the head, which is large in proportion to the body.

By the end of the twelfth week the fetus is unmistakably that of a human baby. Fingers and toes are still joined by webbing. Leg and arm movements are frequent. The heart is now completely formed and pumps blood around the body and to the placenta. The head is still large in proportion to the body. The fetus shown is one and a half times actual size.

By the end of the fourth week of pregnancy, the embryo would be just visible to the naked eye. Here it is shown about seven times actual size. The cells that will form the baby are rapidly developing, and the head can easily be recognized. At this point, the mother-to-be is about one week past her expected menstrual date.

any peculiar eating habits to your health care provider, who may be able to suggest alternative sources of nourishment.

If you are underweight before you become pregnant, you may be advised to put on a little more than the recommended weight gain during pregnancy; if you are overweight, your health care provider may wish to control your weight gain. *Unless supervised by a medical professional, never try to lose weight while you are pregnant; stop dieting when you stop taking contraceptive measures.*

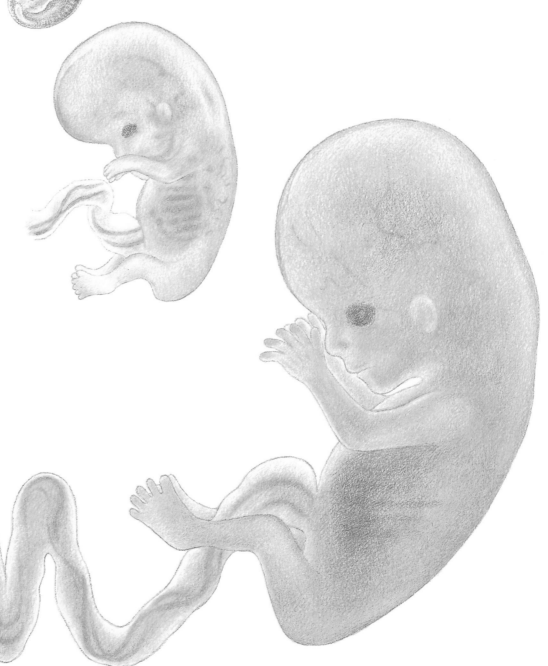

WEIGHT GAIN IN PREGNANCY

Whereas in previous generations specific weight gains were thought to be optimal–usually between 20 and 25 pounds–most health care providers nowadays do not prescribe rigid limits for a woman in good health. Regardless of the actual amount you gain, the percentages should be as indicated.

Most women gain very little weight at the beginning and end of pregnancy; the greatest gains take place during the middle period. The whole gain is put on approximately as follows:

Between 12 and 20 weeks: 25 percent
Between 20 and 30 weeks: 50 percent
Between 30 and 38 weeks: 25 percent

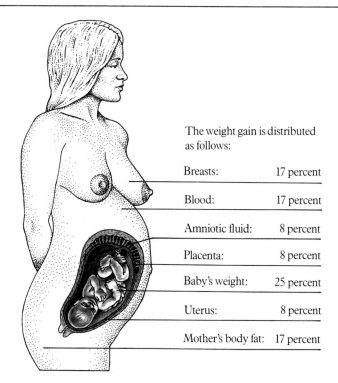

The weight gain is distributed as follows:

Breasts:	17 percent
Blood:	17 percent
Amniotic fluid:	8 percent
Placenta:	8 percent
Baby's weight:	25 percent
Uterus:	8 percent
Mother's body fat:	17 percent

HEALTHY EATING DURING PREGNANCY

During pregnancy it is more important than ever that a balanced diet be followed. Your caloric intake will most likely be increased, but the distribution of those calories among the four basic food groups should remain the same. Even though you may be subject to cravings for particular foods, make an effort not to overload on sweet or fatty foods while neglecting whole grains, fresh vegetables, and sufficient portions of protein.

SELECT EACH DAY FROM EACH OF THE FOLLOWING GROUPS

Vegetables and Fruits (fresh and raw where possible) 4 servings (as indicated) carrots, cauliflower, tomatoes, mushrooms, peas, green beans, turnips, broccoli (½ cup); watercress, sprouts, and other greens (1 cup); apples, oranges and other citrus, pears, bananas, peaches, plums (1 piece)	**Dairy Products** 3 servings (as indicated) lowfat milk and yogurt (8 oz), butter and cream (1 tsp); cheese (1–2 oz)	**Grains** 3 servings whole grain bread (1 slice); whole grain cereals, cooked or dry (1–2 oz); brown rice, pasta, kasha (2–4 oz uncooked weight)	**Animal Protein** 2 servings beef, chicken, lamb, pork, fish (4–6 oz); eggs (1–2) If you follow a vegetarian diet, make up this category with dairy products, legumes, and grains in combinations to provide approximately 75 gram protein.

SELECTION OF MEDICAL CARE

What sort of medical practitioner should you choose to oversee your pregnancy and aid in the delivery? Where do you want to have your baby? Should the birth be natural or drug-assisted? How do you decide on a health care provider for the baby after birth? The choice is ultimately individual, but the details of the many birth care options available today can be bewildering. The basic outline that follows should help.

You may want an obstetrician who is a member of the American College of Obstetricians and Gynecologists and a pediatrician who is a member of the Academy of Pediatrics. This choice, however, would rule out skilled and capable family practitioners and physicians who do not belong to these organizations. In addition, many of the best hospitals and birthing clinics offer birth alternatives, including prenatal care and delivery by capable and caring certified nurse midwives (CNMs)–usually under the supervision of an obstetrician.

Many gynecologists also have obstetrical practices, so your choice of one may include the other. If you have a regular gynecologist who offers a satisfactory obstetrical service, the simplest choice is to continue in his or her care.

Hospitals differ in the delivery suites they have available and in the facilities they offer for the partner or other support people who will be present during the birth. Traditionally a mother-to-be underwent labor in one area, often in a room with several others, and then was moved to another room for delivery. Today many hospitals have completely equipped "birthing rooms" for both labor and delivery. Most hospitals today also permit "rooming in," which means the baby can stay with you all the time if you wish. As well as looking for a hospital with good facilities, monitoring, and neonatalogy, you may want to find one that offers alternatives in these areas.

Obstetricians usually have affiliations with one or more local hospitals. If there are several to choose from, explore the options. Hospitals usually give tours of their maternity floors during which you can ask questions about procedures and practices as well as assess the environment for giving birth. Expectant couples should take these tours before making their final choice.

Choose your pediatrician or family practitioner *before* your baby is born. You will have plenty of other things to do once the baby arrives. Your baby's first scheduled visit will probably be at about four to six weeks of age –though it may be as early as two weeks for a standard weight check, especially if you are breast-feeding.

In addition to investigating a health care provider's medical credentials and reputation among people you trust, ensuring that you have personal rapport is of great importance. You will have a working relationship with your baby's health care provider for some years, so a sense of trust is vital. Your obstetrician or midwife may be able to recommend someone; talking with other parents or with health care providers in other fields may also be useful. You should feel free to interview more than one practitioner before making your choice.

If this is not your first baby, you may already have a health care provider. If you are happy with that relationship, your problem is solved, but be sure to let the practitioner know another customer is on the way. If you are not entirely satisfied, now is the time to make a change.

There is no perfect way to select health care providers, but decide what factors are important to you and make your decision within that framework. Choosing should be done jointly by the two partners.

The checklists provided below are intended to guide you in the selection of medical care for your pregnancy, birth, and the new baby. The answers to some of the more general questions may not be satisfactory, depending on your own feelings and priorities; and you will undoubtedly want to add specific questions that echo your own concerns.

CHOOSING A HOSPITAL
- ☐ Location
- Type
  - ☐ general hospital
  - ☐ maternity hospital only
  - ☐ teaching hospital
  - ☐ medical school affiliation
  - ☐ full-time house staff
- Neonatalogy
  - ☐ full-time staff–i.e., tertiary center
  - ☐ ancillary services available
  - ☐ internal medicine
  - ☐ surgery
  - ☐ other specialists
- ☐ Preregistration requirements
- ☐ Tours of hospital
- Type of delivery facilities
  - ☐ separate labor and delivery areas
  - ☐ birthing suites
  - ☐ association with alternative birth center
- Fathers allowed in labor and delivery room
  - ☐ for vaginal delivery
  - ☐ for Caesarean section
- ☐ Rooming in with the baby allowed
- Visitors
  - ☐ time limits imposed
  - ☐ adult family members allowed
  - ☐ children allowed
  - ☐ anyone allowed

CHOOSING A PRACTITIONER TO MANAGE THE PREGNANCY
- ☐ Credentials
- ☐ Hospital staff appointments
- ☐ Medical school appointments
- ☐ Office location
- ☐ Schedule of visits before and after delivery

Type of practice
- ☐ sole (coverage?)
- ☐ group (will you meet and be examined by any member who may deliver you?)
- ☐ clinic (will you meet and be examined by any member who may deliver you?)

If an M.D., affiliation
- ☐ with nurse practitioner or midwife
- ☐ with alternative birthing center
- ☐ Fees

Referrals
- ☐ from friends
- ☐ from other health care providers
- ☐ Reputation in community

Meeting with practitioner
- ☐ personality, compatibility
- ☐ inspiring confidence

attitude regarding
- ☐ Caesarean section
- ☐ medication
- ☐ amniocentesis
- ☐ other issues

CHOOSING A HEALTH CARE PROVIDER FOR THE BABY
- ☐ Credentials
- ☐ Hospital staff appointments
- ☐ Medical school appointments
- ☐ Office location

Type of practice
- ☐ sole (coverage? someone always on call?)
- ☐ group (will you see same practitioner if possible?)
- ☐ clinic (will you see same practitioner if possible?)
- ☐ Schedule of visits
- ☐ Fees

Referrals
- ☐ from satisfied friends
- ☐ from other health care providers
- ☐ Reputation in community

Meeting with practitioner
- ☐ personality, compatibility
- ☐ inspiring confidence

attitude regarding
- ☐ breastfeeding
- ☐ use of antibiotics
- ☐ other issues

BIRTHING ALTERNATIVES AND CHILDBIRTH EDUCATION

Not so long ago, giving birth meant becoming pregnant, making regular visits to an obstetrician, going to a hospital, receiving a lot of medication and anesthesia, and coming home with a baby. No provision was made for the involvement of the father, and very little was done to dispel for either parent the mystique and fear surrounding an event that should be psychologically strengthening and exciting.

The situation is very different today. Expectant couples now have many choices about all aspects of the experience, and as a result childbirth can be closer to what you think it should be.

Attitudes and practices began to change in the late 1930s when the British obstetrician Grantly Dick-Read published *Childbirth Without Fear*. His theory was that the pain of childbirth is not normal but is a product of tension caused by fear. Dick-Read believed that, by dispelling fear with information and by teaching the ability to relax (thereby releasing tension) during labor and delivery, health educators could significantly reduce pain.

In 1952, the French doctor Fernand Lamaze initiated a method of dealing with labor based on the research of the Russian Poolon. Lamaze's method involves conditioning the brain to respond to stress with breathing exercises. These improve the oxygen supply to the uterine muscles, reducing pain and simultaneously providing distraction from fear.

Further developments of these theories have stressed the importance of support and assistance by the father, who thus shares more fully in the experience. Robert Bradley emphasized the role of the husband as delivery room helper in his book *Husband Coached Childbirth*. Research has confirmed his belief that moral and physical support reduces fear and pain more effectively than drugs and medical personnel. Bradley also stressed the beneficial effect of involving both woman and coach in prenatal visits and childbirth classes (see page 232 for other books on the subject).

Central to all these approaches is what has come to be called "prepared childbirth," in which a couple learns about anatomy and fetal growth and development; physical, emotional, and sexual changes in the mother; minor discomforts and danger signs; the importance of good nutrition, rest, and exercise; basic care of the newborn; and postpartum recovery for both parents. Courses in childbirth education also give intensive training in the delivery exercises—whether those devised by Lamaze, by Bradley, or by a combination of practitioners. These courses are available through maternity hospitals, clinics, and public and private organizations such as local chapters of the Red Cross and "Y" (see addresses on page 230); although most are not directly connected with hospitals, all work in close cooperation with them. Courses vary in

EXERCISING DURING PREGNANCY

These exercises can be continued throughout pregnancy. Gradually increase the number of repetitions until you have reached the maximum number indicated. If you have any doubts about your fitness for these or other exercises, consult your health care provider.

Exercises such as these help keep your body flexible and strengthen arms, shoulders, and torso muscles. Do the sequence once a day at first; then build up to three times a day.

With legs apart, knees straight, and feet flexed up, hold your right foot with your right hand, keeping your torso straight, and lift your left arm above your head.

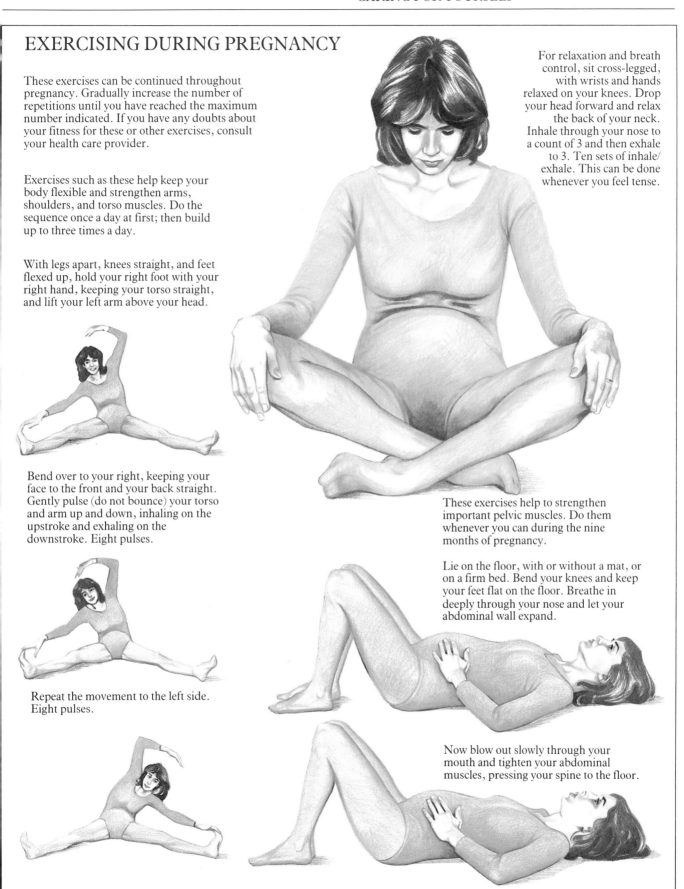

For relaxation and breath control, sit cross-legged, with wrists and hands relaxed on your knees. Drop your head forward and relax the back of your neck. Inhale through your nose to a count of 3 and then exhale to 3. Ten sets of inhale/exhale. This can be done whenever you feel tense.

Bend over to your right, keeping your face to the front and your back straight. Gently pulse (do not bounce) your torso and arm up and down, inhaling on the upstroke and exhaling on the downstroke. Eight pulses.

Repeat the movement to the left side. Eight pulses.

These exercises help to strengthen important pelvic muscles. Do them whenever you can during the nine months of pregnancy.

Lie on the floor, with or without a mat, or on a firm bed. Bend your knees and keep your feet flat on the floor. Breathe in deeply through your nose and let your abdominal wall expand.

Now blow out slowly through your mouth and tighten your abdominal muscles, pressing your spine to the floor.

length from six to twelve weeks, with instruction in the later weeks being devoted to the big event.

Discuss with your health care provider the options available locally. Talk to couples who have recently experienced childbirth. Decide what your needs are as a couple and then select what seems right for you.

Even if this is not your first child, you may feel the need for some review or you may not have been satisfied with the method and circumstances of your last child's birth. Usually childbirth courses concentrate on first-time parents, but refresher courses should also be available in your locality.

DRUG-ASSISTED DELIVERY

So much has been written about what is called "natural" childbirth–delivery without anesthesia or analgesics–that a parent might worry that a delivery in which the mother is given relief from pain through medication is somehow unnatural.

Giving birth is not an endurance test; it is a personal experience. Your choice of type of delivery should be made after you have studied the options and discussed your feelings as a couple. If you decide that the mother should be totally unconscious or given pain-relief medication for the delivery, that is a legitimate personal choice. If you opt for "natural" childbirth and later find that help is needed to withstand the discomfort, you should not feel guilty about that either.

There are advantages and disadvantages to each type of delivery. At present, the medical profession favors using the minimum medication necessary, since the baby will take in medication from the mother's bloodstream until birth, but parents have the right to weigh the risks and advantages for themselves. It is up to you to make the decision after studying the whole subject.

GIVING BIRTH AT HOME

Among the alternatives available today– hospitals, clinics, birthing rooms, alternative birth centers–the home is enjoying new popularity. It is widely held in the medical profession that delivery at home does not make sense today. Most deliveries are uncomplicated, but any one may not be.

For parents concerned that hospital delivery is too "clinical," birthing facilities are available in some hospitals and clinics where the father and possibly other members of the family can be included in a homelike setting. If you wish to explore alternatives, it is essential to consider what facilities are available for immediate help in the event of unexpected complications. No expectant couple should run the risk of tragedy for the baby or mother.

SPECIAL HEALTH CONCERNS DURING PREGNANCY: QUESTIONS AND ANSWERS
What Are the Effects of Smoking During Pregnancy?

Smoking during pregnancy effectively poisons your baby's bloodstream.

Why?
Whether you inhale or not, the nicotine and carbon monoxide in cigarettes pass into your bloodstream and cause the blood vessels in the placenta to constrict. This means that less oxygen and fewer nutrients reach your baby, adversely affecting his heartbeat and respiratory system.

Suppose I continue?
You may still give birth to a good-sized baby, but the overall pattern is that babies born to mothers who smoke weigh less than those born to mothers who do not. (The significance of this difference is unknown at present.) Smoking also reduces the mother's appetite, so she may not eat as well as she should. Smoking in late pregnancy increases the likelihood of premature birth, miscarriage, low birth weight, mental damage to the baby, and hemorrhage in the mother.

How can I stop?
If you are experiencing difficulty kicking the habit, join one of the many support groups dedicated to easing the way. Behavior modification and peer pressure form the basis of most methods. Aversion therapy might be helpful too. If you feel nauseated, think of a cigarette; as the two become associated in your mind, it may stop your wish to smoke. Tell everyone that you are trying to give up the habit, and ask them to encourage you.

Many women find it easier to give up smoking when they are pregnant than at other times. Perhaps they are motivated by the thought that they are ensuring a healthier baby.

What about being in a smoky atmosphere?
It is probably less damaging than smoking yourself, but you will still inhale enough smoke to risk the health of your baby and yourself. If your partner smokes, ask him to give up too. That way you can support each other's efforts.

I can't stop–and I'm a guilty wreck.
Life is hard. Now you are subject to two hazards instead of one. It is false to imagine that smoking is justified by its supposed calming effect–particularly when smoking leads to guilt and a consequent increase in stress and tension. These can affect your

health by raising your blood pressure and increasing your heart rate. Think of other ways besides smoking to relieve tension: eat an apple; take a walk; phone a friend. It is not easy, but constructive support from your partner will help enormously.

The effects of smoking have been conclusively proved to be dangerous to your baby.

What about Drinking?

Heavy drinking, whether regular or occasional, can harm the fetus and should be avoided both when pregnancy is contemplated and during pregnancy.

Can't I drink at all?

Alcohol definitely passes from the mother's bloodstream to the fetus, but opinion is divided about what constitutes a dangerous level of alcohol consumption. In one study, ten single drinks each week increased the mother's risk of bearing a low birthweight baby. Consumption of alcohol has been reported as the cause of various other abnormalities as well.

Suppose I did not know I was pregnant?

A mother-to-be who has had occasional drinks before she knew she was pregnant should not worry that this will affect her baby. It is generally believed that a drink from time to time is not harmful to the fetus. All the same, it is wise to limit drinking to an occasional glass of wine or beer.

What about Drugs and Antibiotics?

The short answer is, "Do not take any." When you stop taking contraceptive measures, flush all the out-of-date drugs in the house down the toilet. Take the rest to your health care provider and ask which, if any, are safe for you to take during this time.

I am already on drugs for a medical condition. What should I do?

Drugs for diabetes, epilepsy, and certain heart conditions may cause difficulties ranging from placental separation to low blood sugar to withdrawal symptoms in the baby. Tell your health care provider you want to become pregnant or think you may be. If the drugs you currently take are unsafe, a safe alternative may be available. In any case, you and your health care provider should seriously weigh the consequences–for mother, for baby–of continuing necessary medication.

What about tranquilizers?

Ask your health care provider before taking any. Some tranquilizers have not been reported to affect the fetus; others are known to do so. Sleeping pills and antinausea drugs may also affect the fetus.

And painkillers?

Again, ask for your health care provider's advice. Present experience indicates that an occasional painkiller such as aspirin or acetominophen does not adversely affect the fetus; but if taken in large quantities, they can cause blood clotting, jaundice, or liver and kidney damage to the fetus. If you are in need of large doses of painkillers, you should be under medical treatment for whatever is causing the symptoms.

And antibiotics?

Penicillin and sulfonamides appear to be harmless, but remind anyone who is treating you that you are taking them and are pregnant. Tetracycline (which can permanently discolor the baby's teeth) should not be taken.

And "recreational" drugs?

"Recreational" drugs, such as cannabis, hallucinogens, and cocaine, should also not be taken during pregnancy. Why risk birth defects or difficulties with pregnancy unnecessarily?

What about X-rays?

Avoid them if possible. Inform your health care provider or dentist that you are or may be pregnant and question whether x-rays are essential.

Vaccinations?

Avoid vaccinations of any kind in the first four months of pregnancy. Vaccination for rubella (German measles) is a particularly serious issue. Because contracting rubella in early pregnancy can result in blindness, deafness, and brain damage to the baby, it is wise before you become pregnant to have a blood test to determine if you are immune– even if you have previously been vaccinated or contracted the disease. If you are not immune, you should be vaccinated and take care not to conceive for three months afterward.

Do not have a rubella vaccination while you are pregnant. If you are pregnant and are not immune, wait until after the birth of your baby to be vaccinated. If you are pregnant and think you may have been exposed to rubella, tell your health care practitioner immediately. If rubella is confirmed early in pregnancy, terminating the pregnancy is an option some may wish to consider.

PREPARING FOR THE HOSPITAL

Few women today go into labor with little knowledge of what lies in store. Most already will have toured the maternity unit where the birth is to take place, will have decided what type of analgesic (if any) to take during labor, and will have attended classes that explain normal birth and some contingency procedures, including episiotomy, Caesarean section, and use of forceps. They will know when to set out for the hospital or clinic, what admission procedure to expect, and the different stages of labor and birth. Ideally, the father-to-be will also have participated in these preliminaries. Thus, when the day at last comes, most couples are more or less prepared.

But before that day arrives, make sure you know the answers to these questions:

How are you getting there? Ambulance, taxi, car–your own or borrowed? If by car, is it working? Does it have enough gas? Do you know the route and the right entrance to the clinic or hospital? Where will you park?

If you have other children, have arrangements been made for their care while the mother is away? Have you arranged for someone to pick them up from school or wherever they may be? If you must leave in the middle of the night, have you arranged for someone to stay with the other children?

Also before that day comes, pack three separate bags: one for the mother, one for the baby, and one for the father.

Here is what might go into the mother's:
four nightgowns, front-opening
bed jacket, dressing gown, and slippers
grooming aids
sanitary napkins (heavy-duty) and elastic belt
nursing bra
outfit to wear home

Extras might be:
writing paper, address book, stamps
stamped birth announcement cards
books, magazines
whatever else makes her feel good–perfume, manicure kit, cosmetics

The baby's going-home kit should include:
receiving blanket
undershirt
diapers
nightgown or stretch suit
hat
outer covering to suit season and climate

And finally, the father will need some items:
a thermos filled with something to drink
a few sandwiches
plenty of change (for pay phones)
a list of phone numbers of friends and relatives

Depending on the length of the labor and the degree of the father's participation:
something to read
a change of clothes

INDUCED LABOR AND CAESAREAN SECTION

Most parents-to-be anticipate an uncomplicated vaginal delivery, and in the majority of cases this expectation is fulfilled. Sometimes, however, complications require that delivery be hastened–by inducing labor with an intravenous drip of a synthetic form of the hormone that controls contraction and dilation of the uterus–or that it be managed with surgical intervention–by Caesarean section.

The need for a Caesarean section is frequently known in advance, allowing the parents to prepare emotionally and practically for a somewhat more complex recovery period. But often the decision is a last-minute matter (though not always an emergency), and parents who are unprepared often experience a degree of fear and disappointment. Educating yourselves about the possibility can help dissipate those feelings.

Twenty years ago, the chance of a Caesarean section on a first delivery was between 1 and 2 percent; for all pregnancies, the incidence was between 5 and 6 percent. Today, the incidence has risen to 10 percent for first deliveries, and to between 15 and 20 percent for subsequent deliveries. Criticism has been leveled at so-called knife-happy doctors, without considering the improved techniques for anticipating health- or even life-threatening conditions before birth. As the number of such deliveries has increased dramatically in recent years, so has the number of women and children who survive.

Ultrasound techniques can ascertain the baby's condition and position even before labor begins. Amniocentesis (the removal of a small sample of the amniotic fluid in which the baby is floating before birth) can be used to detect substances in the fluid that indicate the baby is in danger. External fetal monitoring devices can check and record the baby's heart rate during labor.

A little self-indulgence in pregnancy does no harm as the mother's body prepares for the birth of the baby. Feelings of apprehension and excitement may alternate.

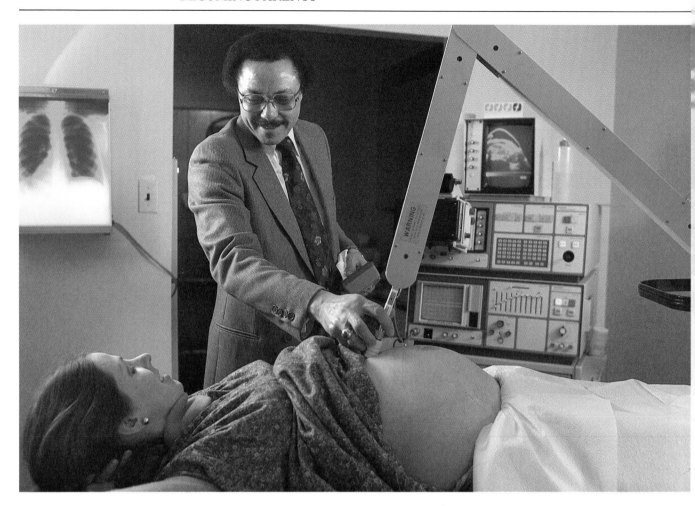

Amniotic fluid is drawn off from the womb for an amniocentesis test. An ultrasound scan shows the technician where the fetus is, to avoid any injury with the needle.

At about sixteen weeks, an ultrasound scan may be given to check the baby's position, health, and size. The scanner is passed over the pregnant woman's abdomen, and sound waves are translated on the screen into a picture of the fetus.

CONDITIONS REQUIRING EITHER INDUCED LABOR OR CAESAREAN DELIVERY

Any sign that delivery should be hastened may also be an indication that Caesarean section is advisable. Some medical practitioners induce labor for a rapid vaginal delivery; others perform an immediate Caesarean.

Among the conditions that could make induced labor or Caesarean birth advisable are:

Diabetes in Pregnancy. The babies of diabetic mothers are usually very large. Diabetes may have been present in the mother before she became pregnant, or it may have developed during pregnancy (gestational diabetes); in either case it is usual to deliver the baby before full term—usually in the thirty-eighth week. Some doctors induce a vaginal delivery, and others choose Caesarean section, but this is unlikely to be a last-minute decision.

Illness of the Mother. The most common illness requiring a speedy delivery is pre-eclamptic toxemia, a serious condition characterized by fluid retention and elevated blood pressure. Depending on the mother's

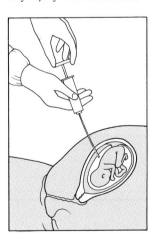

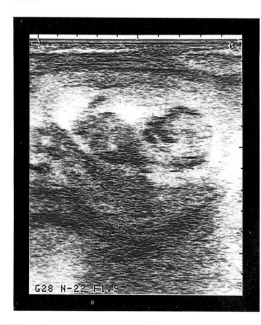

G28 N-22 F1.9

condition, the age of the fetus, and other factors, either a Caesarean will be performed or an early vaginal delivery induced.

Previous Caesarean Delivery. The conventional wisdom used to be, "Once a Caesarean, always a Caesarean"; it was believed that, following a Caesarean, the wall of the abdomen and uterus would never afterward be able to withstand the considerable stresses of labor. Today, unless the condition responsible for the first Caesarean is present in the subsequent pregnancy, many obstetricians will attempt a vaginal delivery. There will be ample opportunity to discuss and plan ahead.

Postmaturity. If the pregnancy is two to three weeks past the expected delivery date and the baby's head is still "floating"–that is, not engaged–or if the cervix is not softening or dilating, tests for fetal distress may be ordered. The tests are not painful to either mother or fetus, but they may be repeated over the course of several days. Their aim is to determine if the baby will be endangered by waiting for labor to begin on its own and whether a successful vaginal delivery can be expected if labor is induced. Depending on the outcome of the tests, the decision will be

to wait, to induce labor for vaginal delivery, or to perform a Caesarean.

Unproductive Labor and Failure of the Cervix to Dilate. If contractions weaken or if they cease altogether for a significant period of time, or if the cervix does not dilate enough, injections of synthetic oxytocin will probably be tried first. If the oxytocin is not effective, a Caesarean section may be recommended. Parents-to-be may not be prepared in advance for this possibility, but most likely they will be able to discuss it with medical personnel when the situation first arises.

Unusual Fetal Presentation. The normal fetal position for birth is head first. If the fetus assumes a position other than this and if attempts to change it fail, vaginal delivery may be difficult or impossible. The most common presentation variation is breech birth, in which the baby arrives bottom first. This occurs in 3 percent of all pregnancies. Many doctors attempt a vaginal delivery; others opt for Caesarean at once. Other positions for which there is no choice but to deliver by Caesarean are feet first, face (rather than head) first, and transverse (the baby is wedged sideways).

Prepared childbirth classes provide the opportunity for both parents-to-be to make friends, discuss feelings and attitudes toward birth, and learn methods of relaxation and baby care. Most important, they learn what to expect of and how best to handle the birth itself. The atmosphere should be informal and should allow plenty of time to ask questions.

BECOMING PARENTS

CONDITIONS REQUIRING CAESAREAN DELIVERY

The following conditions require Caesareans as the only birth choice:

Cephalopelvic Disproportion. This simply means that the head is too big to pass through the mother's pelvic girdle. It does not necessarily imply an unusually large head; the mother may have a small pelvis. Comparative measuring in early pregnancy and throughout the nine months may prepare you in advance for the likelihood of Caesarean delivery for this reason.

Placenta Praevia. In this condition, the placenta is implanted over the cervix, creating an abnormal situation in which the baby's head is prevented from entering the pelvis. It is usually identified before labor begins, so advance planning is possible. Delivery must be by Caesarean, which may be performed at about thirty-eight weeks to reduce the danger of excessive bleeding.

Placenta Abruptio. In this condition, the placenta pulls away from the uterine wall, resulting in hemorrhage and the loss of placental function, which endangers the lives of both mother and child. This is an emergency situation, and a Caesarean must be performed at once.

Genital Herpes. The recent dramatic increase in genital herpetic infection brings increased danger to babies delivered through an infected birth canal. The choice here cannot be optional because of the dangerous risk to the baby of acquiring generalized herpes infection. The medical practitioner and the mother may or may not be aware of the condition in advance. No woman who even suspects she might have herpes should neglect to tell her health care provider so he can watch for active lesions as the due date approaches.

PLANNING AHEAD

In some cases parents will know in advance if their baby is to be delivered by Caesarean, and there may even be a choice. Medical practitioners differ in their assessment of the necessity, so any couple choosing a practitioner should ascertain his or her views on the subject. If a couple is given a chance to plan ahead for a Caesarean, there are several points to consider.

Some hospitals allow the father to be in the delivery room, others do not. This may significantly influence the selection of a hospital. The choice of anesthesia ranges from general, under which the mother is totally unconscious, to various types that block sensation but allow the mother to remain conscious and aware during the birth.

It is helpful to discuss the procedure, its options, and your own preferences with your health care provider and with other couples who have experienced delivery by Caesarean section.

RECOVERY

In addition to making the emotional and physical adjustment to giving birth, the mother who has undergone a Caesarean must recover from abdominal surgery. A longer hospital stay (six or seven days instead of the two to four days for vaginal deliveries) helps, but more aid is essential once the mother and baby are home. The mother's physical activities must be restricted, so family and friends need to pitch in. Whether you rely on this or are able to hire help, make sure everyone understands the importance of helping with housework, cooking, shopping, and fielding well-meaning but too lengthy phone calls and visits; the mother's job during convalescence is to enjoy and care for her baby.

THE POSSIBILITY OF MISCARRIAGE

Miscarriages happen most commonly in the first three months of pregnancy. Saddening though such an event must inevitably be, miscarriage in the early months usually results from the development of an abnormal fetus–though it may be small comfort to the parents to be told that this is nature's way of preventing the birth of a handicapped baby. The first sign of a threatened miscarriage is usually vaginal bleeding; this may, however, occur without a miscarriage taking place. In any event, you should always report bleeding, no matter how slight, to the health care professional who is managing your pregnancy.

Miscarriage during middle pregnancy– from thirteen to twenty-eight weeks–is much less common and may be due to premature opening of the cervix. If this is threatened or has been experienced in a previous pregnancy, a stitch will sometimes be inserted around the cervix, under general anesthetic, to try to keep the cervix closed until labor begins.

A miscarriage is a bereavement; a period of mourning and grief is a necessary part of the process of coming to terms with the loss. Although friends may suggest quickly becoming pregnant again, few who have experienced miscarriage are consoled by this. Social workers, clergy and lay counselors, and support groups (look in the back of this book under *bereavement*) may provide the greatest help during the mourning period.

24

THE FIRST MOMENTS OF LIFE

Don't be alarmed if your baby does not at first sight look like the ideal baby of the advertisements. At birth she may be covered with vernix, a creamlike coating that has protected her skin during her nine months afloat. Her head may be molded by her journey down a narrow passage; her skull bones are not yet fully joined, which allowed them to overlap as she moves down the birth canal. Her face will probably be puckered, her nose may be squashed, and her skin may be pale and even slightly bluish because of the small amount of blood coming to the skin and the decreased oxygen in that blood.

If it all sounds daunting, do not worry. The vernix will be washed off or will wear off in a few days. Head molding will gradually disappear in the first weeks. And her skin will look pink and healthy within a few hours.

It is now customary in most hospitals for the baby to be put on the mother's stomach or handed to her to cuddle even while she is still attached by the cord. When the cord has stopped pulsating, it will be cut and clamped. The baby will be weighed and may need her respiratory tract sucked free of mucus. She will then be rated according to what is called the Apgar scale: Breathing, heart rate, skin color, muscle tone, and reflex response are observed at one and five minutes after birth and scored according to established criteria. In addition, weight, length and size of head are recorded, a check is made to see that the palate is whole, and the legs are gently bent and circled to make sure there is no dislocation of the hip.

In many hospitals, the mother, father, and baby are then left together for some time to become acquainted. It is widely held that learning to love your baby is strengthened and hastened if these early moments of privacy can be enjoyed. It is natural that you should both want to see and hold your baby rather than have her banished to another room.

Because the importance of this early bonding has been emphasized, some parents may worry if the baby is taken off for attention elsewhere, that the delay may interfere with bonding at a later time. Do not be concerned. There is no clear evidence that delayed bonding interferes with the development of a close and loving relationship between parents and child. Of course it is most desirable to cuddle the baby and welcome her into the world at once, but you will find that you all "bond" very well from the first moment she opens her eyes and you take her into your arms.

CIRCUMCISION

One of the questions you will have to consider if your baby is a boy is whether or not you wish him to be circumcised. If you are uncertain about your feelings, do not wait until after he is born and a consent form is thrust into your hands; discuss the subject now with the health care provider you have chosen for your child.

Is routine circumcision justified? What are its advantages and disadvantages? The main advantage is cleanliness, although under normal conditions an uncircumcised penis is not difficult to keep clean, and a boy can be taught proper hygiene at a relatively early age. Another argument put forth in its favor is that it may be important to some children and adults to look the same as their peers or, perhaps, their fathers. If more parents choose not to circumcise their sons, however, this consideration will becomes less important.

Statistics indicate that cancer of the glans is less common among circumcised men, but this cancer is in any case extremely rare. A rare condition that can be corrected by circumcision is phimosis, in which the opening of the foreskin is so small that urine cannot pass through. It is the only medical circumstance requiring circumcision; other reasons are matters of preference.

Opponents of routine circumcision point out that during the diaper years the foreskin unquestionably protects the glans from inflammation and irritation from urine. Prolonged irritation of the opening at the tip of the penis may lead to scarring and narrowing of the opening; an operation may then be required to enlarge the opening and facilitate the passage of urine.

Another argument against the procedure is that the foreskin is a part of the body and thus should not be removed. With any operation there is a risk of bleeding and infection, and it is possible in this operation to remove too much skin.

If you decide on circumcision, have it done within a few days of birth. Otherwise there will be more pain, or more remembered pain, and anesthesia will be required.

If you have any doubts about having your son circumcised right away, do not have it done. Certainly once circumcision is done, it cannot be undone. You or your son can always choose to have it done later.

ITEMS YOU WILL NEED FOR THE NEW BABY

A new baby means new expenses but the expense decreases as your family grows because so much equipment can be passed on. The first baby in the family is usually a great novelty and attracts many presents, which helps to reduce expenses. A lot of equipment can be bought secondhand or borrowed from friends and relations (see page 31).

You may be tempted to begin buying as soon as you know a baby is on the way, but it is wiser to wait a while. Many of the larger pieces of equipment–such as the crib and the highchair–will not be needed right away, so you could defer buying them. In the meantime, you may change your minds about what would best suit you, or you may find that you can buy or borrow from other families–as well as benefiting from their experiences of what is essential.

Mail order catalogs are a source of endless information. Get two or three and compare their offerings and prices. When you buy, remember that safety, not appearance, matters most. The Consumer Product Safety Commission regulates safety standards for many types of products sold in the United States. (See page 33.) Some items, however, may not be subject to CPSC standards for one reason or another, so it is vital to check for yourselves any areas that might present dangers.

You may simplify planning by thinking of the major areas of need: sleeping, clothing, transporting, and feeding.

FOR SLEEPING
Your new baby could sleep happily in a drawer, a laundry basket, or anything flat-bottomed and draftproof. You will probably want a crib with good bumpers, however. You may prefer to begin with a bassinet or a portable baby basket. Many types are available, including some that fit onto baby carriages and lift off for use indoors.

Regardless of the type of bed you choose, you will also need a properly fitting mattress (see page 34). Add to that three or four fitted sheets, at least two waterproof undersheets (the kind that consists of a piece of rubber sandwiched between two pieces of flannel is best), and one or two lightweight blankets. Do not use a pillow for a young baby; not only is it bad for the baby's posture, it could also cause the baby to suffocate if she were unable to turn her head away.

FOR WEARING
Clothing needs vary with the season and climate, but you should resist the temptation to dress your baby too warmly. She may seem frail, but she does not need to be dressed any more warmly than you. Do not buy too many clothes to begin with; the baby will rapidly grow out of the first sizes, and by then you will have a better sense of what you need.

Start with these:
four to six undershirts (the snap type is easier to put on and take off than the pullover styles)
four to six nightgowns or stretch suits
one or two tops with hoods
some sort of baby bag for sleeping outside or riding in a carriage, stroller, or car
half a dozen plastic pants to ward off leaks if you use cloth diapers (see below)

You may also need:
one or two sweaters
one or two hats (or tops with hoods)
one or two shawls (or use receiving blankets)

Booties and mittens are not necessary if your baby is well wrapped in a blanket or covered in a crib, or if her outer garments are the sort equipped with foot and hand coverings.

Stretch suits should have snaps at the legs so you do not have to undress the baby every time you change her diaper. She can wear the same type of clothes day and night (so long as they are treated to be flameproof, as the law requires for all sleepwear), or you may prefer to use a sleeping bag at night. Nightgowns with drawstring bottoms keep toes warm; however, you should avoid drawstring necks, which can become entangled around the baby's neck.

Several choices must be made about diapers–cloth or disposable? wash them yourself or use a diaper service? Each option has its merits, and some combination may be best for you.

Amazingly, the least expensive choice is to buy a washer/dryer and three dozen cloth diapers – particularly if you eventually have more than one child. This enables you to save on diapers *and* to own fewer changes of clothing, since laundering soiled outfits will not involve a trip to the laundromat. You do have to spend time, even though you are saving money.

Disposables are time-saving, but they cost more, and the ultimate disposability of these plastic and paper contraptions may be cause for concern. They are, in any case, a great convenience on trips. Diaper services are a good compromise, but the cost is close to that for disposables and a certain amount of labor on your part is still required.

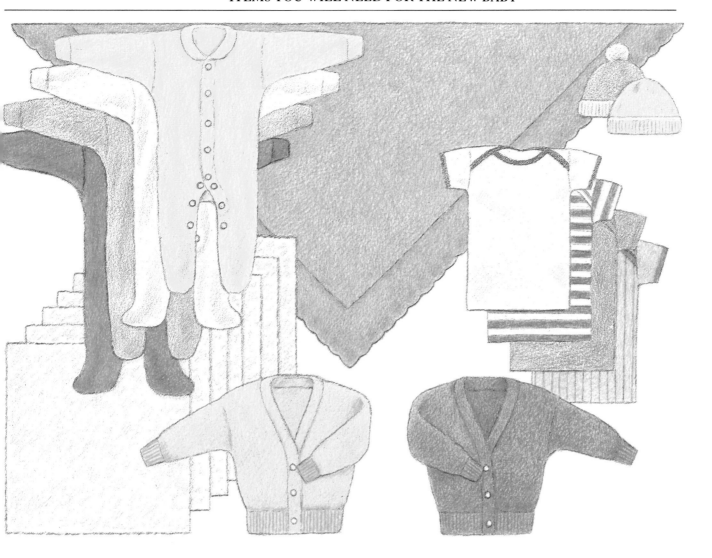

Cloth diapers seem less likely to promote diaper rash, and they are multipurpose items –indispensable for putting over the shoulder when burping the baby and for cleaning up spills. Disposables can be used for nothing other than their designated purpose. Cloth diapers need pinning, which makes some people uneasy. The sticky tapes on disposables stick only once, a particularly frustrating feature when you change the baby only to find she is dry (have some masking tape handy).

A good changing table is extremely useful; make sure it is sturdy and a comfortable height for you. Some have storage space for clothes, diapers, and whatever else you need within reach. For the first month or two, you could give your baby sponge baths on the changing table.

A changing mat is another good idea. Some fold up into carrying bags. You can make your own. A terrycloth envelope into which you can slip a plastic foam pad is all you need.

FOR BATHING
To handle your baby's bathing needs, you
will need:
cotton
soothing occlusive ointment (optional)
round-ended scissors
sponge or washcloth
baby brush and comb
towels
waterproof apron for yourself (optional)

You can buy a special baby tub but you do
not really need one. A large plastic basin or
the kitchen sink will do fine. A washcloth
laid on the bottom of the tub will guard
against slipping. Optional are an inflatable
bath, which stores easily and travels well,
and a sponge bath cushion to provide a
comfortable, nonslip perch for the baby in a
kitchen sink or big bathtub.

FOR FEEDING
A mother who plans to breastfeed (see page
71) will need three supportive bras–either
front opening or with detachable cups. One
of these should be a size larger than was
needed before the baby's birth. It will be
more comfortable during the first week when
the mother's breasts will be quite engorged.

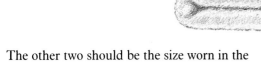

The other two should be the size worn in the
last weeks of pregnancy.

Nursing pads are also needed to absorb the
inevitable leakage in the early days. These
can either be disposable or the washable,
reusable type. Another alternative is to use a
man's cotton handkerchief folded in four.

Several varieties of breast pump are on the
market, manual and electric, although the
expense of the latter hardly seems worth it.
The easiest and most pleasant manual pump
to use is the Marshall-Kaneson.

Three or four bottles for giving water or
expressed breast milk will also be needed.
Many parents like the disposable nursers

since breast milk can be frozen in the plastic liners and no sterilizing is needed. You will also need three or four nipples. Some parents prefer the so-called orthodontic design, which is thought to approximate to the human nipple.

Some women find nipple protectors helpful in preventing sore nipples; others find that they aggravate the trouble. Lanolin or some other nonirritating, unperfumed cream will soothe sore or cracked nipples between feedings.

If you plan to bottle-feed, you will need about twelve bottles, either glass or plastic; if you prefer disposable nursers, a box of 100 liners and six holders will be adequate to begin with. Disposable liners have the advantage of not needing to be sterilized. You will also need twelve nipples, which should be checked regularly and replaced when they become sticky or brittle. You may prefer the traditional style or the so-called orthodontic type. For cleaning, get two brushes, one for bottles and one for nipples. Formulas come in three forms: ready to use, concentrated, or powdered. Study the prices and decide whether you want to pay for someone else to add the water or want to take the time and effort to do the mixing yourself at home.

FOR TRAVELING AND OUTDOORS

In a society that depends on the automobile, the importance of a good car seat cannot be too strongly stressed. Do not think that you can safely hold a child, especially a newborn, in your arms while riding in a car. The force of impact of a car traveling at 30 miles per hour will rip a ten-pound child from an adult's arms with a force of 300 pounds, the equivalent of his falling from a three-story building.

In Tennessee, the first state to enact a car seat law for children under four, the annual death toll in car accidents among that age group dropped from between twenty and twenty-five before the law was passed to fifteen, then ten, and then only six in the three years following the law's passage. Furthermore, toddlers who ride in car seats suffer less from car sickness, are less likely to cause accidents inside the car, and are better behaved.

To be effective, a safety seat/restraint must hold the child securely in place and must itself be firmly anchored to the seat of the car. Many different types exist, but all seats manufactured since January 1, 1981, must conform to federal safety standards. When you are shopping for one, be sure it specifies the new federal standard 213-80 and is compatible with your own car's seat belt system. Although all seats made after January 1, 1981, must meet the standard's safety

Baby carriers make transport easier. Different models and strengths of carriers are available for babies of different ages.

requirements, a hand-me-down or secondhand buy may have been made before then. Even if it was manufactured to meet the standard, a secondhand seat may be cracked, or the straps or fasteners may be worn out. Check carefully.

Do not try to economize in this area by using a light plastic infant seat, a "car bed," or your arms as a substitute. You will, in most states, be breaking the law, and you will be risking a precious life.

Car Seat Checklist
☐ *Can the seat be used in your car?*
☐ *Is it easy to install and remove the seat from the car?*
☐ *Is it easy to install and remove your child from the seat?*
☐ *Does the seat uncomfortably restrict her arms or view?*
☐ *Is it the right model for her age?*
   (It is sensible to buy one that can be adjusted as the child grows so that it suits her from birth to about five years.)

For outings without a car, two new developments have revolutionized baby transport: the wearable baby carrier and the folding stroller. For most parents, the baby carrier is the first choice. There are many different styles, so it makes sense to shop around. A small baby can be carried in front, but make sure the carrier supports her head and holds her snugly against you. The baby will be soothed by the warmth and motion, and the carrier leaves your hands free to get on with other things.

When your baby can sit without much support—usually at about five to seven months—a back pack may suit you both. Again, look for one that gives both of you good back support, has ample leg holes (so as not to cut off blood supply), and provides something soft for her to rest her head against if she wants to sleep.

Folding strollers are easily stored or taken into cars, buses, or trains. If you are going to use a stroller before your baby can sit on her own, get one with a rigid back. The type with two or three adjustable positions is comfortable for children up to three years old.

Unless you stay at home more than is good for you and the baby, you will need something for her to sleep in away from home. Neither the stroller nor the wearable carrier suitably replaces the old-fashioned baby carriage for longer sleep, but various handcarriers are available, ranging from wicker or woven baskets to fold-up units that used to be called car beds. Look for economy here because, by three months, your baby will be too big and too active to sleep in it safely. If the baby will be sleeping outdoors, you may

Strollers, which have virtually replaced baby carriages in convenience-minded families, come in a variety of styles. The kind that folds up easily is popular, largely because it makes storage easy and is usually light enough to carry on public transport or stow in the back of a car. Rain and sun shields are available as accessories.

If you plan to use a stroller for your newborn, look for one with a rigid back that can be lowered to a full reclining position. Some carriages convert to strollers for when the baby is older.

want a mosquito net to cover her sleeping place.

MISCELLANEOUS

Motion does wonders for soothing a restless baby, so an automatic swing can be invaluable if you are trying to eat your dinner and the baby is screaming. Another way to keep your baby nearby while your hands are occupied is to use a portable infant seat that allows three or more sitting angles. Keep it on a solid surface, make sure the seat belt is fastened, and *never* leave the room while the baby is in it. It will no longer be safe once she can sit on her own because she then will be able to tip herself over.

Items such as jumping seats, other hanging seats, and walkers may be helpful when your baby is between six and twelve months of age. They allow her to jump and move about but still stay out of mischief. Remember, though, never to leave a child unattended in one of these contraptions, and when a child is in a walker, keep the cellar door closed and stairways guarded.

If you do not begin with a full-sized crib, you will eventually need to get one. Some cribs on the market convert into youth beds. A highchair is also useful, and some models fold into a low chair and a play or mealtime table and save space that way. You may prefer a seat that clips onto the table for meal times; these are very useful for travel.

In the room where your baby sleeps, make sure you have a comfortable nursing chair. A shelf or wall caddy for odds and ends such as diaper pins, washcloths, and other paraphernalia is useful. A roll of paper towels comes in handy for mopping up.

Lined curtains admit a restful level of light; many parents find a dimmer switch or nightlight useful for quick, sure-footed entries. Look for washable wallpaper and furniture with rounded corners and wipeable surfaces. Carpet, cork tiles, and nonslip vinyl are all warmer than linoleum; bare wood can be splintery, and area rugs are dangerous and slippery (see page 141).

If your baby is sharing your room, you may find that a properly balanced screen provides privacy for you and reduced light for your baby.

IF BUYING SECONDHAND

Although most types of recently manufactured baby equipment must meet federally monitored safety standards, you may be offered secondhand equipment manufactured before the applicable regulations were adopted. When evaluating secondhand equipment, reject any item that has inadequate brakes and locks, flaking paint, surfaces repainted with what might be toxic paint,

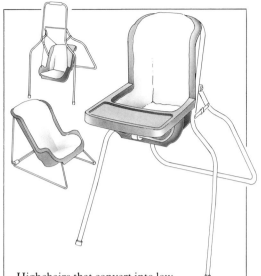

Highchairs that convert into low chairs or swings are space saving and economical.

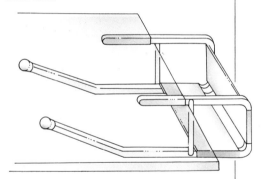

This portable clip-on baby seat grips your tabletop when the child sits in it. An active child could wriggle free, however; never leave a child unattended in this or any other seat.

This highchair converts into a play and mealtime table. Look for highchairs with wide, stable bases.

flammable materials, sharp edges, missing pieces, or equipment that can easily be tipped over by the weight or movements of the baby. If you want information about Consumer Product Safety Commission regulations or have specific questions about a piece of equipment, new or used, called the CPSC's toll-free hotline (page 231). See also page 33.

What you buy for your baby will largely be determined by your life style and space limitations as well as your budget. If you have no room for a carriage, you will probably choose a stroller. If you are short of space, look for multipurpose and collapsible items—changing tables with clothes storage space, inflatable baths, baby seats that attach to a tabletop, and the like. If you have stairs to climb, a collapsible stroller is your best bet. If you already have a toddler, look for a carriage that will accommodate a toddler seat, or a twin stroller, or separate strollers that can be hitched together with a special attachment.

ITEMS YOU WILL NOT NEED

Scales. If your baby is happy and thriving, do not worry about weight gain. If his bowels move regularly, if he needs a diaper change at least six times a day, and if his urine is colorless to pale yellow, chances are he is all right. A rule of thumb is that your baby should gain about 1 ounce per day, 1 pound every two weeks after the first week to ten days.

If you are still concerned, your child's health care provider will probably welcome you to come to the office to weigh the baby and your neighborhood grocer will surely be charmed to let you use his produce scales.

Electric Sterilizers and Bottle Warmers. Any pot that holds water will do in place of these.

Vaporizer/Humidifier. You do not need this unless your health care provider specifies so. The most likely type to be suggested in case of need is a cold-mist vaporizer, which is no less effective than a hot one and avoids the danger of accidental scalding. Better than a humidifier is fresh air. Let your baby sleep with the windows open regardless of the weather.

Multiple Jars and Bottles of Goop. Most creams and lotions contain alcohol and/or irritating substances. A tube of occlusive ointment is enough if you use a dab when redness appears in the diaper area. A washcloth dampened with plain water makes more sense than alcohol-impregnated wiping cloths. Powder and talc are harmful if inhaled. Most soaps and shampoos rob the baby of natural oils, so a clear water bath is probably better until the baby begins to crawl and get dirty that way.

Cotton Swabs and Balls. Cotton swabs can injure delicate eyes, ears, and noses; cotton balls leave lint in eyes and other places. A soft washcloth or a clean fingertip with well-trimmed fingernail is safer and just as effective.

MAKING YOUR HOME SAFE

The best time to take a look at the world your baby is entering is before he arrives. That way you can eliminate danger areas before they turn into accident zones. Do not excuse yourself by thinking "accidents will happen"—they need not, and your job as parents is to make your home as safe as possible. Sometimes protecting your baby means removing hazards; sometimes it means teaching by example. Precautions differ with every home and every person's individual nature.

If your home is safe, your baby need not grow up in an atmosphere where "no" is in frequent use. A prevailing prohibitive attitude can stifle a baby's natural curiosity, curtail his freedom, and turn him into an overanxious toddler. The extent to which you avoid this, though, depends on how much supervision you are willing and able to give. For instance, some parents believe that stair gates are unnecessary and that even a crawling baby can be taught to ascend stairs

on his knees and to back down them to safety. Training him, however, requires time and attention. For those who do not plan to watch every moment until their child has mastered the stairs, two gates—one for the top and one for the bottom—are essential. Playpens may also be useful at times, but they should not be used as prisons.

Make sure you provide a safe area where your child can crawl, explore, push, pull, and tumble onto padded surfaces. He must learn to cope with a certain amount of risk within his own limits. At the same time, he must learn the meaning of warning words—"no," "hot," and "be careful"—but try to limit your use of them so that, when they are used, they are immediately effective.

The early days are the easiest because your baby is reasonably stationary. Even so, instinctively you will be protecting him—supporting his head because his neck muscles are still weak, never leaving him unattended on any elevated surface.

As a child becomes more physically adventurous, he is increasingly exposed to danger. At the same time he is learning new skills and achieving independence in areas in which he previously needed help. At six months, if he sits on your lap you no longer have to support his head, but you do have to keep an eye on hands reaching for your coffee cup.

Physical development always governs the kind of trouble he can get into. You need to stay one step ahead, taking precautions before they are necessary and assessing what his next stage will be.

Try an experiment. Crawl around a room on your hands and knees. You will be amazed at what you find–from trailing electrical cords to sharp-edged tables, from electric sockets to the cat's supper–a treasure trove for a curious baby but a minefield nonetheless. A baby gives no warning that he is crossing from one stage of development to another.

Every baby is different, but a basic time scheme follows on the next pages.

FEDERAL SAFETY REGULATIONS

Federal safety regulations fall into two classes: mandatory ones, which must be met by all relevant products manufactured after the date when the regulation goes into effect; and voluntary ones, which the manufacturers help formulate and then agree to observe without legal penalty for noncompliance. Following are some of the mandatory and voluntary guidelines involving products intended for young children.

Baby Carriers (voluntary):
Base of carrier should be wide for stability.
Bottom surface of carrier should be rough and skid-resistant or should accommodate rough-surfaced adhesive strips.
Entire carrier should be made of sturdy materials and have firm supports.
Safety strap should be built in to all carriers.

Car Seats (mandatory):
Seat must be capable of withstanding a 30-mph crash test without transferring more than a fixed level of force to the test dummy's head and shoulders.
Seat must maintain its structural integrity in the above test.
Harness buckles must resist forces of up to 12 pounds on their opening mechanism without opening, to prevent opening by the child.
Seat must be accompanied by label identifying manufacture date, specifying basic use instructions, and warning against improper use.

Cribs (mandatory):
Slats must be no more than 2⅜ inches apart.
All metal hardware on crib must be safe, with no rough edges.
Dropside locks and latches must be secure and must guard against accidental release or release by crib occupant.
Cribs with mesh sides must have accompanying labels warning of potential suffocation hazard.
Crib carton, headboard, and assembly

instructions must all contain explicit warnings to use a snug-fitting mattress only.

Highchairs (voluntary):
Base of highchair should be wide for stability.
Highchair contours should be smooth and rounded, with no sharp points.
Restraining straps should be easy-fastening and should not attach to tray.
Tray should lock securely onto assembly.

Playpens (voluntary):
Wooden slats should be no more than 2⅜ inches apart.
Hinges and latches on folding models should lock when opened (to prevent scissoring action on fingers) and should have no sharp edges.
Playpens with legs should have firm floor support to prevent collapse.
Mesh netting should have smaller weave than smallest buttons on baby clothing, and instructions should warn against leaving dropside down and exposing baby to risk of suffocation in space between mattress and loose mesh.

Rattles (mandatory):
Rattles must have ends so large that they cannot become lodged in babies' throats.
Rattles must have no sharp edges or points.
Rattles must be made of break- and splinter-resistant material.

Sleepwear (mandatory):
Sleepwear must be treated with flame-retardant chemicals or must be made of flame-retardant fibers.
Sleepwear must cease to burn when ignition source (such as open flame or hot electric coil) is removed from contact with fabric.
Sleepwear exposed to open gas flame along lower edge for 3 seconds under test conditions must not exceed a maximum char length and must have no flaming material 10 seconds after ignition source is removed.

Laundering instructions for maintaining fire-retardant properties must be attached to all sleepwear.

Strollers (voluntary):
Base should be wide enough to prevent tipping even when baby leans over side.
Canopy should lock in place.
Latching devices should secure stroller against collapsing, to eliminate crushing and pinching hazards.
Brakes should operate effectively and reliably.
Seat belts or harness restraints should prevent possibility of infant falls.

Toy Chests (voluntary):
Lids should be equipped with safety hinges to prevent accidental entrapment and head injuries.
Chests should have ventilation holes to prevent suffocation in case of entrapment.

Toys (mandatory):
New toys intended for children under three must not have small, swallowable or inhalable parts (such as removable eyes and noses on dolls and stuffed toys and removable squeakers on squeeze toys).
New toys intended for children under eight must not have sharp points, either on the outside or on the inside where they may become exposed and dangerous if the toy is broken.
New toys intended for children under eight must be free of sharp glass or metal edges.
New toys not intended for young children and therefore not complying with the above requirements must be accompanied by labels specifying age recommendations.

Walkers (voluntary):
Wheel base should be wide for stability.
Seats should be of unbreakable plastic or sturdy fabric with heavy-duty stitching or rugged snaps.
Coil springs and hinges should have protective covers, to avoid finger entrapment.
Locking devices and screws should have no sharp edges or points.

A SAFE ENVIRONMENT FOR YOUR GROWING CHILD

BIRTH TO THREE MONTHS. Your baby has poor head control; he is still learning to coordinate sucking, breathing, and swallowing; he cannot intentionally move away from dangerous situations, but he may make quick nonpurposeful movements that put him in danger.

POSSIBLE INJURIES AND HOW TO PREVENT THEM

Falling
Never leave him unattended on a high surface such as a changing table.
Always keep one hand on him while attending to him.
Keep the crib rails up.

Suffocation
Do not place pillows, heavy blankets, down quilts, or stuffed animals in your baby's crib.
Do not line crib with plastic or cover mattress with removable plastic.

Choking and Strangling
Do not tie his pacifier to a string around his neck.
Do not leave bottles propped for feeding.
Do not give any small toys that can fit in his mouth.

Check that crib bars are not more than 2⅜ inches apart—the maximum under federal regulations. Make sure also that the mattress fits snugly to the sides of the crib so that the baby's fingers and toes cannot become trapped.

THREE TO SIX MONTHS. Your baby can now lift his head and chest off the bed when lying on his stomach; he can reach for small objects, grab them, and pull them to his mouth; he is learning to roll over, and he can sit with some support.

POSSIBLE INJURIES AND HOW TO PREVENT THEM

The previously identified dangers still exist. There are also some new hazards.

Choking
Keep small objects—keys, buttons, coins, small toys—away from him. These are not appropriate playthings. Toys and rattles should be too large to fit in his mouth.

Poisoning
Make certain all toys have lead-free paints or are made of nontoxic materials. If a toy is old or second-hand and may not meet current federal safety requirements, scrape off the old paint and repaint with what you *know* is safe, or simply discard the toy.
Keep pills, medicines, cleansers, alcoholic beverages, and other

Is your kitchen the safest it can be? A young baby is likely to spend much of her time in this room, which is the most dangerous area in the house. Look at this typical scene, and see if you can pinpoint the hazards.
1. Overhanging handles can tip boiling water onto curious faces.
2. Cupboards without childproof locks will swing open to reveal inviting containers with lethal contents.
3. Mugs and kettles too near the edge of worktops can be found by grasping hands; hanging cords and accessible electric sockets are particularly deadly.
4. The knife and fork, matches, and heavy ashtray on the table are all within reach of the child in the highchair, and the handbag is just asking to be explored.
5. A child should never be left alone in a highchair in any room.

Entrapment

Make sure crib bars are no more than 2⅜ inches apart, and that decorative rails and finials do not provide places to be trapped.

Use crib bumpers for further protection against entrapment.

Make sure mattress fits snugly; if you can wedge two fingers between mattress and crib, mattress is too small.

Never leave mesh-sided playpens with side folded down.

Burns and Scalds

Do not use hot water bottles, electric blankets, or heating pads in your baby's crib.

Do not handle hot liquids when holding your baby–his sudden movements may cause a spill.

Do not smoke when holding, feeding, or attending to your baby.

Check bathwater temperature with your elbow before putting your baby in the tub.

Do not let baby touch water faucets while in the bath; if faucet is hot, cover with a washcloth.

Avoid lengthy exposure to sun, and use bonnets and sunshades when possible.

Buy flame-resistant sleepwear and be certain to launder it properly, so as to maintain its flame resistance.

Travel Injuries

Always travel with your infant properly strapped in a car seat that meets federal safety regulations.

Do not have loose objects in the car–they could become projectiles in an accident.

Never leave your baby unattended in the car.

Beginning with your newborn's first ride home and continuing until he is big enough to use a seat belt (age/weight regulations vary by state, but four years/40 pounds is average), he should be strapped into a car seat that meets federal safety requirements every time he sits in a moving car.

potential poisons out of reach or under lock and key.

Post the phone number of the poison control center near the phone and keep a bottle of syrup of ipecac in a locked medicine chest to be used only if the poison center directs. (See pages 223–24.)

SIX TO TWELVE MONTHS.

Your baby learns to sit well alone, to crawl, to pull up to stand, to cruise by holding onto furniture, and even to walk alone; he can begin unwrapping objects and try to remove barriers in his way; his teeth are coming in, and he becomes even more interested in biting or mouthing everything in sight. The major difference is that now not only must you keep trouble away from him, you must keep him away from trouble. He knows what "no" means.

POSSIBLE INJURIES AND HOW TO PREVENT THEM

The previously identified dangers still exist, with some modifications and additions.

Suffocation
Keep plastic bags out of reach.

Drowning
Do not leave child unattended in the bath, even for one moment. Continue bathtime supervision through age five.

Falling
Use stair gates at the top and bottom of stairs.

Use a sturdy highchair for feeding, and always use the safety strap. A footrest will reduce his kicking and lessen the chance of his toppling the chair over.

Stop using an infant seat now that he can climb out of it.

Electric sockets, windows, cupboards, doors–all stand within reach of your crawling/walking baby. Now is the time to make sure that safety covers and locks are in place. The illustrations here and far right show examples of safety devices available in hardware, houseware, and baby equipment stores.

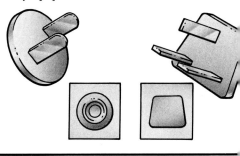

TWELVE TO TWENTY-FOUR MONTHS.

Your infant becomes a toddler and now stands, walks, runs, and climbs; he understands language and begins to use words himself; he can negotiate stairs, with assistance at first and later unaided; he does a great deal of exploring and tests limits that are set for him; he imitates and asks questions about what is going on around him. He resists restrictions and looks for autonomy. "No" is often *his* word now.

POSSIBLE INJURIES AND HOW TO PREVENT THEM

New dangers to add to the list arise.

Falling
When the raised crib railing and lowest mattress position are less than ¾ of his height, chances for climbing out and falling greatly increase. Switch to a youth bed, with a railing if needed, which is lower to the ground.

Choking
Stress the importance of chewing food thoroughly, and avoid chewing gum, peanuts, popcorn, hard candies, whole grapes, large pieces of meat, and hot dogs–all known to present choking dangers in children under three.

Travel Injuries
Continue to use an appropriate car seat, and wear your own seat belt regularly. He will imitate your good habits.

Always hold his hand when crossing the street, and teach him to look both ways first and cross with the light.

General Bumps and Bruises
Encourage him to pick up his own toys, to avoid tripping injuries.

Continue to supervise all water activities –bath, wading pool, and so on.

If you have firearms in the house, be certain that they are kept under lock and key. Keep ammunition in a separate place away from the firearm, and never store a loaded gun.

FIRES

More children die from fires in the United States than in any other country. Fire prevention is of vital importance. The most common place of origin of house fires is the kitchen. Never leave anything unattended while cooking, and keep dishtowels, curtains, and other flammable objects clear of the stove. Keeping a fire extinguisher in the kitchen is a good idea.

Although most fires occur in the kitchen, the most common cause of fatal fires is cigarettes. Try not to smoke at all, for the sake of your health and that of your family; if you must smoke, keep cigarettes and matches where children cannot reach them. Cigarettes and ashes should always be put in large ashtrays–never in wastebaskets. Double-check the house for smoldering cigarettes before going out or going to bed. Do not smoke in bed.

Fires caused by electrical faults can be avoided by not overloading outlets with extension cords. Make sure that large appliances have adequate ventilation. Try not to store combustible materials in the home– and certainly not in cooking areas.

Wood-burning stoves, radiators, kerosene heaters, and fireplaces should have protective screens. If it is impossible to make sure the fire is out before you go to bed or leave the house, leave the screen in place.

Smoke detectors can alert you to fires early enough to enable you to evacuate the house in safety. They are usually battery-operated, although some run on electricity. Since smoke and heat first accumulate high up on walls or ceilings and away from corners, the ideal location for a detector is in the middle of the ceiling. The detector must be situated where it will easily rouse the family–in a hallway near the bedrooms, perhaps–and it must be loud enough to be heard with doors closed. There should be at least one detector on each level of the house.

Make sure that everyone in the household understands where emergency exits are; practice drills are a good idea. A ladder should be kept nearby if the rooms are too high to jump from safely. Rope ladders take

Move crib mattress to its lowest position.
Install window guards, and open windows from top, not bottom.

Strangling

Remove mobiles or toys hanging above the crib before he has a chance to pull them down and become entangled in them.

Burns and Scalds

Be certain you have fireplace screens and freestanding heaters protected.

Turn pot handles on the stove inward, not out over the edge where he might grab at them.

Put safety caps on all electrical outlets.

Keep matches and cigarettes out of sight and out of reach.

General Bumps and Bruises

Remove tablecloths to avoid his pulling off dishes, lamps, and so on.

Remove or hide electric cords behind furniture, away from curious hands.

Pad sharp furniture corners, remove unstable furniture, and keep chairs away from windows.

Keep small snack foods, such as nuts, off low coffee tables.

Check toys for loose parts, sharp corners, or flaking paint.

Use cabinet and drawer latches and doorknob covers to restrict his access to dangerous places.

Poisoning

Remove poisonous plants from the house.

Keep alcoholic beverages locked away.

Never put poisons, plant foods, household cleaners, or anything potentially dangerous in an old soft drink or juice bottle. Keep them locked away out of sight.

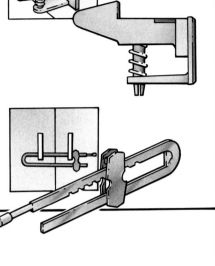

Your child will probably switch from a highchair to a booster seat. Be certain it is stable and that he does not stand up or play in it.

Poisoning

Continue to keep medicines locked up.

Never call medicine candy, and do not let him see you taking medicine. He may imitate you.

TWENTY-FOUR TO THIRTY-SIX MONTHS. He is developing new motor skills and refining old ones; he scribbles and draws, rides a tricycle, throws a ball, and plays games with other children; he separates from his mother easily and seeks some independence; injuries begin to occur outside your home more frequently.

POSSIBLE INJURIES AND WAYS TO PREVENT THEM

Burns and Scalds

Continue to teach the meaning of "hot," and test bath water before bathing.

Keep matches safely out of reach.

Do not allow play near outdoor barbecues or indoor fireplaces.

General Bumps and Bruises

Encourage outdoor play in appropriate areas—for example, do not allow ball games or tag to be played in the street.

Keep play in the yard, and be certain to put away garden tools before the children play.

Do not allow tricycle riding beyond the driveway or sidewalk.

Do not allow him to cross the street alone or unsupervised.

up little space and can be stored near trouble spots; make sure they can be securely fixed to the window sills.

If fire does break out, *think* before you dash out of the house. If a door is closed, feel the air coming under the door. If it is warm or if the door is hot, do not open it; instead, leave through another door (if possible) or through a window. If the door is cool, open it very carefully, bracing your shoulder against it. Heat and pressure can blow the door open very forcefully, enabling the fire to spread rapidly. If you have to go through a smoky area, do not walk, crawl; the purest air is nearest to the floor. Remember that smoke inhalation can be as dangerous as fire.

Above all, do not stop to get dressed or gather your valuables: Concentrate on saving lives.

SCALDING

You can avoid hot water scalds by adjusting the hot water heater so that the maximum temperature is no greater than 130°F. This is hot enough for washing clothes and dishes and will ensure a safe maximum heat for the baby's bath water. If you live in an apartment or are otherwise unable to turn down the water heater's thermostat, temperature-limiting valves can be installed. Always check the temperature of your baby's bath water by testing it with your elbow.

Never leave boiling water within a child's reach. Turn cooking pot handles to the back of the stove. And *never* leave a child alone in a room with a steam vaporizer. If you must moisten the air, use the cold mist type.

POISONOUS PLANTS

Over 7,000 cases involving plant exposure are reported annually to poison centers, and probably many more are unreported. About half of these cases involve children below the age of one year; nearly all result from eating the leaves of plants. If any of the following plants grows in or around your home, dispose of it. Call the poison control center if you suspect your child has ingested any part of a named plant. The list includes the most commonly encountered poisonous plants.

House and Garden Plants

American Plum	Hydrangea
Apple (seeds)	Iris
Apricot	Japanese Yew
Azalea	Jerusalem Cherry
Bird of Paradise	Jonquil
Bunchberry	Laburnum
Caladium	Lantana
Castor Oil Plant (beans)	Larkspur
Choke Cherry	Laurel (berries)
Common Privet	Lily of the Valley
Daffodil	Morning Glory
Daphne	Narcissus
Delphinium	Oleander
Dieffenbachia	Philodendron
Elephant Ear	Rhubarb
English Ivy	Rhododendron
Foxglove	Sweet Pea
Hen-and-Chickens	Swiss Cheese Plant
Holly	Waxed-leaf Ligustrum
Hyacinth	Wisteria

Wild Plants

American Yew	Locoweed
Black Locust	May Apple
Buttercup	Moonseed
Coral Bean Plant	Ohio Buckeye
Death Camas	Pokeweed
Horse Nettle	Poison Hemlock
Jack-in-the-Pulpit	Virginia Creeper
Jimson Weed	Water Hemlock
	White Locust

Nonpoisonous Plants. Some common safe plants for your home or garden are:

Aluminum Plant	Pepperomia
Babies'-Breath	Rubber Plant
Begonia	Spider Plant
German Ivy	Swedish Ivy
Grape Ivy	Wandering Jew
Jade Plant	

A chart of poisonous plants is available through the National Poison Center Network (address below) or your local poison control center.

RESOURCES

For further information on specific topics, contact the appropriate organization below.

Poison Control Centers

The phone numbers of local poison control centers are usually listed on the inside cover of the phone book. But do not wait until you need one. Look up the number now, and post it by every phone. If your area has no local poison control center, call your medical practitioner or local emergency room. Information on poisons can be obtained from The National Poison Center Network, 125 De Soto Street, Pittsburgh, PA 15213, 412-647-5600. This organization will also send you, on request, a public information bulletin; a 50-cent donation to defray postage and handling is requested.

Laws and Regulations

Your city or county department of health has information about local ordinances regulating smoke detectors, window guards, and other home safety features. Information about federal safety laws and regulations is generally available from the agency that administers the particular area of safety involved.

Toy Safety

Try first your local health department or your health care provider for information on the safety of toys or the status of toy recalls. If you need more information, try the Consumer Product Safety Commission (CPSC), 800-638-2772 (toll-free). The CPSC publishes a packet on accidents and product safety; its annual report discusses product recalls. (See also page 165).

Home Safety

Safety devices such as electrical outlet covers, doorknob covers, and cabinet latches can be found in hardware and variety stores; children's equipment stores often carry the most complete assortment. Some companies market groups of devices as accident prevention kits. The CPSC publishes regulations on many types of products for the home.

Automobile Safety

Two good sources on automobile safety are the National Highway Traffic Safety Administration (NHTSA), 800-424-9393 (toll-free), and Consumers Union, 256 Washington Street, Mount Vernon, NY 10553. The NHTSA operates an auto safety hotline at the above number and offers useful pamphlets on car safety and child seat restraints. Consumers Union annually tests a variety of automobile and safety seats and publishes its findings in a monthly periodical, *Consumer Reports*. Back issues are available. The organization's annual *Buying Guide* covers these and many more subjects.

The American Academy of Pediatrics publishes numerous pamphlets on car safety, available through your pediatrician.

First Aid and CPR

The American Academy of Pediatrics publishes an excellent 11- by 17-inch poster on first aid and first aid for poisoning. Ask your pediatrician for a copy.

Thousands of people are educated annually by the American Heart Association in cardiopulmonary resuscitation–CPR. Ask at your local AHA chapter (listed in the phone book) about enrolling in a course. Fees are minimal and the training is extremely valuable. The Red Cross, YM–YWCA, and other organizations offer CPR training too.

Poisonous Plant Safety
A chart is available through the National Poison Center Network or your local poison control center.

FIRST AID KIT
Keep a locked first aid kit out of your child's reach. Do not let him see where you keep the key. The kit should contain:

telephone numbers of your medical practitioner, hospital, ambulance service, police/fire emergency, and poison control center

adhesive bandages of assorted sizes

sterile cotton

disinfectant (isopropyl alcohol or first aid cream)

2- by 2-inch gauze pads

4- by 4-inch gauze pads

roll of stretch gauze

petroleum jelly (in tube for easy application)

adhesive tape (1 and 3 inches wide)

safety pins

calamine lotion

syrup of ipecac

aspirin, baby aspirin, or acetominophen

thermometer

small scissors

two triangular bandages or a scarf large enough to be made into a sling

finger splints

tweezers or sewing needle for removing splinters

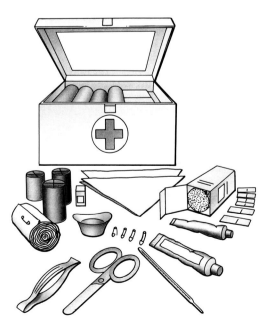

DAILY CARE

For nine months as parents-to-be, you have been objects of interest and even glamor to your relatives and friends. The adjective glamorous may seem far from accurate as, wearied and cumbersome, the mother-to-be enters the last few weeks of pregnancy. Yet a pregnant woman is glamorous, carrying as she does that mysterious quality of giving birth. Daily there are inquiries about her health, her state of mind. She arouses interest, concern; she is treated as special.

Then the baby is born. "It" becomes "he" or "she." Cards, flowers, gifts arrive. Friends come to admire, exclaim, perhaps envy. Excitement and affection are the order of the day. And the mother is still at the center of the universe.

And father? Ideally he will have been home for a few days at least to share the new responsibilities. Particularly with the first baby it will be a time of happiness and heightened emotions. And then, quite suddenly, the visitors depart, gifts stop arriving, and the father goes back to work.

That leaves the mother holding the baby. And she may be overwhelmed by just what she's let herself in for.

The parents of a first baby are unlikely to have anticipated how exhausted they will feel and how endless the new routine of baby care will be. Your baby may be an angel: He may sleep from one feeding to the next, go through the night without waking, and take his nourishment like clockwork. Or he may not. And you as new parents may be coping admirably, with the mother recovering strength and her figure. Or you may not. Either way, the repetition of tasks and the demands on your attention may lead you to wonder if you have turned from people into robots. If the lion's share of the daily tasks most commonly fall on the mother, many fathers also find themselves prisoners of a new routine.

The routine may seem no less formidable when the new baby is not the first in the family, even though the home will be more geared to a life style that includes children. Certainly, the routine that must accommodate the needs of a new baby will vary depending on the age of the older children. A gap of several years, with the older child or children already established in school, may enable you to separate the two routines with a kind of leapfrogging tactic: The baby enjoys undivided attention while his siblings are away from home, and the older children come into their own when the baby is asleep for the evening. If the babies are closer in age, their needs will almost certainly overlap.

In this chapter, you will find suggestions on how to cope with some of the changes that take place in a family to which a new baby has been added. These include both practical matters—teething, how to bathe and feed a baby, when to begin solid foods, handling bedtime and toilet training—and psychological stresses.

Feelings of weariness, bewilderment, and even downright unhappiness are not uncommon in new parents. One of the surest ways of coping with boredom and depression is to acknowledge their existence. It takes time to learn to become a parent, but a supporting kinship exists among parents. If you are able to make friends through self-help groups, local classes, and organizations of people in the same situation as yourselves, a whole world of knowledge and interest will be opened to you.

Meanwhile, the cause of all these complicated reactions is lying passively with an ingratiating, irresistible smile on his face.

"It's only gas, dear," says your mother. "Newborns don't smile."

Who says they don't?

THE EARLY DAYS

It is natural to look on birth as the climax of pregnancy and to forget that it is at the same time the beginning of a new life–for all the family. Let's look for a moment at some of the changes to be expected to go along with it.

Over the first few weeks, the mother is still recovering physically and emotionally from labor and birth. She may be sore when she sits or walks, she may still be discharging locchia as her uterus sheds the extra tissues of pregnancy, and if she is breastfeeding, she may have the added nuisance of leaking nipples until her milk flow begins to regulate itself. As a result, she may feel despairingly that she is not even in control of her own functions. Her figure is not yet back to normal, and even a baby who feeds and sleeps by the book demands an incredible amount of work.

On top of all that, the mother is tired. She sleeps with one ear open; if the baby cries, she fears he is ill; and if he does not, maybe he is too ill to cry. In the traditional setting, where housekeeping and cooking are primarily the mother's responsibility, standards have fallen. If a household necessity runs out, it is no longer an easy matter to drop by the store; going out is like moving an army. A friend offers to babysit so that the parents can enjoy a candlelit supper, but the mother would really rather have one long uninterrupted sleep, and anyway the only thing she has to talk about is the baby. Fatigue becomes a way of life.

To the working father, his partner's preoccupation with new and different demands may seem to have transformed her utterly. The routine dictated by the baby–his insistence on the constant attendance of a mother–leaves only brief recuperative breaks during which husband may inquire after wife. Even at this early stage, the father too is experiencing the emergence of his new parental role. With each diaper he changes or feeding he administers, the father's awareness of his new position in life will grow stronger; and as he shares in handling the responsibilities of parenthood, he too will become familiar with fatigue. The good news is that it will all get better.

ADVICE TO NEW MOTHERS

Some of your initial preoccupation will fade as you begin to feel physically stronger and as the baby settles into a routine. You may not altogether care for the routine, but within reason you will know what to expect. By the

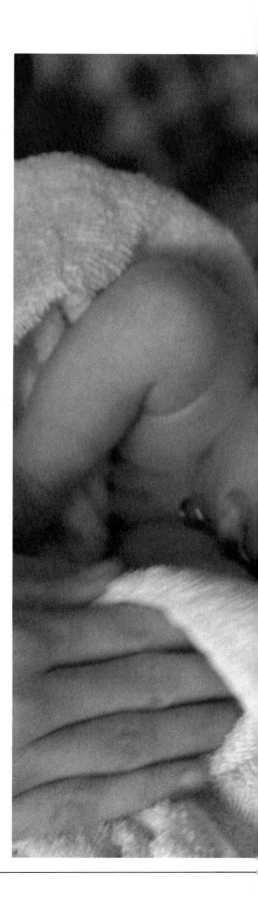

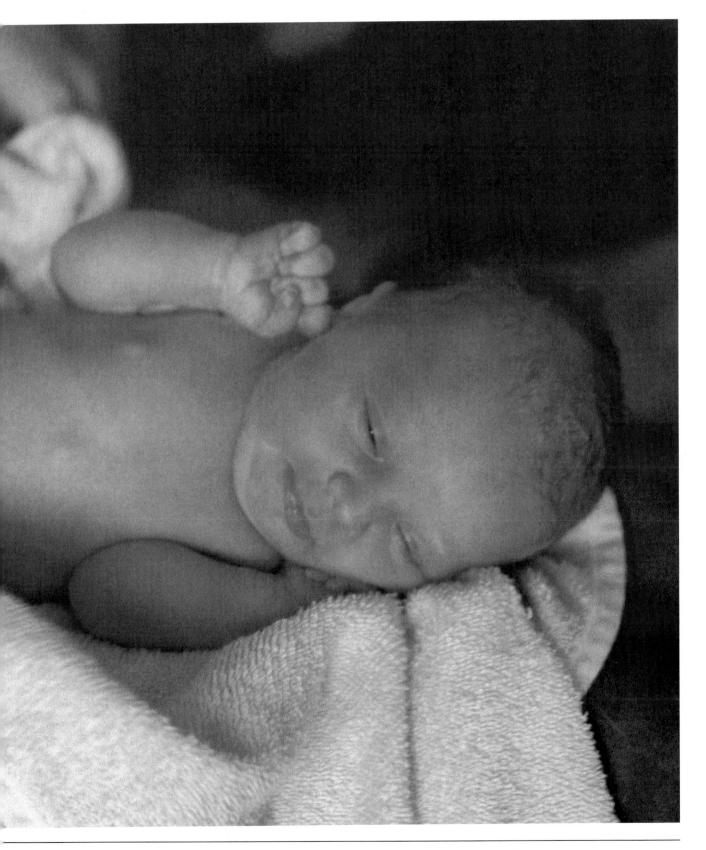

time your baby is a few months old, life will be very different. The work will continue, but you will have the pleasure of dealing with a responding, growing baby, and you will have become more used to the new life.

In the meantime, if your stitches make you sore, sit on a cushion or rubber ring. Rinse with warm water (a plastic squeeze bottle of the sort used to dispense mustard or ketchup is a great aid), rather than using toilet tissue after elimination. Put a handful of salt in your bath water. Do your Kegel exercise regularly (see page 46). Your milk supply will regulate itself, but in the meantime wear nursing pads or tuck a man's all-cotton handkerchief inside each cup of your bra. Change them frequently, as soggy surroundings will give you sore and chapped nipples.

Accept Help
If you are offered help, take it. And if you can afford to hire help, do so.

Limit your visitors; if you want their company, make use of them. Forget the prebaby days when you cooked special meals and generally waited on guests. Instead, ask if they will bring part of the meal. If a relative or friend comes to help regularly, make sure he or she really does help. Suggest dividing the chores between you: You do the cooking and the other person does the shopping, or vice versa. She takes the baby for a walk while you do something else (like having a nap), or you go shopping while she looks after the baby.

This is not being selfish; it is being sensible. The health of the family often depends on the health and attitude of the mother—so look after yourself.

Think About the Home Routine
Most homes are run according to a routine that suits its inhabitants—the order of doing housework, cooking, shopping, and so on. This may be the time to reassess that routine. Think of the end result you are aiming for and, if necessary, change the routine. It may make sense for the father to take on some additional housekeeping tasks; it may make sense to relax some of your housekeeping standards.

Consider the basics: Inhabitants of a comfortable home find adequate warmth, enjoyable meals, reasonable tidiness, clean clothes to wear, and mostly good-tempered housemates. If you get the first four right, you will be well on your way to the fifth, unless you accomplish them by making a martyr of yourself.

Do Not Lose Control
Untidiness does not disturb some people; others find it depressing and overwhelming.

If you are among the latter, an untidy house can make you feel you are losing control. Some simple steps can help. Your baby may not have his own room, but if you isolate the baby equipment—diapers, clothes, bath paraphernalia, and so on—in one room, they will not take over the whole house. Try to keep one other room in the house—the kitchen, the living room, or a bedroom—reasonably tidy so that you will always have at least one oasis

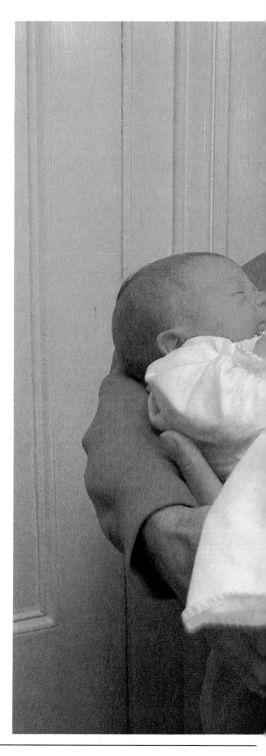

gracious living for yourself (as well as for unexpected visitors).

Then there is laundry. A washing machine is a wonderful thing: You can put the washing in last thing at night before you go to bed and come down in the morning to a load of clean clothes, ready for drying and perhaps even ironing (but do you really need to iron?). If you do not have a washing machine, try to limit trips to the laundromat to twice a week. Some laundromats will charge a bit extra to do the washing for you; it may be worth it.

Simplify Meals

For a while, you may have to forget special sauces and soufflés. If you have a cooperative baby who always sleeps during the evening and if a gracious dinner hour has always been one of the highlights of your days, go on with

CONTINUED ON PAGE 48

Getting to know each other. A father does not always have the same opportunity to be with his baby as does a mother, so time together is doubly important.

POSTPARTUM EXERCISES

Pregnancy and labor put major demands upon a woman's body. Many muscles have been stretched; others have worked intensely. The longer they remain stretched and weak, the longer they will take to recuperate. By beginning postpartum exercises as soon as twenty-four hours after your baby's birth, you will be helping your muscles to regain elasticity and your body to recover. Do not be discouraged if at first you seem to make little progress. Brief but frequent sessions are the answer.

One of the most essential exercises is known as the Kegel exercise. It restores tone to the group of muscles that supports the uterus, bladder, lower bowel, and vaginal wall, all of which have been stressed and stretched throughout pregnancy and childbirth. Women who neglect restoring the strength and tone of these muscles face significantly greater risks in later life of weakened bladders and consequent leaking of urine, prolapsed uterus, and hernias of the rectum and bladder. You should do this exercise several times a day, beginning now and continuing for the rest of your life. Here is how.

You can and should do the exercise standing, sitting, and lying down. It requires no apparent external movement, so no one will know you are exercising at all. Aim for a minimum of 100 contractions a day, but begin with just a few at each session and work your way up. The exercise involves contracting the vaginal muscles, producing a slight fluttering sensation, without moving the pelvis, abdominal muscles, or buttocks. The contraction takes place completely inside. You can acquaint yourself with the proper technique by doing it while urinating: Try to stop the flow of urine several times and note the sensation. That is what you are trying to achieve. Contract the muscles, hold for a few seconds, and then slowly release in stages until the muscles are completely relaxed. Repeat, checking that you are not using the muscles of the abdomen, pelvis, and buttocks.

To help strengthen your back muscles, kneel with head lowered and back rounded and bring one knee up as close as possible to your head, pulling in the stomach and vaginal muscles. Kick your leg back and up, raising your head and keeping your hips parallel to the floor. Bring the leg forward, and then change to the other leg. Repeat three times, and work up to seven or eight times.

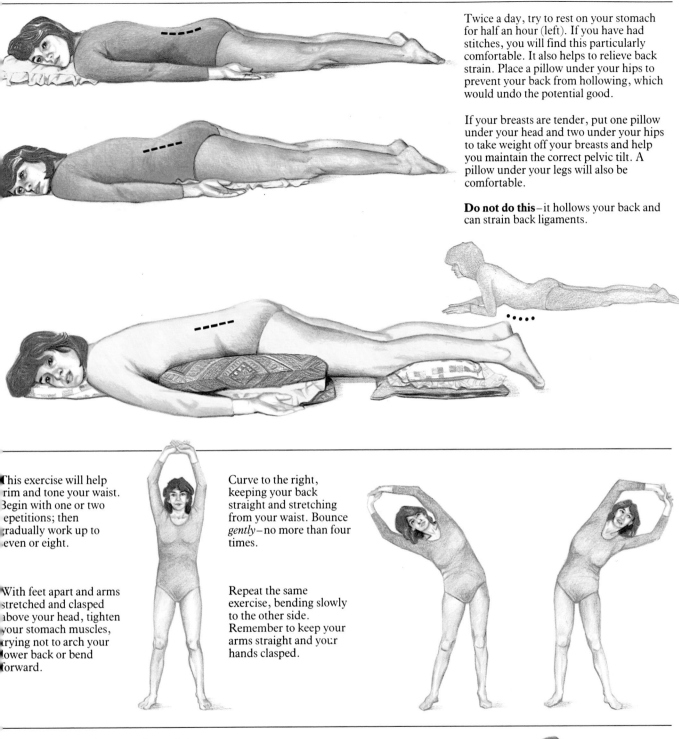

Twice a day, try to rest on your stomach for half an hour (left). If you have had stitches, you will find this particularly comfortable. It also helps to relieve back strain. Place a pillow under your hips to prevent your back from hollowing, which would undo the potential good.

If your breasts are tender, put one pillow under your head and two under your hips to take weight off your breasts and help you maintain the correct pelvic tilt. A pillow under your legs will also be comfortable.

Do not do this – it hollows your back and can strain back ligaments.

This exercise will help trim and tone your waist. Begin with one or two repetitions; then gradually work up to seven or eight.

With feet apart and arms stretched and clasped above your head, tighten your stomach muscles, trying not to arch your lower back or bend forward.

Curve to the right, keeping your back straight and stretching from your waist. Bounce *gently* – no more than four times.

Repeat the same exercise, bending slowly to the other side. Remember to keep your arms straight and your hands clasped.

Here is an exercise for you and your baby; before doing it, check with your health care provider that it is suitable for your baby, and in any case do not begin until he is able to support his head strongly (about six months). Position him so that his chest is on your knees, and hold his hands firmly. Raise your feet slightly as you gently stretch his arms sideways. Lower your legs and bring his hands in to meet. Repeat three or four times. Stop if he does not like it.

that practice. But do not think of it as a test of your ability to cope. If it is important to both of you, perhaps your partner can help. Many fathers will quite willingly take on some of the evening chores–feeding the baby or cooking dinner.

It helps if you are methodical about grocery shopping. Keep a shopping list going and try to avoid running out of things. You will not find it practical to shop every day. A large shopping trip once a week supplemented by what your partner can pick up on his way home is far more efficient. Deliveries to the door are a godsend–many markets offer this service, and if you are already on a dairy delivery service, you will probably find that it carries many other essentials you had not previously thought of buying from it.

Limit Visitors

Unless you live on a desert island, you will probably be besieged by well-wishing friends and relatives who just want to drop by for a few minutes to see the baby. This can be very stressful in the first few weeks, particularly if you feel you must present a clean house, refreshments, a happy and wide-awake baby,

and a slender and smiling self. Set limits on visitors and resist as much as possible the pressure to do more than you can. Husbands and attendant mothers and mothers-in-law are invaluable "front men" in this regard. Limiting visitors means figuring out graceful ways of saying, "No, not now," but it is worth the effort.

Get the Rest You Need

For the first few weeks, your baby will probably wake in the night for a feeding. If this happens at about two in the morning and then he awakens again at five or six, you will not be getting long periods of sleep. During the day, take every opportunity you can to rest or nap.

Feeding times, be they bottle or breast, anchor you to a chair. Put your feet up and take the phone off the hook. You will want to give your baby your attention at feeding times, but as you both become more relaxed about it, you can catch up on your reading at the same time. One young mother fulfilled a lifelong ambition while feeding her first baby: She read *War and Peace*. The baby slept through the whole Battle of Austerlitz.

Most likely your baby will take a morning

At first it may seem that your baby is taking up every minute of your time, and the broad analysis of a typical mother's day (right, top) confirms this. The other two charts at right show how the pattern changes at six months and at two years, allowing more time for you to enjoy for yourself.

In the early days, take advantage of every opportunity to rest. If the baby sleeps, you should sleep too. Enough rest for all of you–father included–is invaluable.

New baby

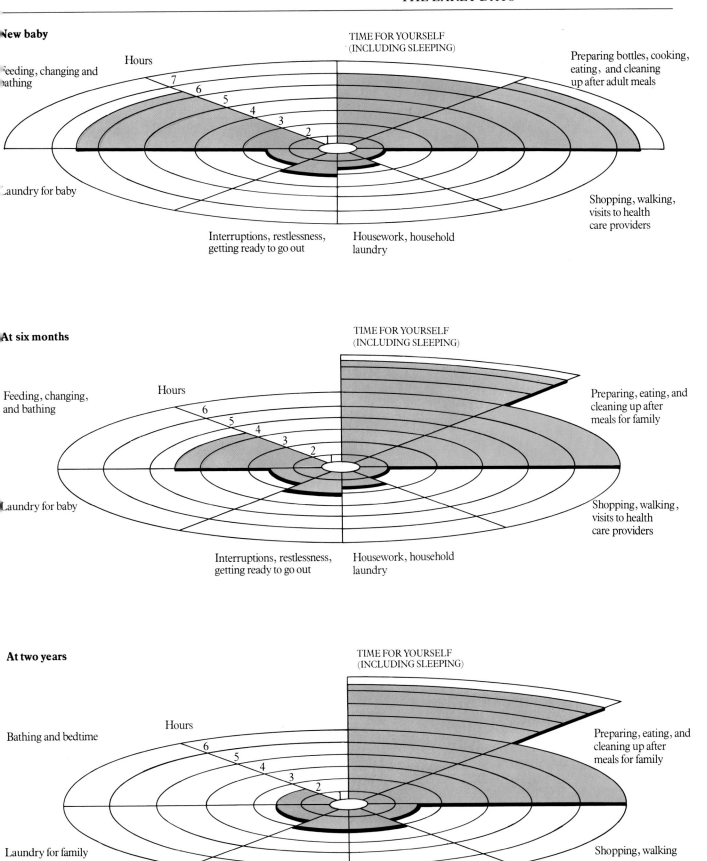

TIME FOR YOURSELF
(INCLUDING SLEEPING)

Feeding, changing and bathing

Hours

Preparing bottles, cooking, eating, and cleaning up after adult meals

7 6 5 4 3 2 1

Laundry for baby

Shopping, walking, visits to health care providers

Interruptions, restlessness, getting ready to go out

Housework, household laundry

At six months

TIME FOR YOURSELF
(INCLUDING SLEEPING)

Feeding, changing, and bathing

Hours

Preparing, eating, and cleaning up after meals for family

6 5 4 3 2

Laundry for baby

Shopping, walking, visits to health care providers

Interruptions, restlessness, getting ready to go out

Housework, household laundry

At two years

TIME FOR YOURSELF
(INCLUDING SLEEPING)

Bathing and bedtime

Hours

Preparing, eating, and cleaning up after meals for family

6 5 4 3 2

Laundry for family

Shopping, walking

Playing, interruptions

Housework

nap, and there is nothing wrong with having a rest then yourself. Take the phone off the hook again, and lay aside your concerns about what chores are as yet undone. The more rested you are, the easier the remainder of the day will be. If he naps again in the afternoon, you may want to follow suit or use the respite for a warm bath and a bit of time with a good book. This is neither lazy nor self-indulgent; it is essential that you have time for yourself if you are to be "on call" for your baby during these early days.

During the first month or two, you will probably have to adapt yourself to his routine. It will be his times of restlessness and quiet, his times of wakefulness and sleep, that dictate what you can do and when you can do it. The fact is, your baby is not a mechanical doll, nor is he exactly like the baby across the street or the one in the book. In time, though, you will be able to help him into a routine that fits in with the rest of the family (see page 95). By two months of age, he will be easier to integrate into your own life. He will be much more responsive then, and more interested in his surroundings. He will enjoy company–especially yours–and be happy to watch you from an infant seat or swing. He will enjoy outings, making it possible to plan a shopping trip or a visit to a friend with greater ease. Normal life–or something close to it–can begin anew.

EMOTIONAL SUPPORT

In these early days, an invaluable source of support is the relationship between both parents. The first few months of a baby's life are a time when mutual reassurance, encouragement, and praise can make the difference between happiness and depression. Sharing tasks and spelling each other can make the difference between simple tiredness and total exhaustion.

The mother needs to be told she is coping well and that she is still desirable and attractive as a woman; she needs to be cared for and looked after. That may seem a tall order for a father only now getting used to his own new role, but the days the mother spends alone with a baby can seem very long. Indeed, for a while it may be that her partner's concern for her is the only reassurance she has that she is valued and interesting apart from her function as a mother.

THE NEWBORN SKIN

If you have never seen a baby at birth, you may be surprised that your newborn does not look quite like the shiny-cheeked creature pictured in the advertisements.

She will probably be covered with a greasy

Here are some of the minor imperfections you may notice on your new baby's skin.

The majority of skin variations are simple alterations of the normal skin, are harmless, and require no treatment but if a birthmark or other variation concerns you, consult your health care provider.

Milia–numerous tiny white pustules over the nose, chin, and forehead caused by blocked oil glands. They need no treatment (do not give in to the temptation to squeeze them) and will clear up soon after birth.

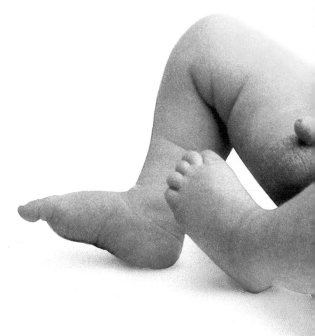

Hemangiomas–flat, red blotches appearing on the nape of the neck, forehead, or bridge of the nose–often referred to as "stork bites." The majority disappear during the first few months of life. Some are soft and raised above the surrounding skin, with a texture resembling a strawberry's. These also mostly shrink and fade away during the first year of life. Others may be large, deep red patches called portwine stains. These too are generally harmless, but they do not fade and they may be associated with other problems such as seizures.

Freckles–similar in appearance to moles but lighter and always flat. They are caused by cells making too much pigment, a process activated by exposure to the sun. Unlike moles, which do not normally change, freckles may grow darker and new ones may appear with frequent sun exposure.

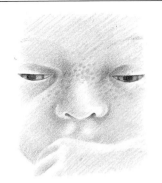

Skin Tags–small protrusions of skin that occur usually on the trunk or in the folds of skin but may appear elsewhere. They are the same color as the surrounding skin, are not painful or harmful but are often easily injured because they may be scratched or snagged in clothing. They can be surgically removed at any age under a local anesthetic in a doctor's office.

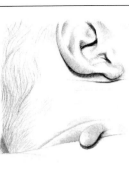

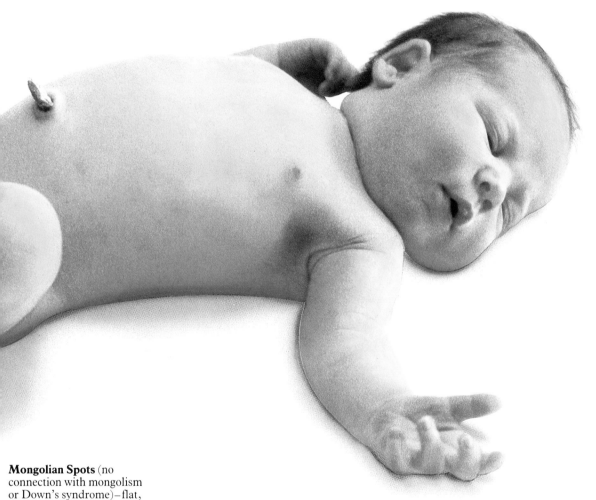

Mongolian Spots (no connection with mongolism or Down's syndrome)–flat, bluish-gray spots, usually about 1 inch (2 cms) in diameter, but sometimes much larger, that most often appear on the lower back. They may occur in groups of three to five and have indistinct borders that gradually fade into the normal surrounding skin. They are most common in dark-skinned races but may also occur in Caucasians; they often fade as the child grows older.

Moles–dense collections of the cells that produce skin color or pigment. Quite dark in appearance with distinct borders, they may be flat or dome-shaped and sometimes have hair growing from them. They are sometimes removed for cosmetic reasons but otherwise require no treatment.

Typically wrinkled skin on the soles of the feet of a full-term baby.

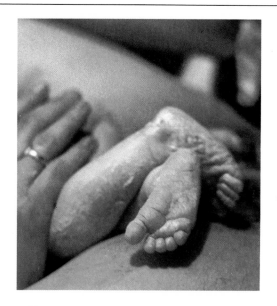

white substance called vernix caseosa. Made up of sloughed skin cells and oils from glands in the skin, it protected her skin during her months of floating in amniotic fluid. This may be washed off by the birth attendant or left to dry out and wear away in the first few days.

At first, the baby appears pale and slightly bluish in color because only a small amount of blood (containing very little oxygen) is coming to the skin in the minutes immediately after birth. As your baby takes her first breaths, more blood flows to the skin and the baby's color becomes brighter; after some hours, her color will be much improved.

Skin textures vary according to whether the baby is premature, full term, or post-term. Premature babies have smooth, relatively thin skin with very few wrinkles; full-term babies have a thicker skin and prominent wrinkles on the palms of their hands and the soles of their feet. The skin of post-term newborns may be cracked and peeling, almost like parchment; deep creases may mark the soles and palms, and the skin itself is quite dry.

Over the next few days, the skin of all these types of babies changes quite dramatically. The outer skin, which was exposed to the amniotic fluid, dries, flakes, and peels, allowing the next layer of skin to come to the surface. This is the soft skin for which babies are renowned. The skin stays as it is for a year or so and then gradually thickens.

THE HEAD'S APPEARANCE

You may be concerned that your baby's head has a peculiar shape–somewhat more pointed than you had expected. This is caused by molding during the tight passage the baby has made down the birth canal; the bones of a baby's skull overlap so that they

can slide over each other to ease this process at birth. The molded head corrects itself into a more conventional shape over the first week or two of life; nothing should be done to hasten it. The fontanel, or soft spot, at the top of the skull where the bones have not yet hardened and closed will remain for eighteen months or so. Nonetheless, it is well protected by the tough scalp tissues, so only a reasonable amount of care need be taken in handling. Do not, for example, hesitate to rub that area of the scalp gently when shampooing the baby's hair.

Pressure against the scalp during delivery sometimes causes tiny blood vessels to burst and bleed in the space between the scalp and the skull, causing a large swollen area. This requires no treatment. The bleeding stops by itself and the excess blood collected in the swelling is gradually reabsorbed by the body over a period of weeks.

Some babies are born with a full head of hair; others are nearly bald. Lanugo, as the hair present at birth is called, usually falls out and only gradually is replaced by permanent hair. This is because hair follicles go through periods of growth and rest, and at birth about 75 percent of the hair follicles are in the resting phase. Over the next few weeks, the follicles that were growing go into their rest period, and the baby may become virtually bald. Between the baby's sixth and twelfth months, however, the hair again moves into its growing phase, and by about age two your child will have a normal head of hair, which may not be the same color as any she was born with.

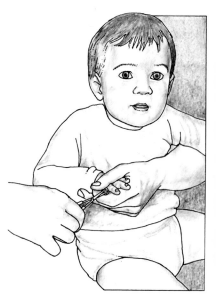

Always use round-ended scissors to cut your baby's nails. It is safer to do this when the baby is asleep. If the nails are still sharp, mittens will prevent her from scratching herself.

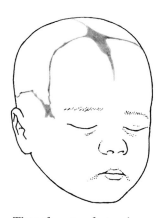

The soft spot or fontanel on your baby's head allows the bones of the skull to overlap during its tight passage down the birth canal. The baby's head may temporarily be molded by its journey, but it regains a more usual shape in a week or two.

52

OTHER NORMAL VARIATIONS

The hormones in the mother's body during pregnancy can cause enlargement of the breasts in both boy and girl babies and of the genitals in baby girls. Sometimes a newborn's breasts secrete a thin white fluid, commonly called witch's milk; the enlargement may persist for several weeks before subsiding as the hormones gradually disappear. Do not squeeze or massage the breasts (this might promote infection) or give any other treatment. The enlargement of the baby girl's genitals is also a temporary condition, although the effect of the hormones may be so strong as to cause her to have some blood-tinged discharge. This is common and needs no treatment, but do mention it to your health care provider.

Your newborn's fingernails may appear well-trimmed or they may be so long that they need to be cut. Use blunt-ended scissors at a time when the baby is passive and relaxed, such as after a feeding or during her sleep. Babies can accidentally scratch themselves if their nails are too long.

COMMON SKIN DISORDERS

Several disorders of the skin that may occur in the first few months of life are minor and easily treated. As your child gets older, the skin problems she may encounter change somewhat. Full discussion of these conditions from the newborn period to toddlerhood can be found in A CHILD'S HEALTH A-Z. See Eczema, Impetigo, Ringworm, Scabies, Seborrhea, Seborrheic Dermatitis, and Urticaria.

Diaper Rash

The most common skin problem your child is likely to have from about two to fifteen months is diaper rash (see page 207, Ammonia Dermatitis). Initially this appears as reddened skin in the diaper area, mostly over the buttocks and genitals. The lower abdomen and upper legs may also be involved, but usually the skin folds of the legs are spared because they are not normally in contact with the wet diaper. As the rash progresses, the skin becomes more intensely red and develops a bumpy texture. Small pustules may develop if the rash becomes infected.

The major cause of diaper rash is prolonged contact of the skin with urine; other causes, such as irritation from the diaper

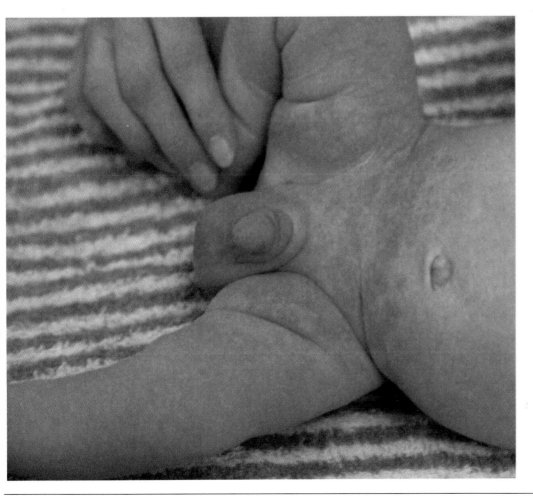

This is the typical appearance of diaper rash – ammonia dermatitis. The skin areas that come in contact with a urine-soaked diaper are markedly inflamed.

itself, may exist but are less common. Simple diaper rashes can get worse for several reasons. Certain bacteria can break down urine into ammonia and other chemicals that are irritating to the skin. Other bacteria and fungi find it easier to grow on this irritated skin and so cause an infection. Different foods are broken down by the body in different ways, leaving different waste products to be passed in the urine. Infection of the skin almost always occurs after the skin has become inflamed.

If your baby develops a rash, change her diaper frequently or leave it off, particularly in the open air during nap time. You might try changing the type of diaper you are using–switch to cloth if you have been using disposables, or try a diaper service, which may be able to disinfect laundered diapers more thoroughly than you can at home. After removing a wet or soiled diaper, thoroughly clean your baby's bottom with a cloth dampened with plain water; then pat dry. The use of baby powder is controversial because powders containing talc are dangerous if inhaled. If you use talcum powder, do not shake it over the baby; rather, put a little in the palm of your hand and apply it gently. Corn starch powders absorb moisture well and do not contain talc, but they may provide a growing medium for the bacteria that cause diaper rash. An ointment that provides a barrier to the moisture may help; those containing petroleum jelly and zinc oxide seem to be effective.

If the rash persists and is severe, your health care provider may prescribe antibiotic or antifungal creams or even oral antibiotics. Other skin problems can be confused with diaper rash–eczema and seborrheic dermatitis, for instance–but a health professional can distinguish these and prescribe treatment.

Other Skin Rashes
As a general rule, any rash accompanied by fever is attributable to an infection until proved otherwise. The majority of such infections are mild and do not last long, but you should consult your health care provider all the same. In the meantime, lowering the baby's temperature with baby aspirin or acetaminophen and sponging with tepid water will make your baby more comfortable, but will not prevent your health care provider from diagnosing the problem.

A rash unaccompanied by fever is a skin problem alone. Most rashes of that sort are caused by contact with an irritating or allergenic substance–for instance, detergent remaining in clothes, metals used in some jewelry, a specific material such as wool, a food, a soap, or a perfume used in skin

creams or disposable wipes. For every substance there is sure to be someone somewhere whose skin will find it irritating; treatment consists of first identifying the substance and then removing it (see page 206, Allergy).

SKIN INJURIES
The most common skin problems among children under three are those accidentally inflicted by toddlers upon themselves–cuts, scrapes, bumps, and bruises. Most require no treatment at all; others need minor first aid. There are, of course, more serious injuries that require the attention of a medical professional or even emergency measures. See A CHILD'S HEALTH A-Z for Abrasions, Bruises, Cuts, Stings, and Sunburn, as well as pages 34-37 on how to prevent accidents by making your child's environment a safe place in which to grow.

Reasonable cleanliness alone will prevent many skin problems from occurring, and timely and appropriate treatment as described here and in the A-Z will limit others. Despite problems that may occur, your child's skin is a durable body covering that requires minimal care.

BATHING
It used to be the practice to bathe an infant every day. Nowadays, "topping and tailing" are considered enough for some days. If it makes you feel better to bathe your baby every day, do so–but for some days a sponge bath or washing the parts that matter is probably sufficient for a new baby. For sponge baths, it is best to use clear warm water alone because rinsing away soap with a sponge bath is notoriously difficult, and the residue can be irritating.

You can use a plastic baby bathtub especially designed for the purpose; some have one sloping end against which the baby can be propped and held with one hand while being washed with the other. The bathroom or kitchen sink may be equally suitable, provided that it is kept clean. If you bathe your baby in a sink, you must be careful to avoid accidentally knocking him against the faucets. It is safest if you put a washcloth or other padding over them before you begin. The hot faucet may also be quite warm to the touch, so padding makes sense for that reason as well.

Make sure that the room is comfortably warm and that you have gathered together all the things you need (see page 28). Fill the bath before you put your baby into it, and test the temperature first by dipping your elbow into the water. It should feel lukewarm.

Put the baby into the water and, using a

mild unscented soap (or clear water and no soap at all) and a soft washcloth, wet or lather all over her body. Rinse the skin thoroughly; soap remaining in skin creases can be irritating to a baby's skin. The same soap can be used to wet and shampoo her hair, or if you wish you can use a baby shampoo, which is less irritating if some accidentally gets into her eyes. The shampoo should be done last. That way the baby does not sit around with a wet head. Also, many babies who delight in or just tolerate a splash in the tub become quite upset for the shampoo part. Saving it for last means the baby can have some fun and you can do a good body wash before the tears begin.

Rinse the hair well, again making sure no soap is left; then lift the baby out onto a towel on your lap and pat her dry. Make sure the creases are quite dry; if your baby's skin is dry or prone to rashes, use a very small amount of occlusive cream to shield the skin from irritation from urine in the diaper area.

The whole bath should take no longer than ten to fifteen minutes, or excessive oil may be lost from the baby's skin and cause drying.

Newborn babies may have some eye drainage for the first few days. Clean this gently away with a soft cloth dampened in clear water–no soap–always wiping from the nose out toward the ear and using a separate corner of the cloth for each eye. If the drainage persists, consult your health care provider.

Do not try to clean the ear canal with a cotton swab. It is unnecessary, and a sudden movement on the baby's part could cause an injury to her eardrum; use a damp washcloth or clean, well-trimmed finger to clean only the part easily reached. Do not probe! Her nose and face can also be wiped with a cloth, but use no soap.

Female genitalia may also be washed gently with a cloth, but do not rub or wash them extensively. Avoid soap in this area. A waxy substance is often present but does not need to be removed. A slight white or blood-stained discharge may also be present, but again this is of no concern unless it persists.

The penis should also be routinely washed. If circumcised, it may still be gently washed after the first day, but any swelling or bleeding should be reported to your health care provider. The foreskin of an uncircumcised penis should not be retracted.

The remains of the umbilical cord can also be gently washed and dried. Normally the stump will drop off within ten days or so, but any discharge or foul odor from it should be reported to your health care provider.

Normally there is no need for creams, ointments, or powders after bathing. Most of these products do little good and can themselves irritate if they are used excessively or improperly. They are best reserved for the problems discussed in the A-Z section or upon specific recommendation of your baby's health care provider.

You will probably find it most convenient to bathe your baby by one of these methods until she begins to be too big or too active for the baby bath (at about six to seven months), and it will then be time to begin to bathe her in the adult tub.

Introduce her gradually to the idea of the bigger bath, which may at first be frightening; some parents begin the process by having the baby in the bath with them–in which case it can begin when the baby is only four or five months old or even sooner. Prop the baby between your legs, supporting his back, and let him play and get used to the water. You will be the best judge of whether your baby is alarmed. If you delay introducing the bath until your baby is older and able to sit unsupported, make the same preparations regarding temperature of the room and water, supplies, and precautions as before. Bending down over a bath can be hard on your back; kneeling on a soft cushion helps.

Never, ever leave a child under five alone in the bath (see page 215).

Whether you need to bathe your baby every day may depend on how active she is–some crawling, walking babies manage to accumulate an amazing amount of dust and dirt, and putting one of these in the tub may be the easiest way of coping with her. At other times, washing hands and face and possibly the diaper area may be enough.

The time of bathing or washing your baby again depends on your individual life style. It is common to bathe a new baby in the morning–usually before the second feeding of the day–and to bathe the older child before bedtime, but there is no hard and fast rule except that you will not want to put a child to bed without washing off the day's grubbiness.

BATHING

It used to be the practice to give a baby a full bath every day–but sponge-bathing or topping and tailing is quite adequate. You do not even have to put the baby in the bath.

When sponge-bathing, hold the baby securely on your lap and remove the minimum amount of clothing necessary. As you sponge (a washcloth works equally well), pay particular attention to the skin creases; you can rinse the baby's hair and gently rub it dry before you put on the undershirt.

Topping and tailing is even quicker and is a good way of washing your baby with the minimum of disturbance. In both cases, use cream around the diaper area sparingly and only when necessary.

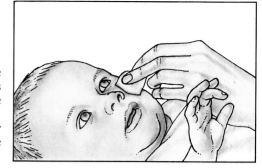

SPONGE-BATHING	TOPPING AND TAILING

1. Sponge baby's front; then pat dry.

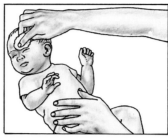

1. Wipe face with moist, soft, lint-free cloth or cotton ball. Dry. Use different corner of cloth or new cotton ball for each eye, and wipe gently from inner to outer corner.

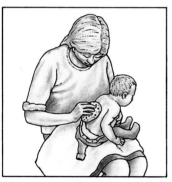

2. Sponge back as you lean baby forward. Pat dry.

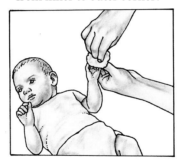

2. Wipe hands with moist cloth.

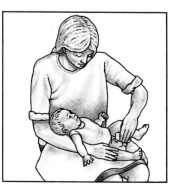

3. Dress baby in undershirt. Sponge bottom first; then legs and feet. Pat dry.

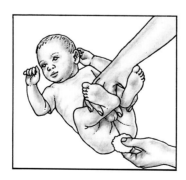

3. Remove diaper and, holding feet securely, use moist cloth or cotton to clean soiled area. Dry gently.

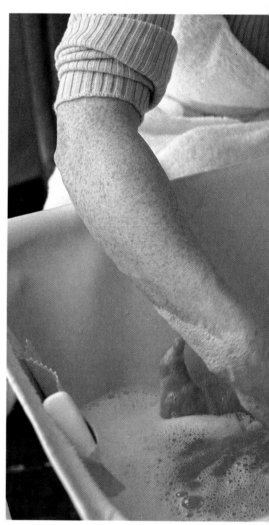

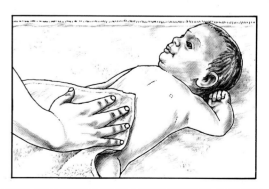

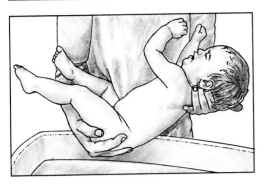
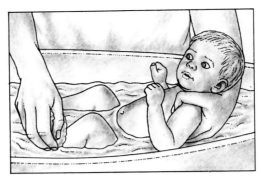

GIVING THE BABY A BATH

First, gather everything you will need. Make sure room is comfortably warm. Fill the bath, and test temperature with your elbow. Water should feel neither too hot nor too cold.

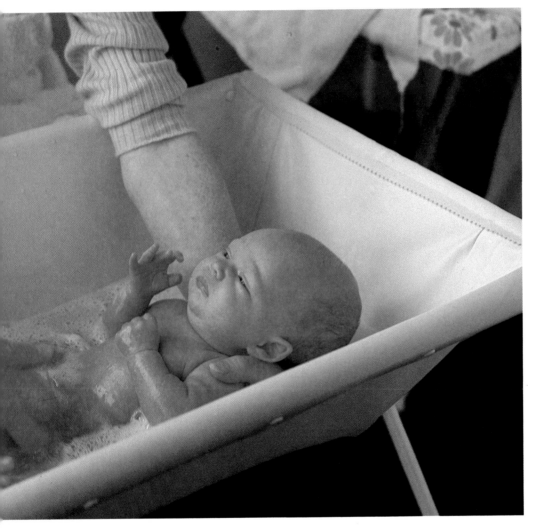

1. Wrap baby in towel. Wipe each eye with new corner of soft, lint-free cloth or separate piece of cotton. Use new piece of cotton or soft cloth to wipe each side of face.

2. Unwrap and gently lower baby into water, taking care to support him as shown.

3. With your arm supporting his head and your hand holding his upper arm, gently wash and rinse his body.

4. Continue washing and rinsing while you smile and talk to baby to reassure him all is well.

5. Lift him out, supporting his head and bottom so he cannot wriggle free. Lay him on towel and wrap him.

6. Holding baby along your left arm as shown, wash hair backwards over bath. Rinse and pat dry.

7. Cuddle baby as you dry his head and body. Pay particular attention to all creases.

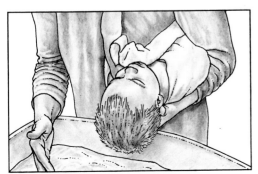
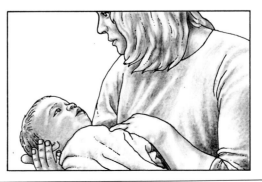

CHANGING DIAPERS AND DRESSING

Shown at right is a range of diapers and waterproof pants available. Cloth diapers can be bought ready-shaped. Protective pants can fasten at the sides or have elastic waists. Disposable diapers (far right) come with a waterproof outer layer.

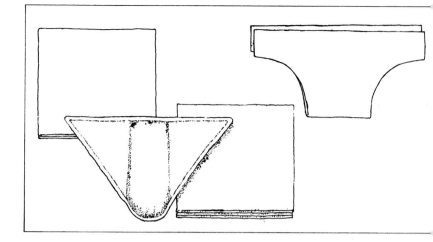

Be careful about where you change and dress your child. Even a new baby can wriggle quickly to the edge of a dangerous drop while your back is turned. You need a firm flat surface: A bed or the floor is suitable for dressing, but a waterproof pad is better for changing. A mobile hung above the dressing and changing area will help to divert the baby's attention.

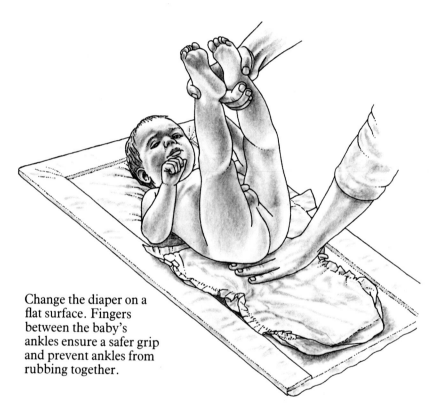

Change the diaper on a flat surface. Fingers between the baby's ankles ensure a safer grip and prevent ankles from rubbing together.

CLOTH DIAPERS

Cloth diapers must be fastened with pins. To avoid pricking the baby, always put a hand between the diaper and the baby's skin. Use a guarded diaper pin, and pin horizontally. Make sure to catch in all the folds.

Cloth diapers are easier to get clean if they are soaked while waiting to be laundered. A solution of washing soda or an enzyme-boosted detergent in water can be kept in a covered bucket to which the soiled diapers are added. Diaper services may not require customers to presoak, but storing soiled diapers in a covered pail between pick-ups is still a must. Whether you use a service or launder your own diapers, flush away stools before putting diapers in a pail.

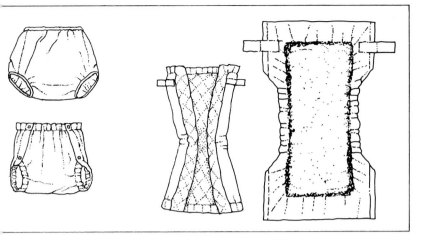

A new parent can find it unnerving to face dressing a baby for the first time. Tiny arms and legs look vulnerable, but babies are tougher than you think. Here are some pointers.

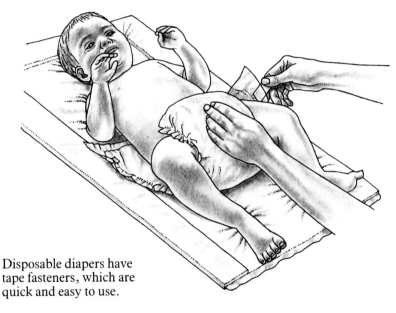

Disposable diapers have tape fasteners, which are quick and easy to use.

Snap-front undershirts are easier to put on and take off, but if you do use pullovers, raise the baby's head slightly and slip the shirt over the head, back to front. Stretch one armhole and gently feed one hand through; then repeat with the other on the other side.

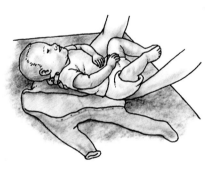

Spread the unsnapped baby suit flat, and lower baby into it.

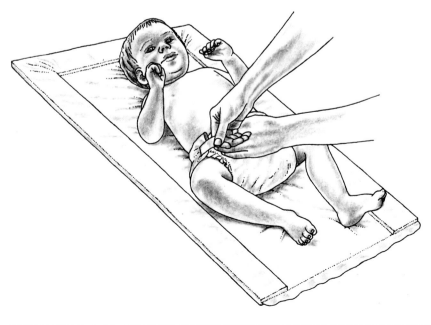

Stretch and accordion the armhole, and push your hand through to draw back the baby's arm. Repeat with the other arm and each leg, and snap closed.

IMMUNIZATION

You may have had measles as a child, or mumps, or German measles–but your child need not. In the last twenty years or so, a number of these childhood ailments have almost been eliminated. In the United States, measles is approaching elimination, paralysis due to poliomyelitis has become very rare, and mumps and rubella (German measles) cases have declined appreciably. Diphtheria, tetanus, and whooping cough, which were killers fifty years ago, have also been largely eradicated. The virus that causes meningitis (Hemophilus influenzae meningitis) and other infections are persistent problems, however.

Immunization against diphtheria, tetanus, whooping cough, measles, mumps, rubella, polio, and Hemophilus influenzae is routinely available and in many localities is required before a child is admitted to school. Parental consent is required before a child can be immunized.

You might ask why, when a disease has become rare, there remains any need to immunize. The answer is that immunization has made the disease rare, but if a child were to contract it and then mix with nonimmunized children, they too would probably catch the same illness. This is how epidemics begin and why immunizations must be continued.

HOW IMMUNIZATION WORKS
When a body is attacked by an organism that causes a disease, it manufactures antibodies to fight that organism. If the illness attacks a second time, the antibodies already present in the bloodstream prevent its taking hold. A vaccine for immunization is made from small quantities of the organisms that cause the disease or from materials produced by those organisms. The vaccine is then either swallowed or injected into the body, and the body reacts by producing antibodies. Sometimes the protection given by the antibodies lasts a lifetime; sometimes it has to be renewed by boosters. If–as happens rarely–a child catches an illness after immunization, the attack will be mild.

A baby is born with antibodies that protect against many childhood infections. These have been passed to him from his mother and make him temporarily immune. This is true whether the baby is breastfed or bottle-fed. The inborn immunity gradually fades during the first several months of life, so immunizations are given to help him build permanent defenses. A baby cannot be successfully immunized while he still carries the innate antibodies because the introduced vaccine will be attacked by these instead of stimulating manufacture of the child's own antibodies. Vaccinations are therefore best given when the natural protection is fading but before the baby becomes exposed to the diseases without protection.

Health care providers usually follow the schedules for immunization drawn up by the American Academy of Pediatrics. The intervals suggested in the following chart represent a typical schedule:

AGE	DIPHTHERIA PERTUSSIS TETANUS	POLIO	MEASLES	RUBELLA	MUMPS	HEMOPHILUS INFLUENZAE
2 months	★	★				
4 months	★	★				
6 months	★	★ (optional)				
15 months			★	★	★	
18 months (booster)	★	★				
2 years						★
4-6 years (booster)	★	★				

Measles, rubella, and mumps vaccines are often given in a combined form at fifteen months of age, by a single injection. Your child should receive a diphtheria-tetanus booster at fourteen to sixteen years of age.

If your child is older than one year and for any reason has not yet received his immunizations, you should have him immunized as soon as possible. The following schedule is a good one for "catching up". Some health care providers may recommend slightly different schedules, but theirs will probably provide comparable protection to the chart shown here.

VISIT	DIPHTHERIA PERTUSSIS TETANUS	POLIO	MEASLES	RUBELLA	MUMPS	HEMOPHILUS INFLUENZAE
first visit	★	★				
1 month after 1st visit			★	★	★	★
2 months after 1st visit	★	★				
4 months after 1st visit		★ (optional)				
10-16 months after 1st visit	★	★				

Notes: Measles, mumps, and rubella vaccines are not routinely given prior to fifteen months of age and may be given together in a single injection. Hemophilus influenzae immunization is usually given only after two years of age. Your child should receive a diphtheria-tetanus booster at fourteen to sixteen years of age.

Immunization has virtually eliminated several childhood ailments in the United States. Protection depends on having your child immunized on schedule.

If for any reason your child has missed his third DPT or polio immunization, it will not be necessary to repeat the whole series. One or two additional immunizations will bring him up to date. If your child is sick with something more serious than a cold, your health care provider may delay immunization until he is well; this will leave him unprotected only during the short waiting period.

Your health care provider will keep a record of your child's immunizations, but you should too. Ask your doctor for an immunization card and have it filled out at each visit. It may be needed in an emergency: For instance, if your child steps on a nail, you will want to know whether his tetanus shots are up to date. Schools, camps, and day-care centers may also ask for immunization information.

DISEASES IMMUNIZED AGAINST

The following discussion covers the symptoms and dangers of the major childhood diseases against which immunization is available. Sometimes the immunization produces side effects that might cause discomfort; those are described as well. In most cases, the side effects are minor, particularly when compared to the symptoms of the diseases themselves. Baby aspirin or acetaminophen usually relieves any temporary discomfort in the period following the shot.

Diphtheria

A serious bacterial infection that usually begins with a sore throat and fever. Patches of membrane form on the back of the tonsils and may extend down to block the windpipe, causing hoarseness, barking cough, difficulty in swallowing, and even suffocation. A skin infection may also develop. Spread by coughing or sneezing or by carriers who themselves remain well, the disease is treatable only in the first few days, after which the bacteria produce a powerful poison that spreads through the body and may cause paralysis or heart failure. About one in ten victims dies.

Immunization against diphtheria is usually given in combination with tetanus and whooping cough vaccines (see the chart for the normal schedule of DPT inoculation). The vaccine protects most children from the disease and makes the disease milder for those who do become ill.

After the booster shown on the chart at four to six years of age, a booster every ten years is needed to retain immunity; it is often combined with tetanus (but not with pertussis) when given to older children and adults.

Side effects of the immunization–if they occur at all–are soreness and swelling at the site of the injection, but this is uncommon in young children. Children over age seven are given a smaller dose of diphtheria vaccine to reduce the chance of local reactions.

Pertussis
Commonly called whooping cough. A highly contagious bacterial disease primarily affecting infants and preschool children. Beginning as a mild coldlike illness, it may be followed by weeks or months of severe coughing, occurring in spasms and causing difficulty with breathing. The cough has a characteristic whooping noise as the child tries to get his breath back. The child may gag and vomit after a coughing spell. Complications may include pneumonia, convulsions, brain damage, and death, most of which occur in babies under six months.

After vaccination, your child may have a slight fever and be irritable for a day or two; sometimes soreness, swelling, or a lump develops at the injection site. The lump may last for several months but is no cause for concern. Your doctor can prescribe medication to relieve the other symptoms.

More serious side effects–high fever, convulsions, abnormal crying, and shock–occur in 1 in 7,000 children. One child in 100,000 will develop inflammation of the brain and may suffer brain damage. The risk of a severe reaction to pertussis vaccine is very small compared to the greater risk of brain damage and death in the unimmunized baby, and recent controversy about the safety of the whooping cough vaccine does not in any way disprove this point. Discuss the subject with your health care provider if you are worried, but please do not neglect to have your child immunized against pertussis unless he has had a very severe reaction to a previous injection. New vaccines are being developed that have far fewer side effects.

Tetanus
Commonly called lockjaw. Caused by bacteria that live in soil and get into the body through a wound contaminated by soil. The poison produced by the bacteria causes painful muscular contractions; the chance of surviving is only 50-50.

The vaccine, which is initially given in combination with diphtheria and pertussis vaccines, is very effective in preventing the disease–99 percent of all children injected are protected. Reactions in children are uncommon. After the booster at four to six years, subsequent boosters should be given at ten-year intervals unless there is a very deep and dirty puncture wound, in which case a shot is necessary if more than five years have elapsed since the last injection.

Poliomyelitis
Also called infantile paralysis. A contagious viral disease primarily affecting children from age one to age sixteen. It may be mild, with fever, nausea, headache, stomach ache, and (occasionally) stiff neck and backache, or it may be severe. In severe cases it attacks the nervous system, causing paralysis of arms and legs and of the muscles used in breathing. One out of ten children with severe polio dies, and paralysis is permanent in over half of the severe cases.

There are two kinds of polio vaccine. The one used and recommended in the United States is the trivalent oral polio vaccine (TOPV or OPV), made from live polio virus that has been so weakened that it no longer causes disease but does stimulate the production of antibodies. Two doses of TOPV in early infancy and a third at eighteen months ensure full protection against polio. Some health care providers give an additional dose at six months, although most babies develop a good antibody response without it. Protection is usually lifelong if a booster dose is given at four to six years of age. The other form is made from killed polio virus and is given by injection (a series of four shots). It is not routinely used in the United States because most polio experts think the oral vaccine is more effective, but killed polio vaccine is used for children who have low resistance to infection or who live in households where others have low resistance. If you have questions about this, your health care provider can help answer them.

Measles
A very contagious viral disease of childhood. It begins with three to seven days of high fever, runny nose, watery eyes, and harsh

cough. A red blotchy rash then starts on head and face and spreads over the entire body, lasting from four to seven days. The illness is usually over in ten days, but it may last as long as three weeks. It is more severe in infants under one year of age, and 1 in every 3,000 cases is fatal. It may lead to complications such as ear infections or pneumonia (1 child in 2,000 may develop inflammation of the brain, with convulsions, deafness, or mental retardation).

The vaccine, which may be given in combination with vaccines for mumps and rubella, usually produces no symptoms; children who do have a reaction usually develop a fever as high as 103°F or a mild rash a week or so after the injection. Your health care provider may recommend acetominophen or aspirin to ease the symptoms. One injection produces long-lasting protection; boosters are unnecessary.

If your child has had *severe* allergic reactions to eggs or to the antibiotic neomycin, he should probably not receive the measles vaccine. Chick embryos are used in its manufacture, and it also contains traces of neomycin. A mild reaction to eggs is not significant, and allergies to chickens or feathers carry no risk. If you are uncertain, discuss the matter with your health care provider.

Your child should also not be vaccinated for measles if he has a fever, although he may be vaccinated if he has a minor illness such as a cold. Children with diseases that cause lowered resistance to infection (leukemia or immune deficiencies) should not receive measles vaccine.

Before receiving a measles vaccine, your child will be given a tuberculosis skin test; this is to detect a mild, unnoticed case of tuberculosis that might be made worse by the vaccination.

Mumps

A contagious viral disease of young children. It develops two to three weeks after exposure and causes fever, headache, earache, and painful swollen saliva glands, most commonly in the face and neck. Often only one gland swells, but both are usually swollen within a day or two. Usually a mild complaint, mumps lasts a week to ten days, but in 15 out of 100 children a mild form of meningitis (inflammation of the brain covering) develops. In 1 out of 400, inflammation of the brain itself develops but usually leaves no permanent damage. In rare cases, mumps causes deafness.

Other complications of mumps include inflammation of the thyroid and kidneys, swelling of the joints, and, in females, inflammation of the ovaries and breasts.

Protection by vaccine probably lasts for life; booster shots are unnecessary. Reaction to the vaccine, which is commonly combined with vaccines for measles and rubella, may be a mild fever and some swelling of the salivary glands one to two weeks after the vaccination, but the symptoms are usually mild and do not require treatment. One child in 1 million develops inflammation of the brain from the vaccine.

As with the measles vaccine, mumps vaccine should not be given to a child with *severe* allergic reaction to eggs or neomycin or to a child with lowered resistance to infection. Neither should it be given if your child has a fever, although it can be given if he has a minor illness such as a cold.

Rubella

Commonly called German measles. A common contagious viral disease. It develops two to three weeks after exposure and generally causes a mild fever, rash, and swelling of the glands, particularly those in the back of the neck. Young women may have temporary stiffness and swelling of their joints. A rare complication (1 in 5,000) is inflammation of the brain. The illness usually lasts only about three days.

Most children will have no symptoms after being vaccinated; others may have a slight rash or swelling in the neck glands a week or two after the injection. One to three weeks after the injection, two to three days of pain and stiffness in the joints may be noticed. About 98 percent of all children who receive a single dose get long-term and probably lifelong protection. A child should not be vaccinated if he has a fever but may be if he has a cold or other minor illness. The strictures about allergies to neomycin and lowered resistance to infection apply to rubella vaccination as well. It is usually given with the vaccine for measles and mumps.

The danger of rubella infection is the effect it has on unborn babies. If a mother contracts rubella early in pregnancy, there is a 20 percent chance that she will give birth to a handicapped baby. She also has a greater than usual risk of having a miscarriage. The most common birth defects caused by rubella infection are blindness, heart and major artery damage, deafness, and mental retardation. In the last major epidemic of rubella in the United States (in 1964), approximately 20,000 babies were born with severe birth defects, and approximately 30,000 women suffered miscarriages. Vaccination of young children eliminates the source of infection and prevents the spread of rubella. The vaccine may be given to a child living in the same household with a pregnant woman without danger to the unborn baby.

ILLNESS	INCUBATION PERIOD	SYMPTOMS	DURATION	COMPLICATIONS
DIPHTHERIA	2–5 days	sore throat, fever, hoarseness, barking cough	2 weeks	inflammation of heart, paralysis, death in 10% of patients
TETANUS	3–21 days (average 8 days)	muscle spasms	2 weeks or more	death in 50% of patients
PERTUSSIS (WHOOPING COUGH)	7–10 days	cold symptoms, severe coughing spells, whooping	weeks or months	pneumonia, brain damage, convulsions
MEASLES	9–12 days	fever, cough, runny nose, red eyes, rash	10–14 days	ear infections, pneumonia, inflammation of brain
MUMPS	16–18 days	swelling of salivary glands in face and neck, earache, fever, headache	7–10 days	inflammation of brain, inflammation of testes
RUBELLA (GERMAN MEASLES)	14–21 days	rash, swollen glands on back of neck, swelling or pain in joints	3 days	inflammation of brain, abnormal bleeding
POLIOMYELITIS	7–14 days	fever, nausea, headache, stomach ache, stiff neck, back ache	1 week	paralysis, death

IMMUNIZATION	AGE AT WHICH GIVEN	AGAINST	POSSIBLE REACTIONS	YOUR CHILD SHOULD NOT BE VACCINATED IF HE HAS
DPT	2 months, 4 months, 6 months, 18 months, 4–6 years (booster), booster every 10 years thereafter	Diphtheria Pertussis Tetanus	*Common:* fever (101°F or less), irritability *Uncommon:* soreness and swelling of injection site *Rare:* high fever (105°F), convulsions, abnormal crying, shock *Very Rare:* brain damage	an illness more serious than a cold; a history of convulsion or other nervous system problems; or a history of serious reaction to previous DPT shot
MMR	15 months or older	Measles Mumps Rubella	*Common:* rash or slight fever *Uncommon:* swelling of glands in neck, aching of swelling of joints *Rare:* mild swelling of salivary glands, pain, numbness or tingling of hands and feet *Very Rare:* inflammation of brain, convulsions	an illness more serious than a cold; an allergy to neomycin; cancer or a disease that lowers the body's resistance to infection, taken drugs such as cortisone that lower the body's resistance to infection; received gamma globulin in the past 3 months; or severe allergy to eggs
POLIO (TOPV)	2 months, 4 months, 6 months (optional), 18 months, 4–6 years (booster)	Poliomyelitis	*Very Rare:* paralysis	cancer or a disease that lowers the body's resistance to infection; taken drugs such as cortisone that lower the body's resistance to infection; a household member who either has a disease or is taking drugs that lower the body's resistance; or an illness more serious than a cold
HEMOPHILUS INFLUENZAE	2 years	Hemophilus flu, meningitis, arthritis, epiglottitis	*Very Rare*	an illness more serious than a cold

Specialists in contagious diseases are working to develop new vaccines to prevent such illnesses as chicken pox, diarrhea, respiratory infections, and other severe infections. As a parent, you are responsible for your child's health; immunizations play an important part in maintaining that health. Some parents worry that their child will be frightened by the needle, but most children soon forget their temporary distress. If you are tense and anxious, you will probably convey your worries to your child. Try to smile and relax, so he can feel that there is nothing much to worry about.

It is important to understand the potential reactions to vaccination. Most health care providers will give you written instructions on what to do if reactions occur, but you may have to ask for them. Remember to have the immunization record filled out, and do not be afraid to ask questions—even if your doubts are minor. It is, above all, important to have your child fully immunized against the common illnesses for which vaccines are available; in general, the vaccines are quite effective and adequately safe.

POSTPARTUM DEPRESSION

So much has been written recently about postpartum depression that you might think it is an inevitable part of giving birth. Feelings of weepiness, inadequacy, and weariness are quite common after a birth, but it is only when this lethargy and depression persist for weeks and color the days to such an extent that everything else seems meaningless that professional help is needed.

NORMAL LOW FEELINGS

It is normal to feel tired when there is a new baby in the house: There is a lot more work to do (unfamiliar work if it is a first baby), and the mother's body has not yet recovered from the hard work of pregnancy, labor, and birth. Not only is her body adjusting to the changes made by the birth, her emotions are also adapting to a new life style and to herself as a different person. The responsibility of a new life is very great, and many parents think, if their baby cries, that somehow they are mismanaging her: Is she in pain? Are we feeding her correctly? What are we doing wrong? (and sometimes) Why won't she go away?

A baby cries, on the average, two hours out of twenty-four. If it comes all at once or regularly in the middle of the night, it can be pretty difficult to bear. On top of that, you will not always know why she is crying. You can try to identify and resolve the main causes—thirst, hunger, discomfort, loneliness—but sometimes all you can do is cuddle and comfort her, and sometimes even that does not help. It is not always crying that is worrisome, anyway; it is the unpredictability of not knowing when you will be summoned by that cry. Parents are attuned to their baby's crying, and it worries them a great deal more than it worries the babysitter, who can leave at day's or evening's end and go home for an uninterrupted night's sleep.

Companionship helps to overcome some of the pressure; it is comforting to find that you are not the only one with those feelings, those

Extra work and responsibility can weigh heavily on a new mother. A mother whose depression is severe should ask for help.

problems. Meeting others in the same situation as yourselves can bring invaluable mutual support. The La Leche League, for instance, is an organization of breastfeeding mothers; other parent resource groups exist on the local level. Babysitting circles or co-ops often evolve from such groups, enabling parents to go out alone or together more often. And then there are the other mothers you meet pushing their strollers on the street or toting their babies while shopping for groceries. Overcome any shyness you might feel and make contact. It can be a big help. (See also pages 44-50 for suggestions about getting extra sleep, help in the home, and so on.)

LOW FEELINGS SIGNALING TROUBLE
Real postpartum depression is a state in which a mother is so depressed that she is ill

and is not responsible for her own actions. If a mother feels she is tipping over into such a state, she should talk to her own health care provider, who may prescribe medication or psychiatric counseling.

In such a situation, a woman might be incapable of assessing her own need for help. This is when her partner or perhaps a relative or friend should be alert to her state and be responsible for getting in touch with her health care provider.

It is rare for a mother to be so depressed that she has to return to hospital for treatment, but if that should happen, many hospitals nowadays make provision for the baby to stay with her mother.

To sum up, postpartum depression is a treatable illness, but it is quite different from being mildly—or even mightily—fed up with the many changes in life that come with a first baby.

CHILD ABUSE

Many parents have at times had violent feelings toward their baby. Indeed, looking back on their children's early days, some have confessed they feel fortunate not to have injured them in the first weeks and months of parenthood.

The teenage mother, the single parent, the divorced and isolated parent who lacks support are more at risk for abusing their young children; that danger is increased if the parent was abused early in life by his or her own parent.

Babies develop to their potential when they have a stable, ongoing relationship with their parents or caregiver. The child who is abused does develop an attachment to his parent, no matter how harmful that parent may be, but the trauma has a profound effect on the child's development and usually leaves lifelong scars. Considerable psychiatric intervention may be needed to help him come to terms with these painful early experiences and develop adult attachments.

If you suspect that a child is being injured or neglected, the law requires you to report it. Most people would prefer to stay out of such distressing situations, but child-protection agencies empowered to investigate such situations exist in all states and communities; you may give them information anonymously if you wish. By doing so, you may save a child's life.

The infant who cries incessantly and the toddler who is disruptive are only two examples of children most parents find taxing. There are many others. If you yourself fear that you will harm your child, try to tell someone—your partner, your

doctor or pediatrician, a child protection agency, a health clinic. You will find people who are willing to help and who do not regard your temptation as disgraceful. Many communities have Parents Anonymous groups (National Office, 2810 Artesia Boulevard, Redondo Beach, CA 90278), where parents who have abused their children or fear they might can meet and support each other's efforts to overcome this impulse.

Never give in to smacking or shaking your baby; even a mild smack could injure him, and there is also the danger that, if you give in to your anger, you might be unable to stop.

Why do parents hurt babies? There are a number of reasons. They may have a son and have wanted a daughter; they may imagine that his wetting the bed and crying are being done on purpose to annoy them; they may consider that he is failing to be the model baby they had dreamed of but instead is showing the world that they are not good parents. Or, as already explained, parents abused in childhood may repeat the model they learned from their parent. Quite suddenly, these hidden thoughts may come to a head, and a parent's patience snaps.

A parent who batters a baby does not necessarily hate the child. Deep down, he or she may be expressing a personal need for attention. But parents must be prepared to give love and attention without expecting anything in return.

Not all battering is physical. A withdrawn, cold parent can emotionally batter a child just as surely as can one who inflicts the bruises and abrasions of less subtle injury.

The result may be a withdrawn, passive child who fails to thrive and grow—perhaps because his parent was not given love as a child and now lacks the ability to give love to others.

As an immediate measure, if your baby's crying so irritates you that you fear you will lose control, put him in a room far away from you (first making certain he is physically safe). Ask someone to listen for you while you walk around the block. Make yourself a cup of coffee. Hit a cushion. Phone a friend or one of the help agencies. A telephone call could make the difference between an unharmed baby and a lifetime filled with remorse.

CHILDREN WITH SPECIAL NEEDS

The birth of a handicapped child is a traumatic experience for her parents and for the whole family. Feelings of guilt, anger, and disbelief, and the realization of the added responsibility that must be undertaken may be overwhelming.

Much of the parents' reaction will depend on the manner in which the news of the child's birth is told to them by the medical staff. Whatever the disability, parents should be told as soon as possible, and they should be allowed to see and hold their baby without delay. Being told that their baby is "not quite right" without being allowed to see her often suggests to their imagination that their child is extremely (even grotesquely) abnormal, when the truth may be that she has a minor condition. Parents of completely healthy and normal children who for some reason do not see their baby for some days (which used to be the practice with babies delivered by forceps) often imagine that they face some conspiracy of silence about a handicap, and they suffer greatly from the lack of understanding of their feelings. The sooner parents are allowed to see and hold their baby, the sooner they will accept her.

BEREAVEMENT AND ADJUSTMENT

The parents of a child with special needs are bereaved parents, for they are bereft of the perfect child they anticipated. Likewise, the brothers and sisters, the grandparents, the relatives, and the friends who looked forward to the birth of the child may be bereaved as well. As such, they must all pass through the stages of loss—disbelief, anger, sorrow, and finally some kind of acceptance—and in these stages they must be supported by information and care.

Much support may come from the intuitive sympathy and sensitivity of those closest to the family, but outside this framework stands a vast and growing number of professional and qualified groups, whose expertise is directed specifically toward help and understanding of particular problems. At no time has more help been available, although paradoxically it might be claimed that at no time has the help been less needed, because so many of the disorders that afflicted children even fifty years ago have been eliminated or are being controlled.

The existence of such help points to the need for a radical rethinking of the attitude toward children with special needs, including: (1) the acknowledgment that a "handicapped" child may mean a "handicapped" family; (2) the recognition that a child with limited physical, emotional, or intellectual potential requires ongoing, often multidisciplinary support to maximize her and her family's happiness; (3) the realization that many health care providers who deal primarily with "normal" children feel unprepared to support handicapped families without being supported themselves by disability specialists; and (4) the awareness that a child with a specific handicap is not handicapped in all areas.

A child in a wheelchair may be treated as though she were deaf; an undersized adult as though he were mentally undersized. When speaking to the blind, many people raise their voices, even though it is well known that blind people often develop a sharpened sense of hearing! The obese child is ostracized; the scarred child may be isolated. Children with special needs present a challenge: Can we accept them without reservation, fairly and without condescension, respecting their right not to be discriminated against? Can we acknowledge the degree to which they make us feel uncomfortable or guilty, causing us to react either with avoidance or with unnatural concern? How hard should we try to maximize their potential?

IDENTIFYING SPECIAL NEEDS

Disability may be physical or emotional. Sometimes one overlaps or causes another: The deaf child, without special care, may find it difficult to keep up intellectually with children of her age group. She may fall behind, becoming isolated and withdrawn as a result.

Physical handicaps are now usually diagnosed earlier, through developmental checks and greater awareness of what problems may exist. Mental and emotional handicaps may not be recognized until the baby fails to react in ways that would be expected of a child her

Handicapped children are children with special needs, but they also have the needs of any child for fun, freedom, and love.

age. The earlier the diagnosis of any handicap is, the better are the chances of optimal treatment for the child and of effective support for the family.

Certain children are known to be at risk because of their history or environment. These are not only babies who come from families with a history of inherited diseases, but also babies who have had severe jaundice, who have had difficult births, whose mothers have contracted certain illnesses during pregnancy, who were very premature, who are born into families where there is emotional turmoil or mental illness, or whose parents are unmarried adolescents. These babies should be carefully and non-disruptively monitored until it has been established that they are progressing normally. Inevitably, some children slip through the net – but not nearly as many as did twenty years ago.

THE STRAIN ON THE FAMILY

A child who needs extra care and attention imposes strains on a marriage and on the rest

of the family. Parents do not always agree on the treatment to seek and may find themselves in conflict about the child's prospects; brothers and sisters may resent the extra attention the handicapped child needs. Where practical, the child should not be overindulged or overhelped. Neither too little nor too much should be expected of her. Even a child with a severe physical or mental disability can become a contributing family member if she is given the right support and education. In these matters, the specialists dealing with the child can give invaluable guidelines. If the child is being cared for by several specialists for various conditions, one should nonetheless act as coordinator and mediator with the parents, so they can discuss their problems.

The child's special needs might be so extensive that her parents fear they will not be able to look after her adequately at home. The decision then has to be made whether the child should be cared for in an institution. This situation is inevitably distressing and requires great soul-searching on the part

A handicapped child puts a strain on all the family, but older siblings are often of enormous help.

of the parents. If they decide that an institution is the best solution for their child, they may still feel that they ought somehow to have managed at home. They may even blame themselves for the child's handicap and feel that now they are adding to their fault by abandoning her. A further burden arises if the parents do not agree on the decision. In such a situation, the supportive advice of a health care provider is invaluable and necessary, not only to help the parents with their decision, but also to help them recognize that caring for the child could be beyond their resources. A self-sacrificing decision to keep the child at home may not be the best solution for the child herself. Most support systems, organizations, and self-help groups for children with special needs were originated by parents with direct experience with such a child. From their suffering has flowered a remarkable quantity of sympathy and practical aid.

It is an easy mistake to attribute all of a child's behavior to her specific disability; a frustrated child can scream with tension whether she is handicapped or not! A child who cannot move cannot work off her energy with physical exercise and must find other outlets. Still, bad behavior need not be excused solely because the child has special needs. (Of course, it is a different matter if her disability has *caused* the behavior—as when a deaf child appears disobedient because she has not heard what is said to her.)

SUPPORT GROUPS

A health care provider may be able to put parents in touch with a local support group or branch of a national organization that could be of help. Member parents of such groups begin with a mutual sympathy, and children with special needs are accepted with understanding. It may be possible to arrange for other parents to babysit, allowing housebound parents some respite while knowing that their child is being cared for by adults who understand her specific problems.

Over 80 percent of children with disabilities are now living at home for most of the time. Facilities for part-time care—whether in the child's own home for a few hours or in residential homes for a few weeks—are essential for the relief and well-being of the family as a whole.

When possible, handicapped children should mix with other children in playgroups and in parent and toddler groups. The parents of a child with special needs may feel uncertain of the welcome she will receive, but a preliminary talk with the supervisor and with other parents can do much to introduce them and their child to beneficial activities and friendships.

Among the specialists trained to help a child with special needs are: teachers, psychologists, medical staff, occupational therapists, physical therapists, music therapists, nurses, play specialists, speech therapists.

The education of handicapped children is now usually administered by the local department of education and not, as previously, by the health or retardation department. Most such children are mainstreamed into regular schools unless their disabilities make attending a special school (for instance, for the blind) more appropriate.

One of the main worries of parents of a child with special needs is what will happen if they can no longer care for the child. Some parents set up trusts for their children so that they are financially provided for when that stage is reached. Sometimes parents arrange to share this responsibility with their other children.

Supervised play for the child with special needs helps him to adjust socially, and gives his family a break.

FEEDING

In the years covered by this book, your child will move from being nourished through the placenta by his mother's bloodstream to eating most of the same things the rest of the family enjoys. Along the way, you (and he) will be making decisions about likes and dislikes; what is good for him and what he may consider "yucky," what he needs from the point of view of sound nutrition and in what form it is most pleasant to eat it.

At first, the feedings will be liquid and administered by someone other than the child. Soon, solids will be introduced, and the adventure of food and eating will begin. Later on, as manual skills and interest develop, your child will make his first (albeit messy) attempts to feed himself. Feedings can be a battleground or they can be a happy time shared with others in the family. We hope, in the pages that follow, to help you make it be the latter. Eating habits that develop under three remain with us for the rest of our lives, and sound nutrition goes a long way toward ensuring a long and healthy life.

CHOOSING BREAST OR BOTTLE
Before your baby's birth you probably made up your mind about how he would be fed: by breast or by bottle. Opinion about the two options seems to vary from decade to decade; bottle-feeding was probably in fashion when

Do not exclude an older child when you are breastfeeding. She could already find it hard enough to accept the new baby.

The father may feel excluded when his baby is young and so much of his partner's attention must be given to their child. Taking his turn bottle-feeding, whether from expressed breast milk or formula, is an opportunity for father and child to become more closely involved. It will also give the mother time for herself.

Breast milk can be expressed, stored in the refrigerator, and given later by bottle.

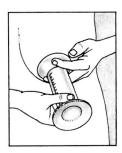
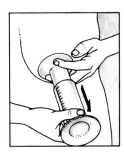

you were a baby, whereas breastfeeding seems to be relatively popular nowadays. All the more reason why the decision to breast-feed or to bottle-feed should be a personal one. It is important to learn as much as possible about the merits of each approach, but when it comes to deciding, both mother and father should be comfortable with the choice for their *own* reasons, not to satisfy others.

The contents of breast milk from a well-nourished mother and of the more widely used of the commercial formulas are compared on page 77. As these charts indicate, both satisfy the nutritional needs of the average infant. That the nursing mother should be well nourished cannot be over-emphasized, since most of the constituents of breast milk depend on the mother's nutritional condition. With the exceptions of vitamins D and K, none of the vitamins required for maintenance and growth are produced by the body and so must be obtained through the foods eaten or through vitamin supplements.

Breastfeeding has some obvious advantages: There are no formulas to mix and no bottles to prepare. The milk comes pre-warmed and is always accessible. It is less expensive, although a nursing mother must maintain a well-balanced, nutritious diet, which may be more costly than careless eating and certainly does require attention. Rarely do babies prefer the bottle to the breast, although some take longer to get used to the breast than others. Breastfeeding offers the mother a unique closeness with her baby. It is furthermore possible to express milk for someone else to give by bottle, freeing the mother somewhat and giving the father (and others) a chance for that closeness too.

There are virtually no known allergies to breast milk per se. A nursing mother might, however, eat foods that her baby is allergic to or simply finds irritating. Highly spiced foods, for example, give mother's milk a zing an infant might find unpalatable. If your baby is restless after feeding, try to remember what you have eaten and leave that out of your diet.

Many breastfeeding mothers find they lose weight and regain their figures without any of the extra exercise or dieting needed by mothers who bottle-feed.

One of the hormones involved in breast-feeding, prolactin, inhibits ovulation, and for this reason breastfeeding is erroneously considered adequate birth control. This is by no means the case, and no one who wishes to avoid conceiving in the months before menstruation resumes should rely on breastfeeding for birth control. About 5 to 10 percent of nursing mothers who have not had a first period after delivery become pregnant. It is therefore advisable to use contraception as soon as you resume sexual activity.

WHEN NOT TO BREASTFEED
A mother with active tuberculosis, typhoid fever, or malaria should not breastfeed.

Women who are taking medication against tuberculosis may breastfeed, but small amounts of the medication will be secreted into her milk, so the baby should have periodic blood tests to check liver function.

In some areas in the United States, Michigan in particular, widespread environmental contamination has resulted in levels of PCBs in human milk that may represent a health hazard to breastfed babies. Unfortunately, not enough is known about long-term effects. If you live in or near Michigan or frequently eat freshwater fish (which may be contaminated with PCBs), ask your health care provider about having your milk tested for PCB content.

Once established, breastfeeding can become a time of mutual satisfaction. Worries that the baby is not getting enough are groundless if he continues to thrive.

Any medication a mother takes is secreted in small quantities into her milk; this is true also for alcohol and recreational drugs. The effects on the baby vary with the substance and the amount taken, but avoiding medication is clearly the best solution. If this is impossible, consult your health care provider. If a safe alternative cannot be tried, it may be best to forgo breastfeeding.

WHEN BREASTFEEDING MAY BE CONTINUED

In the past, breastfeeding was thought to be unwise under a number of conditions that are now not believed to pose problems automatically.

Mastitis, a painful infection of the milk ducts, is in fact alleviated by regular and complete emptying of the breast by a nursing baby. There is no need to fear infecting the infant; indeed, his own oral bacteria most likely caused the infection in the first place.

Inverted nipples may, in the last weeks of pregnancy, correct themselves as the breasts become fuller. They may also be coaxed out with special massages and by wearing nipple shields. (La Leche League can be particularly helpful with this problem.)

Insufficient milk, frequently mentioned as something women fear will make it impossible for them to breastfeed, is more a phantom than a reality. Milk production is basically a supply-and-demand affair—the more the baby sucks, the more milk is made. A woman very rarely produces less milk than is needed. The use of supplementary bottles of formula, sometimes recommended as a solution to "insufficient" milk, can, ironically, bring about the feared shortage. It is better for the mother to keep nursing, get plenty of rest, add to her normal caloric intake one-third again the number of calories, and drink liquids (they need not be milk: even water works) whenever thirsty. The mother should not force herself to drink beyond thirst, and she should limit her intake of alcohol and coffee, both of which can have a dehydrating effect.

So-called **breast milk jaundice**, a condition in which some element in the milk causes a temporary rise in the baby's bilirubin level, is not really dangerous. Some health care providers believe the condition resolves itself within a few days even if breastfeeding continues; others advise a mother to use formula for two or three days and then return to the breast. In the second circumstance, it is wise to express milk regularly with a breast pump during the bottle-feeding period to keep the supply from drying up. The milk may be discarded or frozen to be given by bottle in the future.

Finally, a breastfeeding mother who becomes **pregnant** may find the dual drain on her too exhausting, especially after the first trimester. Her nutritional needs will be prodigious and the stresses on her body significant. Opinions do differ, however, so it is best to discuss the matter with your own health care provider should you be in this situation.

MAKING BREASTFEEDING WORK

In the first three to five days after birth, the mother's breasts are filled with a deep yellow fluid called colostrum, or first milk. High in protein, it is perfectly formulated for the needs of a newborn.

Even though it will be several days before the true milk comes in, it is a good idea to let the baby suckle on each breast for up to three minutes. In addition to giving him colostrum, this accustoms him to the idea of sucking. For you, it stimulates the hormones that produce the milk and promotes uterine contractions, which help your uterus restore itself to normal size and tone.

Once your milk does come in, you will soon learn to recognize the letdown reflex. The flow of milk is stimulated into the breasts by the pituitary gland in the brain. This gland releases oxytocin into the bloodstream, which in turn forces milk from the milk glands into the ducts. The resulting tingling sensation is accompanied by a stream of milk from the nipples. The reaction can be caused by your baby's sucking or even by hearing his hunger cry or by his presence in the room. Some mothers experience letdown when they are away from their babies and simply think of them or hear another baby cry.

The length of time the baby stays on the breast can gradually be extended until a pattern of feeding is established and the nipples are able to tolerate longer sessions. Some babies take five minutes to empty a breast; others take twenty. It is important in the early days to empty both breasts to stimulate production.

If a mother truly wishes to breastfeed but is having difficulty, social or emotional stresses may be causing the situation. If breastfeeding is not widely practiced, accepted, or encouraged among her friends and family members, the mother can experience a lot of stress—particularly if she is unsure of her ability to breastfeed. If difficulties arise, she may be tempted to give up rather than fear risking the well-being of her baby as she fumbles through the first week or so. The truth is, however, that the overwhelming majority of mothers who wish to nurse can do so successfully, even if there are difficulties along the way.

A mother who needs support in establishing or continuing breastfeeding should talk to mothers she knows who have had successful experiences of feeding. The La Leche League (9616 Minneapolis Avenue, Franklin Park, IL 60131) is an organization of mothers dedicated to assisting others.

MAKING BOTTLE-FEEDING WORK

Babies thrive on bottle-feeding, so if you choose to feed your baby this way out of inclination or necessity, you need not worry that her health or well-being will be compromised.

PREPARING FORMULA BOTTLES

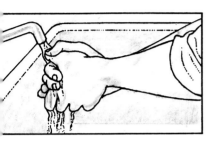

1. Wash your hands thoroughly. If you are using condensed or powdered formula, boil some water and allow it to cool. In most locales, unboiled tap water is safe to use.

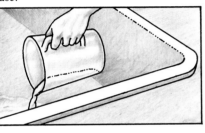

2. Wash and rinse all utensils well in soap and hot water. You may boil them if you prefer.

3. Pour the exact amount of boiled or tap water specified into the mixing vessel.

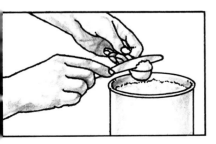

4. Add the prescribed amount of powdered or condensed formula.

5. Stir with a washed or sterilized spoon until well mixed.

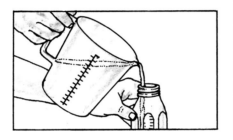

6. Fill bottles. Ready-mixed formula can be poured in directly, skipping previous steps. Some ready-to-use brands come in their own bottles, so you just remove the screw top and replace with a nipple.

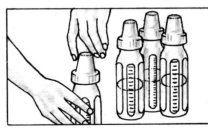

7. Place the nipples upside down and screw on the bottle lids.

8. Refrigerate the covered bottles right away.

CLEANING BOTTLES AND NIPPLES

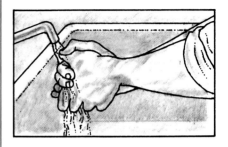

Wash your hands and fill the sink with warm soapy water.

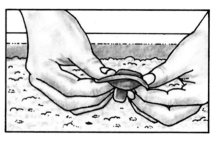

Turn the nipples inside out and rub them with salt. Rinse well with clear water.

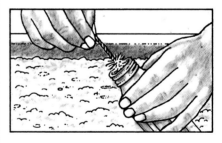

Use a bottle brush to remove all traces of milk from inside the bottles.

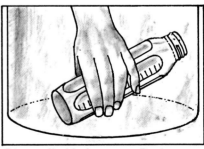

Rinse well with clear water. Bottles may also be washed in an automatic dishwasher. Cleaned bottles may be boiled as well, but this is not essential.

Some advocates of breastfeeding claim that bottle-feeding deprives mother and child of an essential intimacy, but there is no reason why bottle-feeding cannot be an emotionally close experience. Furthermore, it is a closeness that father and child can share as well. Cuddle your baby and talk to her as you feed; maintain eye contact and never *prop* the bottle so that she feeds "automatically" while your attention is elsewhere.

Most formulas suit most babies; choose the one that seems most convenient to use. Ready-mixed formulas, many of which come prebottled and require only that you screw on a nipple, are virtually labor-free; for this reason, though, they are considerably more expensive than formula in powdered form, which must be measured out and mixed with water and then placed into bottles or disposable nursers. Between the two in price and convenience are condensed formulas, which come in cans and must be diluted before use.

If your baby has a sensitivity to any component of ordinary formulas or has other metabolic problems that necessitate her being fed special formula, your health care provider will advise you what to buy and how to use it.

Regular formulas are based on cow's milk that has been specially treated and combined with other ingredients to make it suitable for an infant's immature system. Plain cow's milk should never be given to a newborn, who would be unable to metabolize the proteins in that form. If your baby develops an allergy to cow's milk-based formula (the sign of this is persistent diarrhea), your health care provider will probably advise a soy-based brand. Special formulas can even be prescribed for babies who cannot tolerate milk or soy protein or who have what is called an inborn error of metabolism.

No law says your baby must finish every drop in the bottle. That is important to remember if you are bottle-feeding. Obesity is seen more frequently in bottle-fed babies than in breastfed babies, and this could be because the baby is urged to finish an unreasonable number of ounces at each feeding. Another reason could be that the formula is too concentrated, increasing the calories per ounce. Do not alter the proportions when mixing powdered or condensed formulas either to make them richer or more dilute. It is very important to follow the instructions exactly. If the formula is too dilute, the baby will not receive enough nutrients; if it is too concentrated, a potentially dangerous burden will be put on the baby's immature kidneys.

In the past, much emphasis was placed on methodical sterilizing of bottles and nipples and on boiling the water before mixing with formula. Nowadays it is believed that cleaning these items with detergent and hot water and rinsing well does an adequate job of killing germs, as long as the drinking water is safe.

If you prepare enough bottles to last a full day, seal and refrigerate those to be used later. Do not keep them for more than forty-eight hours. The contents of a bottle with only a few dregs left in it should be thrown away. If your baby takes four ounces or less from an eight-ounce bottle, you may safely refrigerate the remainder until the next feeding, but replace the nipple with a clean one. If the pattern is regular, it would probably make sense to prepare four-ounce bottles until the baby's capacity increases.

Babies can drink formula taken straight from the refrigerator, without it being warmed first; if you do wish to warm it, stand the bottle for a few minutes in warm water. Do not use a microwave to heat milk in bottles – the container will explode.

COMBINATION FEEDING

If a nursing mother must be away from her baby for a period of hours, either for work or for other reasons, she can combine breast-feeding with bottle-feeding. Breast milk can be expressed manually or with a pump; it can be stored in the refrigerator for a day or in the freezer for several months. The La Leche League is a good source of information on expressing techniques. It may be more convenient to use formula for the bottle-feeding. Once a baby has become accustomed to breastfeeding (usually after a month or so), there should be no problem introducing an occasional bottle of mother's milk or formula, and the mother's supply will automatically adjust itself to the change in demand after a few days.

When a mother is away from her baby for several days, it is a good idea for her to express milk during the separation to maintain adequate production.

COW'S MILK

Cow's milk is made for calves, not for humans, and it has no place in a baby's diet until close to the end of the first year. Its high protein and salt content puts a strain on a young baby's kidneys. Skim milk is especially dangerous for babies, primarily for this reason.

Cow's milk is also much higher in saturated fat than mother's milk or formula, and the type of fat is particularly difficult for a baby to absorb. It is low in iron too, and iron-deficiency anemia is common among children overfed with cow's milk. Allergic reactions such as rash and diarrhea are also more common in children fed cow's milk

BREAST MILK AND FORMULA COMPARED

Component	Breast Milk	Formula*	Your Baby's Needs
Salt and water–essential needs	approx. 87% water 7 milliequivalents per liter of salt (adequate)	approx. 87% water between 6.5 and 12 milliequivalents per liter of salt (sometimes oversalted)	both provide sufficient salt and water for normal growth and hydration; neither contains so much salt as to increase the risk of high blood pressure in later life
Calories–energy and growth	20 calories per ounce	20 calories per ounce	both are adequate to provide energy for growth
Protein–building blocks of the body	quantity similar; quality better	quantity similar; quality inferior	both provide the right building blocks for growth
Fats–important for body growth, a source of calories, carriers for absorption of vitamins A, D, C, and K	quantity similar; fats vary according to mother's diet but generally higher in saturated fats and cholesterol if mother's diet is high in these	quantity similar; fats are from vegetable oils, which are high in polyunsaturated fats– "good" fats	both allow equally for absorption of vitamins A, D, C, and K, and for proper growth and development; higher cholesterol level of breast milk is said by some to be an advantage, by others a disadvantage, particularly if there is family history of cardiovascular disease
Carbohydrates–source of calories and important for body growth	quality similar (lactose); quantity similar	quality similar (lactose or sucrose); quantity similar	both provide your baby with adequate carbohydrate content; lactose is preferable to sucrose
Vitamins	may be deficient in vitamin D, in which case supplement may be prescribed	usually enriched to provide sufficient vitamins	
Iron	usually adequate unless mother is anemic	deficient unless fortified	
Fluoride	see page 92	see page 92	

* Formula milks vary in content. Information on the package will identify additives. Contents are listed in diminishing order by weight.

before the latter part of the first year than in those who start on it later.

By ten to twelve months of age, most babies' digestive systems and kidneys have matured enough to cope with cow's milk. The babies also have begun eating several other foods by then, so the deficiencies of cow's milk will in all likelihood be made up by other foods in a well-rounded diet.

FREQUENCY OF FEEDINGS

"Should I feed my baby whenever he cries or strictly by the clock?" This is one of the questions new parents most frequently ask, whether they are feeding by breast or by bottle. The answer is: a little of both. A flexible, semidemand feeding schedule provides a reasonable middleground between the two hard-and-fast methods, although it takes more judgment than either. But bear in mind that, for example, if your baby is crying, it may not be from hunger, so feeding will not always be the answer. If it has been a reasonable amount of time since the last feeding, however, the chances are he wants milk.

The quantity taken and the time between feedings differ from baby to baby, but on average a newborn baby's stomach will hold only two to three ounces at a time and the baby will usually want to be fed at intervals of two to three hours, around the clock. After the first couple of weeks, he progresses to taking four to five ounces every three to five hours (a breastfeeding mother's milk will increase to satisfy the increased demand). Your own baby's pattern will undoubtedly vary, so do not, for goodness sake, wake him for a feeding if he sleeps more than five hours between meals (especially if it is at night!).

As the quantity consumed increases, your baby will gradually adjust himself to your family pattern; as he becomes more active for longer periods during the day and sleeps for longer periods at night, a more regular schedule will probably develop. By four months, your baby may average six ounces per session from bottle or breast and may need to be fed only every four to five hours. By six months, he will be up to seven to eight ounces at each feeding and may need to be fed only every four or five hours–with possibly an eight- to twelve-hour period of solid sleep through the night.

From six to twelve months, formula or breast milk should still remain the primary food for your baby, with solid foods gradually being introduced as supplements. By his first birthday, however, solid foods should be the primary source of nutrition, and liquids should be of secondary importance.

Some babies are happy to give up sucking and seem not to mind having less time at the breast or bottle. Others increase the frequency with which they want to suck, even though they take less at each session. You will know your own child's inclinations, and it is best to go along with them if you possibly can.

As the amount of solid food increases, your baby will decrease on his own the amount of mother's milk or formula he takes. You need not worry too much about measuring portions and counting calories. Look instead for a normal gain in weight and height, good skin color and muscle tone, and a generally alert manner. Do not, however, expect the same rate of growth in the second six months as you saw in the first. (In fact, no period for the rest of your child's life will compare with the phenomenal growth exhibited in the first six months.) Use the chart on page 234, which shows normal average growth rates month by month, to record your own baby's growth.

If the curve is of the same general shape as the example given, everything is fine. If there is much deviation in the shape (not in the actual figures for weight and height), ask your baby's health care provider to evaluate the growth pattern and diet.

As he gets older, your child needs less energy per pound to grow; this may show in temporary decreases in appetite. (See the chart on page 81 for relative calorie requirements at different ages.) At ten months, for example, your previously vigorous eater may seem less interested in food; if he is otherwise well, he is probably just less hungry. His desire for food should be regarded as an accurate measure of how much he needs. Forcing food on an unwilling baby may lead to mealtime battles and, later, to obesity or other eating disorders.

INTRODUCING SOLID FOODS

Solid food has very little place in your baby's diet for the first six months of his life. For the first four months your baby is able to suck and swallow liquids only. The gut is immature and the kidneys can only cope with very dilute loads. Between four and six months, your baby's nervous system becomes more developed, and he can more readily show that he wants or does not want food by opening his mouth or turning his head away. Until then, giving solids could be a type of forced feeding.

Before 1920, solid food was seldom offered to infants before age one; then the first supplements were cod liver oil to prevent rickets and orange juice to prevent scurvy. Aggressive advertising and the availability of a much wider variety of infant foods, as well as parents' wish to see their babies gain weight rapidly, led to the introduction of solid foods earlier than one year. It is now believed that, although mother's milk or formula provides for all of a baby's nutritional needs up to one year, it is a good idea to begin introducing solids some months (six seems about right) before the first birthday just to help the baby get used to the odd new sensation.

When you begin to introduce solid food at about six months, begin with one at a time at weekly intervals. This will allow you to identify any signs of food intolerance–rashes, diarrhea, vomiting. Single grain infant cereals (rice, oats, barley, wheat), which provide additional calories, B vitamins, and iron, are a good first choice. Puréed or mashed fruits (bananas, apples) and vegetables (carrots, peas) are good choices for the next phase. But the truth is that the order of introducing new foods is relatively unimportant, except that it is probably best to hold off on such foods as eggs, meat, potatoes, and pasta until toward the end of the second six months. Among vegetables, beets, spinach, turnips, and mustard or collard greens have high nitrate content, so they too should be held off until near the first birthday. Try for a smooth and fairly soupy texture so that the food passes to the back of the mouth and is easy to swallow. Use a demitasse spoon and be sociable with your baby when you begin. Keep in mind that the first attempts are to educate the baby in a new way of feeding, not to satisfy his nutritional needs. That means making it fun, not fussing about the mess he might make, and *never* forcing the issue. If a new food is not palatable to your baby, take it away; then offer it again in a few weeks, and you may find that he takes it. Do not fight or even cajole; remember that no single food is essential to your baby's nutritional health.

A month or so after these first smooth samples, you may begin "finger foods": toast, crusty ends of bread, and crackers, peeled and sliced apples or pears. These he will hold in his hands and mush with his

It is a messy business, but learning to chew and swallow instead of sucking can be fun if you let it be.

gums, thereby giving him further freedom to choose and feed himself. Do not think that lack of teeth means your baby cannot handle food in that form. It is gums that do the mushing, and even the first teeth are "rippers," not "crushers."

Around this time, too, you can introduce lumpier foods, whether commercially prepared "junior" foods or home-cooked fruits, vegetables, and meats that you chop rather than strain or purée. Introduce them, as before, one at a time and in small amounts. If your baby does not like them, go back to strained foods for a while.

THE TRANSITION FROM LIQUIDS TO SOLIDS

If you think of this period not as weaning, which makes it sound like a problem that has to be battled through, but as a transitional phase in your child's eating career—one during which he moves from being physically and physiologically able to handle food in liquid form only to being able to handle and be interested in new tastes and textures and eventually to enjoy the same foods the rest of the family eats—the whole business will be much easier on you.

When you begin introducing solids at around six months of age, your baby will probably be settled in to four major breast or bottle feedings a day. The solids can be offered at any time, but many parents find that giving them with the morning and evening meals works nicely. At first, save the solid for after the breastfeeding or bottle-feeding so that you can be certain he has had a sufficient amount of his primary source of nutrition first.

By ten to twelve months, he may be down to three bottle- or breastfeedings a day and up to three meals. Some children, particularly large or active ones, may also enjoy light snacks between meals. Crackers and juice, a piece of fruit, or some bread spread with jelly can provide the extra energy some babies regularly need (and most babies need sometimes) to get them through to the next meal.

By one year of age, your child will probably be a confirmed three-meals-a-day person, with snacks when needed, and his foods will resemble those the family eats. He will have enough teeth and sufficiently developed tongue control to be able to handle the coarser textures. By eighteen months, you will probably be able to stop puréeing and mashing foods altogether and simply cut meats into small pieces. Most likely, you will no longer be offering formula; if you have chosen to continue breastfeeding, mother's milk will not be a primary source of nutrition, having been replaced by the balanced menu of solid foods.

It is around this time that your baby will begin to want to feed himself. As soon as he shows an interest in doing so, let him try; it is one of the essential steps to independence. If you worry about the mess or that he is getting more food onto the floor than into his mouth, you will spoil the adventure. Cover the floor with newspaper, cover his front with a large plastic bib (and yourself with an apron if you plan to get involved), and equip him with his own spoon and a straight-sided dish, which is easier to scoop against than one with sloping sides. Keep a second spoon for yourself so that you can slip some food into his mouth while he is experimenting elsewhere. Think of it as fun, and it will be.

WHAT TO FEED

If you use commercial baby foods, you will be reassured to know that they no longer contain added salt; do not be tempted to add salt yourself to improve the bland taste. Too much salt early in life may be associated with an adult risk of hypertension, and your baby's taste in food is naturally for bland, nonsalty foods. Commercial baby foods may have added sugar, but the amount has been reduced in recent years. The addition of monosodium glutamate, sodium nitrate, sodium nitrite, and certain modified food starches has also been discontinued.

There is increasing interest in preparing food for babies at home; if you decide to do this, use only lightly seasoned table foods or high-quality fresh or frozen vegetables and meats that do not contain salt.

Steaming preserves nutrients. Use a baby food grinder or blender early on; later, chopping with a knife or mashing with a fork will give an appropriate texture. Water or formula can be added if you want a more liquid mixture.

As soon as your baby begins to eat food in pieces, be careful about his inhaling bits of food and possibly choking. Any food poses the danger, but certain foods are so dangerous that they should never be given to a child under one year: peanuts, dried carrots, and frankfurters.

Do not forget that a baby responds to food differently than adults do. Babies tolerate tastes few adults would, preferring bland or mildly seasoned foods and accepting combinations that an adult would not particularly like. Tastes change over time. Food refused at eight months may well be accepted at twelve months. Offering a wide variety of tastes and textures early in life is the best way to help your child develop a well-balanced diet in later life.

SPECIAL SITUATIONS
Obesity

Obesity may result from a genetic predisposition, but in most cases it is simply the consequence of an inequality between caloric intake and expenditure of energy. In simple terms, the child eats more than he burns up with activity, and the excess is stored as fat. It is the same as for an adult. The problem in early childhood, however, is that overfeeding before the age of two can permanently increase the number of fat cells a person has. Later dieting may reduce the volume but not the number of these cells, and the risk of regaining weight is therefore always present. Obese babies thus have a greater chance of becoming obese children. These in turn have a greater chance of becoming obese adolescents, who in turn have a greater chance of becoming obese adults.

The best way to prevent obesity in children is to provide a well-balanced diet coupled with adequate physical activity from the very earliest age. Do not be so concerned about preventing obesity that you fail to provide adequate calories for optimal growth. Common sense is the best answer, but consult the charts opposite, on calorie needs, and talk to your child's health care provider if you are concerned about your baby's weight—whether that it is too much or too little.

As a baby grows into a toddler, food should never be used as a bribe, punishment, reward, or substitute for interpersonal relationships. That goes for a child whose weight is in the normal range as well as for one who is obese. An obese child's eating habits may have to be modified so that he does not gain more in weight than is justified by his height. Rarely will a health care provider suggest a reducing diet; rather, the rate of weight gain will be slowed. Never attempt to put a child on a diet without medical advice.

Following are some steps you might try if it is determined that your child is too heavy for his height. If you have a two-year-old junk food junkie, get rid of the junk food in the house. Provide low-calorie snacks, and get the rest of the family to cooperate by forgoing high-calorie snacks themselves. Give small-sized portions, cut food into small pieces, avoid the "clean plate" syndrome, eliminate desserts, and make sure your child does not eat alone but talks to you while he is eating.

Vegetarian Diets

Vegetarian mothers who breastfeed are, for the most part, sufficiently well nourished to provide adequate nutrition for their babies without depleting their own nutritional stores. Because vegetarian diets are so high in bulk, however, they may be deficient in calories. A vegetarian mother must, therefore, increase her caloric intake by one-third to meet the energy requirements of nursing a baby. She should be particularly careful to take a multivitamin and mineral supplement to ensure against possible deficiencies in calcium, riboflavin, iron, and vitamins A, D, and B12.

CONTINUED ON PAGE 84

YOUR BABY'S CALORIE NEEDS

AGE	AVERAGE WEIGHT IN POUNDS	CALORIE REQUIREMENTS PER POUND	AVERAGE DAILY CALORIE REQUIREMENTS
0 to 6 months	birth–7½ pounds	55	400
	6 months–16 pounds	55	800–900
6 to 12 months	6 months–16 pounds	50	800
	12 months–21½ pounds	50	1,100
12 to 36 months	12 months–21½ pounds	45	900–1,000
	36 months–32 pounds	45	1,450

All requirement figures are approximate.

FEEDING A TODDLER

Appetite is the best indicator of hunger; a well-rounded diet will provide adequate nutrients and calories.

The following servings from the four food groups are recommended for daily use from one year of age onward:

Milk	milk, cheese, ice cream, yogurt	at least three servings
Meat	meat, fish, poultry, eggs; alternatives include dry beans, peas, nuts	at least two servings
Vegetables and Fruit	green and yellow vegetables, tomatoes, citrus fruits, melons	at least four servings
Breads and Cereals	crackers, muffins, pasta, noodles, grains, breakfast cereals	at least four servings

WHAT IS A SERVING?

Examples: milk, 4–6 ounces; juice, 3–4 ounces; egg, 1 medium; meat, 2–3 ounces; vegetables and fruit, ½ of orange, apple, or tomato, 1–2 tbsp. of others; cereal, ⅓ cup dry cereal; bread, ½ slice

It is better to serve less and give second helpings than to battle with your child to clean her plate.

CALORIES PER SERVING IN FOODS MOST COMMONLY USED:

Breast and formula milk 20 per oz

Fruit juice 15–18 per oz

Dry Cereal
½ oz (4 tbsp) + 2 oz of formula 90–100 per oz
entire 2½ oz serving 225–250

Junior Foods
Meats
beef 13 per tbsp.
chicken 20 per tbsp.
ham 15 per tbsp.
turkey 18 per tbsp.

Fruits
approx. the same as for strained

Desserts
approx. 10–12 per tbsp.

Vegetables
carrots 3 per tbsp.
peas 9 per tbsp.
squash 4 per tbsp.
sweet potatoes 9 per tbsp.

Strained Foods
Fruits
apple sauce 7 per tbsp.
peaches 10 per tbsp.
pears 8 per tbsp.

Vegetables
all approx. 25–100 per 4½ oz jar

Meats
approx. the same as for junior foods

Desserts
all approx. 50–150 per 4½ oz jar

STAGES OF WEANING

	EARLY MORNING	BREAKFAST	LUNCH
At 5 months	Breast or bottle	Breast or bottle plus teaspoonful of baby cereal	Breast or bottle
Between 5½ and 6½ months	Breast or bottle	Breast or bottle plus cereal	Breast or bottle plus strained broth
Between 7 and 8 months	Breast or bottle	Breast or bottle plus cereal	Puréed vegetables or stewed fruit; try water or fruit juice

You can prepare puréed foods yourself in large batches and freeze it in small portions for later use. Foods with a smooth and creamy texture are most readily accepted.

At 9 months	Breast or bottle	 Cereal, fruit, juice	 Puréed meat or fish with vegetables, fruit, water
At 10 months	Water or fruit juice	 Cereal and fruit, or wholewheat toast and butter, juice	 Cheese, fish, ground meat, chicken, or liver with mashed vegetables; milk-based pudding or stewed fruit; water
Between 11 and 12 months	Water or fruit juice	 Boiled or scrambled egg, wholewheat toast and butter, bacon, milk	 As before, but try chopping coarsely instead of grinding

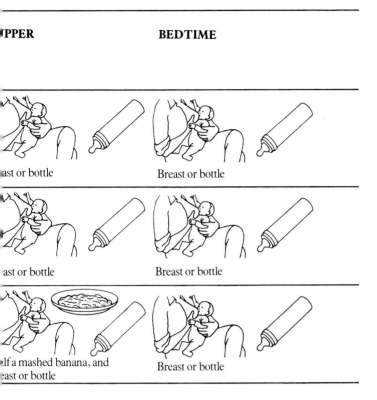

PPER	BEDTIME
...ast or bottle	Breast or bottle
...ast or bottle	Breast or bottle
...lf a mashed banana, and ...east or bottle	Breast or bottle
...eese sandwich, juice	Breast or bottle
...d and butter, cottage ...se, fruit or juice	
...d and butter, cottage ...se or yogurt, fruit	

HIDING FOODS
Hiding milk
cream soups and sauces, mashed potatoes, custard, puddings (including rice), yogurt, fruit and milk shakes
as cheese
soufflés, macaroni and cheese casserole, cheese sauces; grated cheese sprinkled on soups, vegetables, noodles, and rice, mixed into ground meat.
Hiding eggs
French toast, waffles, pancakes, custard, timbales, soufflés, mixed with ground meat for meatloaf, hamburger, or meatballs.

Parents sometimes worry a great deal about weaning their baby. It is sensible to remember that the process is gradual; nothing is achieved by hurrying. The chart at left shows suggestions on stages and times for introducing solids, but be guided by your knowledge of your own baby. If she is fretful, tired, or unwell, do not force her; try again another day.

Once a child begins to eat three meals a day and a wide variety of foods, her menus can more closely resemble those of the rest of the family. Here are some sample main meal and dessert menus for toddlers.

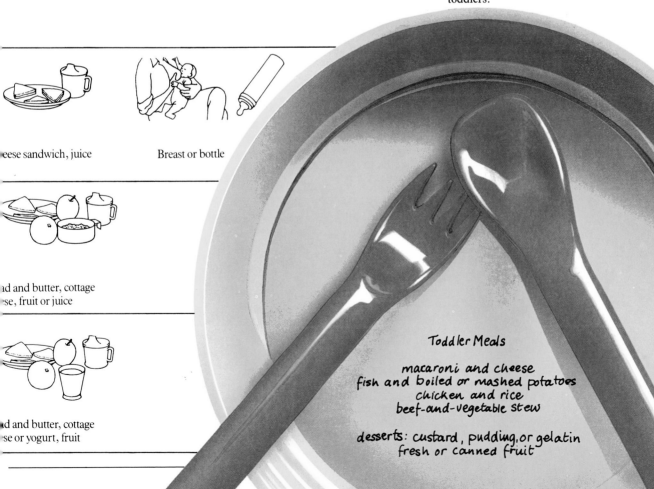

Toddler Meals

macaroni and cheese
fish and boiled or mashed potatoes
chicken and rice
beef-and-vegetable stew

desserts: custard, pudding, or gelatin
fresh or canned fruit

Zen macrobiotic dieters, however, risk undernourishment and secreting inadequately nutritious milk.

Vegetarianism is not new, and certain populations have subsisted for centuries on such diets with apparent good health and normal development. Vegetarian diets can be adequate for the growing child if sufficient care is taken in planning. Plants do not provide as much usable protein as meats, but when certain plants are consumed together in specific proportions (beans combined with wheat or rice, for instance), all necessary proteins are obtained. (*Diet for a Small Planet*, by Frances Moore Lappé, explains this principle in clear and detailed terms.) Milk and/or eggs can also provide adequate protein. If these are not included, green vegetables can be used to provide calcium and riboflavin. Soy milk or supplementary pills provide vitamin B12; nuts, beans, and wheat germ provide zinc; legumes, green and leafy vegetables, whole enriched grains, cereals, and nuts provide iron.

The big challenge in a vegetarian diet is to assemble a variety of foods that offer enough color, form, texture, and flavor to avoid monotony.

Premature Babies

A baby of less than thirty-six weeks gestation usually is not sent home from the hospital until a good feeding pattern has been established and a good weight ain begun. Depending on weight and other factors, it may be from two weeks to two months before the premature baby goes home. He is at first fed either with special formula or expressed breast milk, and because early on he cannot hold much milk in his belly, he usually is fed more frequently than every three to four hours. But like all babies, he eventually settles into a comfortable routine. Supplemental iron and vitamins A, D, and E are often prescribed; a health care provider will advise what special feeding routine (if any) should be continued when the baby comes home.

Picky Eaters

Something about toddlers seems to encourage pickiness in eating. Your two-year-old wants to control the world: he dictates what he wears, when he goes to the bathroom, and what he eats. It is not wrong–only different –if your child has limited tastes and desires, but what can you do if he only wants two or three foods for months on end?

First of all, children will usually take as one of those foods something with a lot of nutritional value–meat, peanut butter, milk, or eggs–and you can also disguise foods so that your resident picky eater gets considerably more of a hateful nutrient than he imagines (see page 83).

As much as possible keep your child thinking of food as something he wants, not as something he is forced to take. If he eats more of one food and less of another at one meal, it does not matter. Over the week, things are likely to be balanced out. If he dislikes vegetables, offer more fruit; if he drinks less milk, give cheese, ice cream, or puddings prepared with milk. If you are still concerned, give him vitamin and mineral supplements in tablet or liquid form–they are available at drug stores without prescription.

DIET AND BEHAVIOR

In the recent past, diet has been linked to behavior, most notably to hyperactive behavior. Studies thus far have not supported claims that either food additives or concentrated amounts of processed sugar adversely affect behavior. On the other hand, malnutrition can cause significant problems in a developing child–among them mental retardation and increased likelihood of infections. Malnutrition remains a serious problem in America today, although it is mostly seen among the very poor and undereducated. It may be convenient to blame a child's behavior on nutritional causes, but it is usually more productive to look at family dynamics and psychosocial concerns.

FOOD AS THE FOUNDATION OF HEALTH

The food your baby eats and the dietary habits he establishes in early childhood can profoundly affect his adult well-being. It is possible to significantly minimize the risk of certain adult diseases by early proper food management.

Salt

Most of us use too much salt. Limit your baby's intake–especially if you have a family history of hypertension, heart attack, stroke, or kidney disease. Breast milk and formula are low in salt.

Cholesterol

If you have a family history of cardiovascular disease due to atherosclerosis, begin a low-cholesterol diet early in your child's life. Breast milk and formula are both ideal. When your child begins on solid foods, limit his intake of such high-cholesterol foods as eggs, cheese, and fatty meats. Skim milk is more harmful than helpful for the average infant, but after one year of age, especially if there is a family history of cardiovascular problems, reduced-fat milk is preferable to whole milk.

Fiber
Fiber is any food component that cannot be digested by the gastrointestinal tract–cellulose, gums, lignins, mucilages, hemicellulose –all of which are found primarily in plants. Fiber increases fecal bulk and often results in softer, more frequent stools. It may play a role in decreasing the risk of colon cancer.

There is some concern that a high-fiber diet can interfere with the absorption of minerals such as calcium, iron, copper, magnesium, phosphorus, and zinc, but this is certainly not an issue for children under one; for older children, include whole grain cereals, bread, fruit, and vegetables but not to the exclusion of the other food groups.

YOUR CHILD'S TEETH

Six weeks after conception, a baby's teeth are already beginning to develop. At her birth, all twenty primary teeth are forming and the first permanent teeth may also be developing. Therefore, even in pregnancy, you should take steps to help your baby's teeth develop healthily. If your diet during pregnancy is adequate (see pages 12-14), your baby's teeth should develop normally; if it is deficient– especially in calcium, phosphrous, or vitamin D–the structure of your baby's teeth may be adversely affected. Abnormalities in either the amount of calcium in the enamel (the outer covering of the teeth) or the quality of the enamel may result. Defects appear as white spots or small linear or round depressions on a baby's teeth. One quart of vitamin D–fortified milk per day during pregnancy provides the developing baby with enough calcium, phosphorus, and vitamin D and thus removes the risk of this sort of defect.

Fluoride protects teeth against cavities and in the past was recommended as a prenatal supplement. Fluoride was thought to combine with calcium in the forming teeth to make them more resistant to decay. There is insufficient evidence to establish that this is effective, however, and the practice is now not widespread. If your health care provider has recommended fluoride supplements, you may wish to discuss the situation; the supplements will certainly do no harm, even if they do not do any good. (See page 91 on fluoride for your child.)

An infection or fever during your pregnancy may also affect the way your baby's teeth develop, resulting in defects such as those appearing for nutritional deficiency.

EFFECTS OF ANTIBIOTICS ON DEVELOPING TEETH
Antibiotics containing tetracycline, if taken during pregnancy, can cause permanent yellow, brown, or gray discoloration of developing teeth. If such antibiotics are taken late in the third trimester, they may also stain the first permanent molars. If an antibiotic is prescribed for you when you are pregnant, be sure to ask your health care provider whether it contains tetracycline; in most cases, an alternative can be prescribed.

BRAND NAMES OF ANTIBIOTICS CONTAINING TETRACYCLINE OR A DERIVATIVE

Generic or Chemical Name	Brand Name*	Manufacturer
Tetracycline	Achromycin	Lederle
	Mysteclin-F	Squibb
	Panmycin	Upjohn
	Robitet	Robins
	Sumycin	Squibb
	Tetracyn	Pfipharmecs
Tetracycline HCl	Achromycin	Lederle
	Mysteclin-F	Squibb
	Robitet	Robins
	Sumycin	Squibb
	Tetracyn	Pfipharmecs
	Tetrastatin	Pfipharmecs
Tetracycline Phosphate	Azotrex	Bristol
	Tetrex	Bristol
Oxytetracycline	Terramycin	Pfizer
	Terrastatin	Pfizer

* If a brand name includes the word *tetracycline* or one of its derivatives, it is not included in the list since it is easily identified as a tetracycline-containing product.

Source: *Physician's Desk Reference*, 39th edition, 1985.

FROM BIRTH TO SIX MONTHS

Your newborn baby has at least twenty primary teeth developing in her jaws. Between birth and six months, in addition to the twenty primary teeth, ten to twelve permanent teeth also start to develop. These comprise the first permanent molars and the incisors (front teeth).

Occasionally a child may be born with a tooth, or one may erupt within the first three or four weeks after birth. These natal teeth most commonly occur in the front part of the lower jaw; they are usually incompletely formed and lack sufficient roots to hold them in place, posing a danger that the baby will swallow the poorly rooted tooth or, worse still, inhale it into her lungs. Consequently, it should be removed as soon as possible. More firmly attached teeth can be a problem, especially to the mother if the baby is nursing–although if the breast is correctly positioned in the mouth, the tooth should not come in contact with it while the baby sucks. If the natal tooth is extracted, the child will be left with three (instead of four) lower incisors for the duration of her primary teeth. This could lead to crowding of the permanent incisors when they come in. Any such problems, should they occur, are correctable through orthodontics in the teen years.

FROM SIX MONTHS TO TWO YEARS

At birth, your baby's lower jaw will be positioned markedly behind her upper jaw. During the first year, however, the lower jaw grows at a faster rate than the upper; by the time all the primary teeth have come into the mouth, the two jaws have reached matching size, and the upper and lower teeth fit properly.

The twenty primary teeth come in some time during the first two years of your child's life, normally beginning at six months. Although there is enormous variation in the ages at which each of the primary teeth appears, two general rules pertain: First, a lower tooth usually appears before its corresponding upper tooth; and second, the teeth usually come into the mouth in sequence from front to back, with the exception of the canines, which erupt after the first molars. The twenty primary teeth – ten in the upper jaw and ten in the lower–consist of pairs of the following (starting from the center of each jaw): central incisor, lateral incisor, canine, first molar, and second molar.

Do not worry if your baby's teeth do not come in exactly as indicated on the chart. Many babies have their first tooth at three months, others will not have a tooth erupt until considerably later than the times suggested above.

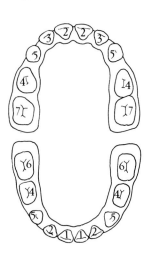

AVERAGE AGE AND ORDER OF ERUPTION OF PRIMARY TEETH

Age of Child	Lower Jaw	Upper Jaw
6 months	2 central incisors	
7 months	2 lateral incisors	2 central incisors
9 months		2 lateral incisors
12–14 months	2 first molars	2 first molars
16–18 months	2 canines	2 canines
20 months	2 second molars	
24 months		2 second molars

TOOTH FACTS

- There are twenty primary teeth and thirty-two permanent teeth, including the wisdom teeth.
- Most primary teeth (which used to be called "milk teeth") are smaller and whiter than the permanent teeth that replace them.
- Inside each tooth—whether primary or permanent—is a chamber containing

Decay can nearly always be prevented by proper cleaning and a good diet. Children up to about three do not have sufficient dexterity to clean their own teeth.

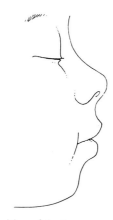

The position of the lower jaw in relation to the upper jaw at birth.

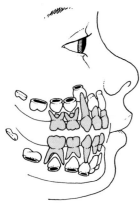

While the primary teeth are erupting the secondary teeth are already in the jaw.

nerves and blood vessels. The presence of these is why a tooth hurts if it is hit or decayed. Protecting this inner pulp are three layers of hard, calcified tissues: dentin, enamel, and cementum. The dentin is covered by the enamel and cementum. Enamel covers the crown of the tooth; cementum covers the roots and helps to anchor the tooth to the jaw.

- All teeth are used to chew food so that it can be swallowed.
- Teeth are necessary for proper speech.
- Primary teeth keep the space ready for their permanent successors. If a primary tooth is lost early, the movement of the adjacent teeth can lead to crowding of permanent teeth when they erupt.
- Some babies do not get a tooth until ten or even twelve months. If you are concerned, consult your health care provider.
- Occasionally a primary tooth may not have developed at all. This may mean that the permanent tooth that replaces it will be missing as well. A dentist may wish to do an x-ray if one or more primary teeth are absent. Nothing will be done to correct the situation while the primary teeth are in the mouth, but if the secondary tooth or teeth fail to appear, orthodontics and bridgework will correct the resulting gap when the child is older.

FROM TWO TO THREE YEARS

By now all the primary teeth probably have erupted and up to twenty-eight permanent teeth are developing within the jaws. At this age, generalized illnesses or high fevers can produce defects in the permanent teeth, as can the antibiotic tetracycline, as previously mentioned. The American Academy of Pediatrics has stated that tetracycline-containing drugs should not be given to a child unless he has an infection or illness for which no other antibiotic can be used.

APPEARANCE OF THE TEETH

Primary teeth that are dark or otherwise abnormally colored when they erupt did not develop correctly. Since the stain is within the tooth it cannot be removed by brushing, although a dentist may be able to improve the appearance through bonding techniques. This is probably not worthwhile with primary teeth, but it may be so with badly stained permanent teeth. Stains that appear after the teeth have erupted are not within the enamel but are caused by germs sticking to the tooth surface. Proper brushing can prevent their formation, but once they are there, they can be removed only by a dentist

using a dental polish that is more abrasive than toothpaste.

Incisors may have small bumps called mamelons along their biting edge; these are normal and will be worn away gradually as your child learns to bite and chew. If they are still there at age four, this may be an indication that your child is not biting correctly; your dentist will advise you if correction is necessary.

It is normal for the primary teeth to have spaces between them; in fact, they should be spaced like a picket fence in order to accommodate the larger permanent teeth.

TEETHING

Teething is a normal and generally painless process, although a variety of signs have been attributed to it—an increase in salivation and mucus production, thumb or fist sucking, irritability, rashes, loose stools, and the need to bite on hard objects. Parents and health professionals must guard against thinking that signs and symptoms of illness are due to teething. If your baby has a fever, diarrhea, bronchitis, or any other sign of infection, she is sick and should be seen by a health care provider. She may be teething at the same time, but the teething has nothing to do with the illness.

If your child seems bothered by teething, there is no harm in offering her a teething ring to chew on or bite. Some contain liquid that can be cooled or frozen to relieve the mild inflammation sometimes seen with newly erupting teeth. Care must be taken that the rings are safe, nontoxic, and unswallowable. A carrot stick too large to be swallowed can be given to the child to chew. Do not give hard teething biscuits; they will soften in the mouth, and the crumbs might get stuck in the windpipe.

A number of products available without prescription from the drugstore may help relieve your baby's discomfort. Most contain benzocaine, a local anesthetic that, when rubbed on the gums, helps relieve the irritation. Do not rub a dissolved aspirin on the gums, because it will burn the tissue.

THUMB-SUCKING

One way your baby has of satisfying her curiosity about the world is to put everything within reach into her mouth. Sucking an object that is not a source of nourishment is called nonnutritive sucking; the most common object that babies suck in this way are their fingers or thumbs.

Various theories have been advanced to explain why children suck their fingers—among them emotional stress, early weaning, and the use of the bottle instead of the breast. But children who suck their fingers have

Babies who suck their fingers or thumbs do so because they enjoy it. The fear that it may result in protruding teeth has been much exaggerated.

been found to be as emotionally stable and secure as other children and as many breast-fed children as bottle-fed ones suck, so none of the theories can be supported. Probably most babies suck their fingers simply because they enjoy it. Of those who do so, 85 percent stop by the time they are four. If the habit persists beyond that age, it may affect the position of the teeth—usually causing a misalignment between the upper and lower front teeth. Until she is four, do not worry if your child sucks her thumb or fingers, and do not try to make her stop. After she reaches four, discuss the subject with your health care provider and work out a strategy to break the habit.

PACIFIERS

Sucking a pacifier has some advantages over sucking a thumb. A pacifier is not attached to the hand and arm, so there are no muscles to pull the teeth forward. In addition, most children will give up their pacifier when it is lost (whether accidentally or purposely by a parent), but fingers and thumbs remain always available.

If you are buying a pacifier, look for one with a large firm shield to prevent accidental swallowing. The shield may even provide resistance against the front teeth being drawn forward. One-piece pacifiers are safe because the single piece—nipple, flange, and ring—makes accidental swallowing difficult. Some have two holes on the side so that even if it did lodge in the throat, the child could still breathe.

Never tie a pacifier by a string around a child's neck, as this presents the danger of strangulation. Never dip a pacifier in honey

or any other type of sweetener. To do so would promote cavities when the teeth are in; moreover, honey frequently contains botulism spores, which can be deadly to an infant even though they represent no real threat to older children and adults. If a baby has to be coaxed into taking a pacifier, she does not need it.

Some pacifiers have a round nipple, and others have a flat nipple (the so-called orthodontic style). Each type has its advocates, but both seem to satisfy the primary purpose of sucking gratification and probably have the same effect on teeth. The current dental literature suggests no advantage in the orthodontic style over the conventional round type; using either is satisfactory. The same applies to nipples used in bottle-feeding.

As far as the baby's teeth are concerned, bottle-feeding does not increase the likelihood that your child will suck her thumb. Do not use either breast or bottle as a pacifier substitute. Allowing the child virtually unrestricted access to either, especially at night, can cause severe cavities once the teeth come in (see page 92).

CLEANING YOUR CHILD'S TEETH

Your baby's teeth are vulnerable to decay as soon as they arrive, but decay can nearly always be prevented by proper cleaning, a proper diet, and the use of fluorides. As parents, you should take this seriously because the early care of your child's teeth is entirely in your hands.

Cavities are formed because a sticky coating called plaque, consisting mostly of germs, adheres to the teeth. These germs

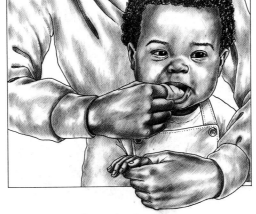

Begin to clean your baby's teeth as soon as the first one appears. Use a piece of gauze to clean both tooth and gums.

convert sugar from the food we eat into acid, which in turn dissolves the teeth. By the time your baby's first teeth erupt, the decay-producing germs are already in her mouth, and it is necessary to clean her teeth every day. The first tooth will be in the front so it will be easy to see and clean. You should clean the teeth at least every night before bed; if you want to do it more often, do so after feeding.

Lay the child on a counter or changing table with the top of her head against your stomach (in the position your dentist adopts when examining your teeth) or sit with her in your lap, her head and back against your stomach as shown. Use a moist face cloth, a cotton-tipped swab, a piece of gauze, or a child-size toothbrush. (When the back teeth come into the mouth, you will need to use a toothbrush.) Clean with a gentle scrubbing motion, and be sure to include gums where particles and germs collect. Once you start to use a toothbrush, also use a small amount of fluoride toothpaste–but teach your child to spit out, not swallow, the paste. Do not use a thick ribbon of toothpaste, as you would for yourself, but just enough to moisten the ends of the bristles, spreading the paste with your fingers.

If your child cries, still clean her teeth. When she opens her mouth to cry, you will get better access to her teeth. Remember when all the teeth have erupted to clean the back teeth as well as the front and to clean all surfaces: the biting surface, those facing the lips and cheek, and those facing the tongue. Children up to three years old do not have the dexterity to clean their own teeth, so a parent has to do it for them.

Once your child's teeth are brushed, do not let her have any food and especially juice and milk. The sugar these contain will remain in contact with the teeth throughout the night and will do enormous damage to the teeth. Enforcing this rule at an early age establishes a routine that will save her much pain in future.

THE EFFECT OF SUGARS

The importance of a nutritious diet on developing teeth has already been emphasized; but once a tooth erupts, it is influenced by what happens to food on the tooth's surface and within the dental plaque, rather than by what nutrition is supplied by the food swallowed. Even if you clean your child's teeth meticulously, a small amount of plaque usually remains on hard-to-clean places.

The sugars in the foods we eat are what cause dental decay. Three factors affect a sugar's potential to do so: its type, its stickiness, and how often it is eaten.

Table sugar, sucrose, is the most common substance that causes decay because its molecules are so small that they can easily get into the dental plaque and be converted into acid. Fructose (fruit sugar) seems to have a smaller role in causing decay.

A sticky sugar-containing food adheres longer to the teeth, thus allowing more time for the acids to form. Sugar in sticky or hard sweets that must be sucked slowly is especially damaging because they are kept in the mouth so long. The acids formed from sugar act on the teeth for about twenty minutes. If a portion of sugar-containing food is divided into five pieces and eaten at five different times during the day, the teeth are subjected to five twenty-minute acid attacks. This is why frequent sweet snacks are so dangerous.

DIETS PROMOTING DENTAL HEALTH

The diet you feed your child can promote or hinder good dental health. Use sucrose (common table sugar) sparingly on foods, in beverages, and in snacks. Do not over-sweeten your child's food; doing so would give her a taste for sweet foods, as well as lead to cavities. Even baby food manufacturers have reduced or eliminated sucrose from their products recently.

Offer fresh fruit, raw vegetable sticks, breadsticks, and nonsugary or nonsalty crackers as snacks–not candy, cakes, and cookies. As your child gets older, nuts and popcorn become healthful snacks, but do not give them to a child under three, since they can be accidentally inhaled.

If you must give sweets, make them "sugar-free" candy. (Not chewing gum, which risks accidental choking.) These products contain sugars (mostly sorbitol and mannitol) that produce very little acid. Be aware of hidden sugars in processed foods. Some presweetened breakfast cereals contain as much as 50 percent (by weight) sugar. Do not use them. Read the labels of all foods, and remember that the order of ingredients indicates the proportion; those listed first

Give snacks of fresh fruit, crackers, or breadsticks rather than candy, cakes, or cookies. Cut out sweet, sticky foods, such as jam and dried fruit; these cling to the teeth and cause decay.

occur in greater quantity than those listed later. Processed foods sometimes contain several different sugars, so the total amount can be large. All the following are sugars, which means they can cause dental decay: corn syrup, honey, sucrose, fructose, glucose, maltose, and dextrose. Reduce or eliminate sweet, sticky foods: toffee, caramels, peanut brittle, glazed popcorn, lollipops, and hard candies are all cavity villains.

Flour and most breads do not cause decay, but once it is chewed, bread becomes sticky and so helps retain other decay-causing foods in the mouth. Jam or jelly spreads, for instance, will cause decay; butter, margarine, or cream cheese will not. Some peanut butters contain sucrose—check the label.

Many medicines are made palatable by being blended in a sweet syrupy liquid. If given several times a day for several weeks, they can cause decay; clean your child's teeth after he takes them.

Soda pop and other soft drinks are far less cavity-producing than was believed some years ago. This is because the rapid passage of liquid through the mouth ensures minimal contact with the teeth. Diet soft drinks contain sugar substitutes or small amounts of sugar, but the use of saccharine and the addition of caffeine to some soft drinks are negative considerations; it is up to you to decide whether moderate amounts of soda pop are acceptable.

Sweets should be given only at mealtimes, not as snacks. During a meal the action of the tongue and the extra flow of saliva help wash debris from the teeth, but be sure to clean your child's teeth well after a meal that contains a sweet, sticky dessert. The decay process begins within minutes. Discourage your child from eating sucrose-containing snack foods. It is impossible and probably undesirable to eliminate all sucrose-containing confections, but remember that it is better to eat the whole serving of candy or cake at once rather than at frequent intervals during the day.

The question of decay-producing sugar in fresh fruit is still being debated; it is not really a question of what is eaten, but how often and when. Orange juice, which is in liquid form, should do little to promote dental decay because it passes rapidly through the mouth, but dried fruits, which are sticky and which contain high concentrations of sugars, are considered to promote decay significantly.

FLUORIDE

Fluoride is an essential nutrient for optimal health and protection against dental decay.

All water contains some fluoride, and only a minute amount is necessary to help prevent decay. In some areas of the country enough occurs naturally to protect the teeth. Where it does not, the level may be adjusted by the water company. Today, half the American population drinks water containing sufficient fluoride to benefit teeth.

Your child's dentist or pediatrician should know how much fluoride is in your drinking water and whether your child should take supplements. You can also find out from the water company; or if you have your own well, you can arrange for a fluoride analysis to be done (usually by the local health department).

If supplementary fluoride is prescribed, it

will be in the form of drops, sometimes in combination with vitamins, to be given once a day. It can be given from the age of two weeks. You may put the drops in water or fruit juice but not in milk: The calcium in milk binds the fluoride and prevents it from combining with the calcium of the developing teeth. The dose is increased as your child gets older. When he is old enough to chew properly, the drops will probably be changed to tablets. Be careful to give only the amount prescribed; too much can cause discoloration of the developing teeth.

Breast milk contains only a trace of fluoride. Even if a mother drinks a lot of fluoridated water, there will not be enough in her milk to protect the baby's teeth against decay. If your baby is being breastfed, discuss the possible need for fluoride supplements with your child's health care provider. Formula made with fluoridated water will meet a baby's needs, however. (For prenatal fluoride supplements, see page 85.)

The first visit to the dentist should be made between two and three years of age. Do not convey anxiety to your child before the visit. Choose a dentist who works well with children.

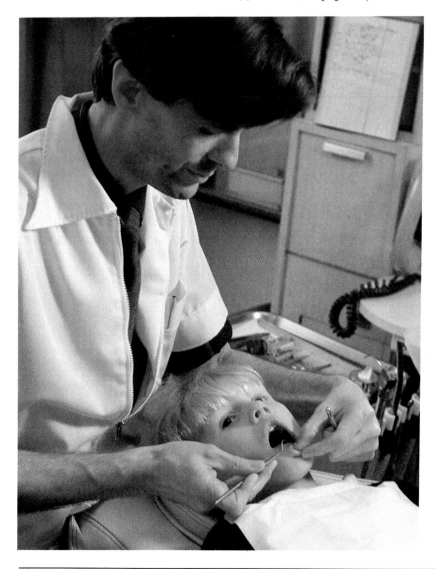

NURSING CARIES

This serious dental condition in infants and young children occurs when a child is permitted to suck a bottle of milk habitually (which contains a sugar called lactose) or fruit juice throughout her sleep. As the child sleeps and sucks, a pool of liquid collects around the necks of the teeth. There it is acted upon by germs in the mouth; acid is formed and the teeth decay severely. See also Dental Caries, page 214.

Nursing caries can be prevented by never putting your child to bed with a bottle of juice, milk, or sweetened water, and by never giving her a pacifier sweetened with honey, jelly, jam, or sugar. You may also want to consider weaning your child from breast or bottle as soon as the primary teeth begin to appear; but as this could be at quite a young age, other considerations might argue against weaning at that point. If you have doubts, discuss the situation with your health care provider.

THE FIRST VISIT TO THE DENTIST

Between the ages of two and three, your child is ready for her first dental visit; of course, if your child has injured her teeth or has obvious cavities, she will need to visit earlier than this.

In choosing a dentist for your child, look for someone who likes working with children. This includes being able to treat children without allowing their behavior to affect the quality of care given.

A pediatric dentist (or pedodontist) specializes in the dental care of young children; one who takes two or three years of extra training becomes skilled in the treatment and management of infants and preschool children. If there is not a pedodontist in your area, ask if your own dentist treats young children or knows of anyone in the neighborhood who does. Friends and neighbors with young children may recommend their dentist or you could try the local dental society, the dental department of a local hospital, or the children's department of a dental school for suggestions. Some dental schools have low-cost clinics with pedodontic services to families in their locale.

Most children have formed an impression from parents, friends, or older siblings of what a visit to a dentist will be like. You will not want your child to be afraid, so your attitude is very important. About two days before the visit (more or less, depending on your child's memory span), tell your child what is going to happen. Explain to her that a dentist takes care of people's teeth and that the one you are going to will count her teeth, will make sure they are healthy, and may clean them with a special toothbrush and oothpaste. That is all that is necessary. Do not tell her that it will not hurt or promise a oy if she is good. Children interpret this to mean that some dentists do hurt and that something is threatening. They are also perceptive enough to read facial expressions and other nonverbal clues, so if you are afraid of dentists, try your best not to convey his to your child by your words or actions.

Some dentists will let you stay with your child during treatment; most recognize that a two- to three-year-old needs the psychological support of a parent. If you are with her, do not talk or grimace. You will probably be allowed to hold your child's hand.

Most dentists tell the child what they are going to do, then show them, and then do it, explaining what is happening as they go along. During the first visit, the dentist will check the number, position, shape, and color of the teeth, and the health of the gums, palate, and tongue. If the drinking water in your area is not fluoridated, the dentist will discuss fluoride supplements. Advice about your child's diet and about how and when to clean your child's teeth will also be available.

The dentist will take x-rays if needed to check for cavities or to examine the bones of the jaws and the developing permanent teeth. You should be aware that, although the small amount of radiation used for dental x-rays has not been proved harmful, neither has it been shown conclusively to be safe; only absolutely necessary x-rays should be taken.

At the end of the visit, the dentist may give your child a small present. This is not a bribe to be good, but positive behavior reinforcement–a reward for good behavior.

If everything is satisfactory, the next visit will probably be scheduled for six months or a year later.

See pages 206 and 214 for Accident to the Teeth and Dental Caries.

The period from birth to age three is of utmost importance to a child's dental health. The presence of teeth aids the normal maturation of the child; without them, she could not chew solid food and take in the nourishment necessary for growth. Nor could she articulate proper speech or have her face mature in the way a young child's face becomes different from a baby's.

So a child's teeth are important. It is the responsibility of the parents to see that they remain clean and disease-free.

SLEEP AND BEDTIME

Sleep is one of the most mysterious benefits conferred on mankind; like most benefits, it is usually underappreciated until it becomes unavailable. It is regulated by a fingertip-sized monitoring center deep in the base of the brain, which protects against overtiredness and loss of alertness. Sleep renews energy; it also allows withdrawal from unpleasant and distressing situations, as well as from boredom. Dreaming offers the opportunity to explore new and imaginative experiences; it especially helps children enter worlds generally unknown to them.

A new baby in the family brings the parents so much extra work and fatigue that they can manage it all only if the baby is peaceful for a reasonable part of the twenty-four hours. Thus the subject of sleep immediately becomes two-sided: The amount of sleep the baby takes inevitably affects the amount the parents get. Unfortunately, the habits of the baby do not always coincide with the needs of the parents.

Your young baby will not stay awake and cry just to be difficult. He may be uncomfortable or unwell or need a cuddle, but when he needs to sleep, he will sleep. Each baby's sleep needs vary, so time charts can do little more than give a general idea. Researchers have identified patterns of sleep–times in the twenty-four hours when most babies sleep and other times when they are probably awake. Parents quickly come to recognize and adjust to this waking and sleeping pattern in their own baby.

DIFFERENT KINDS OF SLEEP
Both children and adults experience two kinds of sleep: REM sleep, which is characterized by rapid eye movements that are visible beneath the closed lids; and non-REM sleep. REM sleep is lighter and more restless than non-REM sleep. Non-REM is the first sleep of the night. It progresses through four stages from light to very deep; a person in the deepest non-REM stage of sleep is very difficult to awaken. REM sleep represents about 25 percent of an adult's total sleep, but in children up to the age of five REM sleep represents the larger part of total sleep. The percentage of REM sleep decreases as the child grows from infancy, as shown in the table below.

Age of Baby	Amount of REM Sleep
Fetus	usually total
Premature newborns	75 percent
Full-term newborns	50 percent
Up to age five	steady decline to 25 percent; thereafter, little change

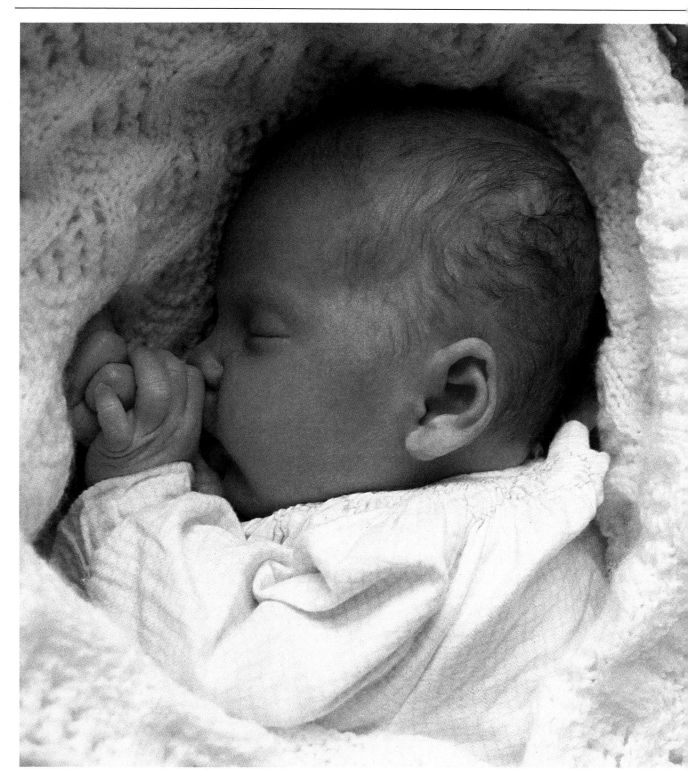

A baby sleeps when he needs to and gradually evolves his own pattern of sleeping and waking times.

Watching your baby, you will be able to distinguish easily the two types of sleep.

During the non-REM phase, the sleeper is indeed "sound asleep." Very little facial or body movement is observable. Half an hour to an hour after stage four (the deepest sleep) has been reached, REM sleep begins.

REM sleep is marked by restlessness, face twitching, irregular breathing, and darting eyes beneath closed lids. It is within this REM sleep that dreaming and dream recall occur, and although it seems that babies do dream, we can only guess this is so because of course they are not able to tell us.

Some parents are frightened to see the change from quiet to active sleep in their babies, but be assured that the transition is quite normal. Scientists are able to measure the two kinds of sleep with an electro-encephalogram, which records brain activity. In non-REM sleep, the EEG shows slow and regular brain activity with an occasional change to a state of wakefulness. In REM sleep, the EEG shows sharp activity with the appearance of special "spike" waves.

THE BABY'S SLEEP REQUIREMENTS

Baby books used to state firmly that, except when awake for a feeding, a new baby sleeps for most of the twenty-four hours. However, a great many babies had not read the books, and their parents not unnaturally thought that either they were handling their babies badly or there was something wrong. We now know that many newborns and older babies need less sleep than was once thought. In any case, sleep needs of individual babies vary as much as the babies. An indication (and indication only) is as follows:

average newborn	16 to 18 hours daily
at 2 months	about 15 hours daily
at 1 year	about 14 hours daily
at 2 years	about 12 hours daily
at 5 years	about 10 hours daily

It makes little difference whether your baby takes her sleep in one long stretch or in several shorter periods–little difference to the baby, that is.

From the first night you spend with your baby, sleep can seem the greatest problem. A misunderstanding of what is normal and what is an idiosyncratic habit that can and should be discouraged is often at the bottom of the harassed parents' trials. If you can understand what can be reasonably expected of your child at various stages, as well as making an honest appraisal of your own level of tolerance, you will be able to set realistic limits, determine when exceptions may be made, and devise a way of dealing with your child's sleeping habits that will satisfy the needs of the child, yourselves, and the household as a whole.

Your baby does not need silence to get to sleep. Sudden loud noises will startle or wake him, but the rhythm of voices, radio, and the sounds of home will not disturb him. If you insist on silence when the baby is going to sleep, you will be establishing a pattern that will be hard to break later. A baby can sleep soundly within yards of a brass band in the park; the background noises of home–the whirr of a lawn mower or the sound of a sewing machine–will in time turn into sounds of comfort and reassurance for your toddler.

Warmth, comfort, security, and a full stomach induce sleep. A new baby feels safer when firmly wrapped, perhaps because it evokes the safety of the womb. As he gets older and moves his limbs more deliberately, he will want to be free of restrictive wraps. In the first weeks after birth, babies fall asleep readily, awaken promptly, commonly cry to be fed, and (after a feeding) quickly return to sleep.

To fit in most conveniently with the rhythm of family life, a new baby would awaken regularly for feedings and sleep most of the time in between. Some babies do; many do not. It takes time for a baby to adjust his inborn sleeping pattern to the habits of the family.

Responding to a crying baby with reason-able promptness leads him to cry less. Presumably this is because he knows reassurance is always at hand; he feels secure that his calls will be answered. All the same, leaping into action at the first whimper is not a good idea. Brief whimpering may often accompany the baby's settling himself in and getting used to things–the feel of crib sheets, the different position of light in the room, being away from his parent. Wait a moment to see if he does settle in without your intervention. This is not the same as leaving him to "cry it out"; that can cause him instead to work himself (and you) into a state of much worse distress.

By six weeks or so, your baby will most likely have one wakeful time each day (it is most convenient if this occurs in late after-noon) during which he can kick, watch what is going on, and generally tire himself out before the evening feeding and bed.

As he grows older, his daytime naps will decrease, but he will be able to amuse himself while he is awake. He will in-creasingly like company and like watching the world go by.

In the course of giving up some of their daytime naps, some babies sleep throughout the afternoon and are then prepared to stay awake all evening. Try to discourage this pattern. As much as you love him, you need some time to yourself. An afternoon walk might help keep him awake, but it might as easily lull him to sleep. Try giving the midday feeding or lunch earlier so that he can have a nap afterwards; wake him after an hour or so to give him time to be awake and grow tired before the evening bedtime. Some ways of coping with the early evening rush– preparing a meal, observing the bedtime routine for the baby, and so on–are sug-gested on pages 44-50.

GETTING THE BABY TO SLEEP

A newborn cannot decide what position he will sleep in. You decide for him–on his back, on one of his sides, on his stomach. He may have a preference; if so, your experiments will show which he likes best. He may sometimes want his position changed, or he may wriggle his bedclothes off and become uncomfortable and chilly. As he begins to be able to turn over or change his positions he will probably go off to sleep in a position of his own choosing. During his first few months of life he will probably settle himself into a favorite way of going to sleep. He may begin to suck his thumb or caress a piece of his blanket, or he may practice some other comfort habit of his own (or your) devising.

Quite often babies awaken several times in the night, amuse themselves, and then go back to sleep on their own. At other times, a baby may need just a bit of reassurance–a cuddle or even just a parent's voice nearby. Once he knows his mother or father is around, he will settle back to sleep. If your baby cries intensely or is very irritable, check first for hunger, an irritatingly wet diaper, feeling cold, and teething discomfort. If the baby seems hot, and particularly if he vomits, an ear infection could be the cause (see page 222). Up until about three months of age, a baby who consistently cries and is difficult or impossible to comfort–especially if this occurs around the same time of day every day, usually after a feeding (which rules out hunger as the cause)–is probably suffering from colic. See page 212 for more information on this trying but happily temporary problem that may underlie difficulty in falling asleep. Try to discover the reason for your baby's irritability, and if it persists, ask your health care provider's advice. Giving a baby a last bottle to settle him down is not recommended, as it promotes tooth decay and fosters a habit that is hard to break. If he is thirsty, however, a little water (unsweetened) might do the trick. In any event, do not assume your very young baby has awakened and is crying simply to annoy you with demands for attention. This is rarely, if ever, the case, and leaving him to "cry it out" will do nothing but make you all miserable.

REACTION AGAINST BEDTIME

When your baby is about nine months old, changes begin to take place. He begins to find it pleasant to be with company and in an atmosphere where a lot is going on. He cannot bear to be separated from you, and he is able to keep himself awake if he wants to. Tension, overexcitement, overtiredness, and other causes as well enable him to keep himself going.

It may be that the abrupt routine of bath, bed, and lights out is no longer acceptable to him. So you must be wily. A regular bedtime

is a good idea because it underscores that daytime is different from nighttime. What you need to do now is merge the day into the night by making the transition less abrupt.

Begin bed preparations reasonably early so that you are not rushed at the end. Make the last feeding leisurely, with gentle talk and play. Give yourself time to putter around within earshot or eyeshot–putting away bath things and so on. He may watch you through an open door. (It could be a good idea to have a low light on a landing and no light at

all in the room.) Hum to yourself or sing and make small domestic noises. If all goes well, he will drift off, contented to know that you are near. If he does not, call to him, and if the voice alone does not help, go in and talk to him quietly. Do not bring him out of his crib, though, or you will confirm his suspicion that it is nicer where everyone else is.

Like other maddening phases, this one will not last forever (although it may seem that way). He will adapt in time, especially if you stay calm and firm in your resolve and make the hour or two leading up to bedtime relaxed and peaceful.

It is important to recognize that your baby may be genuinely frightened at being (as he may think) abandoned. He may also of course be feigning, but real distress slowly reduces from crying into small frightened whimpers and only gradually subsides as you comfort him, whereas feigning can nearly always be turned off like a light—unless you have left him so long that it has turned into real distress.

Some babies find it easier to fall asleep if an adult stays quietly within sight while they are dropping off. Thus day blurs into night.

A drink at bedtime may be
comforting, but if it is juice
or milk, the teeth must be
cleaned afterwards.

HOW TO COMFORT

One useful idea in comforting a young child is to avoid taking him out of the crib but instead to kneel down and comfort him through the bars, gently persuading him to lie down again, offering him a cuddly toy, and covering him up again. This lets him know that the crib is not a bad place out of which he must be taken in order to be comforted but rather is a place that comfort can enter.

The same basic principle of promptly giving your child attention but not taking him out of bed or bedroom applies throughout the toddler years. An uncertain small child may even be reassured by the sight of your knitting or book left on a chair in his room—a talisman that you are still there and will return. The words "I'll be back soon" can also work magic, particularly if you stick to the promise. One desperate father was known to settle his daughter with the phrase "See you in about fourteen hours, okay?" in the hope that he could draw her into compliance. Finally, it is never too early to begin lullabies, bedtime rhymes, and stories.

VISITS AFTER BEDTIME

A face appears around the door. The smile may be a little uncertain, unsure of the welcome, or it may show triumph. "Look, I've saved you a journey: I've come to you!" it may seem to say. Whether he is a toddler or a dexterous crawler, your child has discovered how to climb out of his crib and find you.

Greet him with politeness, patience, and if possible a straight face. "Did you want something? A drink of water? Another goodnight kiss?" Then, back he goes. If he comes back again, repeat the treatment. Show him by your calm firmness that bedtime really means bedtime.

He may also appear at your bedside during the night. Advice about what to do has become more relaxed lately, and some experts advise letting him come in. The comfort of your warmth will send him off to sleep, and (in their view) he will break the habit when he is ready to. If he does not, you will have shown that your sleeping quarters are not a battleground, and you can say quite calmly, "I'd rather you stayed in your own bed, so will you please?" When he does, thank him without being overly effusive about it. Other experts disagree, believing that children should never be allowed to share a bed with their parents. This is one of those areas that must be left to the choice of individual parents, since it is clear the experts do not have the definitive word on it.

Sometimes toddlers come into their parents' bedroom, check that all is well with them, and go back to their own room. On other occasions, they may have had a bad dream or been awakened and been frightened. If there has been a genuine fright, it may seem hard to return the toddler to his own bed, but if you wish to do so, take him back, make sure he is comfortable, give him a drink of water if necessary, have a few quiet words, and leave him. Do not turn it into a chatting session. You can leave his door open, leave a low light on, reassure him that you are not far away—and see if it works. If you are consistent, firm, and calm, it most likely will.

MAKING BEDTIME PLEASANT

If you make bed a threat or punishment for your toddler—"Any more of that and you'll go straight to bed"—you are asking for trouble for yourself. The message clearly is: "Bed is a bad place to which I am sent for being naughty." But is normal bedtime a punishment? A child can become conditioned to think so.

The trick is to make bedtime seem almost a privilege. Gear the day to wind down gradually, beginning with a mention of bringing a game to an end or putting toys to bed; give one or two mentions, and then proceed to the ritual of last wash or bath, toothbrushing, storytime, and last-minute kisses. Some artful parents begin the story in the bathroom and finish it when the child is warm and tucked in bed.

Avoid playing exciting games just before bedtime; your child will not be able to wind down suddenly. If bedtime coincides with the mother or father coming home, one or the other parent could take over the bedtime routine. This becomes a time for deepening relationships, exchanging confidences, and sharing news of the day.

SLEEPING SCHEDULES AND BEDTIME RITUALS

Even when you have established a comfortable sleeping schedule, be prepared for alterations. Your child undergoes changes as he grows, and his needs alter. He may have off-days when he sleeps more or less than usual, or he may have a cold or a minor pain. If your child is under twelve months old and has difficulty going to sleep, it is unlikely to be because he is stubborn or spoiled. Instead, the reason is probably physical—hunger, discomfort from overeating, irritation from diaper rash, teething, or earache. Try to discover the underlying cause of the restlessness and treat that. You cannot always relieve every discomfort a baby experiences; sometimes hugging and comfort are the best you can offer.

There is a railway track outside a big city

where trains run through a steep cutting, the sides of which are thick with tall, spindly trees whose tops are just level with the train windows. In one of those treetops, inaccessible except from the trains, hangs a teddy bear. It could only have been flung from a train window–probably in a moment of wild toddler excitement–but imagine the despair, the loss, and the inconsolable anguish of the next few bedtimes.

The moral is: If your baby has a cuddly toy or other special object, duplicate it without delay. It is easiest if he chooses a diaper or a piece of cloth, but make sure the standby is sometimes used so that it will have the familiar smell as well as feel he likes. With a standby to fall back on, the loss of his primary object will not be so traumatic.

Bedtime rituals usually develop gradually; the ceremonial folding of the object– sometimes this is a very elaborate process– the placing of the toy in bed, the arrangement of various other toys without which bedtime cannot take place. Part of the time he is putting you on and you both know it, but on the whole you should be able to maneuver it into a fairly good-humored relationship.

BABYSITTERS

Occasional nights out are good for both baby and parent. A grandparent or friend whom the baby already knows makes the best babysitter. If that is not possible, make sure the child has at least seen the babysitter previously so that, should he awaken, he will not be greeted by a complete stranger.

Leave the telephone numbers for where you will be, a willing neighbor, the doctor, ambulance, emergency police and fire, and poison control center. Tell the babysitter about any particular names your child has for his cuddly toy or object, wanting to go to the bathroom, drinks, and so on, as well as any special habits he has. Describe your usual practice in responding to cries and requests. Leave a bottle of formula, expressed milk, or other drink your child may need. Come back when you say you will.

If your child has been rampaging all the evening, do not feel so guilty that you never go out again. The babysitter is not as emotionally involved as you are and will be less disturbed by the experience than you would have been.

Should you tell your child that you are going out? Honesty is usually the best policy, but avoid being so heavy-handed about it that he realizes you expect him to react against the idea. If he usually sleeps all evening and all night, you may be tempted not to tell him–that is something you have to decide for yourself. Of course, he may enjoy an evening away from you just as much as you enjoy an evening away from him: He might really like having a different person read the story and make a bedtime fuss.

It also does not hurt a young child to have an occasional night out with his parents, provided it is not too tiring or too stimulating. Chances are he will feel very privileged and grown up.

PROBLEMS ASSOCIATED WITH SLEEP

Occasionally in sleep young children will grind their teeth, jerk their limbs, and (sometimes) sweat profusely and cry out. These are not normally indications of a disease or disorder but are often manifestations of anxiety. If you can identify the basic anxiety and are able to relieve it or remove the cause, the symptoms will generally stop. If they persist, it is advisable to consult your child's health care provider. Some possible areas of concern are the arrival of a new baby, a move to a new house in a new town, friction among family members, and illness or death of someone close. It will, of course, not always be possible to eliminate the underlying cause, but you may be able– perhaps with professional help–to provide reassurance and relief.

It is during the deep phase of non-REM sleep that sleeptalking, sleepwalking, and night terrors may occur in young children, beginning when they are as young as six months of age (see page 222). Bedwetting, another sleep-associated problem with a possible emotional background, is not an issue with children under three, who in any event are primarily still in diapers at night.

Although more common in adolescents, sleepwalking can occur even in toddlers. Often the walking is directed toward the parents' room, but on occasion it may be more dangerous–near an open window or stairway, for instance. It is best not to awaken the child, even when he is in a fairly precarious position; instead, gently guide him safely back to bed and settle him in.

In rare cases, sleepwalking may be a manifestation of epilepsy; it is then usually accompanied by undesirable acts such as urinating on the floor. A child who exhibits such a behavior pattern should be examined by a health care provider (see page 216).

Like two other essential natural functions –eating and elimination–sleeping is a subject that elicits a great deal of parental concern and expert (and inexpert) opinion. Putting your child to bed can be a trial and a terror lasting months and even years, or it can be a natural part of family life, an aspect of your child's growth and independence, and even a special time to be together. So much depends on the attitude that you as parents adopt. If you are firm and consistent, yet warm and caring, your child will come to understand that bedtime is a pleasant and important part of his day, just as eating, playing, bathing, and other activities are.

TOILET TRAINING

Toilet training is a natural milestone for a child and in many ways is not particularly difficult. Nonetheless, it is yet another area that normally causes parents quite a bit of concern.

To avoid oversimplifying the process, it is best to begin by looking at the organs involved with the process. The gastrointestinal tract is essentially a double-layered tube that begins at the mouth and ends at the anus. The function of the inner layer is to absorb nutrients and water; the function of the muscular outer layer is to propel food and drink along the length of this absorbing surface. Along the way, the tract takes on different shapes appropriate to the successive jobs it has to do. The mouth is designed for sucking and chewing; the esophagus propels the food to the stomach, where it is mixed; the food is then passed into the small intestine, where most of the nutrients are absorbed and the residue is emptied into the large intestine, whose job it is to absorb water and to store the now depleted food, or feces, temporarily before it is eliminated.

The absorption of water in the large intestine is one of the most important functions of the gut. As long as the feces remains in the intestine, the extraction of water continues. Soon the feces becomes the familiar formed stool. Children need much more water proportionate to their size than adults. A 150-pound adult could survive quite comfortably on 2 quarts of water a day, but a one-year-old child weighing about 22 pounds needs 1 quart.

Once food goes into the mouth, the gastrointestinal system takes over without conscious control. A person's first indication of the process is when discomfort signals that it is time for a bowel movement. At this point the adult has conscious control, but it may take up to three years for your child to gain this control. In infants, especially those under the age of one, the movement of feces through the gut is a matter of reflex. In a motion known as peristalsis, the muscular layer of the large intestine contracts in little segments, moving the food toward the anus in much the same way as a surfer rides a wave toward the beach. The movement is regulated by nerves within the intestine and by the autonomic nervous system, which is able to increase or decrease the movements. The infant has none of this process under conscious control.

ELIMINATION IN THE YOUNG BABY

Usually within twelve hours of birth, most babies begin to pass green-black jellylike stools called meconium. The dark color comes from the accumulated material produced by the liver and gut of the fetus before birth. Although the fetus passes urine into the amniotic fluid during gestation, it does not pass any stools. Occasionally, if a baby is subjected to intense stress just before birth, she may pass this meconium in the womb, staining herself and the surrounding fluid.

If a baby does not pass meconium within three days of birth, it may indicate a medical problem—an intestinal obstruction, failure of development of the anus, cystic fibrosis, or more rarely absence of the nervous control system of the gut. If your baby is still in the hospital for the first three days, the passing of the meconium will be monitored. If she is at home, you should watch for it and tell your doctor promptly if it has not occurred.

Newborn babies may have six to twelve stools each day. By two months, these begin to decrease to about three to six; and by the second year of life, a single daily stool is usual. Some children have them every other day, and some have two a day. Do not worry if your baby has more or less than the average: It may be quite normal for your child, and as long as your health care provider is satisfied with her progress there is no need to be concerned.

Texture, consistency, and odor of stool change with age. Breastfed babies usually have pasty yellow-green stools that tend to be sour-smelling and to be expelled with great vigor. Formula-fed babies tend to have paler stools with a less objectionable odor. Because of rapid movement through the bowels, both types of stool are soft and unformed. Breast milk stools, in contrast to formula stools, usually cling to the diaper. Vitamins containing iron may cause the stool to turn dark green as excess iron is eliminated. Foods eaten by your child may also color the stool: Tomato juice and beets both tend to produce red stools that can look quite alarming. Call your health care provider if you are concerned, but think back to what your child has eaten in the last few meals.

BEGINNING TOILET TRAINING

Toilet training is a learned behavior that a child picks up in much the same way she does other skills—by mastering parts of the skill separately as she becomes capable of each and eventually putting them together, not by becoming successful all at once.

Is there any harm in pushing a child to learn sooner rather than later? This is a controversial question–one that is probably best answered by looking at the entire development of toilet training skills. It is especially important throughout to maintain a balance between your expectations and your child's abilities.

ACHIEVING BOWEL CONTROL

It seems to be generally true that bowel control is achieved at the same time as, or before urinary control. Bowel movements are, by the time a child reaches the age of readiness, down to one or two a day whereas a child of one, two, or even older may urinate as often as a dozen times a day. The feeling of urgency with a bowel movement is more impressive than that for urination. Let us look for a moment at what goes on inside the body when a bowel movement is about to take place.

A stool is expelled when the lowest part of the large intestine (the rectum) becomes filled with and distended by fecal material. The sensation of fullness causes impulses to move through nerve fibers to a group of nerve cells located in the lowest portion of the spinal cord. The end of the intestine or anus is usually kept tightly closed by rings of muscle, but when the nerve group receives the "stretch" signals, it orders these valves to open. The muscles on the floor of the abdomen begin to lift the opening of the intestine toward the stool and a contraction of the chest muscles and diaphragm expels the mass. After its passage, the rings of muscle return the anus to its resting, closed

position to await the arrival of more material and a repetition of the process.

At first, your baby has no control over this process, but in the first year to eighteen months changes in her central nervous system will bring increasing voluntary control of the reflex. As connections are made in parts of the brain and spinal cord, your baby will become increasingly aware of associating the feeling of the need to defecate with her ability to control or inhibit the movement.

Before your child begins to learn toilet control, there must be some physiological readiness. By fifteen months or so, when the bowel movements have likely decreased to an average of one every day, you will probably have become aware of the facial gestures and body squirms she makes when preparing to have a movement. By acting quickly, you may succeed in having your child deposit it in a pot, but this is not training and there seems little point in doing so. Sometimes her movements will be so regular that you may think your toddler is trained by eighteen or twenty months, but this is not usually the case: She is ready but not trained.

At the stage when your child is aware of her need to have a movement, you can help by developing your own word for the process. She will thus begin to make associations between the feeling, the physical act, and the word you use. When she has begun to associate these you will be able to extend the association. During the readiness period, when your child has a movement, you might say to her, "Jenny is having a BM"; and now, adding an association, you can include a phrase such as, "Time for Jenny to go to the potty."

This of course presupposes that there is a pot for your child to go to. Two types of toilets are in general use: the small potty seat, either with a chair attached or just a plastic bowl; and the adapter seat that fits on the adult-sized toilet. The individual potty has the advantage of making the child feel she is really in control, without her legs dangling precariously or her buttocks being suspended in midair above the water. A small potty can also be taken on outings. If you choose the type that fits on a full-size toilet, be sure to give your child something to rest her feet on. (This will serve the additional purpose of providing a step up to the seat later on when she will want to go by herself.) Having support when she is pushing the movement out will make it easier and avoid straining the muscles of the anus.

If your child does not make the necessary association, ask yourself if you are giving a clear enough message. That is more likely to be the cause than that your child is being willfully difficult.

Mouth
sucking, crushing

Esophagus
propelling

Stomach
mixing

Small Intestine
absorption of nutrients

Large Intestine
absorption of water

Anus
elimination

The human digestive system is a tube stretching from mouth to anus, modified along its length to perform various tasks. Food is propelled along by involuntary muscular contractions. Until fifteen months of age, the baby will move her bowels automatically; some time after this, she will develop control.

Never forget how significantly your praise and approval encourage your child. Make regular times during the day (usually after meals) when she can sit on her potty and wait for a movement. It is fine to let her eat something or look at a book while sitting. The idea is to get the child familiar with the potty, not to make her actually perform every time she sits on it. Children who are familiar with the potty are more likely to want to use it. Let her use it as a seat she sits on with no pants. At first, you will probably have to pull her underpants down for her, but when she does it herself, do not fail to praise her. The learning process begins with the child making the association and then acquiring the skill. Progress can thus be measured by how many associations she has made—the word for bowel movement, the potty, and so on, rather than the number of times she achieves a movement in the right place. It is at about the age of eighteen to twenty months that

A toddler usually takes great interest in toilet training when she begins to understand what is expected of her.

Success! Bladder and bowel control are not easy to achieve, and your toddler should be praised when he deserves it.

PATTERNS OF TRAINING READINESS

The average age for successful toilet training in the United States is twenty-seven months. First children are usually a month slower, suggesting that younger children may learn from their elder siblings or that their parents have become more skillful in training. Boys are usually two months later in acquiring control than girls.

The following chart shows what you may expect your child to achieve at various stages of readiness. Remember that children vary in the timetables according to which they acquire skills. If you feel that no progress is being made, ask yourself if you have begun the process before your child is ready.

AGE	CHILD	PARENT
0 to 12 months	She is gaining control over reflexes, learning how to meet needs, and distinguishing self from others.	Enjoy your baby; it is too early to think about training; have patience.
12 to 18 months	She is developing anatomical and neurological ability to control bowel movement. She will be interested in order and arrangement, show willingness to try new things on her own, and become aware of stool and potty, telling others by word and action.	Obtain potty and make association as explained in text – using house word when she has (or appears to be having) a bowel movement.
18 to 30 months	She has movement and urine in potty; she knows when she wants to go and goes to potty, at first with you, then alone; she cleans herself and is interested in pleasing you.	Continue to associate potty and act of passing movement; praise always, as soon as possible afterward; keep balance between what you expect and what she can achieve; recognize that setbacks are part of the process, are temporary, and will be solved with your patience.

See in the A-Z. Constipation, Diarrhea, Gastroenteritis, Intestinal Infections, Motion Sickness, Projectile Vomiting, Urinary Infections, and Vomiting.

Bowel Problems	Action
constipation one or two loose or watery stools unusual color unusual odor excessive gas passage	If mild, these symptoms need attention only if they persist; mention them to your health care provider on your next visit.
abdominal pain with any of the above blood in the stool frequent watery diarrhea, with little drunk or eaten vomiting, with one or two loose or watery stools	These symptoms are urgent and should be brought immediately to your health care provider's attention.

your child becomes interested in grouping and order; she also is beginning to use language to communicate. These are signs that she is becoming ready to learn toilet skills.

Adding personal hygiene at this time – using toilet tissue and washing hands – may confuse her and impede learning. Children at this age can usually handle only one thing at a time; introducing the issue of hygiene raises the confusing question, "If something that is a part of me is dirty, does that mean I am dirty?" Concentrate on one thing at a time, allowing your child time to indicate her readiness to progress to the next stage.

ACHIEVING URINARY CONTROL

Urine is formed in the kidneys, a pair of organs composed of a great number of microscopic filters through which all the blood in the body flows. The filters allow liquids to pass but retain blood cells and other larger molecules such as proteins. Each filter is connected to a similarly tiny tube that twists its way toward the center of the kidney; it is the job of this tube to reabsorb needed substances and excrete unneeded ones into the urine. The urine then flows down to larger tubes called ureters, each about a centimeter wide, which empty into the bladder, a muscular sac. The bladder is emptied through the urethra, a tube ending in a circular, muscular ring (the sphincter) that is normally tightly closed.

Like the large intestine, the bladder is richly equipped with nerves that sense its increasing distension, and in a young infant it is this sensation that reflexively causes the bladder muscles to contract and squeeze the urine down. The sphincter in turn relaxes to allow urine to pass outside. As your child matures, he will be able to control this reflex.

If urine is unable to leave the kidney or the bladder, it can lead to kidney damage. Often such an abnormality can be noted before the child is born, since very little amniotic fluid will be produced and the mother will gain much less weight and size than is normally to be expected.

It is important to notice a normal urine flow soon after birth. Most babies of both sexes pass urine within the first few hours, boys sending a strong arcing stream a foot or more. Few parents are not caught off guard! The absence of such a stream calls for prompt medical attention.

Your baby's urine will normally be clear, becoming pale yellow as she gets older. After sleep, when the urine is more concentrated, it may be darker in color; it will also be darker if your child has a fever or if the weather is hot. In both cases this is an indication that she needs more fluids. If left standing, urine may become cloudy or form a white deposit, but this is normal, as (usually) is a pink spot on the diaper, which may be caused by uric acid. Urine that is cloudy when passed, however, is abnormal. The smell of ammonia you may notice when changing a diaper is caused by the breakdown of the urine and is nothing to worry about (see page 207), but if there is an unusual smell, consult your health care provider.

As your child becomes familiar with her potty, introduce a word for urine, and remark to your child when there is urine in the potty. As with bowel training, praise, encouragement, and reinforcement lead to success.

Usually, staying dry during the day precedes staying dry at night by six months to a year. Because it is so much a matter of conscious control, you cannot expect your child to resist the impulse to urinate when she is asleep. Occasionally a child may be so anxious to please her parents that she will not be able to sleep at night, fearing an accident during sleep. This occurrence is most usual during the second year of life. If it happens, you can help by limiting liquids before bedtime, and by slowing down the training process to lessen her anxiety–using diapers at bedtime even though she has stopped using them during the day.

The age at which a child learns control is subject to many variables, including family attitudes, gender, and birth order, but it is generally true that a child who is learning to use the potty will make progress in fits and starts. Illness, times of emotional and family change (such as the arrival of a new baby), or excitement may cause temporary setbacks, but here, as with bowel training, patience is the best policy.

SOME TRAINING ISSUES

Do not get angry or punish your child if she wants to play with her urine and stool or if your son directs his stream in every direction but the pot. These are all normal experiments, and he or she will get over them in time. Try to be patient and gradually introduce the notion of acceptable behavior, rather than expressing horror or disgust.

Can you speed the training process by letting your child come into the bathroom while you urinate or have a movement? Since training can be accomplished without this, the practice is unnecessary; however, there is no harm in it either.

Training pants can be used as a way of graduating from diapers while still allowing a margin of safety in case of an occasional miss after the child has been trained. It is not a good idea to introduce them before this point, however, since giving your child "big boy or girl pants" does not send a clear message to the child about what you want or expect. This form of garment is best used to relieve tension for both of you in catching the unanticipated miss rather than to increase tension by raising the level of skill you expect from your child.

If your child is unwell during the training process, she will not lose much ground, even though during the illness she may seem to regress. It may be wiser to wait until she is better before resuming training. This is something you may want to discuss with your health care provider.

Toilet training will take place during the latter half of the period covered by this book, and it may well extend into your child's fourth year. By the time she reaches that age, you will be well-acquainted with her as an individual and your relationship will be firmly established. Unlike mysteries that arise in the early days, when first-time parents often feel uncertain that they are doing the right thing, toilet training lends itself to being conducted in a relaxed and assured manner. Waiting until your child is ready, communicating clearly about expectations and approval, and exercising patience and support throughout the process are the keys to success.

When your toddler is old enough to use the adult toilet, her feet must be supported; otherwise, she will strain when having a bowel movement.

MEDICAL CARE FOR YOUR CHILD

Many babies go through the first few years of life with hardly a sniffle or rash, while others seem plagued with minor ailments. All parents should learn to feel comfortable about managing the usual illnesses and to know what signs or symptoms indicate a more serious problem.

You will spend many hours with your baby and get to know his habits and feelings. When his habits are not changed much during an illness, you can be reassured that the ailment is minor; major changes in behavior, sleeping patterns, eating and drinking, and liveliness are warnings of more serious illnesses.

CHOOSING A HEALTH CARE PROVIDER

If possible, choose a health care provider for your baby before he is born. The obstetrician and hospital maternity unit will need to know whom to contact when the baby is born. Parents differ in their need for advice, and health care providers differ in their ability to discern the guidance parents may need. Your choice will be easier if you already know health care providers in your area. If you do not, discuss the subject with friends who have children. Ask them to describe the type of practice and personality of their health care provider so you can choose one who is right for you. You might want to interview the health care provider before your baby's birth and get an idea of his or her approach to feeding and management, and its compatibility to your own. Ask about emergency calls and fees, and do not hesitate to talk to several health care providers if necessary.

SCHEDULED MEDICAL VISITS

The timing of visits depends on the need to follow up any difficulties with the newborn and on the schedule established for monitoring growth and development and providing immunizations.

If all has gone well at the birth, your health care provider will probably want to see your baby two to three weeks afterward. This checkup will establish that he is being adequately nourished, that you are adapting to each other, and that he has no major physical problems.

If you are experienced parents, this visit may be omitted. Subsequent visits will be timed to coincide with immunizations, and additional visits may be required for advice on specific medical problems. A typical schedule of routine visits might be: at three

weeks; then at two, four, six, nine, twelve, and fifteen months; then at six-month intervals until age three; and then at yearly intervals. The purpose of these visits is to handle questions or problems, discuss diet and habits, and oversee physical well-being. Typically, your child will be weighed and measured; his eyes, ears, mouth, and throat will be examined; his chest will be listened to, his limbs and joints observed for normal development, his reflexes tested, and at prescribed intervals his blood and urine evaluated.

To make the most of these visits, parents should write down any questions they have—however minor they seem—and insist that the health care provider take the time to answer them fully. Queries about normal development and well-baby care are as important as those relating to illness. A good health care provider will take the time to discuss and explain these issues.

THE ROUTINE OF TREATMENT AT HOME

Many illnesses that once required a child to be hospitalized can now be treated at home. As long as the household can provide satisfactory care, remaining at home is clearly better for the child, who thereby avoids adding separation from the family to the unpleasant effects of the illness.

Rest and Activity

Your health care provider will tell you if your child should stay in bed; generally, though, if the child feels well enough to get up, he should be allowed to. He will be happier participating in family activities than lying isolated in bed. If a toddler gets tired, he usually will go back to bed on his own. In the meantime, set him up on a couch or comfortable chair in a location where he can see what is going on. A younger baby will let you know in his own way (usually by falling asleep, whether in bed or not) when he is ready to be put back in bed. In most cases, ill infants can be made as comfortable in infant seats or playpens as in their cribs. If your child must stay in bed, try to make the bedroom inviting and interesting. It is often possible to do household jobs in the same room, to keep him company.

A child who is not feeling well may nap more frequently than usual during the day, sometimes delaying his normal bedtime. You can discourage napping in the latter part of the afternoon or early evening by keeping

A sick child needs company and the reassurance that she is still part of family life.

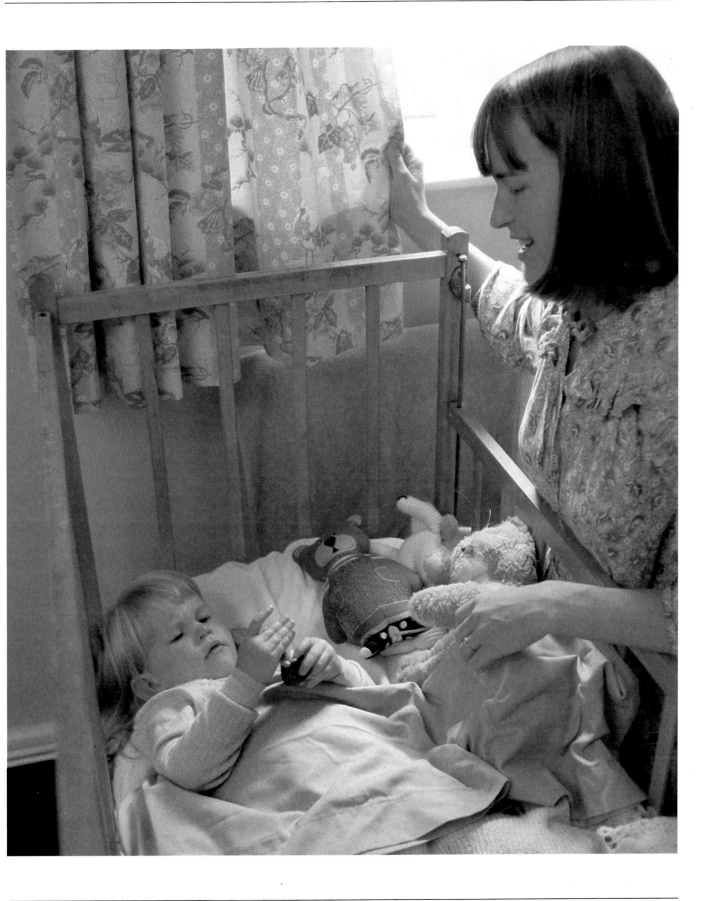

him interested in quiet activities. For a young baby, human company is the best bet. An older child may be kept awake and entertained by a radio or record player in the bedroom, or some favorite toys, books, games, and pets. Telephone calls (with reasonable limits on time and cost) to grandparents or favorite friends and relatives can be a great treat. Puzzles, scrapbooks, coloring, cutting and pasting, and playing with construction toys can all be done in bed. (Coloring pencils and paste in stick form are kinder than crayons, paints, and glue to sheets and blankets.)

Visitors and Family Members

Contagious diseases can be spread to others during the first few days of illness—frequently before you know what the child has or even that he is sick at all. Ask your health care provider if isolation is necessary; this will depend on the seriousness of the illness, how contagious it is, and whether or not others have been immunized. Provided

---

WORRISOME SIGNS
Any of the following should receive professional medical attention.

Eye Infections
Red, pussy eye in a child under three months of age
Frequent blinking and tearing (can result from a foreign body in the eye)
Sudden swelling of one or both eyelids
A lot of pus from the eye at any age
A lot of eye pain
Steady worsening of any eye complaint
Fever of over 101°F. (38.3°C.)
Listlessness

Respiratory Infections
Suddenly worsened breathing (noiser and more labored)
Tendency to tire easily while drinking; or refusal to drink
Inability to sleep
Inability to be made comfortable
Tendency to become agitated
Blue or pale appearance
Sudden chest pain
Drooling
Sudden high fever with congested cough

Vomiting and/or Diarrhea
Inability to hold anything down
Severely dry lips and mouth
Decreased urine output
Decreased tears
Blood in stool or vomit
Listlessness
Abdominal pain
Abdominal bloating
Inability to sleep
Sunken eyes
Fever

---

that they do not tire or disturb the child, visitors can be invaluable. A sick child may be comforted simply by the sight of others—grandparents or other children—chatting or working quietly in the room.

Meals

Unless your health care provider advises differently, your sick child probably will not need a special diet. Infants who are still on the breast or the bottle should continue to be fed as usual. Sometimes a stuffy nose makes breathing while sucking difficult. Your health care provider may suggest using a nose syringe before feeding to clear the breathing passages, but do not try this without medical advice. An older child with a sore throat will naturally prefer soft, easy-to-swallow food, so do not be alarmed if your toddler stops taking solids for a day or two. Help him to drink as much as possible—fruit juices, uncaffeinated soft drinks, soup and clear broth, and milk or flavored milk drinks (if diarrhea is not a problem). A milk or yogurt shake can provide extra calories and protein, but again it is best to avoid milk and milk products if the child has loose stools.

A sick child will probably want to eat smaller portions than usual but more often. Prepare food that is attractive and that he likes. The appeal is needed to encourage his sluggish appetite and to bolster his morale by making him feel cared for. Do not, however, feel or communicate any anxiety if he eats little or no food for a few days. As long as his fluid intake is maintained, no harm will be done. Keep in mind that children with vomiting illnesses will naturally cut down on their intake because of nausea and should not be pressed to eat.

GIVING MEDICATION

Accurate measurement of dosages is of prime importance when giving medication to a child. Do not use household spoons, which vary enormously in size; rather, use the callibrated droppers, syringes, cups, and medicine spoons designed and sold for this purpose at most pharmacies. Pharmaceutical manufacturers do try to make medicine palatable for children, and it is usually not difficult to get a child to take required medication. If you have anxieties about giving the medicine, they, more than any nasty taste, may make the child resist. Try not to let your attitude show through if upset or nervous.

It is easy to give liquid medication to infants under three or four months of age by pouring the accurately measured dose into a rubber nipple. Most babies will suck the medication readily through the nipple, particularly if they are hungry. Or use a medicine dropper or syringe designed for this purpose to squeeze the measured dose into the mouth. This works well with older infants and children too. At between eight and eighteen months of age, children will become able to drink the medication from a little cup. If you keep smiling and are lavish with praise, you will find it goes down even easier the next time.

By two to three years of age, children may begin to resist taking medication. Coaxing in a firm way–pointing out that the medicine will make him feel better and that the doctor wants him to take it–usually works. Tougher cases may require a reward such as a favorite cool drink or a spoonful of ice cream afterward. Even when faced with particularly stubborn refusal, avoid trying to hide the medicine in juice, formula, or other food. The child may not eat or drink the whole thing so you cannot be sure how much medication was taken. Furthermore, the altered taste may cause the child to refuse that food or drink for some time afterward. Even more serious, interaction between the beverage or food and the medication could interfere with absorption of the needed medicine.

What happens if your child steadfastly refuses? First, *you* must be convinced that the medication is indeed needed. Why struggle to give medicine for a drippy nose? If you are not sure, call your child's health care provider. If the medication is essential, you will need to restrain your child. The most effective way to do this involves two adults, a table, and a small cup, eye dropper, or syringe filled with the measured dosage. Lay the child on the table, with one person holding his arms extended above and alongside his head (this helps prevent his turning away). The second person leans over the child's middle (thereby restraining the lower half of his body) and, using one hand to keep his mouth open, slowly pours small amounts of medicine into his mouth with the other hand. Give the child a chance to swallow before pouring again; if he cries, wait for a swallow, then pour some more in. Do not be surprised–but do be prepared–if your child bites under these circumstances. It is a normal reaction and should not be condemned.

This procedure may seem cruel, but it works and most children quickly learn to avoid the struggle by cooperating. Chances are you will have to do this only once, if at all. It is important to reward your child with praise, kisses, sympathy, and that cool drink, even though he has made a fuss. Try not to be angry, as this will only add to the child's fury.

Forms of Medication

Most medication intended for children under three is dispensed in liquid form to be taken orally. Occasionally, however, you may have to administer medication as eyedrops, nasal spray, suppositories, or tablets. Here is a brief outline of how best to deal with each.

Many children will resist eyedrops, so it is easiest to instill them when your baby is asleep, if this is at all possible. If you cannot do it then, you may need the help of a second person to hold the child's arms while you do the job as described earlier. The child may be lying down or, if he is cooperative, sitting upright. Gently pull down the lower lid, taking care to use the pad of your index finger rather than the nail. Drop one drop (or a small amount of ointment, if it is in that form) into the little pouch produced by your finger on the lid. Then release the lid. As the child blinks in natural reaction to this, the medication will spread across the eyeball. He need not keep his eyes closed afterward, nor rub his eyes. Do not be concerned if some liquid seeps from the corner of the eye. It is tears, not the medication, which is already at work by the time the natural tear mechanism is triggered.

When using nasal sprays avoid releasing pressure on the spray bottle before you remove the tip from your child's nostril. The sudden intake of air can injure delicate membranes in the nose and draw mucus from the nose into the bottle, thus contaminating it. Quickly position the tip of the bottle just at the nostril opening (do not jam it inside the nostril), squeeze, remove, and then release pressure, before repeating for the other nostril.

To give suppository medication to a baby, lay him face down across your lap, put a thin rubber glove or plastic bag on your hand, place a dollop of petroleum jelly on the rectal opening, then slowly push the suppository inside until no part of it is visible (otherwise it is likely to come out right away). An older child should be positioned on his side on a table or bed, with his back toward you and his legs bent against his abdomen. This position will allow you to restrain his legs if necessary. Proceed as described for an infant.

Tablets are rarely used for children under three, but chewable vitamins and children's-dose aspirin and acetaminophen are available in tablet form and may be tried from nine months onward. Your baby may be interested enough to pick up the tablet and pop it into his mouth; the tablets are made palatable, so the experience will be a pleasant one. If you give tablets, however, be sure never to refer to the medication as candy and always keep the container in which it comes

MODE	USUALLY USED FOR	LIMITATIONS AND SPECIFICATIONS
oral	cooperative child over age 5	cooperation needed; understanding needed; erratic if hot or cold liquids have been recently drunk; will read approximately 1°F. lower than rectal temperature; may underestimate fever in child who mouth-breathes; must remain in place for 2 minutes
rectal	child under age 5; uncooperative older child	adequate restraining required in child under age 2; may trigger bowel movement in child with diarrhea; must remain in place for 1 minute
axillary	newborn; child with diarrhea; child of age 1 to 5 who is too upset by rectal method	accuracy depends on skin temperature; must remain in place 4–5 minutes; will read 0.5° to 1°F. lower than rectal temperature; not as accurate as oral or rectal method

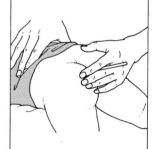

Three methods of taking a young child's temperature are shown. Choose the one that suits your child's age and level of cooperation.

Use a stubby-ended thermometer for taking the rectal temperature of a young baby or a toddler. Secure the child with one hand and hold the thermometer as shown to prevent its being knocked out or forced inward if the child kicks or wriggles.

A thermometer with a longer, thinner end is used in the mouth or, more rarely, under the arm.

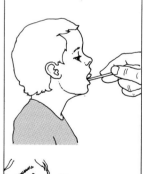

out of sight and out of reach. This, of course, is true with all medications in whatever form.

Safety of Aspirin

The two most commonly used medicines for fever control are acetaminophen and aspirin. Follow the labeled recommended dose–ask your child's health care provider if you are in doubt–and keep all such medicines well out of reach. If taken in large quantities, either can produce serious illness.

Aspirin can accumulate to toxic levels if a child is not drinking well. Fever, poor appetite, and vomiting can result.

The relationship of aspirin to the occurrence of Reye's syndrome has been much discussed recently, and the FDA now requires all aspirin-containing products to warn of a possible link on their labels. Reye's syndrome, an uncommon illness that may begin with sleepiness and vomiting and result in liver failure and coma, is thought to be a toxic reaction to viral infections; it can occur after viral illnesses such as chicken pox or influenza. It is recommended that aspirin not be given to children with viral illnesses. It is wiser to give acetaminophen for fever control.

TAKING TEMPERATURE

You can sometimes tell if a child is feverish if his forehead is hot to the touch or if his face appears flushed. This, coupled with other early signs of illness, may be all the evidence you need to tell you that something is brewing. Feeling the forehead is not the most reliable way to measure body temperature, of course, but it does help parents decide whether or not to get the thermometer out.

Every home should have at least two glass thermometers (in case one breaks). Hospitals are now using electronic thermometers, but the better ones are quite expensive. You can break quite a few glass ones before an electronic one would become cost-effective.

Temperature disks or strips designed to be pressed against the skin and to change color to indicate the skin's approximate temperature are not much more reliable than feeling the child's skin by hand, so they are not recommended for accurate measurement.

A glass thermometer can be used three ways: rectally, orally, or much more rarely axillarily (under the arm). It should be cleaned before and after use with alcohol or cool water and soap. Hold it firmly, and with a few snaps of the wrist shake down the red line until it is below the 95°F. (35°C.) mark. If you are using it rectally, lubricate the tip with a bit of petroleum jelly. Always clean it, shake it down, and return it to its case after use.

The body's temperature normally varies a little during the day. Babies have temperatures of around 99°F./37.2°C. (ranging from 98° to 100°F./36.6°C.–37.7°C.). Older children have a greater change in temperature through the day, the lowest occurring in the morning and the highest in late afternoon (ranging from 97° to 100°F./36.1°–37.7°C.). Fever usually means a temperature of over 101°F. (38.3°C.) taken rectally.

HOSPITALS

Even though your child might never need hospital treatment as an inpatient, as an outpatient, or in an emergency room, it is a good idea to prepare yourself and him for such an eventuality. As opportunities arise, let him know casually that a hospital is a place where people go to be treated for injuries or serious illness and that they usually get better. In the same way that you read him stories about farms, stores, and fire departments, read him stories about hospitals. Many books for very young children mention visits to a hospital as a matter of course, and several specifically prepare a child for a visit (see page 232).

Point out your local health care facility as

you go past it. Do not refer to it as though it were a mysterious place or talk in hushed tones to other adults about what dreadful things go on there.

Children do not have to be patients before they can visit a hospital. Many hospitals now welcome children as visitors; if this situation arises naturally, take advantage of it. If an older child in the family is admitted or must go to an outpatient clinic, take the younger child for a visit. Puzzles, books, or similar quiet games will keep both of them occupied. Some hospitals have small playrooms in the children's outpatient or emergency department. The Association for the Care of Children's Health (3615 Wisconsin Avenue, NW, Washington D.C. 20016) offers additional information on all aspects of this subject, including an annotated bibliography of books for children about hospitalization, illness, and handicapping conditions.

Preparing Your Child and Yourselves
Children love playing at doctors and nurses. Encourage your child to do so with the emphasis on patients who improve and who are treated kindly and made comfortable.

If you know your child will have to go to the hospital—to have a hernia repaired, for instance—begin by getting all the information you can from your health care provider. Ask lots of questions; if you think you may forget them, jot them down. Ask about anything that makes you anxious or scared. Make a note also of any symptoms you may have noticed that you think may be helpful for the health care provider to know. It is better that your child not be present during such a discussion, so take along another adult with whom you can leave your child while you speak with the health care provider.

Once you are fully informed, prepare your child gradually by mentioning it from time to time as casually as you can. Explain about the procedure and anesthetics in a way that is appropriate to his age and ability to understand—explain that it is like being asleep—he will feel very comfortable and drowsy. And tell him you will be there when he wakes up.

Try not to be anxious yourself, but if you are, do your best not to communicate this feeling to your child. Do not deceive your child by saying that something will not hurt if you know it might. A better approach by both parents and health care providers is to say, "This will hurt just for a moment," and to explain if possible just what is happening.

The Hospital Stay
If your child has to be admitted to the hospital, bring in some of his own blankets and toys, as well as pajamas, slippers, and a robe. Happily, unrestricted visiting is be-

coming more common in many hospitals, but this does not mean that all relatives and family members can drop in whenever they want. Usually the parents and sometimes the grandparents and siblings can stay with the child for most of the time. On occasion, if medical procedures are performed, you may wish to leave but assure your child that you will be back soon. Tell the nurse in charge that you wish to be present when the child returns from an operation and ask to be permitted to accompany him to the operating room and remain with him until he is given his anesthetic.

Sitting by a bed can be very boring, especially if your child is playing happily with the child in the next bed and takes no notice of you. Visiting for brief periods may be better because your child is probably used to your coming and going at home—to shop, to pick up other children from school, to go to work, and so on.

In some hospitals, a parent is allowed to sleep in the child's room; if this is something you would like to do, check in advance. Overnight stays and other visits can be very tiring; if it is possible for mother and father to alternate, you will probably become less fatigued. Remember that when your child comes home from the hospital there will be nursing to do and adjustments to make that may involve extra work.

A parent who stays in the hospital with a child can be of great help to the nursing staff. The parent can help amuse other children whose parents are not there or can participate in feeding or distributing meals, bathing, and dressing. Much of this depends on the attitude of the nurse in charge.

Some hospitals allow sand and water play and quiet and noisy games. Silence and clinical order are not now always regarded as essentials to recovery.

The Convalescent Child at Home
Many children are so occupied and busy in the hospital that they find home a very dull place when they return. There may be no constant companions and no chance to observe the life of a hospital unit going on around them. But your child might also feel that being in the hospital was some sort of punishment, and now he may display disruptive behavior, anger, or coldness toward members of the family—usually his mother. Patience and understanding of this new aggression are usually rewarded by its swift resolution. Talking to the head nurse, the hospital social worker, and other personnel who have worked with your child could help you prepare yourself and the rest of the family for what may be temporarily antagonistic behavior once your child is home.

YOUR GROWING CHILD

No child can grow in isolation. Although at birth she possesses an innate ability to progress–to learn to walk, talk, and understand according to a normal pattern of development–she is but newly launched into the deep and delightful waters of living. You, the parents, are the navigators here, providing the compass, marking the reefs; in a very real sense, you oversee the direction of your child's development in her early years. If you are intimidated by the notion that your child's development of physical, cognitive, and communications skills–indeed, of her personality–is in your hands, you need not be. You, as parents, are perfectly situated to be experts on your own child. Nonetheless acquired knowledge helps, and this is where professional advice comes in.

Research in child development has uncovered both the constants underlying developmental behavior and the numberless varieties of individual behavior possible. Perhaps the rarest of all babies would be one who followed "the book" in every detail. Consequently it is important to realize that part of your baby's being human consists of her being a unique individual. That means she possesses the singular inconsistencies, preferences, and frailties characteristic of human beings, as well as the singular glories, talents, and potential.

Although it is practical to write about different areas of development in separate sections–seeing, moving, talking, and so on–your baby obviously does not grow in a series of isolated steps. Each area of growth affects the others in a shifting pattern of development, the whole of which is intricately structured and wonderfully interwoven. Sometimes development in one area supports and strengthens growth in another. Sometimes a slowing down takes place in one skill while a spurt occurs in another because energy is being channeled in the latter direction. An early talker may not be an early walker, an early walker may not yet have ease of speech. Another baby may progress steadily and predictably through each stage of development.

To lighten the burden of togetherness, nature artfully loads the dice. When it seems life is all broken nights and feedings, your baby will stare at you for a long, considering moment and–deliberately and devastatingly–*smile*. When you are worn out with lugging her around, she will begin to crawl. Along the tortuous toddler trail to maturity, nature has prepared a whole series of rewards to lure you onward. And every time you respond with delight to her achievements, your baby is stimulated by this encouragement to undertake further efforts. Love works both ways, and the involved process of growing up frequently relies on love for both motive and reward.

A baby learns through her senses but not through one sense at a time. She sees that a red book is different from a blue book but cannot tell you about it because speech has yet to catch up with sight. But in time all the boundaries among the senses will blur, and the landscape will merge into a whole. Seeing, hearing, understanding, talking, and loving–your child will stand at the frontier, and before her will stretch the unexplored land known as living.

SEEING

Until comparatively recently, it was thought that newborns could see very little, if at all. Now, however, research confirms what parents have always thought–that from birth the baby not only can see but also seems able to focus his eyes. "He's looking directly at me. I'm sure he can see me." How many mothers and fathers have entertained that thought in the first moments of welcoming their new baby? It now appears that a newborn, if held quietly, may keep his eyes open for up to an hour after birth and that during that time he will appear to be studying the face of the person holding him.

FROM THE BEGINNING . . .
At birth, your baby possesses an innate sensitivity to light known as photophobia. Unlike a kitten, he is born with the ability to open and close his eyes, and he does so in response to variations in the level of light. We have the same reaction when we go from darkness into bright light and instinctively narrow our eyes against the glare. As most babies come from the sheltered darkness of the womb into bright light, the ability to protect the eyes by closing them is very important. Our increased awareness of the discomfort to newborns that glare may cause has led to the practice in many hospitals of dimming the lights at the moment of delivery. Similarly, because we know now that a baby's hearing is more acute than was previously thought, voices are lowered and noises kept to a minimum during delivery.

Your newborn can see fairly big and bright objects at a distance of between about 6 and 12 inches. He can focus for a short while and follow an object for a short distance. Babies also appear to be more attracted to curved than to straight lines; they have been observed to study an arc for a consistently longer period than they do a straight line. If these preferences and abilities are put together–a fairly big object without too much detail, a curved outline, a distance of about 6 to 12 inches–one object clearly meets all of the requirements and, moreover, is the one thing the baby is most likely to see in the course of his daily life: the human face.

It is probably only the outline and not the detail of your face that your baby first sees. Later, eyebrows and eyes seem particularly important facial features; and all parents know how, while the baby is feeding, his eyes seem locked on theirs.

Your face, at which your baby stares with such attention, appears blurred to him but

By four months of age, a baby begins to see colors; by six months, he begins to perceive depth; and by twelve months, he can focus almost as well as an adult.

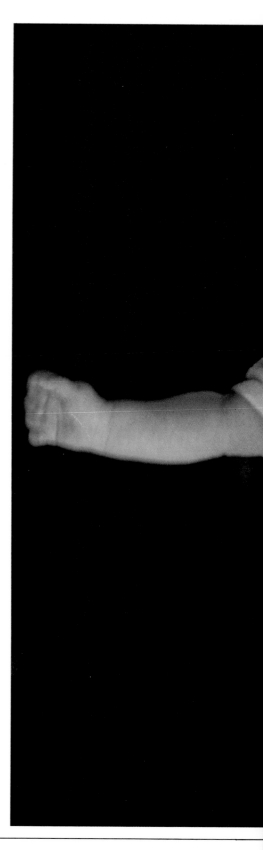

neither silent nor static. It nods, turns, shifts about, and produces reassuring, gentle noises–for few mothers and fathers do not talk to the baby they are holding. These gentle words of encouragement and affection are nearly always accompanied by nodding movements of the head.

Your baby soon learns that the face he sees so frequently produces its own particular voice, and these are the face and the voice that he associates with comfort, warmth, and security.

But won't any face or voice do? Can your baby really distinguish your face and your voice? Although other faces and other voices can comfort a baby, proof exists that very young babies can not only associate their mothers' face and voice, they can also tell when the two are separated. A series of simple tests carried out in Boston and London some years ago established that it is the voice linked to the face that holds the baby's attention. First, each baby was shown his mother's face without its appearing to speak. Instead the mother's recorded voice was played behind the baby, who either took very little notice or else seemed quite displeased. In the second stage, the baby was shown his mother's face, but a stranger's recorded voice was played to him in such a way that his mother appeared to be speaking

with a different voice. Again the baby was uninterested. The third step was to show a stranger's face miming to his mother's recorded voice. Little reaction and very little interest followed on the baby's part. It was only when his mother's face and her recorded voice were put together to simulate the way he would normally see and hear them that the baby reacted with his usual enthusiasm.

Within about three weeks of birth, then, your baby has learned that only your face goes with your voice. Naturally, he has not got it quite sorted out yet–which is why a six-week-old baby, who prefers people to objects, can sometimes be seen smiling appreciatively at an object that has roughly the same detail as the human face and that nods at him, seeming thereby to show some of the same reactions that the human face does.

Not only can your baby follow the first steps of associated sight and sound, he can also choose to see only what he wants to see, blanking out anything else either by going glassy-eyed or by turning his head away. "Put the mobile away," he seems to be saying, "I've had enough." Another trick is to let his eyelids droop until a new distraction comes along that interests him–then the lids lift and a look of alertness comes back into

The picture at right shows what a newborn probably sees when he looks up at a human face. He sees the outline, and although most details are blurred, eyebrows and eyes will catch his attention.

Inset left: In time, the face he gazes on appears more sharply focused; concurrently, he begins to associate that face with a certain voice.

Inset right: At four months– perhaps even earlier–he can distinguish nose and mouth. Familiar faces are now greeted with squirms of delight.

A newborn's range of focus is limited to between 6 and 12 inches, just far enough to see what matters most: the faces of his mother and father.

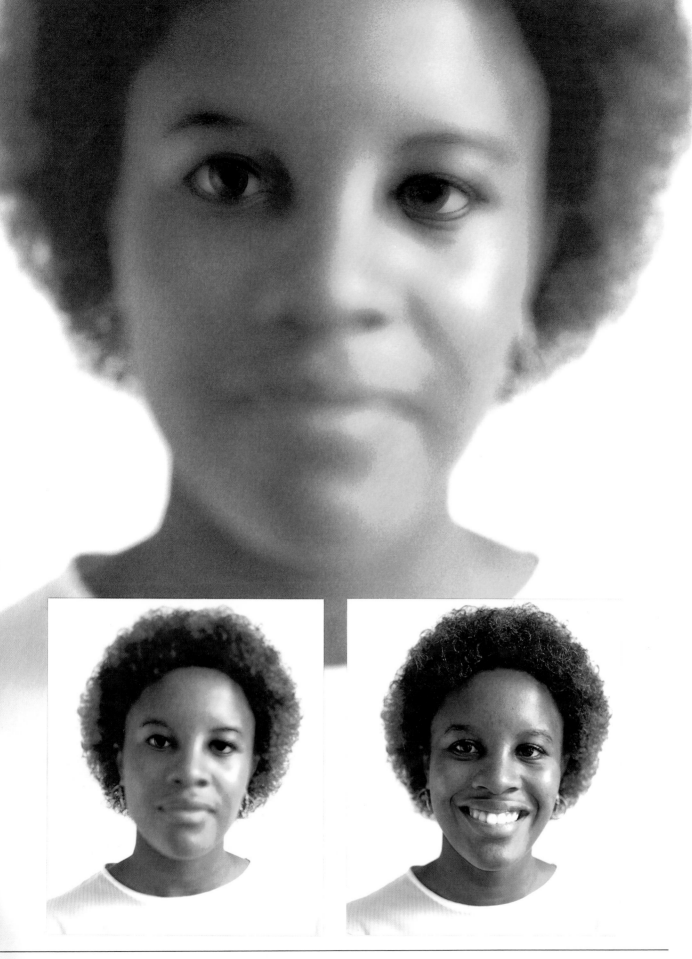

Memory is linked to sight as a baby stares at his mother's face. As eye muscles strengthen, he is more able to direct his gaze at what he wants to see.

his eyes. The newborn's attention span is, however, quite limited and tends to wax and wane. Sometimes even the most vigorous stimulation may not elicit a response from your baby until he is once again ready to pay attention.

Although you learn these things through daily care and contact with your baby, it is only when they are recorded and analyzed that the extraordinary abilities and rapid development of your baby can be seen for the achievements they are. Within a few weeks of his emergence from the lightless world of prebirth, he can see, associate, choose, and discriminate. Do any of us at any other time in our lives learn so much?

PATTERNS OF DEVELOPMENT

It is the gradual cross-association of the senses that leads to growth and awareness. Much of what your baby sees will mean little to him because his mental ability is still so limited. As the weeks pass, though, abilities and opportunity advance together. As your baby's eyes develop and his eyesight improves, he can keep his eyes open for longer periods and can focus on objects at increasingly greater distances; consequently, he is exposed to and receives more visual stimulation. From two to three months of age, your baby begins to grow more aware of his environment because he becomes better able to explore it. Studies have shown that, up to the age of about two months, most babies seem to prefer looking at pictures showing only eyes and eyebrows to looking at pictures showing only a nose and mouth. Eyes and eyebrows are what your baby sees most frequently as he lies in your arms looking up. His preference for pictures of those facial features shows that he *remembers* what he sees most often. Memory has thus become linked to sight.

By the third month of life, muscles around the eye are becoming stronger, and the eyes are working together more efficiently. Previously, your baby may occasionally have shown a "wandering eye," which can be alarming for inexperienced parents. One eye suddenly moves off in a different direction from the other. This stops happening as the eye muscles strengthen, and it generally does not persist after three months. If it seems to be doing so, however, consult your baby's health care provider. An eye muscle imbalance, caught early on, is easy to correct. Uncorrected, it may lead to serious vision problems. Even though routine vision checks are not done until preschool age (usually between three and four years), do not hesitate to bring any concerns you have to the attention of your health care provider. (See Amblyopia and Strabismus, pages 206 and 227.)

As time goes on, your baby appears to stare straight through you much less often. At ages up to three months, he may still be able to focus only on objects within 7 to 12 inches of his eyes, but by three to four months he will be able to focus at greater distances. Earlier in life, he had trouble keeping both eyes on an object for any length of time, but now he is able to watch for some moments, to follow an object through movements, and to study it.

By eight or nine weeks, your baby begins to reach out and swipe at objects. He begins to realize that the world is three-dimensional. At first, he bats out and seems surprised if he happens accidentally to touch anything. He will swipe at little toys strung across the crib or carriage, or at a mobile within reach, and he will display increased interest if the thing he touches makes a pleasant noise. At first the movements are primitive, but after a very short time (as his visual motor skills develop) he never misses–his hands locate accurately and purposefully the object his eyes see.

By three to four months, he is really taking off. His scope has broadened so much that, when he looks at faces, eyes and eyebrows are not enough: He wants to see nose and mouth as well. Objects that used to appear to him as either light or dark are now beginning to assume colors; probably by now he can see red, yellow, green, and blue. He will also– from about six months–begin to perceive depth.

Sight and memory are improving. Favorite toys are remembered and welcomed; family members are greeted with smiles and squirms of delight. This "reward" that he gives so generously stimulates your own delighted reaction, and the mutual bonds of affection and response are thus continually strengthened. A baby's developing skills naturally evoke the most positive reaction from his parents, whose encouragement and pleasure, in turn, help their baby to develop still further.

Life is not all sunny smiles, however. Now that your baby remembers familiar faces, he also recognizes the unfamiliar. At about six to eight months, he begins to equate the familiar with security, and the unfamiliar with uncertainty; this is when the well-known "stranger anxiety" may appear. You will find a good example of how this develops on visits to your health care provider for

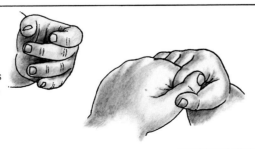
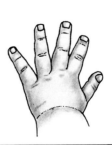
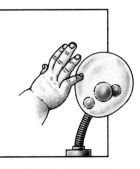

Hands have a particular fascination for the three-month-old. He moves and flexes his fingers and begins to swipe at objects. His aim will be uncertain for some weeks.

checkups or immunizations. At two months, your baby is utterly unimpressed by the new face; at four months, he inspects it a lot more closely but is still not too worried. At six months, he may prefer to hold tight to you, and by nine months, he may want nothing to do with this white-coated, stethoscope-wielding stranger. This is an appropriate reaction in light of the baby's development, and the health care provider should not mind the loud protest.

By the end of the first year of your baby's life, his eyes work well together and can focus close up and far away very efficiently–although still not quite as well as an adult's eyes can. The ability to see objects of different sizes clearly at various distances is known as visual acuity. Visual acuity continues to improve throughout the second twelve months and after, until "perfect" vision (designated as 20/20 vision) is reached at about age four or five.

In his second year, your child sees different colors, sizes, shapes, distances, depths, and textures, but of course he may not yet be able to talk about what he sees with ease. He can recognize big, little, square, round, in, out, and many more concepts, but he may not yet be able to verbalize them. During his second and third years, his speech will catch up with what he sees, and he will be able to tell you about it.

Physical skills are also improving, and sight is now aiding movement a great deal. Visual-motor skills increase as, with developing dexterity, his hands do whatever his mind has signaled them to, wherever his eyes have guided them–to reach for an object, for instance. During his second year, your baby can direct most of a spoonful of food to his mouth; by his third year, he will be able to feed himself well. In the second year of life, he also begins to take things apart and to examine complex toys. Sight-memory is developing constantly: not only can your two-year-old hide your car keys, he can later remember where they are.

He enjoys looking at books and may recognize numbers or letters. He recognizes animals and begins to imitate the sounds that you teach him they make.

But although your two- to three-year-old can see almost as well as an adult, he may still be unable to translate what he sees into speech or action. Skills of visual discrimination are often as yet imperfectly developed, properties such as straight or curved may not be fully appreciated, and certain letters such as D and O may be easily confused.

A classic example of a young child's still-immature visual skills is shown by what is called the property of rotation. Up until now, it has not mattered to him whether his

teddy bear was facing right, left, upside down, forward, or backward. Whatever its position, it remained a teddy bear. Once you begin looking at letters of the alphabet with him, though, it becomes important to you that he see and recognize things the right way up. You want him to take the "picture" b and make it a different picture when it is reversed and becomes d. Then you want him to turn it upside down and make it p or inside out and make it q. At ages from two to three, young children consider these things important only if an adult makes them seem so; as they grow older, however, they understand for themselves that such things as which way a letter faces are important. This realization is an enormous developmental step.

From personal experience, your child will come to understand that some things must face certain ways and that changing their position will either change the things themselves or change their meaning. But arriving at this understanding takes time and is one of the reasons why a child's formal education begins at about five years and not earlier.

DEVELOPMENT AND ENJOYMENT
Because so much is now known about a young baby's ability to see, you can encourage your child's development and increase his enjoyment by providing the right kind of stimulus at each stage.

Mobiles are probably among the first toys or decorations you thought of buying for your baby. Now that you know a baby's visual range, you can make sure that you put them in just the right place.

Do not hang a mobile directly overhead in your baby's crib, carriage, or playpen. If you

Babies are essentially fun-loving. They enter whole-heartedly into games and playing–and particularly into mimicry–from the surprisingly early age of a few weeks.

These shifting colors and movements delight the baby–but never leave a child under five alone with a balloon. Burst or otherwise deflated, it can be sucked in and can suffocate the child.

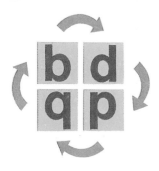

The property of rotation–in this case, the same shape has decidedly different meanings when turned in different directions. But it has little significance to a child until about age three.

watch your baby carefully, you will see that he does not look straight up or straight ahead because his neck muscles are as yet insufficiently strong to fight gravity and maintain his head facing directly up while he is lying down.

Hang it where he is looking–to the right or left. Better still, hang one on each side, and position each the correct distance from his eyes (about 10 to 12 inches). Mobiles should be simple and brightly colored, and they should have curved shapes without too many details. You could make your own, using shapes like those of a kite face and remembering to draw in the eyes and eyebrows in bold, bright colors. Since your new baby is not yet able to reach out and swipe at them, the mobiles can be suspended on a string.

By your baby's second or third month of life–when he is beginning to reach and touch–you should replace the first mobiles with a sturdier type. The first can remain up at a distance (on the ceiling or elsewhere out of reach), but the second is the one your baby is really interested in.

This second mobile can have the same fairly simple outlines–not too much detail–

but it should have a fixed base so that, when knocked, it comes back quickly to its original position. A mobile that is attached only at the top and that swings freely will, when knocked, disappear from the baby's sight range, then reappear, then disappear, then reappear again–in short, it will behave in a totally confusing way. A mobile with a fixed base returns to its original position rapidly so that the baby can practice swiping at it again and again.

From about eight weeks on your baby will take great delight in looking into a small mirror. Choose an unbreakable one with protected edges, about 6 inches across, and fix it out of his reach but within his sight range, to his right or left.

Certainly by two to three months, he enjoys company and will appreciate being part of the family–perhaps propped up in a stroller, swing, carrier, or infant seat so that he can follow you around the room with his eyes. If you use a baby carrier or infant seat, make sure it is the kind that supports your baby's back and neck properly. If you put his carrier on a worktop or table to improve his view, it is essential that you observe the

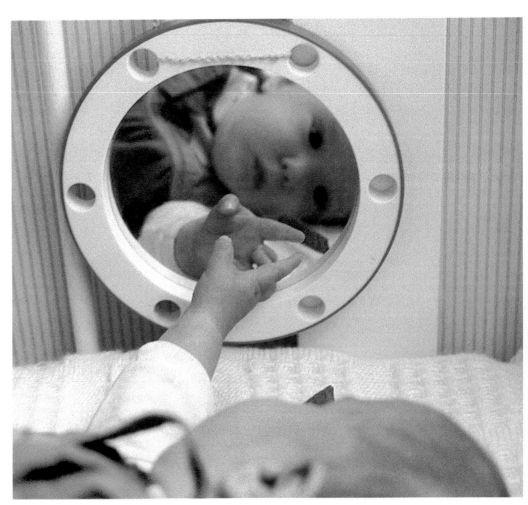

An unbreakable mirror fastened securely to the side of the crib gives hours of amusement as the baby studies his reflection.

safety precautions noted on page 34.

When your baby's focus develops, the outdoor world vies with the indoor for his interest. He can watch the shifting clouds, the patterns of leaves, the sudden miracle of a robin on a park bench or a butterfly on a bush. By four months, he is beginning to haul himself up a little, and he can see what lies beyond his immediate surroundings. Being small, a baby is much nearer (and newer) to the natural world than an adult is, and he will examine for long sessions the marvelous intricacy of interwoven grasses or a clutch of leaves.

At about four months, he may for the first time stare at a place from which an object has just disappeared. Soon thereafter he will learn to follow a falling object with his eyes. The next stage is that endlessly fascinating (to the baby) occupation, the "where did it go" game. The rattle gets thrown over the side of the stroller repeatedly; the teddy bear gets dropped from the high chair times without number. Not only will your imperious playmate yell for you to pick it up again, but even as you straighten up from retrieving it, good old Mr. Bear will bop you on the head as he departs on his next downward flight. But the endless game of throw and return does have a point: Your baby is learning to improve his grasp and release. He is also learning that he can cause something to happen by his action and that things that disappear can also reappear. In a similar way, he is learning that when you go out of the room you do not cease to exist; you, like the teddy bear, will come back and he need not cry.

AVOIDING OVERSTIMULATION

Stimulation is good, but you do not want to overdo it. It is not necessarily true that the more you offer your baby, the quicker he will develop. He might indeed suffer from over-

Cause and effect! Your baby soon learns that he can cause a happening: When he pulls on the ring, the puppet moves.

When your baby swipes out at a mobile that has a fixed base (like this one), it will bounce back in a predictable manner.

exposure and take his own way out–blanking out experiences and stimuli he cannot cope with. All learning must be leisurely, with one stage leading to the next. Trying to force learning on your baby at too early an age can be counterproductive. There is certainly nothing wrong with beginning to expose your child quite early in life to the world's immense variety, but the brain is capable of understanding only so much at a given age. Its limitations as well as its capacities must be respected. The child himself is often the best guide–showing when he is eagerly receptive to new experiences and when he wants time and privacy to explore or consolidate on his own.

You will find that a broad range of parental attentiveness is possible between the undesirable extremes of indifference and over-intrusiveness. A normal, warm, caring home in which the baby is accepted from birth as part of the family provides plenty of natural stimulus for the baby to develop into an affectionate, alert child. To a baby, the world is an educational playground, and his first lessons are learned at home. Shapes, colors, sights, smells, and noise are all present at home. Later, as his consciousness of the world extends, you can spread before your child the riches of wider experience, but anxious parents intent upon teaching academic skills or a sophisticated knowledge of the world at earlier and earlier ages will only succeed in communicating their anxiety to the child.

More information about how and when to "teach" a child is given in the discussion of becoming a person (page 168) and in the section on learning through play (page 158). For the time being, it is sensible to remember that babies need babyhood just as children need childhood–and that leading is nearly always more effective than pushing.

Swiping, reaching, stretching, your baby is endlessly amused by the routines of home. He is learning through involvement.

It may be tiring and frustrating to the adult who has to pick up the toy, but this child is practicing his ability to grasp and let go.

READING WITH YOUR CHILD

"Story!"

Your eighteen-month-old toddler drops the book on your lap. Laboriously, he hauls himself into the chair at your side, draws his favorite toy or comfort blanket up after him, wriggles to make sure he has more than his fair share of the seat, and taps the page peremptorily. "Story," he repeats in a decisive tone, and another storytelling session is in progress.

To give your child a love of reading is to give him the key to discovering life itself, from lists of sports scores in the daily paper to books revealing the humor, wisdom, and mistakes of the past, present, and future. And you can begin imparting this gift almost from birth, for the first "stories" do not require reading: They are the rhymes and lullabies of our oral tradition. Later, your voice will be connected to reading from a page, and even a young child recognizes the magical fact that a certain book produces the same story or the same pictures. From your

baby's earliest days, storytime and books can be associated with the security of being cuddled, with togetherness, with the special privilege of individual attention.

The aim here should be enjoyment–not teaching. If you can think of the daily storytelling or reading sessions as a source of enjoyment for *you*, then it will be a source of enjoyment for both you and your child. There is, after all, no hardship in sitting comfortably and reading from one of the multitude of wonderful children's books being produced today. A four- or five-month-old baby will sit happily propped at your side, chewing his rattle and occasionally swiping at the pages of the book you are holding. You may simply be *talking* about the pictures in the book–"There's a beautiful red apple. What a fat little baby!"– it really does not matter. Your baby is enjoying the caring, the comfort, the proximity, and the rhythms of your voice. And so are you. Once you get over any initial self-consciousness, you will find it is a great

Secure and absorbed, this baby enjoys the comfort of being cuddled and the appeal of the inviting shapes and colors as much as the older child enjoys the story she is being read.

ego-booster to be declaiming like Laurence Olivier. Do not feel aggrieved, though, if your audience of one has fallen into a sound slumber at your side or has quietly dribbled over the text. He is meant to enjoy the storytime in his own way too. In any case, make your reading a performance! Do it with style!

The best first books to read to your baby have one or perhaps two clear, simple pictures on each page, possibly with the names of the objects illustrated written underneath. Laminated cardboard pages may help books to last longer; your baby is bound to want to suck or chew on them as soon as he gets a hold of them. Important as books are, you have to anticipate this type of handling and recognize that a baby is simply not going to be careful with books, however much you prize them. As time goes on, he will learn to hold books properly, to turn their pages carefully, and to treasure them as well as a child can.

The big pictures, and rhymes, and the verses will soon encourage your baby to join in, especially if the objects and animals in the pictures have their own characteristic noises. Certainly by his first birthday, he will recognize his favorite book and will be able to imitate the appropriate sounds. He will also know at once if you try to skip any of the pages when you read it.

Later, he will enjoy simple stories, perhaps associated with familiar situations, such as visiting grandparents or going shopping, and he will enjoy stories that contain a surprise or discovery–pop-up books, books with tabs to pull that make things happen, or books where the "surprise" is in the picture.

Children around two years old can begin to appreciate unfamiliar situations described in books–pictures of animals and scenes they are unlikely to see or experience for years, if at all. Have you ever seen a zebra in the wild? Yet doubtless you recognized it at first sight in the zoo because pictures had made it familiar.

Situation books help children come to terms with real life. Books about going to the doctor, the new baby, and other such subjects can help prepare your child for an event before it happens. A two- or three-year-old can well understand the subtleties of meaning these books carry without being able to express them verbally. Fairy tales nearly always take into account the physical disadvantage of a small child living in a large world. How often does the smallest creature triumph, the poor become rich, the third son (always the downtrodden one!) win the princess? Such tales reassure the young child; he can identify with the weakling turned conqueror because he lives in an environment that he is largely powerless to control. For the same reason, children often delight in what may strike parents as bloodthirsty deeds. A child with no chance of getting his own way in real life may take comfort in seeing, for example, the devastating explosion of a volcano in pictures.

WHEN YOUR CHILD BEGINS TO READ

If you have instilled in your child a love of books and stories, he will want to read for himself quite naturally. Learning to read is a complex business. You will know when your child is poised on the brink of reading readiness, but it is unlikely to occur while he is within the age range of this book. What you can do is show him the combination of shapes that spell his name, so he can recognize that combination when he sees it. If he seems ready for it, you can then show him the shapes that make up simple words– *bed*, *cat*, and so on. Always use lower-case letters (*a*, *b*, *c*) rather than capital letters (*A*, *B*, *C*) because they are the ones that appear in print most often. No more formal teaching is necessary at this age.

One thing you can do that will be fun for you both is to make him his very own book. Buy or make a scrapbook and on the front write his name and stick his photograph. Underneath you might write, "This is me," and your child's name. Inside you can write, draw, or stick whatever the two of you like– the bus ticket from when he went to see his aunt, a bit of wrapping paper from the present his cousin gave him, a drawing of his new shoes, a sentence about what he did today or ate for his dinner. It is *his* book, a record of *his* life and no one else's, and it will be very precious to him.

TELEVISION

At its current level of accessibility, television for children cannot and should not be ignored. Programs on television for very young children are frequently excellent. They can be imaginative and humorous, and they often employ among the best illustrative and dramatic talent going. But what television for children demands is the involved presence of an adult to watch with the child. Monitor the menu first; then decide when the set goes on. When the designated program is over, switch the television off. Remember that a TV set is not a babysitter.

You should also remember that your child cannot always take things in as quickly as you can; this is why programs for children often proceed at a slower pace. The child can best understand what is going on when the action is not too noisy, not too quick, not too complicated, and not too frightening. Of

Magnetic letters stuck on the refrigerator door can be one of the earliest games to teach that shape and position have meaning.

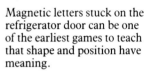

Television should not be used as a babysitter. Young children benefit from its positive effects and suffer least from its negative ones when they watch with an adult.

course this varies from child to child, and what frightens one will delight another – but you are the expert here. The essential rule is not too much and not alone. Watching without an interested, involved, and loving adult is a sterile business for a child. Take care, too, to help your child distinguish between the program and the commercials. This is an uphill battle, but it will be worthwhile to have won it in the years to come. Encourage your child to sit no closer than three feet from the television set. If he needs to sit closer than that, it may be an indication of a vision or hearing problem that should be checked by a health care provider.

If you really think your two- to three-year-old is getting too interested in television for too long a time every day, ask yourself whether life outside TV is interesting enough for him. Do not make television another battleground. Try distracting instead of prohibiting; try involving your child in independent play or activities that complement your own. Children love to imitate and help with adult tasks, even housework. Watching a fast-moving cartoon might be fun, but it hardly compares in appeal to making cookies in the kitchen with you.

STAGES IN THE DEVELOPMENT OF SIGHT

At Birth
He can distinguish light and dark and can close his eyes against too-bright lights. He can also focus at distances of from 7 to 12 inches.

First Month
He stares at his parents' eyes, making eye-to-eye contact, and is relaxed when doing it. He also stares at objects but does not yet reach for them.

Second Month
He prefers people to objects and becomes excited when he sees a familiar person. He can watch moving objects, and he begins to swipe at objects and to explore his hands.

Third Month
He recognizes familiar people, and he explores and flexes his fingers.

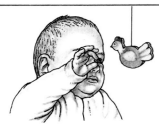

Fourth Month
He stares at himself in a mirror. He appears puzzled when an object disappears from sight. He focuses well, and his swipes at objects are more accurate.

Fifth Month
He notices and seems to measure the space between his hand and an object, and he begins to look when an object falls. He recognizes his toys.

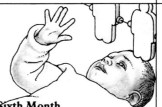

Sixth Month
His eyes direct his hand for reaching and pulling. When he drops toys, he begins to retrieve them. *As muscle control develops, sight increasingly directs movement so that the two abilities overlap and coordinate.*

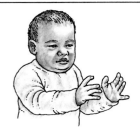

Seventh Month
He can grasp with one hand and can hold different objects in each hand. He claps and he can anticipate actions.

Eighth Month
He can pick up small objects, sighting and reaching for them accurately. He can point at the objects he sees, and he follows with his eyes when an object is pointed out. He turns objects over to examine them, and he watches his own hands as they learn to hold and drop. He may be wary of strangers.

Ninth Month
He knows that small objects can be approached with a finger and thumb grasp, while a large object (a ball) requires both hands. He will search for and uncover a toy he has seen hidden, and he remembers things he has not liked and things he has. *His powers of reasoning and thinking are now aiding and influencing his reaction to what he sees.*

Tenth Month
He is able to fit things together and to push simple shapes through the correct holes in his sorting-box toy. He searches for things, and he imitates gestures and expressions readily.

Eleventh Month
He begins to be able to feed himself—at first with finger foods but then, with increasing dexterity, with a spoon. He will search for an object that is out of sight.

Twelfth Month
He can now reach accurately for an object while looking the other way (his sight has gauged the distance). He recognizes pictures and colors, and he is able to stack toys reasonably accurately, to build with blocks, and to hammer pegs into a pegboard.

Note: All these stages are guidelines only. Each baby varies in his development, and although the progression follows the same pattern, each baby is an individual and may achieve these milestones at slightly different ages.

MOVEMENT

Your child's rapid growth in the first three years of life is nowhere more evident than in the astounding maturation of her movements. Within a few months, the flailing movements of your newborn are transformed into graceful and coordinated motions. In less than a year, her sitting and standing become second nature. Before her second year is complete, she walks expertly and has precise control of her hands. By her third birthday, she has mastered all of the basic movement skills and is ready to explore with ease and confidence the largest vistas and smallest corners of her world.

How are these skills so quickly accomplished? Certainly the naturally accelerated growth of a child's brain and nerves, which control the body, are primarily responsible. Yet only by constant practice could she have refined these movements into such an incredible repertoire in such a short time. Watching her, you soon realize how intensely she works to gain control of her body and how tirelessly she rehearses her emerging movements (through play), despite misses and spills. As she begins to crawl and later to walk, she frequently loses her balance and sprawls face-down on the floor. Nevertheless, she instantly pushes herself up to try again. Over and over, she reaches for a toy, missing it repeatedly, but then finally succeeding (and usually stuffing it triumphantly into her mouth).

There appears to be a natural drive that propels children into this endless rehearsal. It is a mixture of burning curiosity to explore the world and joyful satisfaction at gaining control over their bodies.

You can encourage your child's growing abilities by providing interesting and challenging surroundings in which she can practice her emerging skills. Playtime together, however, should be relaxed and enjoyable for both of you. Trying to force her progress through different stages of development—rolling, crawling, standing, and walking—will only lead to mutual frustration. Instead, she needs to be presented with new objects and settings that naturally stimulate her curiosity and help her to learn to move. By allowing your child to investigate in her own way and at her own pace, so that she both seeks and succeeds, you enable her to gain confidence in her own abilities. This gift of confidence and motivation to explore is one of the greatest you can bestow.

It is important to realize that your help may not cause her to learn more quickly. No amount of pushing or coaxing can make her move before her body is ready to. Each child has her own normal pace of development, a

Most of your newborn's movements are reflexes, which he makes involuntarily. The most common of the reflex actions you will see are shown here.

A newborn clings strongly to supporting hands in what is known as the prehensile grip.

Lying on his back, a new baby will stretch out one arm in the direction he is facing and draw the other arm across his chest. Known as the asymmetric tonic neck reflex, it will begin to disappear at about four months.

Held in the position known as ventral suspension, the new baby's head droops, the limbs hang down, and the hips are flexed.

Supported under the arms, a newborn will attempt to stand and make definite stepping movements.

This baby is supported by a hand and forearm. As his head droops back, his arms are flung out in the startle reflex.

This baby turns instinctively toward the nipple. This reaction is known as the rooting reflex. Notice how her hand clasps her mother's finger. This too is a reflex reaction; she will grasp any object put into her palm.

pace in tune with the continued development of the brain and nerves that takes place well into the first decade of life. You can, however, recognize when her body is ready, provide her with opportunities to test and sharpen her skills, and thus encourage her motor development. For example, she may be pulling herself up by the furniture, taking a few stumbling steps, and then falling. Help her by letting her walk between you and another person so that her walking is refined in an enjoyable manner.

Do not imagine that you can raise your child's future IQ by encouraging movement skills. Little relation exists between the two—so do not rush to enroll her at Harvard if she walks at eight months, and do not worry about academic underachievement if she only starts walking at eighteen months. Early movement skills seem to have little bearing on future intelligence. There are, however, a small percentage of children whose move-

ment is delayed because of physical or mental problems. If your child is not sitting at nine months, is not propelling herself around the house by creeping, by crawling, or by scooting along on her bottom at twelve months, or is not walking at eighteen months, it is sensible to discuss the situation with your health care provider. Many children learn these skills at even later ages, but it is wise to try to detect possible problems early on and perhaps save yourself unnecessary worry.

PATTERNS OF DEVELOPMENT

Every child is an individual and develops at her own pace. Although the general sequence of movement development (sitting before standing, for example) is the same for all children, each child moves according to her own timetable—one sitting at six months, another at eight. The style of movement may also differ: One child crawls, while another scoots on her bottom; one first learns to roll from back to stomach, while another first rolls from stomach to back. Finally, children's temperaments vary too. Some children prefer quiet skills, such as drawing or hand activities, whereas others prefer to jump and tumble. As a result, many children naturally show more advancement in some skills than they do in others. Your best course, therefore, is not to try to fit your baby into a rigid schedule or style of movement. Only the average ages of attaining skills are described here; a great deal of healthy and perfectly normal variation exists among children. If you note a considerable discrepancy between your child's development and the average, discuss it with your child's health care provider before becoming alarmed. In this chapter, movement is described for the full-term infant only (at least thirty-seven weeks of gestation). Premature infants show slightly different movement patterns—often until they are eighteen to twenty-four months of age.

AT BIRTH

At first sight, a new baby seems a helpless little creature. Once placed, she cannot move but lies with limbs tightly tucked up to her body. She can circle her arms and kick her legs, but her movements are aimless and often jerky. Twitches and startles are common.

But your baby has been learning to move before she was born. Since body control develops from the head toward the toes, the first evidence of it appears when, laid on her stomach, she can lift her head a few inches and turn it to one side to breathe more easily. This ability is so limited, however, that she cannot indefinitely hold her head clear of an obstruction. This is why pillows or a plastic sheet that might be sucked in can cause suffocation. Your newborn will also try to balance her head momentarily when held up on your shoulder before letting it drop back down.

Most of her other movements are reflexes and not directly under her control. When she is laid on her back, her head falls to the side due to neck weakness. This often provokes what is called the asymmetric tonic neck reflex or the "fencer" position, in which the limbs on the face side straighten and the limbs on the opposite side bend. Other simple reflex actions she can perform include sucking on anything placed in her mouth and grasping anything put into her palm. She may also wriggle across her bed on her stomach, stand when held up, and even make a few stepping motions. None of these movements is voluntary; they will all gradually fade, and within two to six months they will begin to be replaced by voluntary movements. At birth, only the more primitive areas of the brain, which govern reflex movements, are mature; then as the brain grows, most of these reflexes subside. Gradually, development of the more complicated brain areas that govern intentional movement allow your child to gain control over her body.

It is similar to transferring weights between pans of a scale. In one pan is the reflex reaction (at birth, the dominant weight), and in the other is voluntary control. As the reflexes diminish, voluntary control takes on greater weight. As maturation progresses, the scales become even, and then they gradually tip as voluntary control dominates and dictates actions. Soon reflex reactions appear to vanish, lying dormant in some recess of the brain until a stressful incident— illness, emotional upset, or an accident, perhaps—triggers them into action. You can see this in the heightened startle reaction of an adult to some unexpected incident.

There is not a great deal you can do to encourage movement in the first weeks of life, nor is it necessary to do so. Your baby is recovering from the trauma of birth and is coming to terms with her new surroundings. At this stage, priority is given to getting to know each other and learning to function as a team. During her brief awake periods, you may wish to stimulate her visual interest by putting a mobile or simple drawing on the side of the crib in her line of vision (see page 124).

THE FIRST THREE MONTHS
In her first three months of life, a baby is usually still in a twilight zone of sleep and wakefulness. Gradually the wakeful periods increase, as does the baby's awareness of her environment. The sight of your face or of a familiar toy sets her wriggling with excitement, arms and legs waving in wide circles. Some active babies manage to roll and squirm along on their stomachs when agitated; this is an automatic reaction not under their control. If she lifts her head up and back to the side, your baby may roll over. She may also creep across the mattress if she digs her heels in and then kicks her legs straight. Watch out for this even before she is able to move voluntarily. Do not, for example, ever leave her unattended on a high surface or in the center of your bed, even if you fence her in with pillows. If she is on a high surface and the telephone rings or you get called away for some other reason, either take her with you or put her into her crib.

Over the first few weeks, she finds it increasingly easy to lift her head. Placed on her stomach, she can just manage to clear her chin from the supporting surface for a few seconds. Her arms are not sufficiently developed to enable her to push up on them, so they remain tightly tucked up to her chest.

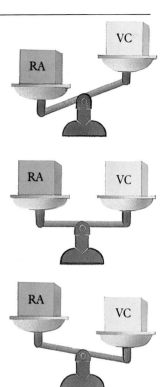

As the reflex reactions fade, voluntary control takes over and eventually dictates actions while reflex reactions lie dormant.

Everything now goes in her mouth to be sucked, explored, bitten, and generally tested.

Lying on her back, she turns her head more and more easily from side to side, but she still does not have the strength to hold it evenly in the center for more than a few seconds.

By three months of age, however, she has enough control to hold her head firmly face-up, and now if you put a mobile directly overhead, she could watch it for some time. Her increased neck strength enables her to lift her head and chest while lying on her stomach. Setting her forearms slightly away from her body (but keeping her elbows behind her shoulders), she pushes up on them until her chest clears the supporting surface. For several minutes, she gazes eagerly around before lowering herself more and more smoothly down.

Hand skills, too, are developing. By her third month, your child begins to observe her hands intently and to wriggle her fingers. No longer the tightly clenched fists of the newborn, they are now loosely curled or fully open, and their movements fascinate her. She begins to swipe at objects within reach at her side and her hands close as she reaches. At first she overshoots the mark; it will be months before she coordinates the skills of reaching out, opening her hand, and closing it on target. She does not yet have the strength to reach up directly overhead. This reaching movement can be encouraged if you put toys, mobiles, or simple pictures to the side of her crib or changing table. Do not always hand her the toy—she needs to practice—but at the same time do not make it too difficult for her to reach, and do not let the game go on so long that she becomes frustrated. At times, she will need some helping out.

The grasping reflex is still strong. If you touch anything to her palm, she automatically clutches it, although she still cannot release the object at will. You will find yourself prying her hands loose from objects for months to come because her ability to release is still immature.

She excels in hand-to-mouth movements. Shape, taste, and smell notwithstanding, everything goes into her mouth. However much you are appalled at her lack of discrimination, try (within reason) not to worry too much about the offense to hygiene. The mouth is a magnificent sense organ for both taste and touch, and it is giving your baby valuable direct experience in the world.

At this period, your child still depends on you to change her position. By doing so, you will help her exercise different parts of her body. Being carried on your shoulder helps her practice holding her head up. Lying on her stomach helps her strengthen essential arm, back, and neck muscles as she lifts her head. Some babies dislike the position, but a short while on the floor—even just two to three minutes twice a day—is beneficial. Encourage her by singing or talking to her or by showing her little toys; as she learns to push up to see around herself, she will gradually come to enjoy the position.

Let her play on a blanket on the floor as much as possible. It will improve her view of the world and stimulate her curiosity, as well as allowing her more room to explore. Leaving her confined in a crib or carriage for excessive periods of time can only serve to bore her and may reduce her mobility. When she becomes more active, a playpen will be useful at times for safety's sake, but in the early weeks it is unnecessary (see page 33).

Growing mobility inevitably brings its own hazards. Some baby equipment, although excellent when used at the appropriate time in the baby's development, can be dangerous if used either too soon or too late.

The momentum of a wind-up baby swing can cause your child to fall forward if she has insufficient control of her body; and although at times a swing can be a parent's best friend for soothing a fractious infant, the child needs to be padded firmly into place with rolled towels at sides and front. A safety strap is a must!

A reclining infant seat set on your work surface allows you to entertain your baby while you get on with the chores, but it must have a wide, stable base so that it cannot tip over. Always use the safety strap and adjust the angle of recline to suit the baby's back strength—beginning with it set at its most reclined position. Babies as young as two months may be able to arch and plunge head first off a counter while still strapped into the seat. Discontinue using an infant seat at the first sign of this.

Baby carriers worn on your front must support the wobbling head of your new baby; check its head support as well as the strength of the shoulder straps. When your baby is around four to six months old, you may switch to a frame-type backpack, since by then her head and upper back will be stronger and will not need such constant support.

Some experts believe that walkers and jumping seats put excessive strain on undeveloped bones and muscles and prefer that a child stand and walk when nature dictates. Before using any of these devices, ask your health care provider's advice. They should never be used before a child develops enough head and body control to sit when you are holding her at her hips. In addition, children in walkers have been known to tumble down unguarded stairs or to pull down objects that were formerly out of reach. Jumping seats have swung babies into too-narrow door frames. Whatever its potential usefulness, any device can be detrimental if it is pressed into service before the baby is ready for it, if it gives inadequate support, if it is unstable, or if it is overused–that is, if it is used for longer than about one hour at a time.

THE FOURTH THROUGH SIXTH MONTHS

Your baby's world is still mainly horizontal in her second season of life, but her development of movement is gradually progressing, according to plan. Head, shoulders, arms, and hands are now in active use, and she has just discovered two more delightful objects: her feet.

Lying on her back, she makes a grab for them, misses, and gets her knees instead. Constant practice at this entertaining game helps to strengthen her muscles and also makes her body more flexible. Before long, her toes are in her mouth. (At the instant of accomplishing this, her back may momentarily be so rounded that she topples over to one side.)

Lying on her stomach, she pushes herself up onto her forearms, with elbows no longer tucked close to her chest but aligned directly underneath her strong shoulders. Cautiously she tests her skill, supporting herself first on one forearm and then the other. Next, she leans on one arm and quickly reaches out with the other to try to sweep a toy toward herself, sliding this arm along the floor because she still lacks the balance to lift it completely off the ground. At first she probably misses the toy, or her fingers close reflexively before reaching it, but gradually she improves.

It is a great achievement to estimate distance and to coordinate reaching and grasping while balancing on a forearm. You can help your child by putting rattles or other graspable objects within her reach. Keys or rattles hung on the sides of her

changing table will amuse her and help her practice reaching and grasping. Small objects and anything sharp or toxic must be kept away. Objects now travel from hand to mouth at a rapid rate.

At about five months, she accidentally rolls over (usually from front to back) as she reaches to the side for something, loses her balance, and topples over. She may begin the other way, turning first from back to front; but whichever way she does it, she will learn control within a few weeks and the movement will quickly become smoother. In the meantime, if she can roll in only one direction, you may have to turn her back over yourself as she becomes frustrated at her own inability to do so.

Your child's newfound ability to rock, roll, or twist herself allows her to move with increased freedom. More than ever, you need to guard against possible accidents. She may brace her feet against a firm surface, such as the floor or furniture, and push

When her toes are in her mouth, her back may be so rounded that she topples over to one side. From such mishaps a new skill–turning over–is learned.

At about five months a baby learns to "airplane." Head lifted, back arched, and legs lifted straight behind her, she bounces gently on her stomach. Supporting herself on one forearm, she can reach the other arm out deliberately.

herself along–or even propel herself into space if she is left unattended for an instant on a high surface. It can happen so rapidly that she should never be left in such a situation.

Your child is also learning to "airplane" or "swim." While on her stomach, she lifts her head, arches her back, lifts her arms with elbows bent behind her, and lifts her straightened legs. She bounces gently up and down in this position, collapses in momentary exhaustion, rests, and then begins again.

By six months of age, she can push herself up from her stomach on fully straightened arms. Legs, too, are straightened, and her fingers, which are curled at first with the effort of staying up, later relax as she gains strength. To reach anything, she must still drop down, lean on one forearm, and reach out with the other.

All this time, she is preparing for sitting and standing. When she is held up in sitting position, her head balances well; when supported in standing position, she stands on straight, sturdy legs. These movements are voluntary, not reflexive. Her back is not yet strong enough to enable her to sit alone, but you can help her practice by sitting with her on the floor two or three times a day, supporting her between your legs. Or she can sit next to you on the couch, propped up on either side with cushions, as you look at a picture book together. She will love being sat on your knees, facing you as you gently bounce her up and down and sing to her. A few minutes at a time is probably enough for her to begin with.

From four months on, she stops simply gazing at her hands and instead begins to play actively with them and with her fingers. She locks them together over her chest and then pulls them apart with a snap. Later, she moves her fingers against each other. She can lift toys to the center of her chest and manipulate them with both hands; if you put a toy in one hand, she quickly lifts the other hand to join in feeling it.

By six months, your child's arms sweep only slightly to the sides as she circles smoothly in to pick up a toy and hold it triumphantly above her chest with straight arms. Underreaching is still common, so she may need a little help if she gets too frustrated. Her hands are no longer primitively flexed but always open, and she can close them over larger toys, squeezing them awkwardly into one of her palms because her thumbs are not yet mature enough to help her grasp. Her release is also immature, so dropping things is still inadvertent.

Anything within arms' reach is a sure target. Avidly she samples color, texture, taste, and sound as she constantly practices reaching and grasping. By putting toys and objects in her pathway, you will add to her interest and delight. Discard anything flimsy, however; it will only end up in pieces, probably in her mouth.

Toys can also aid mobility, but although it is tempting to buy some of the impressive "educational" varieties, household objects are often more stimulating and a lot cheaper. Measuring spoons, sponges, brushes, kitchen pots and pans, and mobiles constructed from ribbons, will all teach your child basic concepts such as "full," "empty," "above," and "below," as well as helping her learn to move and to increase her dexterity with objects of different shapes (see page 161).

THE SEVENTH THROUGH NINTH MONTHS

Wobbly but resolute, your child leans forward and sits with arms placed between spread legs. At first, she can sit for only a few seconds before toppling sideways. Her stomach muscles were being strengthened in preparation for this posture when, lying on her back, she would lift her legs straight up and grab her feet. Now, as her muscles grow stronger, she sits straighter and straighter for longer and longer periods, gradually relinquishing the support of her arms. With both hands free she can now bring toys to her mouth. Her balance, however, may still be precarious, and she may fall quite heavily as she reaches sideways, so pad the area around her with rugs or cushions.

Gradually, your child prepares for creeping and crawling. On her stomach, she pushes herself up on extended arms and looks around. She may even push herself backwards as she lifts, pushes inch by inch, and to her surprise and annoyance finds herself retreating from, instead of advancing toward, her toys. She can reach out for a toy, balancing on one extended arm. She can even turn her body and reach out to the side or behind her for a toy, while maintaining control. She may dig her toes into the floor and push up on straight arms and legs, with bottom in the air–her own version of push-ups. From here, she may bend her knees and go into a hands-and-knees position. Other children push up onto hands and knees from a lying-on-stomach posture. Regardless of the method used, her hands and knees are set wide apart for stability and her stomach hangs low; then she tests her balance by rocking back and forth. The engine is running, but the brakes are still on.

Some children at nine months pivot on their stomachs, propelling themselves in circles. Others may pull themselves by the arms across the floor, keeping their stomachs on the floor (a method known as creeping).

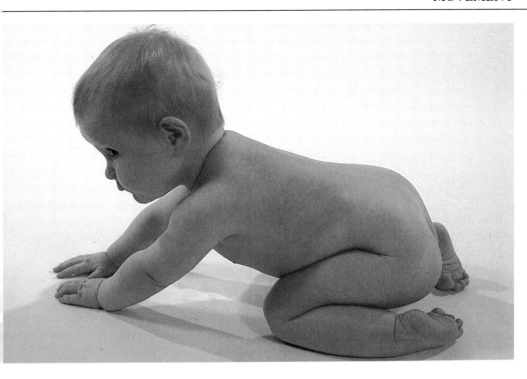

One of the early stages of crawling: She pushes herself up on extended arms.

Toes may be dug into the floor to help, but the arms do most of the work. Later, creeping babies learn to push more with their legs. Other babies prefer to scoot around on their bottoms or proceed directly to crawling. Whatever the method chosen, your baby is on the move. She can sit with a straight back for long periods, turning and leaning forward with wonderful agility. Her agility now extends to standing as well. One day, you will go into her room and find her standing casually in her crib, holding onto the rail. But do not expect her to know how to get down again; until she learns, pitching backwards and falling is likely to be the technique she uses. Now is the time for the home to change. Take away crib mobiles that could twist around her neck as she stands; pad sharp corners of pieces of furniture that cannot be moved to safe places. Coffee tables can be lethal. They have sharp corners, are the right height to grab hold of, and may well tip over if your child hangs onto one end. It is safest to remove coffee tables from any room she is in. She will probably have favorite standing spots, too, and furniture there may have to be padded. Be especially cautious around doors. She will get behind them just as you open them, or she will close them and–realizing that she has shut herself in and you out–will yell in distress. In this connection, self-locking doors that cannot be opened from both sides are to be avoided. Fingers can be caught in the hinge edges of a door, which narrow as the door closes. Your child can reach higher than you think, so remove breakables and watch out for table-cloths, curtains, and electrical cords within her grasp (see pages 34-35).

The growing dexterity of her hands allows her to move a toy from one hand to the other, but since she cannot yet release her first grip, she must press the toy firmly into her other hand so that it can pluck the toy away. Hands

She supports herself on the furniture and pulls herself up to a standing position – often in a favorite spot.

137

open wide with excitement as you offer her an interesting object, and she will smoothly reach for it with a single hand. She still shows some overreaching and circling, but these will improve at about eight months. With increasing coordination, she uses her thumb, opposing her fingers, to close over a toy–though at first only if it is large or medium-sized. Tiny objects are only raked at with the fingers and pressed clumsily into the palm. By eight or nine months of age she pinches her thumb against her index finger in a scissorlike grip that allows her to pick up small pieces of food. The "pincer" grip–thumb pinching together with the index and middle fingers–is used to pick up medium-sized objects. She does not yet have sufficient control of the pincer grip to pick up tiny objects as delicately as an adult does, pinching thumb to index finger.

Cause and effect become a new interest of your child. She shakes different rattles and listens to their different sounds; she "talks" into a cup to hear the hollow echo; she bangs objects together to feel the impact. Providing opportunities for these explorations also aids in the development of her movement.

THE TENTH THROUGH TWELFTH MONTHS

Sitting, she seems to think, was yesterday's achievement; now, creeping, crawling, and standing offer greater delights. So, as she sits, she turns her body sideways and swings her arms down; leaning forward, she rests her weight on her arms and rolls over onto her hands and knees. Soon she learns to reverse this trick. She may prefer to continue creeping or scooting around on her bottom, but most children have been rocking backwards and forwards on their hands and knees in preparation for crawling. Some children skip crawling and proceed directly to standing–learning to crawl later or dispensing with that phase entirely. When the right moment comes, she puts one knee forward; then, cautiously testing her balance, she advances the other. Practice makes perfect, and by eleven months–with hands and arms close together–she is crawling easily and speedily, ceaselessly on the prowl for unguarded stairs, open cupboard doors, and any tight corner she can get into. She often crawls with a toy clutched in one hand, but make sure it is neither sharp nor potentially dangerous in some other way; her arm could still collapse or slip, jabbing the toy upward into her face. A cupboard full of safe utensils –plastic bowls, strainers, and so on–offers her endless delight as she disappears into the depths and riotously explores its contents.

Some children crawl on the foot of one leg and the knee of the other, but this is soon replaced by walking. Standing now comes more easily, and your child can hold a toy in one hand and pull herself up with her other hand in order to stand.

Next, she begins to move while standing, still cautiously holding onto furniture while she rocks forward on one foot and back on the other. Then one day she shifts her weight onto one leg, picks up the other leg, and steps sideways. The great migration is about to begin (and so, too, is the migration of objects in your home up the walls, as her mobility and reach increase).

Her control and speed in transferring weight from one leg to the other increase daily as she practices turning from standing at the couch to standing at the chair beside it. She holds on with one hand, while twisting her body around and reaching with the other. Soon she is walking around the furniture with ease. One day, she stands alone, wavering precariously and then grabbing for support. But her balance rapidly improves until she can stand without wobbling. Some days later, you hear an almighty din and find one of your chairs moving steadily across the room, with the little one pushing it from behind. Occasionally, she leans so far forward that her feet cannot keep up, and for one wavering moment she becomes the bridge between feet and chair. Tumbles are frequent, but her courage is amazing as she tries and tries again. With legs wide apart and arms high in the air for added stability, she tries walking, unaided; after staggering a few steps, her legs cannot keep up and she falls forward. If she has a walker, this may be the time to put it away. Be sure stairways are securely closed off at all times.

By ten months, her hands' release ability has improved considerably. She cannot accurately drop tiny objects, like raisins, into a small bottle until about eighteen months, but she starts practicing now, and food and toys begin flying through the air. Annoying though this may be, it is for her a remarkable accomplishment. Not only is she coordinating release, she is also watching the effects of gravity and the properties of objects: One thing rolls, another clunks, and so on. To save yourself the irritation of constantly picking up toys for her, you may decide to tie them to her highchair–but watch constantly that the string does not wind around her neck or hands.

The ability to pick up small objects with index finger and thumb fascinates her. She examines her finds with enormous interest. By the end of her first year, her pincer grip has so matured that she uses only the tips of her index finger and thumb; like a hawk she can swoop down on whatever takes her ancy. She also points, using her index finger, and pokes into holes, nooks, and crannies you did not even know existed. (All electrical sockets should be covered.)

THE THIRTEENTH THROUGH EIGHTEENTH MONTHS

Your child's world has reached dizzying heights. She now strolls the length of the room, still with an occasional wobble and with arms held up and legs spread for balance. Falls are frequent, but slowly they become less so. If she needs speed, she may still drop to her knees and crawl, sometimes in an advanced crawl with hands and feet on the floor and bottom waving. Then she pushes off with her hands and rises carefully to stand.

Climbing seems to obsess her. Beware of silence. She could well be clambering up chairs, tables, or stairs—babies have even been known to scale bookshelves. Climbing is one thing; getting down is another. It is wise to leave safety gates in place until your child can descend stairs on her bottom or crawl down tail first. Supervised stair climbing is a good idea to help her master the skill.

Once climbing becomes a favorite activity, beware of silence. She is probably up to mischief.

Crawling is gradually replaced by steady walking. She now holds her arms lower or even down at her sides, and her legs closer together as her balance improves. She can adjust her balance to the weight of a toy she is carrying and is seldom seen without a toy in hand. By this time, she can also squat, wobbling down to pick up a toy and supporting herself with one hand to the floor. By eighteen months, she squats down smoothly to play, without hand supports. She walks sideways and backward, turns corners, and may attempt to kick a ball—usually by walking into or onto it. Crouching and jumping off the floor may be beyond her, but she may try to jump off a low stair—one foot first, and then the other.

The daily walk can last for hours as she explores every leaf, examines every crack in the pavement, and stares at any animal she meets on the way. All the time, she is learning to balance on such varied surfaces as gravel, grass, and concrete. She loves playing ball, although her poorly timed release causes her to send it off in a variety of directions, including straight up in the air and dribbling at her feet. When reaching, her hand no longer fans out but adapts more and more to the contour and size of what she is reaching for. She loves putting small things into containers (cheese cubes and certain dry cereal shapes are safe even if they end up in her mouth) with her neat pincer grip. Because her release is much improved, she can put one block on top of another without knocking the first down with a clumsy release. Manipulating a crayon is more difficult. At first she holds it squeezed tightly in her fist, swinging it awkwardly with a whole-arm movement, but by eighteen months she has enough control to scribble light wavy lines. With experience, these become firmer. She will love to watch you draw and to join in—but do not leave crayons within unsupervised reach: Walls and library books are tempting canvases for your budding artist.

Her world is full of gadgets to explore: locks, wheels, light switches, and more. She tinkers endlessly, opens and closes drawers, and piles things up. Nothing she can reach is safe from her, and the aim from now on is to give her freedom to explore while keeping her out of trouble.

THE NINETEENTH THROUGH TWENTY-FOURTH MONTHS

She runs everywhere; you wonder if she will ever walk again. She can speed up, slow down, and take wide corners with ease. Sudden, sharp corners, however, are still difficult for her to negotiate. She rearranges furniture and pushes everything around;

The daily walk may take hours, as he studies every inch of the route.

and, like a kangaroo, will soon jump several times in a row.

Her walking steps are longer and her gait smoother (although these will not be totally fluid and adultlike until she is four). Her running is graceful and powerful. With nimble feet, she turns sharp corners and maneuvers to avoid obstacles. She can walk fairly well along a straight line and can balance on one foot for several seconds. She clatters upstairs on alternating feet, but she still might use two feet on each step to come down safely. While pedaling her tricycle, she can turn and twist it with amazing agility as she patrols the driveway. With arms extended stiffly in front of her, she can clutch a thrown ball to her chest if it falls directly into her arms. Timing and coordination are still maturing, so she may not yet be able to throw the ball back directly to you, but she can throw it farther and farther.

Because her ability to release her grip has matured, she can construct a ten-block tower and with nimble fingers can dress and undress herself without much help (small buttons and zippers may still defeat her). You may have to set her clothes out in proper order, however, or she may put them on back to front or with inner garments over outer ones.

Controlling her crayon in the curl of her fingers with opposing thumb, instead of in her fist, she can make smaller and more precise marks. Not until four to six years will she grasp it as an adult does, with crayon held between index finger and thumb and resting on a curled middle finger. Her present finger grip allows her to make smoother and firmer marks, circles, and horizontal and vertical lines. These skills help develop the basic control needed later in life for writing.

The three-year-old child's movements are fluid, graceful, and mature. Her natural zest and curiosity have helped propel her through her first three years of accelerated motor development and have equipped her with efficient skills of mobility and manipulation. She is free to reach out, touch, and make her place in the world.

later she learns to pull too. (Watch out for chairs pushed or pulled over to windows and install window guards to prevent a potentially tragic fall.)

Outdoors, she climbs on park benches, on tree stumps, and on any low wall. She may step-jump off a low height, but she cannot yet consistently lift both feet off the ground as she jumps. (Occasionally her feet just clear the floor.) She can kick a large ball, and she loves to play catch. Her throwing skill is still relatively crude; nevertheless, her accuracy is improving all the time as she adjusts the turn of her body to the timing of her release.

She begins switching on lights, unscrewing bottle tops, and turning doorknobs. Be prepared. She also loves undressing. A prolonged hush now may mean that she soon will appear, prancing around without clothes on. (Clothes that fasten at the back may be the solution here.) Drawing skill is improving significantly; by two years, her scribbling has progressed to wavy lines and wobbly ovals. She can draw horizontal or vertical lines and may attempt to copy circles that you draw for her.

THE THIRD YEAR

Confident and daring, your child is romping with abandon and independence. A thirty-month-old can jump in the air but still lands roughly on stiffened legs. Later, she will learn to bend her knees to absorb the impact

SHOES AND SOCKS

Do not start worrying about shoes until your baby begins to walk. Until then tights, stretch suits, socks, booties, or sleeping bags will keep her feet warm. (If you use a walker, though, your child will need some sort of foot covering when you take her outdoors.)

Let her go barefoot as much as possible. When she begins to walk, her grip on the ground will enable her to balance more easily and will also help develop her foot muscles. Carpeting provides a safe surface, but beware of throw rugs, which might move out from under her. Do not let her wear only plain socks or tights, which might be slippery; some socks and tights on the market come equipped with rubber soles to aid her grip.

When she needs shoes for warmth and protection, have them fitted properly. Make sure she stands down when trying on a shoe, since her weight makes her foot spread a little. A thumb-width space should exist between her big toe and the tips of the shoe. Do not pass on shoes from one child to another because these will have molded to the first wearer's feet. Shoes may need to be replaced as often as every eight weeks, so there is no point in keeping one pair aside for special occasions. Check frequently to see

that your child's shoes are not too narrow and that there is plenty of toe room.

Leather shoes were once considered essential to support growing feet. Many health care providers now think sneakers and soft cloth shoes are better because they do not compress the feet. They are certainly cheaper so the temptation to use them too long is minimal.

Stretch suits and socks can also be outgrown and can cause your child's feet to become curled up inside. If this happens, cut the feet off the too-small suits and add proper-size socks separately to keep her feet warm. Make sure that socks are sufficiently stretchy, that they have not shrunk, and that they do not impede circulation at the tops.

STAGES IN THE DEVELOPMENT OF MOVEMENT

About Six Months
She holds her arms up to be lifted. She can turn, twist, kick strongly, and bounce up and down with alternating legs. If supported, she can stand; lying down, she can turn over.

About One Month
She holds her head up for a few seconds. She turns her head and eyes toward light or a familiar voice. Her eye-to-eye contact begins to strengthen.

About Three Months
She holds her head up from her stomach and supports weight on her arms. She watches people and her own hands. She swipes at objects.

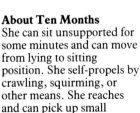

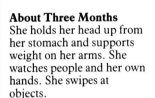

About Ten Months
She can sit unsupported for some minutes and can move from lying to sitting position. She self-propels by crawling, squirming, or other means. She reaches and can pick up small objects.

One Year to Fifteen Months
She sits, crawls, and stands. She may walk unaided or by pushing something along to aid balance. She climbs stairs. She can reach out for a toy while holding another in her other hand.

From Fifteen Months On
She walks and feeds herself. She climbs obsessively and seems to get into everything. She becomes adept at playing ball and begins to scribble and draw.

Note: All of the stages outlined here are generalized guidelines only. Your baby may reach some earlier and some later than this chart shows. Girls often reach various milestones before boys. Do not worry if your child does not match the blueprint exactly, and above all do not try to force her to progress.

COMMUNICATION

"I'm here! I've arrived! But I'm not sure I like it."

A baby pushes head first into a world of light, noise, chill, and change, signaling his arrival with a cry. With the umbilical cord still pulsating, he is lifted and given to his mother, to be greeted with embraces and sounds, if not words, of comfort and welcome. The baby stops crying. Vocal communicating has begun.

But of course communication begins long before the moment when the father, the mother, and the child first meet face to face. It has grown steadily with the sentience of the child in the womb—in his increasing awareness of the warm, comfortable liquid that surrounds him, of the rhythm of his mother's life, of her muffled heartbeat, and of the distant sound of her voice. Human beings communicate through all five senses, and babies do so more than most.

So communication to a baby is touch (soft bedding, the security of familiar arms), taste (the warm, life-giving milk), smell (the scents of the mother, the father, milk, and home), sight (the pleasing features of a familiar face), and especially sound. Within a very few weeks, the sounds of home become increasingly meaningful to your baby—the bark of a dog, the whirring of a washing machine, the lullaby of a lawn mower heard on a sleepy summer evening. But for now, the sound that the new baby associates with comfort is the voice—until later, when "sound" turns into "speech" and takes precedence over those earlier and more primitive means of contact.

Learning to speak is the everyday miracle. In the first few years of life, the small child masters a subject whose like in complexity and subtlety he will probably never be required to master in the rest of his life. It is the skill that separates human beings from animals, and it is at once the most commonplace and the most mysterious of achievements.

Let us look at how "voice-sound" turns into speech and what happens in the course of the rainbow of achievement that spans from the baby's first cry to the time when he has exploded into the flow of talk, chatter, monologue, commentary, and questions with which the typical three-year-old greets each day—and an occasional night as well.

We will also examine how you can help guide your living bundle of energy toward the best speech possible, some of the common problems that may develop, and what to do if they should.

Communication is a two-way business, but it does not always need words. We convey messages with expressions, gestures, eye contact, touch—and even by just being within sight of others.

Communication begins in the womb – the warm comfort of the liquid that surrounds the fetus and the sound of the mother's heartbeat.

THE NATURE OF COMMUNICATION
The basic tools necessary for the miracle called communication to occur are language and speech. Language is what the baby thinks ("I want some more milk!"), and speech is how he verbally lets you know his thought. Of course this communication of a thought may and usually does involve more than "speech"; your baby will wiggle, point, and cry to help you understand his thoughts. In any case, language must come before speech, since your baby must think of what to say before he says it.

Although no one knows exactly how this communication develops, it is certain that you as parents are the most important ingredient. A baby surrounded by speech will pick up for himself the skills of speech, but he will learn those skills much more easily, quickly, and fluently if he is encouraged and helped by those who care for him. Most of the time, that means parents.

No one can overestimate the part that parents – or whoever provides full-time care – play in helping a child into speech. Children who are deprived of this early loving stage of learning (preverbal communication is its formal name) may never catch up on verbal skills in later life. Of course, they will learn to speak and to express themselves, but they seldom achieve the fluency of those who, from birth, have been surrounded by the to and fro of loving dialogue. Ideally, the baby learns the mystery of speech in the merry-go-round of home and family, long before he is exposed to the more formal teaching of school.

The process of teaching seems to begin with the baby's first cry. At that moment, the baby is using one of the few tools he possesses: his voice. Is it an utterance of distress or greeting? A cry for help or a vocal visiting card proffered to the world? The child developing in the womb does not live in silence. He hears his mother's heartbeat and the noises of her digestion. He will start at a sudden loud noise and may seem to grow peaceful if the mother sings a lullaby. At birth, therefore, sound is not a new experience for the baby. And because (as far as we know) it has already been associated with comfort and security, sound is not a new means of communication, either.

Communication is a two-way business, requiring both a speaker and a listener. At first it is the parent who listens and learns to interpret the meaning of the baby's cry. The development of the dialogue that eventually takes place between the baby and his parents progresses in a series of steps, each of which has to be successfully negotiated before the next can be tackled. It is similar to climbing a ladder – and just as one child may take longer to climb than another, so each child's development proceeds at its own individual speed and should not be forced into an unnatural pace. Half the art of parenting is knowing when to follow and when to lead a child.

A single child frequently progresses at different paces in different activities within each stage of development. The child who speaks early may be slower in walking. While you have a crawling little chatterbox on your hands, a walking – but not talking – tornado of energy may live next door. It is as though nature sometimes chooses to direct energy into one channel at a time. Other children tramp steadily onward, each skill keeping pace with the others. Comparing children's achievements – which sometimes seems to be a parental obsession – is quite useless and could cause both you and your child a lot of distress.

THE LADDER OF LANGUAGE
To a stranger, all babies' cries may sound the same, but not so to the parents or primary caregivers who spend a lot of time with the baby. You rapidly learn to distinguish among the different kinds of cry – pain, hunger, fear, boredom – and you react instinctively to each. You speak to the baby, and your tone varies according to the signal that prompted your response. If it is a whining, grumbling, getting-off-to-sleep sort of noise, you will probably be somewhat matter-of-fact; a cry of pain or real distress, however, will be met with a softened and much more sympathetic tone. The remarkable duet between caregiver and child has begun: the baby cries; someone responds; the crying stops. The crying has achieved its object of bringing action.

Within a very few weeks of birth comes the baby's first voluntary communicative act: reaction to a familiar voice. He is perhaps whimpering a little in his crib, when the telephone rings. He may stop for a moment or two, but then he begins again. As you go

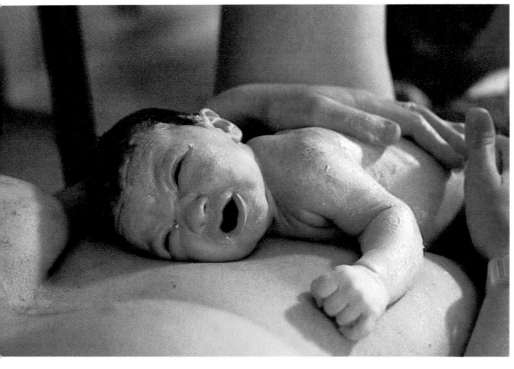

A baby's first cry signals his arrival in the world.

past him to answer the phone, you may try assuring him: "All right, I'm coming. I won't be long."

He stops crying. The baby is listening. He recognizes your voice, and more significantly he has learned that your voice means attention is coming. He would not be so soothed if, for example, you turned on the television or the vacuum cleaner or if the dog barked. It is your voice (and not anyone else's) that does the trick.

The tone of voice is what matters at this point. If you react in pain or anger to a sudden occurrence–crying out after sticking your finger with a pin, or shouting at the cat for climbing on the table–the baby almost certainly will begin to cry. But if your voice "smiles" with the warm gentleness of love and contentment, pleasurable sounds will greet you.

Before very long, you will find that if the baby is lying in his bed and you go near and talk to him he will begin to wriggle and wave his arms in excitement at the sound of your voice. If he already happens to be wriggling, he will stop; either way, he is responding to your voice.

So the baby has already taken several steps up the ladder of language development. He is listening and learning. He has sorted through his noisy world to discover that voices and sounds have meaning. The next important step is when looking and listening are coordinated. Previously he may have reacted to your voice without turning toward you, but now comes the ability to match sight (an object) to particular sounds. This moment has arrived when, having carefully scanned his world after you say something to him, he looks you in the eyes and presents you with his first smile.

How many steps up the communication ladder is the baby now?
1. Sound has meaning.
2. Voices have meaning.
3. One voice has more meaning than the others.
4. That voice belongs to one face only.
5. That face and that voice make things happen.
6. This is the combination of voice and face–so when it appears, I will acknowledge it.

And he is still under six months old.

SMILES AND SOUNDS

Now smiling comes easily. You smile; he smiles back. He smiles first, and you reward him by smiling, picking him up, cuddling him, telling him how sweet he is, talking to him.

A week or two later he "talks" back. Small experimental sounds come from him–not those early reflex sounds of hunger, pain, or boredom, but small overtures of sound. Much as an orchestra tunes up, your baby begins playing with his voice, getting the right notes, trying out new sounds. He will practice on his own, and he will practice with you–solos and duets.

On his own, the baby "talks" to himself a great deal. You will hear him repeating the

A baby learns speech at home, long before he is exposed to formal teaching.

Sounds come before words. To a baby, the sounds of home and his parents' voices give comfort and security and encourage him to join in.

same sounds over and over; listening to him, you will notice that he makes a sound, pauses as though he is thinking about it, and then makes the same sound again. If you join in, he will stop as though a little surprised at being overheard and interrupted. But after a moment, he may join in with you quite amicably.

The baby uses these sounds first for his own amusement and then as a two-way sharing of pleasure and content with you. Rather than trying to *tell* you anything specific, he is just interacting and being friendly. He also practices a conversational politeness you may miss in certain later years. He makes a few remarks, and then you join in. When you have finished, he will start again. He knows all about the to and fro of conversation already.

These first sounds, which begin at about three and a half to six months, are among the most delightful and endearing of experiences for the new parents. The baby invariably begins to make the vowel sounds first—aah, eee, ooh, especially—and he sounds just like a small dove, cooing with contentment. Soon he vowels will be joined by the consonants; but for the brief time when only the vowels are being vocalized, all of the sounds he makes are pure joy.

The next rung of the ladder is the consonants, or at least the ones that are easily produced at the front of the mouth–*p*, *b*, *t*, and *d*–to be followed swiftly by the nasal sounds of *m* and *n*. At this stage, quite accidentally, the baby may produce sounds such as "mama" or "dada." No doubt you will pick him up joyfully, tell him how clever he is, and repeat "Mama, Dada" to him several times, hoping he will say it again. The chances are he will regard you with a confused stare and eventually will smile at you, since by now he knows that smiling is always met with approval. You may now rush to your spouse and announce that you have a genius on your hands.

Do not be misled. The sound was accidental; he was not "naming" you. Even as your baby was bringing joy to your heart by that accidental combination of sounds, little Russian babies in painted wooden cribs and little Eskimo babies slung on their mothers' backs were probably producing the same sound. All over the world, babies begin by making the same sounds, only later discarding the ones that they do not hear around them all day and retaining the ones they do. That is the way your baby first begins to speak English, and Russian babies Russian. That is also the way regional accents are passed on and kept alive.

TALKATIVE PARENTS/TALKATIVE BABIES

Talkativeness begets talkativeness, but not if the talking goes on above your baby's head—if the conversation is too quick and too adult—and certainly not if you never give your baby a chance to join in. Patience and praise are what encourage your baby to try out his voice still more. It is an old psychological trick: Reinforce the behavior you want repeated. And partly because the baby values your approval and partly because it is in his nature to experiment with his voice, he will go on progressing.

Although a baby who is talked to and encouraged to join in will probably babble more fluently and in later life will be more easily articulate, a neglected baby will (to a lesser extent) babble, too. So will a deaf baby — babbling is built into his system. Only later, when he cannot reinforce his babbling with the sound of other voices, will the deaf baby fall silent. Therefore, while he is still under six months old, you cannot accurately conclude that a baby's hearing is normal simply because he is making the usual baby sounds. It is only in the second half of his first year that a baby's "speaking" behavior may provide evidence of a hearing difficulty. But of course caring and informed parents will by then have noticed if the baby's reactions to phones ringing, dogs barking, and other everyday noises are not normal (see page 150).

But now the noises coming from the carriage, the infant seat, the playpen, or the crib begin to take on a different quality. Inflections and tones are creeping in. Before, the baby seemed to be practicing a five-finger exercise; now, he is doing scales. His voice will question, harangue, express disgust, cajole, sympathize, and scold—and all without a single word. He will understand the variations in your tonal quality, too. Ask a baby a question and he will begin to look surprised. "Where's the dog?" "What did I do with my shoes?" Of course, he does not know what you are talking about, but the tone is asking a question. Gradually, by the association of sounds and objects, he will come to understand that sounds have particular meanings. Sounds put together, in fact, are words.

Just as your baby knows that his voice can control you, you will find that your voice can control him. "Oh, look what you've done!" you exclaim as a bowl of sticky cereal trickles steadily onto the carpet. His face crumples and his eyes fill with tears. Clearly he has done something wrong. But then–"It's all right, you couldn't help it. There, see? It's easy to clean up." Miraculously the face straightens; the eyes beam. All, it seems, is well. The concerto of noise, action, and interaction continues.

Admittedly, babies are not always the most stimulating of companions, particularly if you do not have much adult company either. Sometimes the prospect of weeks of prattle can seem very bleak indeed. But the amount of stimulation your baby is given now is vital, and it will have a profound effect on his later ability to communicate and to make relationships. Up to the age of two, the foundations of his future intellectual development are being laid.

Live language directed to the child is the most consistently favorable kind of educational experience an infant can have during the eleven to sixteen month period. Neither language from a television set nor language engaged in by nearby people and overheard by an infant seem to play a substantial role in the process of acquisition of intellectual or linguistic skill.

This quote is from *Origins of Human Competence: The Final Report of the Harvard Preschool Project* (Burton L. White et al., Lexington Press, 1979) – a thirteen-year study of the development of the child in his

Talk to, not *at*, your child. Overheard conversation is not as helpful to a child who is learning language as direct involvement with a caring adult.

own home during the first years of life. The Harvard Preschool Project constitutes one of the most intensive examinations of child development yet undertaken.

A noisy, communicative baby is a contented baby. Unhappy babies often do not "talk." You may be able to cajole your baby out of an unhappy mood by your voice or your antics, eliciting his babbling sounds again, but the rule is: While he is chatting, he is happy.

Words have meaning, but sounds will have meaning before words do. The months of babbling and chatter have taught the baby (or rather allowed him to find out) that sounds have meaning – "grr . . . yum yum . . . yuk . . . ." They are not words in the adult sense, but each has a very definite meaning.

Many parents worry because their baby is not saying recognizable words. "He's nearly one and hasn't said anything yet. The baby next door is only ten months old, and she says lots of words." This does not matter at all if the baby proves he understands words, if he reacts to simple commands: "Play peek-a-boo. Wave bye-bye." Can he imitate some of your sounds? Can he meow with the cat or bark with the dog? If so, the prerequisites for speech are all there, ready to burst the banks – and when that happens, the flood follows quickly.

The first word may come at about one year or so, sometimes even earlier, and it is usually rapidly followed by others. By his first birthday, a baby may know from one to ten words; the brightest children are not always in the forefront of the early-to-speak.

As your baby turns into a toddler, his

world expands. He understands more as he needs more, and quite naturally he is propelled into learning more words to communicate his growing concerns and experiences. He explores the house–looking, touching, pulling, and pushing–and the adult with him will naturally begin naming the objects the baby is touching. "Chair. Stool. Ball. Car."

If you listen to yourself speaking to a baby or young child, you will hear yourself speaking slowly, distinctly, and with pauses between the words. You may also repeat words several times. "Car, car, car." You are likely to extend and elaborate on the words the baby uses. "Car," he will say, and after he vocalizes or otherwise acknowledges he has seen a car, you will reply, "It's a nice car, isn't it? A pretty red car."

You will also put his thoughts into words. A dog barks. "Listen. Spot is hungry," you say. You give the dog food. "Now he's happy," you say. "Pat Spot." The back door slams. "There's Daddy," you say. The day will come, of course, when you will have to be careful. An acquaintance blessed with the ability to create furniture accidently strikes her finger with a hammer: "Ow! Damn!" – a phrase joyfully repeated by the two-year-old to his astonished grandparents at their next visit.

The chances are that you also serve as interpreter-in-chief; that first word, so lovingly welcomed and heralded by you, very likely could not be understood by anyone else. "What's he saying?" friends ask, and you spring into translation. No wonder the baby is so bonded with the adults who look after him most.

BABY TALK
Baby talk can be very endearing – when the baby is doing the talking. It is not altogether so charming when a grownup erupts into a stream of gibberish among which only the terms "blanky" and "nicey picey" may be understandable.

Parents may be tempted to prolong baby talk by encouraging and imitating it. But this is not very wise because sooner or later your baby will need to use the right words – words that people besides you can understand. The best solution is to use the right words yourself while letting your baby know that you understand what he means by his version of the word. In the beginning, you will have to settle for his simpler version and mark time until he is able to cope with the adult pronunciation. Words do not come fully formed, and baby talk may be the order of things for many months.

Pronunciation is a very complex skill. It depends on a combination of hearing, intellectual and emotional development, and the

148

ability to use tongue, lips, teeth, and jaw with correct coordination. This is a tall order for a rising two-year-old.

Here is an example to explain the processes. Slowly make the sound "bay" as it is pronounced in "baby." Now consider what happened as you made that sound. First, your vocal mechanism had to be alerted to produce a sound. Second, your lips had to come together to form a seal. Third, your tongue had to rest on the floor of your mouth. Fourth, air pressure had to be built up behind your closed lips. Fifth, at the right moment, your lips had to open for the small explosion to come through (which produced the "bay" sound). To corroborate this, put your hand in front of your mouth as you say the word, and you will feel what is happening.

Try some other sounds – the "ca" in "cat," the "da" in "dad," the "mmm" sound in "mom." Many of these sounds require vast and complicated movements of tongue, lips, teeth, jaw, and voice. To make each sound separately is difficult enough; to put them all together in the right order for a word is at first impossible for a child.

Fortunately, a lot of these sounds can also be seen. In addition to hearing what you say, your baby can watch you saying it. This is why he will be most successful in pronouncing correctly the words he can most easily see – "bay" in "baby" and "mmm" in "mom" are among them.

Some sounds are very difficult to see pronounced: the "s" in "soup," for instance, and the "z" in "zebra." Although pronunciation will gradually improve, some of the more difficult sounds may not be mastered until about age five.

What is certain is that, if you try to extract correct pronunciation from a baby by holding out a cookie but not giving it to him until he says "cookie" and not "coo-coo," you will end up with tears of frustration. Early on correct pronunciation does not matter; it will usually come naturally if you do not actively deter it (by adopting the child's incorrect pronunciation or by making a child who is not yet capable of saying the word properly try to correct himself). He is *trying* to sound like you, and what matters now is that you should understand each other. Accept and reward his effort because the purpose of communication is to serve understanding.

Your child knows a great many words before he says them. Suppose you have a cat named Ralph. All day long, your child probably hears the word "Ralph." "Where's Ralph?" "Ralph, come and eat your dinner." "Good kitty, Ralph." So the sound "Ralph" goes into his computer without your realizing it. Suddenly something happens to press the "print-out" button, and presto, the child throws his arms around the cat's neck and says, "Ralph."

He might, however, call the cat "bed" if that is a word he has often heard. It really does not matter at this point. He is not slow or stupid, and he will get it all comfortably sorted out in time if you do not start fussing and overcorrecting him.

The months between the first and second birthdays are composed of days of wonder. Your baby is an explorer, and the whole world is a marvel. Under the bed, behind the furniture, inside kitchen cupboards – the days are not long enough to satisfy his urge to discover. Shopping, housework, gardening, and driving are all new and stupendously exciting. With the security of his parents as a base, he can make little forays into the unknown. And each new discovery provides the chance to learn new words. Finger games, rhyming games, singing, talking, looking at books, and naming things he touches enable him to expand his vocabulary by leaps and bounds. "Ba" somehow ensures that a ball is given to him; "din" produces food; "dink" produces drink. Words are useful and wonderful things, he recognizes. They make things happen. He is now more than halfway up the ladder toward acceptable communication.

Between the ages of two and three, single words are turned into doubles: "Mommy go," "More milk." The effect is as though the child is sending telegrams in which every word has to be paid for. But soon he is past this stage, and more complicated concepts are beginning to be learned. "On the table" means something, as do "in the cupboard" and "outside the door." Small joining words such as "and" and "but" are developed, and the possessive assumes enormous importance: "Mommy's hat. Daddy's shoes." The verb ending "-ing" is sprinkled among the phrases now – "Mommy singing," "Daddy working," "Daddy sleeping," "Mommy laughing."

Pictures in books are correctly named. Your child realizes that not every animal with four legs is a dog.

From now on, the steps up the ladder of communication are sure and swift. Tricky moments still lie ahead, but the rise is rapid. The ultimate triumph comes when the child is able to express his needs, wants, and feelings in words that are totally understandable to those around him.

DELAYED SPEECH DEVELOPMENT

Every child grows up in different circumstances. Position in the family, parents' disposition, and heredity all affect his development. The youngest child in a family is

Do not worry if your child's early words are not fully formed. Pronunciation is a complex skill to acquire. It is important for your child to watch your lips speaking a word correctly. Here is a baby's-eye view of his mother saying *baby*. The text explains the coordinated movements of jaw, lips, and tongue required to produce just the first syllable.

FIND YOUR CHILD'S SPEECH AND HEARING AGE

AGE	HEARING AND UNDERSTANDING	YES	NO	TALKING	YES	NO
Birth	Does your child listen to speech?	☐	☐	Does your child coo or gurgle?	☐	☐
	Does your child startle or cry at noise?	☐	☐			
	Does your child awaken at loud sounds?	☐	☐			
3 Months	Does your child try to turn toward the speaker?	☐	☐	Does your child babble?	☐	☐
	Does your child smile when spoken to?	☐	☐	Does your child cry differently for different needs?	☐	☐
	Does your child stop playing and appear to listen to sounds or speech?	☐	☐	Does your child repeat the same sounds a lot?	☐	☐
	Does your child seem to recognize mother's voice?	☐	☐			
6 Months	Does your child respond to "no" and her/his name?	☐	☐	Does your child's babbling sound like the parent's speech, only not clear?	☐	☐
	Does your child notice and look around for the source of new sounds?	☐	☐	Does your child make lots of different sounds?	☐	☐
	Does your child turn her/his head toward the side where the sound is coming from?	☐	☐			
9 Months–1 Year	Has your child begun to respond to requests ("come here," "do you want more")?	☐	☐	Does your child say words (8–10 words at age 1½; 2–3 words at age 1)? (Words may not be clear.)	☐	☐
	Does your child turn or look up when you call?	☐	☐	Does your child enjoy imitating sounds?	☐	☐
	Does your child search or look around when hearing new sounds?	☐	☐	Does your child use jargon (babbling that sounds like real speech)?	☐	☐
	Does your child listen to people talking?	☐	☐	Does your child use voice to get attention?	☐	☐
1½–2 Years	Can your child follow two requests ("get the ball and put it on the table")?	☐	☐	Does your child have 10–15 words (by age 2)?	☐	☐
				Does your child sometimes repeat requests?	☐	☐
				Does your child ask 1–2 word questions? ("where kitty?" "go bye-bye?" "more?")	☐	☐
				Does your child put 2 words together ("more cookie")?	☐	☐
2½–4 Years	Does your child understand differences in meaning ("go/stop;" "the car pushed the truck/the truck pushed the car")?	☐	☐	Does your child say most sounds, except perhaps *r*, *s*, *th*, and *l*?	☐	☐
	Can you child point to pictures in a book upon hearing them named?	☐	☐	Does your child sometimes repeat words in a sentence?	☐	☐
	Does your child notice sounds (dog barking, telephone ringing, television sound, knocking at door, and so on)?	☐	☐	Does your child use 200–300 words?	☐	☐
				Does your child use 2- to 3-word sentences?	☐	☐
	Does your child understand conversation easily?	☐	☐	Does your child ask lots of why and what questions?	☐	☐
	Does your child hear you when you call from another room?	☐	☐	Has your child's jargon and repeating disappeared?	☐	☐
	Does your child hear television or radio at the same loudness level as other members of the family?	☐	☐	Does your child like to name things?	☐	☐

TOTAL ☐ ☐ TOTAL ☐ ☐

often a rapid learner, pulled on and encouraged by the increased attention and stimulation of there being other children around. This can also have the opposite effect. An older child can interpret so successfully for him that the younger one makes no effort at all to speak for himself. The caring parent will soon know if the speech is there and just lying dormant or whether some other cause may be responsible for the lack of speech.

The main point to remember is that if by age one your child does not understand you and if by eighteen months he is not speaking a few meaningful words so that you–or whoever is with him most–can understand them it would be wise to ask your health care provider's advice about obtaining a further evaluation. Today, sophisticated methods of testing are readily available that do not require the baby's cooperation.

One cause of a child's not speaking properly when he could reasonably be expected to is impaired hearing (see Deafness, page 213). Severe deafness is almost certain to be noticed very rapidly, but pinpointing a slight hearing impairment is more difficult. A child

Success comes when a child uses words to make friends and communicate needs and feelings to those around her.

Use this chart to follow the development of your child's speech and hearing ability. If at any age all your answers are *yes*, your child is developing hearing, speech, and language normally. If, however, you score between one and three in the *no* column, your child may be developing more slowly; and if you score more than three in the *no* column, it would be wise to seek professional advice.

might be thought stubborn or inattentive, when all the time the trouble is that he cannot hear properly.

If you think your child may have hearing problems, ask yourself: Does he not hear the sound of a knock on the door? Has he ever appeared startled by a loud sound? Does he regularly want the television turned up? Does he not hear you when you call him from a different room? These are elementary observations, but they may point to a possible difficulty.

A slight hearing loss can follow a cold or an ear infection, which is one reason why either ailment should always be taken seriously and a health care provider consulted. Such a loss is nearly always temporary, but children catch a great many of these infections in the early years, so parents should be especially watchful at this time.

If a hearing impairment is confirmed, a great deal can be done to help. Children with extreme problems of deafness can be helped toward acceptable and "normal" pronunciation. Parents of such children should associate themselves with a center that specializes in the treatment of hearing disorders. Hearing aids and therapy are available; they are essential if the child is to develop language and speech to his maximum potential.

STUTTERING

Many children in the process of learning to communicate hesitate, search for words, and go back and repeat phrases. This could be because the child is thinking out what he is trying to say or is being distracted by something else or is trying to formulate the right words. Boys seem to be more liable to stutter than girls. If a child is going to show

signs of stuttering, he will usually do so between the ages of two and five. It can take the form of sudden long silences in the middle of a conversation, of drawing out one of the sounds in a word, or of repeating sounds or phrases. It can come on very suddenly, and usually the child is not aware of what is happening.

So far, this is a normal stage of development; if properly handled, it will disappear as rapidly as it came. If you become anxious, try to correct the hesitations, draw attention to them, and generally set up tension during your child's efforts at communication, the problem could move on to a second and more serious stage at which correction is far more difficult, if not impossible. At this second stage, the child struggles to correct his speech. His face grimaces, he may squirm with distress—he has now become aware of the problem.

A child in the first stage of stuttering should not be made aware that he is doing anything unusual. Just ignore it. Reward his effort with warm attentiveness, and the symptoms should subside. If they do not, and if the child becomes upset over his speech, seek professional help.

EMOTIONAL ASPECTS OF SLOWNESS IN SPEAKING

Parents of the slow-to-speak child or the child with a speech disorder often worry that their child may suffer emotionally from the teasing of peers or from the impatience of other adults. Interestingly enough, children rarely notice or are critical of the speech efforts of themselves or others. As long as one child is able to understand another, they seem satisfied.

Visual aids now help a child who is hard of hearing to pronounce correctly. This computer translates sound into a trace on a screen. A correctly pronounced word is rendered on the screen, and then the child tries to match the pictured trace – by making matching sounds.

It is often the parents who are unable to accept less than perfect speech in their child. Try asking yourself some questions to see how you measure up in this respect. Are you embarrassed when your child speaks at home or in public? Do you correct him, or do you try to accept him as he is? Do you try to talk for him, to protect him from embarrassment (or perhaps to protect yourself from embarrassment)?

The way you react to your child's speech efforts significantly influences the way others react. Begin by looking at the disorder as a whole. If the problem is such that, after reading this, you think that your child will not outgrow it, you should seek help.

A speech therapist, however, can only do part of the job. She can point the way and show you how to help your child to better speech. (It will help you if you think of the problem as being temporary – one that will be improved through the combined efforts of your child, yourself, and the therapist. Given patience and time, most, if not all, communication problems can be lessened; the majority can be entirely cured.)

It is best to look forward to the result of the treatment rather than to question why this has happened to your child. You will find

that – because you stand midway between expert and layperson – family and friends will look to you for understanding of your child's problem. A positive approach will help you accept your child's disability, and this will supply the most necessary emotional foundation for the relationship between you and your child.

Always give your child *time* to speak. Do not appear unwilling to wait or impatient for him to complete his thought. Do not fill in the word or complete the thought for him – let him finish for himself. Look at your child while he is communicating. This may be difficult, especially if he is having a problem with stammering, but it is necessary. Relax while he is speaking, thereby showing him that he has time and so do you. And unless specifically requested to do so by the therapist, never correct his speech efforts or allow anyone else to do so.

Even if you think your child will outgrow his disorder without special help, following these rules will lessen the emotional tension you may feel.

A great many worries and fears are based on myth rather than fact, so take every opportunity to ask professionals about the particular type of problem your child has. Each problem has many different aspects. Your understanding of these will go a long way toward alleviating your worries and concerns about the problem and – most importantly – toward helping your child.

ONE LANGUAGE OR TWO?

Julio is nearly six months old. His mother and father are Hispanic. They live in the United States, and when they are at home Julio's parents speak to each other in a mixture of Spanish and English, often unaware of which language they are using. Should they teach Julio to speak Spanish or English or both languages simultaneously?

It is a difficult question. Some children manage to acquire two languages at once without much trouble; others find it difficult to learn two names for each object, and development is slowed as a result. Unfortunately, it is not possible, as yet, to find out in advance which type of child you have.

One way to avoid possible confusion is to teach the child one language only, and then to introduce the second when he is reasonably fluent. Parents who do this usually teach first the language of the country they are *not* living in – perhaps reasoning that when the child grows and mixes more he will have every opportunity of learning the language being spoken around him every day. So in this case, Julio would be taught to speak Spanish first and then English.

One possible hazard of this method is that

it may, in the early years, limit the child's ability to mix easily, since he would have to rely–in Julio's case – on being understood only by adults and other children who speak Spanish. He could easily become isolated, unable to visit the woman next door or to talk to the shopkeeper, a small child's invaluable first steps into a social world. You could of course figure that, until he is about two and a half, Julio would not be making many of his own contacts anyway–that in his social encounters he would always have an attendant adult, who presumably would act as both caretaker and interpreter.

As with most things having to do with children, the answer may well be to let the child set the pace. If he seems confused and not making headway in either language, it is time to think again. It is certainly much easier to become fluent in a second language if you learn it during childhood or adolescence rather than waiting until you are an adult; for this reason, it is unfortunate to waste the rich opportunity to make use of both languages spoken in one family.

SPEECH PRONUNCIATION DISORDERS

Parents frequently become concerned as their child begins to talk that his pronunciation is not "normal." Friends' and neighbors' children may be able to pronounce words better than your baby; and even though you have followed the advice given earlier in this chapter about not correcting, your baby may not be learning the exact pronunciation of words as rapidly as you think he should. Lisping and other common sound substitutions of one sound for another ("wabbit" for "rabbit," "thoop" for "soup") sometimes seem like they will never go away. Remember, though, that pronunciation is a very difficult task–as you doubtless noticed when you made and analyzed certain sounds described earlier–and that learning correct pronunciation is a real struggle for your child. The ability to pronounce sounds accurately depends upon having the lips, tongue, and teeth working together. As long as your child is able to suck, swallow, and chew effectively (which is the primary function of the muscles and mechanisms that are used in pronouncing words) and is able to understand you easily and follow directions without difficulty, be assured that appropriate pronunciation will probably develop. If, however, your child is not able to pronounce all sounds accurately by the time he is five years old, seek professional advice.

Cleft lip and cleft palate, two defects in the formation of the mouth present at birth, can interfere with proper pronunciation even after surgical repair of these conditions. For that reason, treatment customarily includes work with a speech therapist as well as surgical and dental specialists. See page 211 for more detailed discussion of these two conditions.

HOW YOU CAN HELP YOUR CHILD DEVELOP SPEECH SKILLS

Talk–talk–talk!

And talk *to* your child, not *at* him. "Did you like your dinner?" "Look at the rain." "We will get wet." Give him the chance to reply. Keep your speech simple and short. Do not use long, involved sentences. Repeat a word several times, slowly but distinctly. Make sure your child can see your face as well as hear you. He needs to "see" the sound you are making.

A new baby with a couple of older children already in the family may be bewildered and overcome by their expertise in language. In response, they will usually modify their language to suit him, using simple words, repeating them, and saying them slowly.

Finger games, rhymes, singing, and talking all help a baby's vocabulary grow as he listens. In time, he will imitate these activities.

Language opens the door to friendship, love, learning, and understanding.

Nonetheless, try to see to it that the baby has some time alone with you for his own talk.

Talk, play, chat, read, point–but do not drown the baby in too much speech. Keep it simple. Match your pace to his. The younger he is, the more repetition will help his learning.

Use every opportunity that each day presents to help with sounds and vocabulary. But talk about things he can see and touch. At first, the abstract idea of yesterday will mean nothing to him. Talk about what is happening now.

Talk about things he likes to hear about: going shopping, what he has done today, a favorite story. Children love to have a favorite story repeated. While this may drive you crazy after the hundredth repetition, the very repetition helps to fix language and speech concepts in your child's mind.

Never laugh at or try to correct mispronunciations. Do not repeat your child's mistake, but instead praise his effort. If he has taken a stab at a really difficult word, it is essential to praise him for attempting it; at the same time, bring the word–correctly pronounced–into your own sentence. "What funny chibleys," he may say. "Yes, they are funny chimneys, aren't they?"

Use everyday words frequently so that he learns them as he goes along. "Where's the broom?" rather than "Where is it?" "Is that the bell?" rather than "What's that?"

Do not compare his progress with that of

other children. Never frustrate him by withholding something he wants just because he is not using the correct word. Be prepared for regressions into baby talk, sounds, and noises if he is tired or not feeling well.

Make words fun. Spend time singing and looking at books together. Up to age two, he will best appreciate books that have one picture and one word per page.

Expand his own words and interpret his needs with speech. When he lifts his arms to be picked up and says "Up! Up!" say, "Up comes John" as you lift him. When he is at the "why" stage, try to answer questions simply. "Why is the cat mewing?" "Because she is thirsty."

Help your child to mix with others. Young children do not so much play together as play side by side, but they are learning to enjoy company and to be accustomed to others.

Later this will help them learn to share and to learn new words as well. Music, songs, and rhyming games are all part of communicating. Even young babies jog happily up and down to catchy tunes on the radio or the television. They do not need to understand the words; the rhythm and sense of enjoyment are enough. Later—perhaps from eighteen months onward—they will enjoy having their own record or tape player and their own recordings of songs and stories. But these are additions to, not substitutes for, your caring human voice. It is the give and take of daily speech that has the greatest influence on your child's developing skills of communication.

Finally, if you feel your child may have a problem, seek professional help. Never attempt to bring about change yourself. Your job is to be a good model for your child to imitate and a source of praise for his efforts.

STAGES IN THE DEVELOPMENT OF LANGUAGE			
From Birth to Four Weeks He vocalizes distress by crying and wriggling. He begins to respond to his parents' voices and to be soothed by their sound.	**From Four to Eight Weeks** He smiles and gurgles. He vocalizes pleasure. He acknowledges his parents' voices.	**From Eight Weeks to Six Months** He begins to turn toward sources of sound. He communicates to parents by cooing and grunting. He begins using vowel and consonant sounds to babble.	**From Six to Ten Months** He begins to imitate sounds. He vocalizes more consonant sounds.
From Twelve to Eighteen Months He begins to use single words and baby jargon. By twelve months, he understands simple commands such as, "Say bye-bye," and "Peek-a-boo."	**From Eighteen Months to Two Years** He begins to use two-word sentences, verbs, and pronouns.	**About Three Years** He begins to ask questions and to use four- to seven-word sentences. His speech pronunciation is still distorted, but the intelligibility of his words is improving.	
Note: Keep in mind that all these stages and ages are approximate.			

THINKING

In the past, parents as well as professionals generally believed that infants were passive creatures who spent most of their time sleeping and eating. They were not seen as problem solvers and active explorers of their environment. The daily parent-infant contacts—diaper changing, feeding, bathing—were rarely considered anything more than necessary baby care, although the possible pleasures to be derived from those contacts were well understood by parents. As it turns out, these contacts are also important to a baby's mental development.

In fact we know now that babies are keen observers and adventurers, actively involved in their immediate environment. From the first day of life, your baby begins to learn and build a foundation of knowledge that continues to grow with each new experience. She looks around, sucks, listens attentively to her

parents' voices. She twists and turns to find out what is going on in her small world. Her senses supply her with information, and gradually her developing mental and physical abilities begin to interpret that information. She learns to draw conclusions, to think, and to understand the world she lives and acts in.

When—at a few weeks of age—your baby wriggles with delight when she sees your face, she will be unaware that she is learning to differentiate among faces. When she stops crying because she hears your voice, she will not know that she has linked your voice with comfort. But your affectionate and informed observation will tell you that your baby is not only assessing and storing information but solving problems, reasoning.

Later she will begin to understand concepts and categories; and later still, when

A baby is an explorer. Senses feed her information, and her developing abilities begin to interpret that information. She draws conclusions.

speech is added to her other skills, she will be able to express in words what she is doing and what she is thinking. Speech is one of the skills that divides humans from other animals, but so also are thought, judgment, reasoning, and the ability to understand abstract ideas. The growth of these abilities is called cognitive development.

During the first few years of life, your baby's brain grows at an amazing rate, and its growth is paralleled by the rapid development of the child's cognitive abilities. By the time you first wave good-bye to your five-year-old at the school door, she will already have developed most of these basic thinking skills.

This does not mean—and the fact cannot be overstressed—that all children develop at exactly the same rate. One child may take a while to understand something, while another may grasp it right away. Yet they may both have similar intellectual abilities. Two other children may keep pace with each other for a long time, and then one will surge forward. So if your baby seems to be a slow developer, do not worry; she will almost certainly catch up. If you notice, however, that her development seems markedly delayed (and you can see the outlines of the time scales involved by checking the development summaries on pages 159-164), ask for professional advice before you begin to worry unduly. The chances are that–like a toothache carried into a dentist's waiting room–the cause of your anxiety will disappear as soon as you do something about it. But it is important not to fuss or force; your baby is sensitive to your moods, and stress is infectious.

INFLUENCES ON COGNITIVE DEVELOPMENT

A child's abilities are determined in part by her genetic make-up, but dozens of other factors can impede or encourage progress. Your child perceives, adapts, and reacts to her world in her own special way. Environment is of paramount importance–whether her world stimulates, bores, or merely confuses her with too much activity and noise. Fatigue, illness, and emotional strain can all affect a child's rate of cognitive development, as (more obviously) can physical deficiencies of hearing or sight, or an underdeveloped sense such as of taste or smell.

Physical activity may also affect the rate of development. A physically active baby explores her surroundings earlier than a passive child does; the latter, nevertheless, may be learning through observation rather than through participation. A three-year-old may sit mute in a corner in company but later launch into a detailed account of what was said, done, and worn that would be the envy of a gossip columnist.

Socializing, too, is an important factor in cognitive development. It involves not only parents but grandparents, uncles and aunts, the children next door, the mail carrier, and the storekeeper. The whole *involving* world of human contact provides the social environment within which a baby grows.

THE PATTERN OF COGNITIVE DEVELOPMENT

Just as your baby grows physically in an orderly sequence–sitting, crawling, walking, running–so her thinking and reasoning powers progress in a pattern that is common to all children, although the speed at which different children advance from step to step varies widely and has no bearing on their eventual intelligence.

Mental growth depends on the organization of received and perceived information. As your child encounters new experiences, she tries to fit them into her exisiting knowledge and image of the world. Take, for example, a two-year-old who sees a bird picking up seeds from a windowsill and then flying away. From watching this happen, she formulates an idea of what a bird is. A few months later, she is taken to a zoo and sees an ostrich–also a bird, but a very large and flightless one. Now her idea of "bird" must be broadened to include birds that do not fly. Later your child may ask, "Why doesn't the ostrich fly, if it has wings?" You may answer, "Well, birds fly so they can get out of danger quickly, but an ostrich has such strong legs that it can run very fast and doesn't need to fly. And because it hasn't used its wings for so long, they've probably gotten weak."

Children make social contacts in the casual friendliness of home: window cleaner, mail deliverer, and neighbor all share their experiences.

More layers of knowledge are being added to your child's existing store. Later she may think further and ask, "If I didn't use my legs, would I stop being able to walk?" And your answer would be, "If you didn't for long enough."

Further thought may lead her to the conclusion that, since she has legs for running, she does not need wings–and later still she may well put all this theory into practice by sitting still and asking you to wait on her, "Because my legs won't work because I haven't been using them!" She is not being difficult; she is playing out the idea of being a bird that cannot fly.

In this way, your child gathers knowledge, fills in the cracks, and organizes what she has learned.

LEARNING IS PLAY; PLAY IS LEARNING

No one works harder than a child at play, but then a child sees no difference between work and play. It is only later that people learn to separate the two. An educational game can be one as simple as rolling an orange across the floor.

The orange is brightly colored, and when you release it your baby can follow its progress with her eyes. If she can crawl she will probably try to follow it and then grasp it. (Already sight, movement, and grasp have been involved.) She will probably try to bite it and discover that the skin is bitter, thereby learning one of the basic tastes. She may try to roll it as you have done, or she may retrieve it for you to roll again. Physical skills, mental skills, and reasoning are all being used. You have also exposed your baby to a physical law: a round thing rolls because it is round. (The invention of the wheel was founded on that understanding.)

The process is of course not as complicated as the words required to describe what goes on, and you do not have to think it all through whenever you play with your baby. Your main thought is that you and your baby are enjoying a game together. But beyond that, she is learning with leisure in a relaxed and enjoyable atmosphere, and you are helping her to learn.

PHYSICAL INFLUENCES ON DEVELOPMENT

Among the physical problems that may adversely affect intelligence are glandular (thyroid) disorders, nutritional deficiencies, certain prenatal infections–if the mother had

A round thing rolls, a square thing does not; neither does a triangle or a rectangle. Without words or explanations, this child has learned that rolling is a property of round things.

German measles (rubella) in early pregnancy, for instance–and prebirth exposure to smoking or alcohol. Birth injuries and abnormal brain or body structure can also retard development. Depending on the particular deficiency, these may affect either the inborn capacity to develop or the ability to acquire knowledge. Thanks to present-day knowledge and resources, such problems are considerably less frequent than in previous years. Immunization before pregnancy prevents rubella in the mother (see pages 19 and 53), malnutrition is not common in the Western world (see pages 12-14), and enormous strides in prenatal and postnatal care have eliminated some former hazards.

Because babies learn as a result of input from their senses, the growth of their reasoning and thinking is influenced by the maturity of their senses; inevitably, one area of growth overlaps another. Babies also grow continuously yet unevenly, not in neat divisions of progress and rest or at a fixed rate throughout development, so it is no good trying to set your watch (or your baby's IQ) by her achievements on a chart. Certain developmental stages do take place during certain time intervals, and this fact justifies making a rough timetable of the development taking place in your baby at different stages. But developmental stages are not lessons for your child to do and for you to grade; they are periods for enjoying and discovering different experiences and for growing together.

FROM BIRTH THROUGH THE THIRD MONTH

At birth, your baby's behavior is largely reflexive. Most movements are involuntary reactions to a variety of stimuli; but whereas some reflexes–sneezing, for instance, or the startle reflex–do not appear to influence a baby's cognitive development, others such as sucking at a nipple or looking at an object can.

Most babies' senses function normally at birth. Babies see, hear, touch, smell, and taste. They do not, however, arrive with an inborn sense of what things look like, how a voice should sound, or how milk should taste. All of these things have to be learned, and learning starts from the moment the baby sees the light of the world.

Learning is not channeled through one ability at a time. Sight can direct movement, hearing can stimulate memory. At about five to six weeks, your baby first notices her hands, but she cannot yet control them and therefore does not yet use them for exploration. By the third month, she has learned to grasp toys and has begun to look at her hands as she moves them. She soon discovers how to put her hands in her mouth. More and more, she is learning to direct her movements and to assess what effect they have.

How You Can Help

Choose the right kind of mobiles for your baby's crib or playpen (see page 122). Move a colorful ball slowly across her field of vision. She will turn her head to follow its movement and will stop at the midpoint of her body.

While her hands are still fisted, up to five or six weeks, put your finger into her hand so that she can practice grasping it. She will also be exercising her muscles as she grasps. Put different objects into her hand–the handle of a rattle, for instance–so that she begins to understand about different textures. Let her clutch her blanket.

When she puts her hands into her mouth do not pull them away; this is a natural form of exploration. Her mouth is her most effective and available tool. If you discourage her from using it as such or constantly keep it occupied with a pacifier, you will prevent her from effectively exploring other objects. (Naturally, pins, pencils and other sharp and swallowable items should be kept well away.)

When she begins to swipe out at things, change her mobile (see page 124). Give her some crib or carriage toys, particularly ones that make a noise when moved. Let her grasp a rattle. Talk and play with her, and sing to her as you rock her. Prop her up so that she can watch the family and look around her. Let her kick her legs to exercise her muscles.

THE FOURTH THROUGH SIXTH MONTHS

Her senses are becoming integrated, and her ability to focus her eyes has improved so much that she can see at nearly all distances an adult can. Sound now stimulates movement; she looks for the source of sound, and follows well with her eyes. She is interested in everything. As she is learning to coordinate her hands and eyes, she can begin to focus on an object and then reach out for it. She will not succeed every time because grasping a toy is a complex task. The toy must be located with the eyes, and its distance must be estimated; then the arm must be moved forward with the hand in the right position, and the fingers must be adjusted to grasp. It will not be many weeks before she becomes expert at getting things, but in the meantime let her try and practice for a while. Although it is tempting to hand her what she is reaching for, do not obviate all her efforts.

Between her fourth and sixth months, your baby can see objects at almost any distance in her immediate environment, and

For the umpteenth time, she sends the teddy bear over the side. She is learning concepts: cause and effect, disappearance and return. If you decide to make the game easier on you by tying a ribbon to the bear and her chair, make sure the ribbon is no more than 5 inches long to avoid the risk of strangulation.

she can follow them visually in most directions. She does not have to look first at her hands and then at the object she wants; instead, she focuses on the object and then reaches out and grasps it. By six months, she can bring her arm directly to the object; her hand will be open until she touches the object, and then she will grasp it.

This development is not only a significant motor accomplishment but also an important cognitive task, the mastery of which is essential in many daily activities of her future life.

How You Can Help

She will love being propped up in a reclining infant seat or chair so that she can see what is going on around her–although she will still need to be supported. Put her on a rug on the floor and place toys at different distances so that she can reach out and try to grasp them. She will also love repeating activities. Give her a rattle or a soft squeaky toy so that she can practice the same movement and get the same result over and over again. Sing to her, listen with her, talk to her, and imitate sounds for her. Bathtime becomes more fun for her. She will enjoy smacking the surface of the water, and–although she still needs to be supported in her bath–she will enjoy water play with toys that float, sink, squirt, and bubble.

THE SEVENTH THROUGH TWELFTH MONTHS

She gets into everything and is increasingly mobile as she crawls, shuffles along, and grasps everything within reach. She is aware of strangers and may be frightened by them, but she still goes out to meet the world instead of letting it come to her. She looks at, feels, and examines objects; she is becoming familiar with the textures of things–not only of toys, but of the bare floor or carpet or grass or sand she crawls on.

She learns to use her forearms and hands independently and picks up small objects (see page 138). Memory and judgment are being added to the physical skills of opening her fingers, releasing the contents of her hand, and flinging an object away–causing something to happen. Remember the drop-the-toy game and the amazing number of things your young Sherlock Holmes was discovering through that obsessively repetitive action? The baby of seven or eight months, flinging a toy over the side of her highchair, may after a few trial runs flinch at the exact moment the toy is due to hit the ground.

She knows and remembers where things are–for example, her dinner in the refrigerator–and she will wait outside for opening

time. She knows that things exist even when she cannot see them. Her actions are more meaningful; she may give you a pot at dinner time, for instance. She can fit things inside each other and can pull a toy along by a string.

How You Can Help

Within the limits of safety, let her explore her world. Let her go barefoot and feel the difference between wooden floors (watch for splinters) and carpets, grass and sand. She will like water and mucky play, so give her the chance to splash and play with water and sand. She needs to be watched in the bath, and she is likely to try to eat the soap.

Offer her small safe objects to pick up so that she can practice her grasping reflexes–seedless raisins are good for this. Involve her in things that are happening and talk to her about them–the washing machine going around, for example, or the doorbell ringing. Make the daily walk enjoyable with talk.

She will love to crumple paper, shake rattles, wave from the wrist, and play games

Toddlers love messy play. They learn the different properties of mud, water, and sand through touch–and sometimes through taste as well. Obviously, such play must be supervised by an adult at all times.

of "find the toy." Show her a toy; then, while she watches, cover it. She will joyfully look for and find it. You may find that if you repeatedly hide the toy under one cover but then change where you hide it, she will first check the earlier hiding place–even though she saw you hide it elsewhere. In the following months, she will learn to search for the toy only at the place where she last saw it.

THE SECOND YEAR

Your baby now becomes a toddler–no longer the "helpless" bundle of yesterday, but a small being aware of her independence, learning that she is separate from those around her. Still dependent on her caregiver for support, love, care, and protection, she nonetheless asserts her own individuality and makes clear her likes and dislikes. She soon masters the word "no" and uses it to express her disagreement.

The one-year-old lives in a here-and-now world and is not yet ready to conceive of past or future. She cannot think ahead. She might, for instance, climb onto a chair and then onto a table without thinking about how she is going to get down. She still views the world exclusively from her own point of view and does not want to share anything. This is known as the stage of "egocentric growth."

She recognizes familiar objects seen from different angles and can identify objects by touch, without seeing them. She also recognizes familiar voices. She may be walking; if not, she crawls or shuffles along at incredible speed. With so many things to explore, she is seldom bored and moves around constantly from one thing to another, discovering and absorbing new facts all the time.

A few months into her second year, she may soak a sponge full of water and squeeze it out, discovering that a sponge holds water. She may find out for herself that a ball always rolls and never slides, that blocks can be stacked, and that clay can be molded. She may not understand gravity; but she knows that a ball, when dropped, falls to the floor and that water squeezed from a sponge also falls down.

She learns something new every day about textures (rough sandpaper/glossy photograph), shapes (circle/square), tastes (bitter/sweet) and sounds (high pitch/low voice). She compares and sorts all these things out in her mind for future use.

She may now seem increasingly interested in the world beyond the home–watching out the window or exploring the yard. Outdoors, she listens to the wind, watches leaves fall, and sees her reflection in a puddle. She is progressing from baby talk and a few real words to short phrases and sentences, and she begins to use her voice to get your

attention, to make something happen, or to express her feelings. She listens intently when you read to her and attempts to imitate you as you name the animals in a book.

She still does not understand abstract concepts describing emotions–a sad boy, a happy puppy–and may not until her third or fourth year of life. But she is now learning to contrast and compare. For instance, your black cat, the tabby next door, and the Siamese cat in a picture book are all cats even though each looks a little different.

How You Can Help

Play the guessing game. Take turns shutting your eyes and feeling what toy it is. Make a feely box where the two of you handle hidden toys and guess what they are. Play hide and seek with her, and teach her to crawl downstairs backwards so that she has freedom to explore. Provide her with squishy playthings such as nontoxic fingerpaint and clay dough. Teach her the names of everyday objects: flowers, birds, leaves, cars, and people. Imitate sounds with her. Look at books together and talk to her about them. Let her sort out objects in the house–plastic forks from plastic spoons, red socks from green socks. Her visual-motor ability, the coordination of what she sees and what she does with her hands, is becoming more highly developed. Help her practice this with simple jigsaw puzzles to put together and crayons for scribbling and drawing.

Play a "matching" game with her: two balls alike or different; two faces alike or different. Help her to sort her toys into different colored boxes and ask her to hand you named objects: a lid, a spoon, a pan. Exploring cupboards will be her greatest joy, so show her what to do with the objects she finds there–brushes sweep, lids fit on jars, pans have different sizes. Teach her the names of the parts of her body. Above all, be patient; the time of endless questions is now beginning.

THE THIRD YEAR

The first two years have been spent exploring and discovering. Now your child is reflecting and evaluating. Increasingly she is interested in new circumstances, objects, and people. She watches details intently–the colors of a butterfly, perhaps, or a cat playing with a ball of yarn. What is going on in her mind may be unclear to you, but her concentrated expression tells you that an important learning process is taking place.

Out of sight is no longer out of mind. She is increasingly able to reflect upon events and situations. As her speech improves, she continually asks questions; it may exasperate you, but she is collecting vital information.

Working puzzles, matching shapes, pounding, pushing, and stacking–all this apparent play is children's work as they learn about the world around them.

By the age of three, your child will be ready for play group and all the delights of friends and new experiences.

She begins to play with friends rather than merely alongside them, and her play is increasingly imaginative.

When she listens to your heartbeat, she really is the doctor; when she sells you the contents of your refrigerator, she really is a grocery clerk. She plays out happenings–going for a ride, visiting friends, going shopping.

In these activities she exhibits "symbolic thought"; that is, the block she sits astride really is a truck to her. She ascribes feelings and attributes actions to inanimate objects– "Mr. Bear broke the jug." "The stairs came up and hit me"–a process known as "animism."

She does not always understand "tomorrow" and "yesterday," but she knows about "soon" and "later." She draws with more control. Gradually she learns to share and begins to understand the difference between "giving" and "lending." Still, it is best not to pressure children into sharing. At a time when the concepts of self and others are newly solidified, it is important for a child to have her own things.

She is increasingly interested in books and begins to learn about feelings–sad, happy, excited, tired.

How You Can Help
Encourage her independence by letting her stay overnight with her aunt and uncle or her grandparents. At three years, she may be ready for a play group, although each child is different and you must be the judge; some children can take only about an hour of group activity before needing to return to more familiar surroundings.

Help her to understand about quantity and opposites. A small pile of sand added to another small pile makes a bigger pile; some things are hot (soup), and other things are cold (ice cubes). Praise her drawings and always listen to what she is saying. Help her begin to understand time—for example, one way of explaining "tomorrow" is to say that it is "after you have had one bedtime."

LEARNING THROUGH PLAY
Through play, a child learns, explores, grows, rids herself of fears, copes with emotions, and makes friends. Toys are the tools of play, but they need not be exclusively objects bought in a toy store. Your child's first toy is your face—its texture, warmth, smell, and reaction. A child can turn anything she chooses into a toy to play with—from the third step on the stairs (which is a magic carpet and not to be stepped on) to a battered wooden spoon (which one two-year-old identified as her "own dear love").

Play has no rules; when rules appear, play becomes a game. If you try systematically to turn playing into "learning," you will spoil the spontaneity of play and with it some creative and free-spirited part of childhood. This is why too much worry about "educational" toys is useless. Every object and activity your child meets is educational—and that includes sorting spoons from forks or making piles of different colors of clothes to go into the washing machine. You may be working when you do this, but your child is playing.

Still, certain toys do meet a child's needs at particular times: soft toys for comfort and caring; sturdy, rough-play toys for getting rid of aggression; hypnotic toys (like mobiles or snow scenes in which flakes drift down inside a glass ball) that allow the watcher to withdraw and meditate or sort out a problem. Some toys exercise the imagination— doll houses, garages, farms, with people and animals—and some toys teach skills, stretch muscles, or help with coordination. At different times, a cardboard box can be a boat on a sea seething with sharks or a castle enclosing captives to be rescued. Play comes from inside the child and is one of the ways she deals with stress.

It can also be used for letting off steam ("Mr. Bear, stop that at once!"), for role play ("Another glass of juice, my dear?"), or for power play ("We'll have to cut that leg off, I'm afraid!"). You will learn almost as much from watching and listening to your child's play as she will.

A child's imagination is unlimited. When she plays with a simple truck, she could be a garage mechanic. A box on her head turns her into an astronaut. The best toys are often the least expensive.

Try not to interfere with your child's play or try to make her play differently from the way she's chosen. Whose play is it, anyway? There are examples of play being remembered from as early as six months of age; those influences must be extremely powerful in later life.

PLAYING SAFELY

Toy manufacturing is a multibillion-dollar industry, and the variety of toys it produces is endless. Through federal legislation, administrative regulation, and some voluntary industrial standards, toys have become safer, but the utterly safe toy simply cannot be devised.

When selecting a toy for your child, always remember her abilities and skills. Do not buy a toy for her to "grow into"–something disastrous could happen if she plays with it too early. Many toys now clearly identify on their packages the age range for which they are recommended. The manufacturing company in each case will have taken into account the developmental skills required for the toy's proper use, as well as the possible consequences of its improper use.

Not only is a two-year-old unable to fathom the game of checkers; she is very likely to put the pieces into her mouth. Toys for children under three must be large enough not to be swallowed. Look for simplicity in design; fewer moving parts means fewer parts that might come loose, be swallowed, or cause cuts.

Occasionally, the reverse of the developmental rule is true. For instance, a mobile hung out of reach of a five-month-old is stimulating for her to look at; at fifteen months, though, she could reach up and be strangled by its strings. Look around the house regularly (once a month is a good interval), and reconsider the accident potential of your belongings in view of your child's development.

If you have more than one child, you may find that toys suitable for one are dangerous for another. The answer is to supervise when they are playing with such toys. If you cannot supervise, they must only be allowed to play with toys that are safe for both.

You cannot expect other people's homes to have been made accident-proof for your child's benefit, so when visiting friends or relations take along one or two of her toys for quiet play–stuffed animals instead of trucks, for instance. A portable playpen might also be an answer, or a bedroom that you can quickly make child-proof–covering electrical sockets and anything exposing sharp edges, removing fragile objects and anything small enough to be swallowed–might serve as a restricted play area.

POTENTIAL DANGERS IN TOYS

☐ Wood or plastic that might splinter
☐ Toys that break easily
☐ Sharp edges
☐ Small swallowable parts
☐ Stuffing or granules that are sharp and protrude through their casing
☐ Toys that might tip if a child sits on them
☐ Older, secondhand toys that may have been manufactured before laws and regulations against sharp glass, metal edges, sharp points, small parts, and high-lead paint in toys for young children came into effect
☐ Toys with long strings or cords
☐ Wheels that run away too fast on baby walkers or other vehicles
☐ Machinery or clockwork insufficiently cased
☐ Inflammable material or material giving off toxic fumes
☐ Soft toys with eyes inadequately attached or attached with pins
☐ Nails instead of screws
☐ Heavy lids on toy chests that could fall and injure the child's neck or head as she looks inside

WATCH OUT FOR . . .

soft toys with eyes that are insecurely fastened

toys that come apart easily, exposing sharp edges and pieces small enough to swallow

wooden toys with sharp nails that can easily become exposed

bright and colorful toys with paint suspected to contain lead

toys made from plastic that can split or splinter with age

small toys in shapes that can block the windpipe if swallowed or inhaled.

Here is a range of toys to suit your newborn and toddler up to three years old. They have been chosen from the catalogs of major manufacturers; these and similar toys are designed to be both safe and stimulating to use.

Nine Months to Eighteen Months
Stacking by color and shape is an important play activity; both the beads (left) and the truck (right) are designed to encourage this.

Eighteen Months to Three Years
Toys that can be pulled or pushed along give confidence to the young walker. (Trim pull cords to 5 inches to avoid the risk of strangulation.) A stacking tower helps your child develop logical thinking and ideas of order and significance.

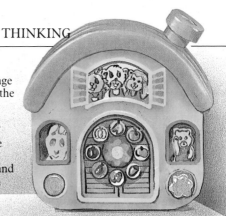

Birth to Three Months

Toys to suspend over the crib (left and center) encourage your baby first to watch and then to swipe and grab at the interesting colors and shapes. (To avoid the risk of strangulation, be sure to remove any device that hangs across the crib when your child reaches five months of age or begins to pull herself to standing, should that be earlier.) The musical activity house (right) and similar items strapped to the crib provide a variety of sounds and motions—at first with an adult's help and later through the baby's own efforts.

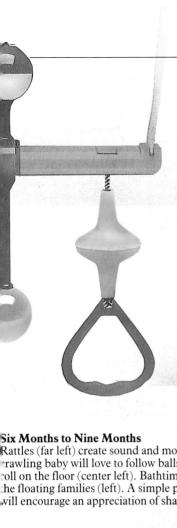

Three Months to Six Months

Soft, cuddly toys, such as the bunnies at far left, can provide comfort and security. If they squeak when squeezed, so much the better. Toys like the push-along train rattle (right) encourage finger manipulation and two-handed coordination.

Six Months to Nine Months

Rattles (far left) create sound and movement. Your crawling baby will love to follow balls and other toys that roll on the floor (center left). Bathtime is more fun with the floating families (left). A simple posting box (right) will encourage an appreciation of shape and space.

The Consumer Product Safety Commission is empowered to ban unsafe products, to issue mandatory safety standards governing types of products, and to participate in notification about and recall of dangerous products. It is the primary federal regulatory agency in charge of overseeing the safe design and manufacture of toys. Notices of defective toys are sent to physicians, health clinics, and toy stores, and they are usually prominently displayed. If you have a question about the safety of a toy, contact your local health department or the Consumer Product Safety Commission (toll-free hotline: 800-638-2772).

Toys are also tested for safety and performance by the Consumers Union and the Underwriters Laboratories. The Consumers Union tests products it considers most interesting to the average consumer. As a result, although it provides impartial evaluations of all products tested (being beholden to no commerical interest), its testing is selective and it may not have evaluated the toy you buy.

The Underwriters Laboratories tests only toys submitted to it by companies. U.L. approval may be nice to have, but it is not required nor often sought by manufacturers of toys.

Information on products tested by either of these groups is available by direct contact or (for Consumers Union testing) by reviewing past issues of *Consumer Reports* at your local library. Some daily papers in large metropolitan areas have a regular question-and-answer consumer column that could help. Local legislation regarding product safety varies from state to state; your local health department can inform you of relevant standards in your area.

PETS

Sooner or later most children want a pet; if you agree to one, the question is which animal is most suitable. The decision inevitably depends on your lifestyle and your personal preference.

It is worth thinking about why so many children seem to want pets. A child needs to love as well as be loved, and a pet in the house provides a focus for her love and her sense of protection and responsibility. Obviously a young child cannot take full responsibility for an animal, but she will learn that a pet has to be fed regularly (usually) exercised, kept clean, and provided for when the family goes away. Having a pet may also help teach her about mating and birth. A cuddly pet seems to release tension in a child, and its loyalty is reassuring when everything else in the world seems to be going wrong.

The death of a pet inevitably causes suffering to a child, but a period of mourning is necessary and natural. Do not immediately rush out and buy another animal to replace the first. If the first is eventually replaced, do not encourage thinking of the second as the first "coming back again"; each should have its own place in the family's affections.

If you already have a dog or cat before the baby arrives, there is a danger that the animal will become aggressively territorial in response to the newcomer. Never leave the baby alone with the pet; do continue to shower the pet with as much attention as before so it does not feel displaced.

PET PRECAUTIONS
- Dogs, cats, hamsters, and several other types of domestic pets can all bite and scratch; a child must be taught not to tease animals (see page 207).
- Fleas and mites can cause skin rashes on your child, so care should be taken to rid the pet of these.
- Cage birds–notably parakeets and parrots–can cause psittacosis, but they can be bought already vaccinated.
- Teach your child the extra hygiene necessary when a pet is in the house: Animal dishes should never be washed with the family's, and hands should always be washed before meals after touching a pet.
- Roundworms can spread from dogs and cats to children and can be transmitted from the soil a pet has used. This can happen whether the family has a pet or not. Happily, the condition is easily treated (see page 225).
- Rabies from pet dogs and cats is not at present a threat in most countries, provided the laws of quarantine are observed.
- A healthy well-cared-for pet rarely causes any problems of disease in a family.

BECOMING A PERSON

"What color eyes will he have?" "Suppose she has Grandpa's nose or Uncle Willie's feet?" "I hope she has your nature . . . my mother's common sense . . . your father's wit . . . my father's dexterity . . . ." "Do you think?" "Suppose . . . ."

You have been asking the questions for nine months; now, at last, some of them have been answered. "It" has become "our son" or "our daughter"; birth-blue eyes are settling to their permanent color, you have checked the nose in profile against Grandpa's and breathed a sigh of relief–though you are not sure yet about the size of the feet. Those sorts

Parents are always eager to
know what temperament
and character their child will
have. The future is being
made in the present.

of questions have been answered, but only the future will answer others: "What character, temperament, and personality will he have?"

But the future is being made in the present. So far, observing physical progress has been easy. Baby book in hand, you have checked reflex and grasp, and you have applauded the first smile. On Monday, you thought you had a genius; on Tuesday, you were not so sure. Understanding the development of personality, however–the characteristics that make your child uniquely himself and different from anyone else–can seem more complicated, particularly when you know that his personality is being shaped in part by your handling. Character, temperament, or personality is formed by a combination of the traits your child was born with and the influence you and others bring to bear. Given his basic temperament, your job is to help him master his environment, to be aware of him as a separate person, and to judge and assess the moments when he is ready to be helped to new stages of development.

Because "readiness" is a familiar word, its particular importance as applied to learning is easy to overlook. Readiness exists on the brink of learning a particular skill. It signals that the child has reached a requisite level of motivation, competence, and maturity: He must want to be able to do the new thing, be physically able to do it, and be mature enough to do it. It could be likened to the moment in midair when a swimmer has left the side of the swimming pool but has not yet hit the water. Your sensitive ability to recognize this stage of readiness will help your child tremendously in forming a healthy personality. You can provide the essential basis for a healthy personality whether you are a single parent, a married couple, divorced, or part of an extended family. The cornerstones are a loving, steady relationship, continuity of care and affection, adequate stimulation, and opportunity for attachment–initially to one person, and later to others.

To watch a child coming to terms with his body and his world is to see an awesome single-mindedness at work. At four months, he tries over and over again to roll from his front to his back or vice versa. He tries, fails, tries again, pauses to rest, and then resumes the struggle. To be able to turn from back to front, your four-month-old must have the ability to push off selectively with one arm and leg while holding the other against the body and at the same time suppressing the asymmetric tonic neck reflex. This may seem to be a tall order for a four-month-old, yet most babies do it. Watching those frantic scrabblings on the rug, you know that though your baby has not quite achieved success he is at the stage of readiness. And just as the physical progress of movement takes place in a logical and orderly sequence–sitting, crawling, and then walking–so will the developmental steps toward personality.

Even before birth you know your baby to be a unique individual. Birth deepens that knowledge in the first amazing face-to-face confrontation between the parent and the new human being. Awe often overrides love in those first moments of encounter. The multitude of other possible emotions–weariness, apprehension, fear of inadequacy, as well as physical relief, may not allow love to be an immediate reaction, but with a properly managed pregnancy and birth love grows rapidly.

And with love grows sensitivity. Within hours of your baby's birth you will know what his particular cry means, and you will begin learning his individual likes and dislikes. Your dedication and commitment grow so that you respond automatically, despite your own weariness, to his daily and nightly demands. He has forced changes in your life, and you have responded by modifying your own behavior to meet his needs and tempo.

The baby's welfare thus takes precedence over your own; and by this means, the cornerstones of personality are being laid, for within his abilities the baby learns that he is loved. And he meets you halfway: the more intensely he reacts to you, the stronger you become attached to him; and the stronger your attachment is to him, the more his is to you.

He listens to your voice, responds to your face, snuggles into your arms. Your baby makes deliberate efforts to hold your attention, and the interaction between you and your child marks the beginning of an important process in the formation of personality. A three-month-old baby will wriggle, smile, and make efforts to attract a parent. One study of a three-month-old's efforts to attract his parent's attention showed that if the parent sat impassively and did not respond, the baby after a while would cry or else become quiet and look away, sucking his fingers for comfort. The parent in this case had blocked interaction. When the parent responded by smiling and talking, however, the baby's movements became stronger and more rhythmic and he was obviously pleased.

When your baby "flirts" with you in this way, you will have an opportunity to see this in action. What you are doing is showing him that he is of interest to you and that you value him as a person. You are helping him toward the beginnings of self-respect.

But you are still allowed to be human. On off-days, the foundations may show hairline cracks but the structure will survive. Other demands and inclinations will occasionally dictate that he has to wait a little longer for his feeding or for his rattle to be picked up. Such moments will not leave permanent scars on his personality. Babies are surprisingly resilient, and unless a baby is subjected to very severe deprivation or outright injury, he can tolerate a fair amount of stress for short periods without lasting effect.

Severe deprivation would include being left alone in a crib without stimulation for most of the day and night over a period of several months, for example, or being fed for days or weeks with a propped-up bottle instead of being cuddled. A temporary upset or family stress will not leave lasting damage; in fact, some stress is needed to build a healthy personality since everyone experiences it to some degree. An early childhood entirely without stress could lead to a vulnerable blandness. It is only when stress is prolonged – for instance, if a parent is seriously depressed or ill for a considerable length of time – that you might fairly be concerned about the effect on your baby and should ask a health care provider for advice.

No single style of parenting, family pattern, or ideal surroundings exist that are right for all children. If they did, everyone might be raising near-clones instead of individuals. The goal for parents is to provide the best environment and support system they can for their baby. You are as individual as your baby, and simply being yourself will provide the right background. You cannot force your baby to develop, but what you can do is provide conditions in which he will be encouraged to develop.

EASY, DIFFICULT, AND SLOW-TO-WARM CHILDREN

Researchers have been able to identify three broad categories of temperament: the placid or "easy" child, the irritable or "difficult" child, and the uncertain or "slow-to-warm" child. Within days of birth – perhaps even before birth – you may know what sort of baby you have. Of course, the dominant characteristic may change at times, for varying reasons and periods; of a group of babies studied from birth to the age of seven, 65 percent showed the same temperament the whole time, while the remaining 35 percent showed basic changes in temperament.

Researchers have also sought to discover whether one particular characteristic in a child might underlie the basic temperament he exhibited. They found evidence that, for all temperaments, the presence or absence of timidity was the key characteristic. Both the difficult child and the slow-to-warm child have elements of timidity in their natures, though they evidence these in different ways. The difficult child becomes awkward and irritable, whereas the slow-to-warm child becomes passive and withdrawn. The easy child, on the contrary, seems to lack timidity and tends to take new experiences in stride, without obvious trouble. Research of this type suggests that difficult and slow-to-warm children will benefit most from being treated with a balanced mixture of firmness and affection, since such a balance is best calculated to dispel the underlying timidity.

Part of the difference between a difficult child and a slow-to-warm child lies in the intensity of their reactions. The difficult

The difficult child leaves you in no doubt about his wishes; reactions are quite clear.

The slow-to-warm child is less violent in his reactions and may be persuaded against his inclinations.

child tends to react intensely–to throw a tantrum when confronted with a new situation, to fight being held by a stranger, to spit out unaccustomed food, to clamp his jaws shut. The slow-to-warm child shrinks back from new situations, may whine and not snuggle rather than fight if embraced by a stranger, and in general is more passive. He may turn up his nose at new food and push the dish away, but he is less likely than the difficult child to resist actively if he is offered a taste. He may not like it, but he may in time put up with being fed it.

Any child in any category of temperament may switch from one to another quite suddenly. Once again, firmness and affection are the best ways to see him–and you–through.

DEALING WITH PHASES

Some general principles may help you deal with the various phases your child enters, as well as helping him assimilate new experiences and move on to further development. These principles apply to all types of children, and they are closely tied to your own interaction with others and especially with your partner. Some of the goals to aim for are identified below.

Agreement Between Parents

Make sure, as parents, that the two of you discuss together in advance your approach to various situations, so your behavior in dealing with them does not conflict. If the child misbehaves and the father would like to send him out of the room, but the mother would prefer to ignore the behavior, you must both make the effort to support each other in front of the child. Do not discuss your respective attitudes in front of him and do not undo your decision with hugs and kisses that signify, "We didn't really mean it."

Consistency in Treatment

Without being overly rigid in your reaction, try to settle on and maintain a single method of dealing with a particular situation–for example, going to pick up the baby as soon as he cries, allowing an older child into your bed, or sending a child to his room for disobedience. A helpful hint: the fewer the rules, the easier they are to keep.

Tolerance for Immaturity

Try not to allow your own feelings of shame, embarrassment, or inadequacy to spill over onto the child. *He* does not mind if he is still in diapers at two years of age or still wants to drink from a bottle. Perhaps *you* mind because you take his behavior as a sign that you have not done *your* job properly. This is an unreasonable projection of an idealized norm onto your child and yourself, and it is

unfair to both of you. Similarly, if he wants to take his comforter–piece of torn blanket–with him when meeting your classy friends, let him take it. Do not be ashamed of him for being himself.

Foresight and Tact

Think ahead for the child and anticipate situations, avoiding them if you know he will not be able to cope with them or gently encouraging him so that he gradually gains the confidence to manage them. Sometimes you will find him in the midst of a situation it is too late to avert–for example, juggling with your best china. If you give a gasp of horror now, he will simply drop it in surprise. Your best move is to approach him smoothly, whisk the china away calmly but briskly, and substitute. Give him brightly colored plastic replicas or miniatures of similar shape: plastic pots, barrels, blocks, and so on. The substitution will allow him the same pleasure and you somewhat more.

When a big, potentially scary event is impending, tell him what is going to happen, and let him "play it out." A few days before the first visit to the dentist, tell him about the chair that goes up and down, the special toothpaste, and the whirring brush, and explain that the dentist will look in his mouth with a tiny mirror on a stick.

Diversion and Retreat

Distractions can provide made-to-order relief when the going gets sticky. Invent them yourself. "Look at that cat" and "Just see what I've got in my bag" sometimes work wonders. If the child cannot be distracted and his behavior is unacceptably disruptive (tantrums in a supermarket, for instance, when you are in the midst of shopping), give up, go home, and arrange to do the shopping alone next time. If your child wants to accompany you again, he must regard it as a privilege, for which reasonable behavior is expected.

Taking Things Gently

He makes it clear that he does not like carrots or new people. Do not turn this into a high-noon showdown. Take them both away, and try again a few days later. Not liking strangers can be a sign of intelligence and self-preservation, and not liking carrots is at worst a matter of taste. Anyway, how would you like to be made to kiss aunts, stroke cats, and eat carrots on demand?

Keeping Your Cool

No one denies that children at times are frustrating and infuriating. Try to keep your sense of humor, and remember that most stages pass. Look after yourself, too, physically and mentally. A tired, out-of-sorts parent will not be able to cope, and you can easily get into a vicious spiral of depression. If you feel you are losing your sense of balance, seek professional help.

STAGES OF PERSONALITY DEVELOPMENT

You cannot think about the development of your child's personality without taking into account the development of his movement, speech, and understanding. Physical and mental development may also lie behind your child's change in temperament. An eight-month-old baby may suddenly begin to cry at the sight of his father if he has been used to being at home all day with his mother. A new walker may be more irritable at certain times of the day—his frustration level lowered by the greater physical demands he is facing. These are stages that may last only a few weeks. Do not try to rush him; the behavior will probably end as unexpectedly as it began.

The Swiss psychologist Jean Piaget defined guidelines to the stages of development based on his observations of children. Many of his theories have since been extended or modified, but they remain interesting and valuable.

Encouraging the Desire to Learn

Readiness to tackle a new step or skill depends on maturity (natural physical and mental growth), previous training (the experience that parents have provided), and motivation (natural curiosity and desire to learn).

The support and praise of parents is vital to a growing child because a child can all too easily become sensitive to failure and thereupon lose the wish to learn. Parental assessment of readiness is not as difficult as it may sound on paper. Just as you have to anticipate dangers for your child ("When he learns to crawl I must watch out for hazards in the home"), so you will come to anticipate his developmental preparedness and needs.

A very young child is not able to understand cause and effect; he does not know that the coffee pot fell on him because he pulled the tablecloth or that his hand was burned because the radiator was hot. He cannot make decisions about his movements in his own surroundings. But by the time he reaches two years of age, basic reasoning has developed. Your two-year-old knows that he can push his stuffed toy through the bars of the crib only if he turns it first in a certain way; he will not need to experiment.

It is a toddler's job to become independent and a parent's job to let him. He may stagger off on his own but keep turning back for reassurance. Sensible praise and support will encourage him all the way. Even as a baby of six or seven months, before he can feed himself, he puts his hand on yours in a charming gesture of companionship as you take the spoon to his mouth. When he first feeds himself, he makes a mess, but he must

---

SOME OF PIAGET'S BASIC DIVISIONS

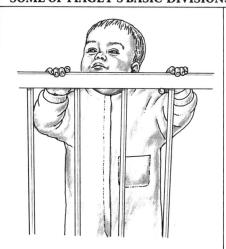

Between Five and Eight Months
The baby lives in the present but acts on his environment instead of waiting for the environment to come to him. He shakes his crib or playpen bars, and he reaches out for things he wants.

Approaching One Year
He knows that objects exist even when he cannot see them. He can discriminate among sounds but not use them. He knows what objects are and may recognize the words *shoe* and *walk* but not be able to say them. In the same way he knows what purposes objects serve but may not be able to use them. The family car driven up to the door may mean an outing, and he will become excited.

Between Eighteen Months and Two Years
He makes use of things that are not there by making "pretend" games. He speaks in more complex sentences and can use language to translate awareness of what he is doing into telling you about it. He knows the sequence of the day—when it is time for a walk, a shopping trip, a story—but he does not understand hours, minutes, weeks, or months. He can see things only from his own point of view (egocentric growth). He attributes feelings and actions to inanimate objects: "The slide threw me off"; "The floor hit me."

Be interested in what your child is doing and enter into her successes; praise her efforts.

Dressing is an arduous process, and the order in which clothes go on and come off is difficult to sort out. Try to encourage these early steps toward independence.

be allowed to do so. When he first dresses himself, he gets both legs through one side of his pants (the first time he does this and you see him lurching into the room, you will think in horror that he has injured one of his legs!).

When he is about fifteen months old, you may find you have to set limits on his activities. "No" is effective in inverse proportion to the frequency of its use. Say it twenty times a day, and it will mean nothing; reserve it for occasions when you must have control and obedience, and it will elicit them. "No" can save your child's life, if you see a danger that he does not. To lessen your use of "no," consider providing a distraction or an alternative activity.

Toddlers like pets but have to be stopped from hurting them. Your child might have an inborn talent for pulling the cat's tail, but he can learn from you how to stroke it gently. He must learn not only how not to hurt the cat (which might react by hurting him) but also how to relate properly to an animal.

CONSISTENCY LEADS TO SECURITY
The fast pace and active demands of modern society often leave people little time to establish and maintain basic relationships. Many parents find it extremely difficult to observe a consistent course of conduct toward their children or to slow down their lives to their children's pace. But inconsistency only bewilders a child—for example,

if you laugh one day when he throws sand in the sand box and then spank him the next day because when he does it again some sand gets in another child's eye. So, if his behavior needs to be halted or corrected, do not yell across the playground at him. Go to him and speak calmly but not hesitantly, bearing in mind how what he has done and how you are now reacting fit into the overall pattern of behavior and interaction you have and want to have with him. All of this takes time and self-discipline. Do not, however, be misled into thinking that you are being liberal-minded if you let your child get away with everything. "Not wanting to curb his spirit" can simply be a pretext for parental laziness, indifference, or distaste for conflict on any level.

By about eighteen months, the child who has been handled consistently is able to exercise the beginnings of self-control and to respond to simple directions. He can also make the connection between statements and events. "Oh dear, the truck is broken. Put it aside and we will try to fix it after our walk."

By about two to two and a half, your child has begun to form attitudes toward the people in his world. "No" and "I won't" are well established in his vocabulary; you, as the setter of limits, are probably on the receiving end of much of their use. In a two-parent family, one parent should not be saddled with the whole job of providing the discipline ("Just wait till your father gets home!"), while the other provides the comfort. Shared responsibilities promote easy, comfortable communication among all family members, and this helps the child become a happy, congenial person. Occasionally, too, his "no" may be right. Be reasonable: If he is really tired, he just may not be able to pick up his toys before bedtime.

Aggressiveness needs to be channeled. Frequent use of "no," aggression, and anxiety about being separated are all natural to the two- to three-year-old. It is best to offer alternative solutions rather than head-on battle. Not all conflicts need be avoided, however. Suppose your child of two-and-a-half was under the weather last week, so you stayed with him until he went to sleep. Now he refuses to sleep without you and threatens a tantrum. Offer an alternative: a few minutes' cuddle, a story, or a drink (just one).

Tantrums are distressing to both of you. If you possibly can, ignore them; shouting, spanking, and other overt forms of punishment are all ways of paying attention. It is the lack of attention that is most punishing, and this is why good behavior and effort should always be rewarded with praise. Giving your child a choice is also giving him a measure of control–"Would you like the red bib or the green one?" "Shall we have a story before you brush your teeth or afterwards?"

SPANKING

Spanking is not usually effective as a deterrent. It may make you feel better, but it does not offer your child an alternative way to act, and it may teach him that physical violence is an acceptable way to control others. Too frequent spanking can become something the child expects; he can come to think of it as a kind of fixed price he must pay for certain conduct – a view that annuls any idea of moral force or personal responsibility attaching to his own action.

A child who is given insufficient attention and support by his parents may commit misdeeds to provoke spanking because then the parents will at least take notice of him. You can sometimes see this in the mutinous expression on some children's faces. "Well, I'll show them," they are saying–but it is a sad reflection on their environment that they have to be naughty to be noticed.

Spanking, if used at all, should be reserved for exceptional occasions when perhaps the child is doing something dangerous to himself or others, such as running into the road or going near an unattended swimming pool.

Tantrums in public can be embarrassing. Keep as calm as you can, and if possible, ignore him. No attention often means no tantrum.

Setting limits is important. The child who does not hear the word "no" too often will respect it when he does.

But remember always that when you are worried and frightened it is easy to lose control and harm a child.

Tantrums sometimes serve to announce the stage of readiness for greater independence. Very often they are expressions of frustration – when the child cannot physically or mentally cope with a situation, and his immediate sense of inadequacy erupts into yells and screams. Anticipate if you can, divert if you can, punish only if it is absolutely necessary; avoid battles unless you intend to win (and then not by force). Above all, praise when you can.

"Stars" for achievements are very much appreciated by the rising threes. If your child is trying to do something or learn something, put up a chart with his name and the days of the week on the refrigerator door. Buy a packet of stars and stick one on the chart every day he picks up his toys. At the end of a good week, he could have a bigger star; and when he has had several good weeks, the behavior pattern will have become fairly well established, and he will probably forget about the stars.

What you are doing is using a "positive reinforcement" system, not negative punishment. If you promise a reward, give it. It need only be small. You are not buying good behavior; you are rewarding it.

The word "discipline" has come to mean "punishment" or "restriction," but what you are teaching your child is self-discipline – the internalizing of reasonable external standards of behavior. Parents should be models of what they teach. This is not always easy, partly because adults often let their own self-discipline slip and partly because adults are to an extent the products of their own childhood. Parents whose own upbringing was harsh or perhaps too lax may need to change their own behavior in order to pass on acceptable standards to their children. Most adults have learned to cover up their less attractive traits when they want to. Nonetheless, it is sometimes necessary to recognize that one has unpleasant traits or received wrong handling as a child, in order not to pass them on to or make the same mistakes with the new generation.

GRANDPARENTS

Grandparents can be your greatest resource. Usually they are as delighted to be grandparents as you are to be parents. If you are fortunate to live within easy visiting distance, they may even be eager to babysit (for short periods) or to provide regular care if you are working away from home.

The birth of a baby often brings greatly deepened relationships between parents and grandparents and sometimes provides an opportunity to resolve certain longstanding conflicts between the two. Parents may still have holdover feelings of dependency or inadequacy, but having a child marks the beginning of a new role–one that parents' own parents often come to recognize and respect.

If a grandparent is to look after your baby for any length of time, you should sort out as early as possible your own ideas about the baby, while at the same time respecting the older person's experience and concerns. Your mother's experience of weaning, for instance, may be different from the method you intend to follow, so you will have to make the differences clear (without rancor) from the beginning. If a difference in treatment still persists, then you may have to arrange matters so that the grandparent cares for the baby only between feedings, thereby avoiding the possible conflict. On the other hand, grandparents are usually wonderful at comforting children and at distracting them before a tantrum erupts.

Grandparents have rights too. Do not burden them with too much babysitting. They have their own lives to lead, and young children can be tiring or meddlesome in an older person's home.

Grandparents have a very special relationship with young children. Often they have a great deal of time and patience to give, and small children can learn much from them. A warm and enduring relationship between grandparents and grandchildren also gives the children a beneficial image of older people–the sense of security to be gained from them and also some of their needs (a young child can take great pleasure in "helping" them). For their part, grandparents are usually adept at finding ways for children to amuse themselves and are masters at reading children's books aloud, as well as at telling stories of their own childhood. For a small child, grandparents can be both a loving presence and a window on the world.

LIVING WITH OTHERS

Babies have to learn to give as well as take, and where better than in the tumult of a family?

A baby who is not the first in the family inherits a different world from a first-born. He never has to learn to share because from birth sharing is part of his life. Parents and professionals widely believe that second and subsequent children are less trouble than the first. This may be because the parents, having practiced on the first-born, are more relaxed; then, too, the baby has a lot more to interest him in surroundings filled with other children to watch, play with, and learn from.

For a first-born child, it must be bewildering to have a new baby join the family. A sensitive approach is needed to ease him over from being the star of the show to being a member of the cast. The old adage is true–it is not the quantity of time you give a child but the quality that counts. Make sure that each child has a daily time with you–however brief–that is his alone. It can be done, no matter how fragmented parents occasionally feel as they try to reconcile a

Grandparents are very special people. Often they have more time and patience than parents, and "helping" them can be a special treat for the grandchild.

score of conflicting demands.

Suggestions for easing a new baby into the family are given on page 95 and some specific strategies for preparing your child for a new arrival can be found on page 197. Here are some further thoughts on the subject.

Never exclude the older child from the room where you are attending to the younger. If possible, ask him to help—fetching towels, holding the wash cloth during diapering, and so on.

If changes in a toddler's routine will be necessary when the new baby arrives, anticipate them before the birth so that these become established habits in advance.

Do not expect an older child to be willing to give up his possessions, clothes, room, or equipment to the baby. He may choose to do so, or necessity may require it, but he should be consulted first, and any reluctance on his part should be respected.

Make a regular time and activity that is specifically his, such as bathtime with his father, story with his mother, or watching a television program together. What it is matters far less than that it is consistently his own.

Helping your child become a person involves a series of complex interactions between the physical characteristics of the child and the world around him. It cannot be pointed out too often that a child has to develop one set of skills before being able to learn the next, and that children differ in the amount of time they take to progress— though the order of development is usually the same.

When a baby is young, he is totally dependent. Once mobile, he seeks independence, becomes aware of his separateness, and begins to experiment on the road to self-control. Give and take is crucial from now on: Children need limits so that they feel safe, and they need freedom so that they can explore. Providing this balance is one of the most difficult and rewarding tasks of parenthood. It is also one of the most necessary.

A child evidences his surroundings but is not a mirror image. A doormat parent, for example, may produce a selfish child. The parents' job is to build a foundation of trust so that the child learns to value himself while recognizing that he is part of a larger social structure whose members have their own rights and needs. The child who knows he is loved also knows he is worthy of love.

Observing his parents' interaction between themselves and with others, the child learns continual lessons about becoming a person. For a child to grow courteous, he must see courtesy in action; for him to become considerate toward others, he must see consideration practiced around him. The example his parents and siblings set for him in their daily conduct provides the model upon which he patterns his own behavior.

A baby cries if his mother cries, but not because his mother is sad: He cries because somehow the atmosphere makes *him* feel bad. A child of two and a half or three who sees his mother crying, however, will be sad *for* his mother. This is where another adult can help. "What can we do to make Mommy/Daddy happier? Let's make her/him a special meal." The child thus learns that you do not have to give a present; giving a service, something of yourself, can be much more valuable.

Love, unlike praise, cannot be contingent on good behavior. It applies to a deeper, more permanent aspect of your child and of your relationship to him than any fleeting controversy can touch. If you are angry at your child's conduct, try to make clear that the cause is at the level of deeds, not of underlying attachment.

Throughout the laborious process of becoming a person, your child depends on your love. Give him enough supportive affection, and you will be giving him the gift of loving.

Children need limits to feel safe, but they also need freedom so they can explore. Once a child becomes aware that she is a separate person, she begins to travel the road toward self-control.

FAMILY MATTERS

A mother once said that she regarded her job as teaching her children "to pack their bags." That summarizes the relationship between parents and children. From the moment the umbilical cord is severed, a child begins learning to pack her bags, and parents who do not anticipate the inevitable separation are sowing for themselves the seeds of loneliness in later life.

It is easy to become immersed in parenthood, especially in the very early days when a baby needs almost continuous care and protection. But children grow up. Babies become toddlers who need to explore a wider world than the home. They go next door to play; they stay with relatives and friends. Other gods appear, threatening your infallibility: "But my teacher says . . . ." "But Bobby's parents let him . . . ." In the constantly changing picture of life a child sees, her parents slip into the background surprisingly quickly. Before they are quite ready for it, parents are likely to detect in their child's eyes the same faint boredom with them that, scant years before, they had occasionally felt with her.

Separation is an intrinsic part of growing up, but the process is gradual and requires that parents continually reassess needs and make new decisions for themselves and for their children. Getting the timing right–knowing when a child needs support and when she needs to fend for herself–is an essential part of the alchemy of parenthood, through whose operation a baby becomes a child and a child an adult.

Learning to separate comes about most easily when it is allowed to occur gradually in stages of readiness–when child and parents are prepared for the new stage. For the baby, this is governed by her natural physical and mental development. First she explores but looks back to make sure that a friendly adult is still there if she needs to make a quick retreat to base. After a few forays, she concentrates more on the goal ahead and looks back less. Finally she appears not to look back at

all, but it is the heritage of security gained in those early supportive days that enables her to assert her independence. For parents, the challenge is rather to anticipate and support their child's progress toward independence, expecting neither too much nor too little of her at each stage.

When both parents work outside the home, they may be concerned that the reduced amount of time they spend with their child may negatively affect her development. The important thing to remember, however, is that the quality of time spent with a child is much more important than the quantity. In fact, under certain circumstances, physical separation may be less difficult for a child to cope with than emotional separation. For example, an abstracted, cold, and distant parent who is always physically present is much less valuable to a baby's development than an involved parent who spends considerably less time in the child's company. Parents who are caring, interested, and listening when they are with their children are successfully laying the foundations of lifelong security.

Weaning your child to greater independence often entails insisting upon your own rights and preferences. Parents owe it to their children as well as to themselves to assert and preserve their own individuality. By defining areas of time, space, and privacy for yourself, you teach your child that others have rights that exist apart from her needs and wishes. The boundaries obviously must be elastic, but by the time your toddler is going on three she will recognize your right to your own preferences, will take pleasure (within her limits) in helping you achieve them, and will be encouraged by your appreciation.

To become loving and caring, your child needs to be loved and cared for. She needs to have her own preferences respected, because through being respected a child learns self-respect. If you give your child dignity–the dignity of having time to finish a game before being whisked off to bed, the

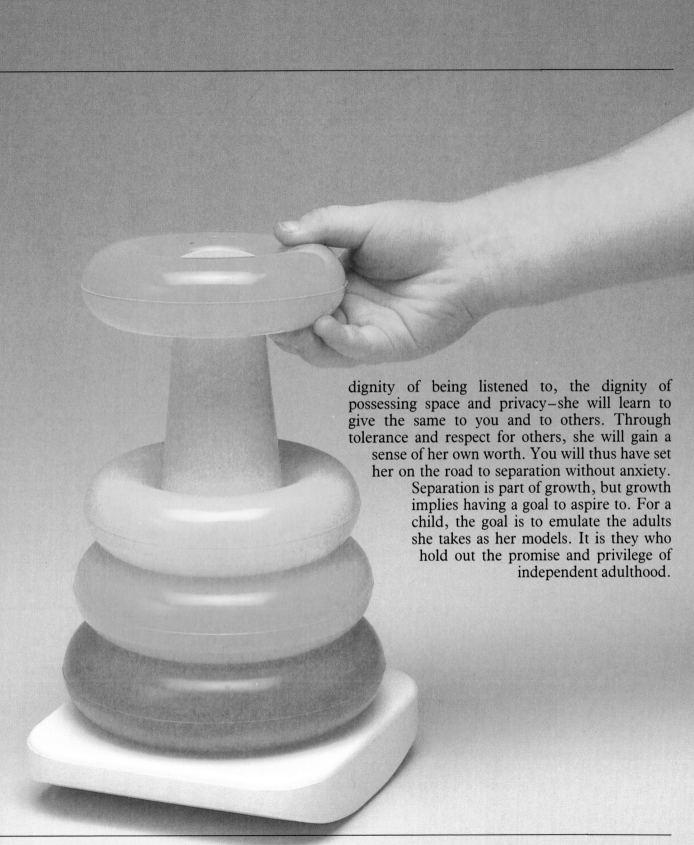

dignity of being listened to, the dignity of possessing space and privacy–she will learn to give the same to you and to others. Through tolerance and respect for others, she will gain a sense of her own worth. You will thus have set her on the road to separation without anxiety.

Separation is part of growth, but growth implies having a goal to aspire to. For a child, the goal is to emulate the adults she takes as her models. It is they who hold out the promise and privilege of independent adulthood.

THE WORKING MOTHER AND SEPARATION

By the end of this decade, two out of three American mothers will hold paying jobs outside the home; over half of these will be leaving at least one preschool child in the care of someone else. If you, as parents, both decide to work outside the home, you need not feel you are in a minority.

Complicating this decision is the large amount of child-rearing literature that seems to imply that the mother (and only the mother) should bring up the child. Parents may worry that relinquishing even some of this care to someone else may jeopardize the child's future development, stunt his intellect, and undermine his emotional and possibly his physical health. Separation is only one aspect of this many-sided issue. The decision you make will be influenced by your own circumstances and those of others in your family, the personality of your child, and the resources available in your community.

Before you become involved in the details of the decision, though, it may help you to stand back and consider why so many women today work outside the home. Usually it is for one or more of four main reasons: they need the money; they miss the imposed discipline of outside work; they are lonely; or they feel a need to exercise their talents or training in order to retain their identity. Some of these needs can be partially met without going out to work—although not always easily or satisfactorily. A woman may find it possible to earn money working at home, but she is likely to be poorly paid. She may impose her own discipline of work at home, but this may be difficult with a baby in the house. On the other hand, she may make friends with people who are in similar circumstances—probably through parent resource groups, by meeting them at the playground, or by finding names on community bulletin boards—and she may find that her new lifestyle encourages her to master skills she was unable to develop previously or to study for a different career when her family is older.

If in the end you decide that you will both work, you will probably be most concerned with two questions. Will the separation harm your baby? Who will care for him?

WILL THE SEPARATION HARM YOUR BABY?

In baby-care jargon, a baby "bonds with his primary caregiver"—the adult who looks after him most. Usually in the first few weeks that

For many mothers, working from home with a young child is preferable to leaving her to be cared for by someone else. Even with a cooperative child, though, it will take a lot of organization; and be warned: Home workers are notoriously underpaid.

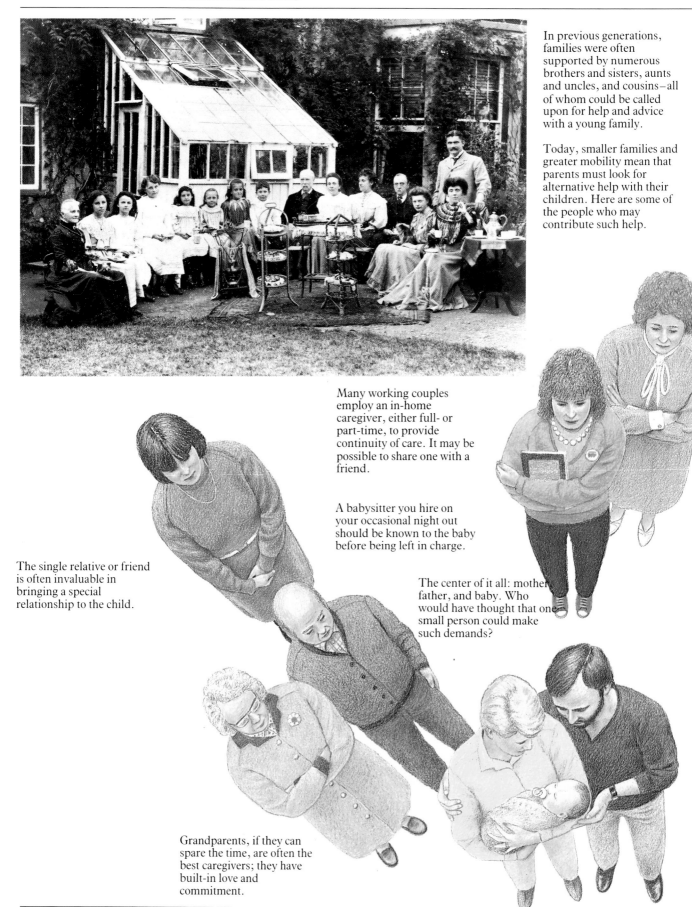

In previous generations, families were often supported by numerous brothers and sisters, aunts and uncles, and cousins—all of whom could be called upon for help and advice with a young family.

Today, smaller families and greater mobility mean that parents must look for alternative help with their children. Here are some of the people who may contribute such help.

Many working couples employ an in-home caregiver, either full- or part-time, to provide continuity of care. It may be possible to share one with a friend.

A babysitter you hire on your occasional night out should be known to the baby before being left in charge.

The single relative or friend is often invaluable in bringing a special relationship to the child.

The center of it all: mother, father, and baby. Who would have thought that one small person could make such demands?

Grandparents, if they can spare the time, are often the best caregivers; they have built-in love and commitment.

person is the mother, but it need not be. If the father or grandmother or someone else fills the bill, the baby will not complain. But whoever it is, there is no doubt that a special relationship and affinity between that person and the child is essential to the child's development. In the first two years of life, continual and gentle attention to his needs generates a trust and confidence that carries over into all his other relationships.

The primary caregiver need not be the only caregiver. In past generations, grandparents, aunts, uncles, and older siblings were all involved to a degree in child-rearing. A child was not limited to the viewpoints, influences, and role-modeling of one or two close adults; he was exposed to the diverse ideas and styles of an extended family. A continuous, warm, satisfying interaction with a mother figure in the first one or two years of life is essential to a child's future emotional health, but sometimes this is seen as an all or nothing proposition. Does having a substitute mother for part of each day compromise the mothering? A number of studies have been done on the questions of separation, and their conclusions are reassuring to parents who share the care of their children with others in order to work.

According to these studies, mothering is no less important than it ever was, but well-planned, creative substitute care is not only safe, it may well provide distinct advantages to a child. Children of some nonworking mothers have been noted to be more timid and less willing to explore, experiment, and enter into new situations than children who spend some of their time in day care. These tendencies were particularly apparent among boys. When it comes to learning new skills and collecting information, children of working mothers seem to do as well as or better than children whose mothers are at home. They seem to have fewer stereotyped ideas of "a woman's place" (which could be useful in view of the world they will probably live in). It is also worth remembering that a child who is in the care of another person for 3 hours each weekday morning spends only 15 hours per week away from home–and 153 hours per week at home.

Ultimately, the differences found among children of working and nonworking mothers have been minor and cannot be judged as good or bad. Neither is it possible to say whether the differences are due to the mother's working or not.

RETURNING TO WORK
The degree of a baby's dependency changes with his age. In general, it changes as follows.

Up to Six Months. A baby will smile more readily at his mother or father or at the adult who cares for him most but will not object to strangers. He does not regard himself as separate from the adult giving him care.

Six to Twelve Months. He begins to separate himself from his caregiver but clings to the familiar adult and demonstrates fear of

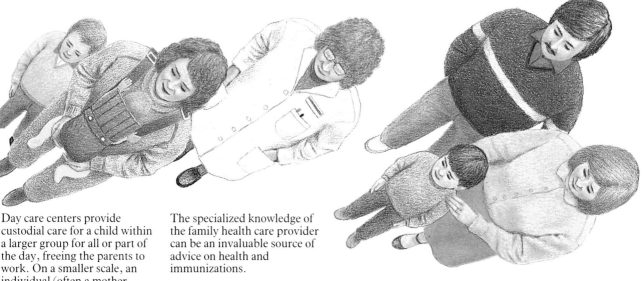

Day care centers provide custodial care for a child within a larger group for all or part of the day, freeing the parents to work. On a smaller scale, an individual (often a mother herself) may take care of several children in her own home.

The specialized knowledge of the family health care provider can be an invaluable source of advice on health and immunizations.

Friends and neighbors with children of their own are often the best caregiving solution. It is often possible to work out reciprocal schemes of help; babysitting co-ops represent such an arrangement.

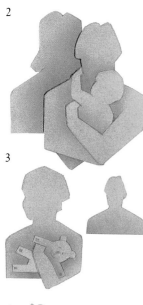

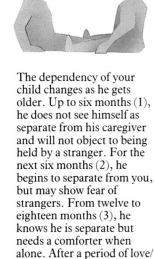

The dependency of your child changes as he gets older. Up to six months (1), he does not see himself as separate from his caregiver and will not object to being held by a stranger. For the next six months (2), he begins to separate from you, but may show fear of strangers. From twelve to eighteen months (3), he knows he is separate but needs a comforter when alone. After a period of love/hate for you and intense shyness, he will find separation more tolerable at around two years (4), and he will start to function as an individual, trusting others.

strangers. He begins to explore, crawling away from you but looking back to see if you are still there. If danger threatens, he quickly returns to homebase.

Twelve to Eighteen Months. He knows that he is a separate person, but he still needs to be looked after. Walking brings greater independence, although he still likes to be able to return to homebase if the need arises. His movement is outward–away from you– but he cannot always bear real separation and often finds a mother substitute to comfort him. This could be a blanket or a favorite toy that he uses as a support when his mother is not there.

Eighteen to Twenty-four Months. Love and hate battle as he both needs and resents needing you. He feels close to you but knows he is separate from you, and this leads to conflicts, frustration, and temper tantrums. He will bring back experiences, words, and objects to share with you and may be intensely shy with strangers. This does not mean that you cannot leave him, however; you must, so he can learn that you will return and that you have a separate life.

Two Years and Older. His nurturing has been sufficiently supportive that he now feels confidence and trust in others. Separation is more tolerable and the image of you as parents has become part of him so that he will incorporate your rules of behavior and conscience. Although he is able to function as an individual, separate from you, his attachment to you will last for life.

Here are some of the ways by which you can help him develop this sturdiness of growth:

Your . . .	teaches him . . .
love	to return love to you and to others.
regularity and reliability	trust.
ability to tolerate his anger	to accept limits and still love.
allowing him freedom to learn and to explore while still supporting him	confidence to move outward to a world beyond the family.

No chart of a child's development can ever be exact–your child is an individual–but from the stages of development and attachment shown above, it follows that a mother who intends to go back to work outside the home had best to do so before her baby shows fear of strangers, which usually begins at about six months. Conversely, if by this age he is used to the substitute mother who

will be caring for him, his mother may be able to go back to work knowing that her baby is content to be left behind. If circumstances allow, however, she may prefer to wait until the baby is more independent and sociable (usually from twelve months on).

EFFECTS OF SEPARATION ON THE MOTHER

Even if you decided before the birth that you would return to work, putting it into practice will not be painless. Mothers sometimes miss their babies more than babies miss their mothers. Apart from practical considerations (and despite all reassurances), she may still experience feelings of guilt. Acquaintances may imply not only that she ought to stay at home but that she ought to be happy to do so–and that to do otherwise signifies failure as a mother.

This is not a comfortable situation, particularly when you may have mixed feelings about it yourself, but bear in mind that the ideal of twenty-four-hour motherhood is not necessarily valid. In recent years, social changes have given many more women the incentive to pursue a career outside the home. They have also encouraged men and women to form greater expectations of fulfillment and companionship within marriage, and the homebound mother may find it difficult to maintain those expectations without outside stimulus.

If you are a single parent, you may have no choice but to return to work, and your priorities and needs may be different from those of adults sharing a stable relationship. But if you are one of a pair, the first essential is to make sure you are agreed on what you are doing. Adding conflict to all the other emotions present at this time will be destructive; an atmosphere of resentment or begrudging martyrdom is not a healthful one to bring up your baby in.

To work or not to work is something you may have to discuss together at some length; if your wishes do not coincide, you will have to concentrate on reaching a workable compromise. However efficient your baby-minding arrangements are, concessions will probably have to be made on both sides: Domestic responsibilities may have to be shared and baby routines reallocated. It is best to establish the framework early.

A mother who does go back to work may be shocked by the special relationship her baby develops with whomever looks after him while she is away. She may feel as though her place has been usurped in the child's affections–even though this is only partially true. But the alternative–that he cries every time she hands him over and is unhappy whenever she is away–is not very attractive either. The caregiver will give the child one sort of care, and the mother will give him another; in the end, the working mother must be satisfied with that situation. One trap she must not fall into is to undermine the caregiver's authority. That is why the choice of substitute care is so important (see pages 190-91).

One alternative to working full-time may be to work part-time or to share a job. Part-time work varies in type and availability, but there often are occasional Saturday, evening, or holiday rush jobs to be had. Job-sharing–where two people share one job, working mornings or afternoons or for half the week in turn–is a new idea, but some large corporations have instituted it and the idea may grow. Employers convinced of the practicability of job-sharing believe that they get a day and a half's work out of two people rather than a day out of one! It is easiest to convince an employer to let you try job sharing if you worked there before your baby was born and are a valued employee. But even if you are looking for such a position with a new company, it is not out of the question. Try writing to firms stating your qualifications and experience and suggesting the idea. Another method is to offer yourself and a friend for a single job; that might enable you not only to share a job but to share the care of each other's families.

WHO WILL CARE FOR YOUR BABY?
Finding the right kind of care may be difficult and may take time. In theory, at least, several alternatives exist.

The Father. If his temperament is suited to it and you are both agreed, the father may well be the best alternative. The possibility may arise if he works at home, if his job is less well paid than the mother's and he is happy to give it up, or if he does not have a job. Some parents work outside the home on a shift system, but this usually means you have very little family life together.

If he works outside the home, the father is traditionally expected to leave his wife and new baby and return to work after a few days' paternity leave, if indeed he takes off any time at all. But many fathers today are intimately concerned with the arrival and nurturing of their children and increasingly are taking an active and knowledgeable part

The father may well be the best alternative caregiver to the mother, if this is agreeable and feasible to both.

Grandparents often work out wonderfully as caregivers, but they may have different ideas on discipline and feeding.

in their upbringing. The father who wishes to be involved but must return to work may well feel a sense of loss. It should not be difficult, however, to arrange a routine that allows the father to remain involved with the baby in the hours he spends at home. In the early days, diapering, bottle-feeding, putting to rest, and soothing would help a new father develop an attachment for his baby that will grow as the baby does.

It is a mistake to bring up children in such a way that only one parent can satisfy their needs to the exclusion of the other.

Friends, Relatives and Neighbors. This arrangement may be fine provided the details are agreed upon. How many hours a week? Is it accepted willingly or grudgingly? Do your ideas on feeding, "spoiling," cuddling, discipline, and other child-rearing issues coincide? If not, are you all prepared to compromise? Is the minder likely to become possessive and undermine the mother's place in her baby's affections? Grandparents often work out wonderfully as caregivers because they already have a built-in commitment to the baby even before he arrives, but the older generation sometimes has different ideas on discipline and feeding. Be sure to sort all this out before you begin the arrangement.

In-Home Care. If you can afford it, you may decide to employ someone to care for your child in your home. This can be an ideal arrangement because it provides one-to-one attention in a familiar environment. You will need to choose with great care; it is essential to talk to the caregiver's previous employers. Obviously you will look for warmth, gentleness, stamina, experience, and knowledge—but flexibility is no less important. Although many approaches and solutions exist to virtually all child-rearing issues, all parents have their own values, styles, and goals. Try to find someone who is willing to function as an extension of your family, not as a rigid, possessive competitor who will insist on the superiority of her knowledge. Someone who qualifies under your particular standards could offer a great deal to all the family, in both sensitivity and experience (see page 191).

Family Day Care. In family day care, your child is cared for in the home of a caregiver who is also caring for other children who may range from infancy to school age. This may be a practical and more economical alternative to individual care in your own home, providing the comfortableness of a home away from home for your child as well as the stimulation of the company of other children of differing ages. It is essential to interview the prospective caregiver in that person's own home at a time when other children are there. You will then be able to see the caregiver's attitude toward the children, managerial and peace-making abilities, patience, and personal involvement with them. Facilities are important (see page 191).

Not every caregiver chooses to be one through love of children or interest in their development. With children of her own, a mother may find that caring for other children is a way of adding to family income without having to work outside the home. It is reasonable to ask, "Why did you choose this work?" Of course, the care given can still be excellent even if financial need was the primary motivation.

Day Care Centers. A day care center is a facility other than a home where groups of children spend a few hours or all day. There are many kinds of centers—specialized centers for the exceptional child, those following a particular developmental philosophy, others catering to specific religions—but not all may exist where you live. In some centers, parents take part in the child care; in others, the center is run through administrators. Some are run for profit, others are part of a chain, and yet others are partially funded by federal, state, or local government agencies. Such centers have a sliding scale of fees to make them accessible to everyone. Unfortunately, there are also centers that are little more than depositories offering children shelter and an adult within reach in case of disaster.

All states regulate day care centers, but requirements may vary considerably. Most specify a certain amount of space (indoor and outdoor) for each child, minimum safety and hygiene standards, a minimum ratio of adults to children, medical backup in case of emergencies, and general requirements regarding qualifications for the staff of the center. Applicable regulations can be obtained from the licensing agency responsible for day care oversight in your state. Federal day care regulations (applicable to all day care centers that receive federal funds) can be obtained by writing to the Day Care Division, Administration for Children, Youth and Families, Box 1182, Washington, D.C. 20013.

HEALTH PROBLEMS AND DAY CARE
The more your child mixes, the greater is the chance of his catching one of the infections children are so prone to. In a well-staffed and well-run center that provides adequate space and attention to hygiene, the overall rates of infection are little (if at all) higher than for children cared for at home and playing with friends. Routine exclusion of every child who has a cold rarely protects the other children to any significant degree, but do inquire about the regulations that apply

when you visit the center. Skin infections such as impetigo and ringworm and infestations of lice or scabies worry parents a great deal, but all are easily managed problems that require only prompt attention and (probably) a brief exclusion from the center while treatment is begun. Problems such as these occur even in the cleanest of surroundings and do not necessarily reflect adversely on the center or the children there.

Outbreaks of serious diseases, hepatitis among them, are the exception rather than the rule, but it is important that everyone involved in day care be alert to possible dangers and know when to react quickly. Scrupulous attention to hygiene, especially by employees who prepare food, change diapers, or both, is essential. The American Academy of Pediatrics' Committee on Infants and Preschool Children has recommended preventive procedures. Ask if the center is familiar with these recommendations when you make your preliminary visits.

HOW YOUR CHILD MAY REACT TO SEPARATION

There is no certain way of anticipating what effect separation will have on a baby or young child. It could take the form of tears, extra clinging, apathy, or aggressive or regressive behavior—bedwetting, tantrums, thumb-sucking. Handled with affection, sensitivity, and (above all) patience, these are temporary setbacks.

Many centers have plans for the gradual introduction of the child into the new situation. This often requires a parent to be present for a few days or even a few weeks while the child adjusts. If you are concerned about how the transition period will be handled and especially if your own schedule will have to be rearranged to permit your presence, inquire in advance about this. The transition may not be easy for any of you, but children—like adults—cannot grow without anxiety. It is up to the adult who cares for the child to monitor the child's level of anxiety and to support the child as he learns to grow.

Regardless of the type of care you choose, a period away from home will seem long and exhausting to a child, and he may well have reached saturation point before you are there to pick him up. If you can manage it, a child under three should not be left for more than four to six hours a day, which may mean that one parent can work only part-time. Alternatively you could arrange for a friend or relative to pick up the child and care for him until you return.

Be prepared for tears or shyness at the beginning of some days. Some children withdraw into a corner and refuse to enter into activities. These are normal reactions;

an experienced caregiver will be able to help your child through these stages. It is one more reason to have regular talks with the caregiver about your child's behavior. Try leaving him a small object to take care of for you until you return. Have a plan for what you will do when you meet again—something special for lunch, a visit to his grandparents, a shopping expedition—so that he has something to look forward to.

One of the rituals all children love and find consoling is a kind of debriefing session in which they tell you what they did during the day. It fixes the day and the experiences in a child's mind, and allows both of you to share and talk about them. Bathtime, bedtime, and mealtime can be good moments for this, but so can the walk home. Do not force the pace: Being left without a familiar parent causes your child to expend a lot of energy, and he may be tired and want to relax a bit before he begins to share his thoughts with you. Some children flatly refuse to give information on demand. Remaining silent, on the other hand, is a great way of getting people (including your child) to confide in you.

Some children fear that somehow home will change while they are away. A favorite doll or stuffed animal left to "keep an eye on things" can bridge the gap. They are also sometimes alarmed by a parent's new hairstyle or unfamiliar clothes. Mention changes before they take place, if you can.

If your child continues to resist separation despite all your care, this might indicate a problem that goes deeper than a temporary reaction. In such a case, consider getting professional advice rather than shelving the problem by discontinuing day care.

DAY CARE CHECKLIST

The following checklist of points to note when deciding on day care for your child has been adapted from *A Parent's Guide to Day Care* published by the Day Care Division of the Administration for Children, Youth and Families of the Department of Health and Human Services. You can order your own copy of this very useful booklet by writing to them at Box 1182, Washington, DC 20013.

In general, when you are deciding on in-home care, interview the prospective caregiver in your own home with your child present so that you can see how they interact. When considering family day care or a day care center, you will find it less distracting to visit alone, perhaps taking your child with you for a second or third visit. Do not expect, however, to be warmly welcomed if you just drop in; a good caregiver has a program with planned activities and routines, and visitors can be a disruption. Planned exploratory visits are necessary, and you will be welcomed if you make arrangements in advance.

In-Home Care

☐ Does the prospective caregiver appear warm, friendly, gentle, and relaxed, with a sense of humor?

☐ Does she have child care experience?

☐ Can she provide verifiable references from previous employers?

☐ Does she appear happy about herself and her job?

☐ Is she someone with whom your child would be happy?

☐ Is she someone with whom you might share attitudes and ideas about child-rearing?

☐ Will she treat your child as an individual, taking time to listen, and to understand his needs at different ages?

☐ Is she prepared to cuddle, comfort, feed, and change a young baby and concurrently to play with him and talk constructively, pointing out things to look at, listen to, and touch?

☐ Will she cooperate with your chosen approach to toilet training?

☐ Does she satisfy you as to her hygiene and (if applicable) as to the food she prepares for your child?

☐ Does she appear able to help your child grow mentally and physically by letting him explore and think things through, and by providing stimulating companionship and support?

Family Day Care

To the requirements for in-home care add:

☐ Does she seem to have enough time to look after all the children in her care?

☐ Is the state regulation governing the caregiver-to-children ratio (if one exists) being observed?

☐ Will she help your child become independent, to mix with others, respecting others' backgrounds and cultures?

☐ Will she take time to discuss your child regularly with you?

☐ Can she provide routines and rules your child can understand?

☐ Will she arrrange for yearly health assessments for herself?

☐ Does she provide art and music supplies suited to the ages of the children?

☐ Does she provide safe, child-proof settings, enabling a baby to crawl freely and a toddler to explore freely?

☐ Does she provide space and opportunities for toddlers to play quietly and actively indoors and out, whether they are playing alone or with others?

☐ Will she allow your child to watch special programs on television that have been approved by you?

☐ Will she otherwise limit or forbid television viewing to prevent its becoming a substitute for her attention?

☐ Will she allow the child to speak both English and the family's native language if it is different?

☐ Does the site look clean and comfortable, with enough space for all children to move freely and safely?

☐ Are safety precautions adequate—are there caps on electrical outlets, safe storage places for anything potentially dangerous, safety plans for exits, protected radiators, smoke detectors, fire extinguishers, and so on?

☐ Are there safety bars on windows above the first floor and gates at the top and the bottom of stairs?

☐ Is there a potty or child seat in the bathroom?

☐ Is there a clean and safe place to change diapers?

☐ Is hygiene (washing hands after diaper changes and before meals) attended to?

Day Care Center

To the requirements for in-home care and family day care, add:

☐ Does the center have an up-to-date license, if one is required by the state?

☐ Are there enough furniture, playthings, and equipment for all the children in care, and is the equipment safe, in good repair, and suitable for children of the ages present?

☐ Does the center have enough bathrooms?

☐ Does it have enough mats or cribs so that children can take naps?

☐ Are there separate crib sheets for each baby in care?

☐ Is there sufficient heat and light?

☐ Is the outdoor play area fenced and clean?

☐ Is the food provided sufficient, acceptable, and nutritious?

☐ Are there adequate facilities for sick children, first aid kits, and a backup emergency plan if the caregivers are unable to reach you—that is, is medical help on call?

When you visit a center take note if the children seem happy and occupied and if they interact happily with the staff, climbing on laps and chatting freely. Be wary of a center that is overly tidy and quiet: Such virtues do not belong to childhood! Ask what arrangements would be made if the principal caregiver were called away or taken ill. Would there be adequate substitutes so that the center could remain open?

OTHER SEPARATIONS

Children experience separation because of things other than parents working outside the home: marital estrangement and divorce, hospitalization (whether their own–see pages 112-13–or that of a close family member), death, placement in a foster home, even the birth of a new baby in the family. As much as you wish to protect your child from the pain associated with any of these other separations, that may not always be possible.

BEREAVEMENT

The death of a family member or of a close family friend is a traumatic experience for adults and may be more or less so for a child, depending on the closeness of the relationship, the circumstances of the home, and the age and character of the child.

Any death in the family has an impact on the children–whether what is involved is a miscarriage (when the child is old enough to know that a baby is on the way), a stillbirth, or the death of a relative or friend with whom the child has a close relationship. The painful event becomes part of the family's story and colors the child's viewpoint in many ways.

Babies up to six months of age show little or no response to a death, even a parent's death. From six months to three years of age, the young child will be much more likely to react to the loss of a close familiar.

The death of a sister or brother may lead the child to feel guilty, as though anger she may at times have felt toward the sibling caused the death. She may also fear that she too will die.

Death of a Parent

The death of a parent is certain to affect a child, and more so if the parent who died was the child's primary caregiver. At about the age of three or four, a boy or girl will tend to be particularly affected by the loss of a parent of his or her own sex because that is the stage when the child is beginning to depend on same-sex role models. If bereavement should happen at this age, it is a great help if a relative or friend of the sex of the lost parent is able to step in with interest and involvement.

To the bewilderment and grief of the child whose primary caregiver dies, the surviving parent must add the practical difficulties of arranging care for the child. If the baby or young child is, out of necessity, cared for by several relatives or friends for short periods while a permanent solution is being sought, the child may learn to trust no one–believing that, if she allows herself to love and become attached to another, she will only lose that person.

A young child also has no idea of time. She may mourn and wait for the parent to return much longer than might be expected. The stages of grief in children most often follow the same pattern as in adults: disbelief, anger, sadness, and finally some kind of acceptance or almost indifference–as though he has forgotten the loss. The stages have to be worked through, and it is only when this has been done that the child will be able to develop a trusting relationship with someone who, it is hoped, will provide lasting care.

If a substitute caregiver is to be provided, the main prerequisite is kindness. Natural parents are interested in the child's development and take care to foster it. If one parent dies, the child needs to find the lost support and interest elsewhere. However much the remaining parent tries to fill the gap, the involvement of another encouraging adult is valuable.

Helping a Child Grieve

Death must be properly explained to a child, though in terms simple enough to suit her age and ability to comprehend. It is useless to imply that the dead person will come back. If the child is about three, she may be old enough to attend the funeral, but those surrounding the child must assess the individual nature of the child and decide whether under the particular circumstances she should attend.

Children need to express their pain, they should not be discouraged from crying and talking about the loss, since expressing grief may lead to less distorted and painful memories later. Sometimes, however, a child may show little sadness. This may be an example of children's tendency to repress distressing experiences, or it may be that the interested adults, preoccupied with their own grief, are simply unaware of all the undercurrents in the child's expressions. The support of professionals or people in like circumstances can help sustain parent and child through these distressing periods.

A period of sorrow and adjustment may be inevitable in your child's life, but you must become her support system at that time. What affects your child will also affect you; what affects you will affect the child. If you yourself are suffering from any event or experience, it may be doubly difficult for you to give your child wholehearted attention,

Children may experience loss through divorce, illness, or death. In all of these situations, a period of sorrow may be inevitable.

but parents who have experienced distressing times invariably say that their children supported them.

Like other single parents, widows and widowers should maintain outside interests so that the children do not become too dependent on the one-parent relationship nor the adult too dependent on the children (either of which would make the inevitable later separation more difficult).

SEPARATION AND DIVORCE

In the United States today it is projected that one in two marriages will end in divorce. Unless a different agreement has been reached before divorce, custody of any children involved is usually given to one parent, with the other allowed varying degrees of access. The father of the children is most commonly made responsible for financial maintenance. Usually custody of the children, when decided by the court, is given to the mother, although in recent years fathers have assumed responsibility or joint custody has been decreed with increasing frequency. Joint custody of the children—when the relationship between the partners is amicable—is often very satisfactory and allows the children to maintain a relationship with each parent. Difficulties may arise, however, if the parents live at some distance from each other.

In the past, mothers who were not given custody often felt inadequate and sensitive to the implication that they were less capable of caring for the children than the fathers were. This need not apply nowadays when fathers frequently assume equal care of the children even before separation and when women's expectations and opportunities in life have changed.

Effects of Divorce on Children

If the divorce has been preceded by a period of quarreling, fighting, and discord in the home, the final separation may come as a relief to the children. But a child who loves the parent who is no longer living with her suffers bereavement, and everything should be done to help her over her sorrow. Divorce is seldom entirely amicable. Amidst the heightened emotions of this time, it is not uncommon for parents to use their children as weapons (or targets), venting the anger they feel toward each other through (or on) the child. At such a time, professional counseling may be imperative (see page 230). The children's reaction to divorce may well mirror the parents': relief, spite, anger, guilt, failure, loneliness, or bewilderment. Through conscious effort on the part of one or both parents to continue providing stability, warmth, and consistency, the long-term effects of divorce can be overcome. But it may take years for a child to accept the divorce or to give up the idea that her parents will one day reunite.

The Children's Reaction

If the divorce is the culmination of a period of dissension, quarreling, and even physical violence, the child may during those preceding months exhibit all the symptoms of strain listed on page 190 as consequences of separation. If the parent who is the child's primary caregiver is depressed and withdrawn, that person is unlikely to be able to give the child warmth and attention, instead perhaps ignoring the child or treating her harshly and with impatience. If the parent is apathetic, he or she may indulge the child too much, ignoring bad behavior.

One of the pitfalls to be avoided in divorce is the temptation to maneuver the child into siding with one of her parents against the other. This puts the psychological burden of the split onto the child by demanding that she decide where her loyalties lie. It would be no wonder if the toddler retaliated by playing off one parent against the other.

Children are frighteningly vulnerable to the stress and difficulties of their elders. Once again, the adult may have to come to terms with personal suffering in order to explain *in terms the child can understand* just what is happening. The withdrawal of love is an experience that can mar a lifetime.

If the aim is to keep bitterness away from the child, what happens if the absent parent does not visit, write, or take responsibility for the child? Clearly, the burden of sustaining the child falls on the custodial parent (see section on single parents, below).

Within limits, a child of two or three can understand parental sadness, but its intensity needs to be diluted because the aim must always be that the child feel wanted and worthy of love. To pass on the ability to love may be the greatest achievement most humans can aspire to, and it begins with valuing oneself as a person. Children from broken homes have been shown to become subsequently delinquent less often than children from unbroken homes dominated by neglect and disharmony.

SINGLE PARENTHOOD

A single parent can provide the emotional stability needed to enable a child to thrive, but it undoubtedly takes more courage and commitment than if the parent were supported by a partner.

A single parent needs support. Under fortunate circumstances, it will be offered by friends and family. Such help should at all times be welcomed, not only because of its practical and emotional benefits to the parent but because it will enable the child to develop wider social relationships.

Single parents are not always lone parents. A parent may be bringing up a child alone following divorce or bereavement, in which case the absent parent has been a presence in the child's life. In these cases, it is right to keep alive by occasional reference a certain memory of the absent parent's existence.

If a mother is single because the father has drifted away before or soon after the birth, her loneliness may be extreme. She may decide to stay home, supporting herself and her child on public assistance, or she may decide to go out to work. If she chooses the latter and her baby is well cared for, that may be a good solution because then the mother will have a life outside the home. Staying at home with a baby all day, without the support of a partner, can lead to a feeling of aimlessness; babies are not always the most stimulating of companions. She also needs to look ahead to when the baby will have become a toddler and then a schoolchild, and when she will herself not be so needed. She may miss the child's company excessively if that has been the focus of her entire life.

For a single working parent, day care for the child is of paramount importance. All of the qualities of care listed previously (pages 190-91) must be met, but continuity of care and warmth of affection must go to the top of the list. Through these, the child will learn to trust others and to make continuing attachments – and the parent also will have support and peace of mind.

One difficulty the lone parent may experience is that the child has little opportunity to develop relationships with adults of the same sex as the absent parent. Involving members of the extended family – grandparents, aunts, uncles, older siblings – offers a possible solution. This is particularly important at about the age of three if the child is the same sex as the absent parent because then the child will want to begin to identify with an adult of the same sex. Having a succession of boyfriends or girlfriends may not be the answer. Even though they may have affection for the child, the frequent temporariness of their involvement can only lead the child to experience further uncertainty and distrust of personal relationships.

A single parent should never hesitate to take advantage of any help offered by

A divorced father can miss his child as much as the child misses him. His continued involvement may be important to the family's well-being.

friends. Professional counseling is also available if needed. With stable resolve and commitment, a single parent can be confident of rearing children successfully.

STEP-FAMILIES

When a parent remarries, the child must adapt to the step-parent, particularly when that person is living in the same household. A child under three is more likely to adapt quickly than an older child with longstanding ties to the absent parent. But a child of any age who has been the sole object of one parent's attention will find it hard suddenly to have to share that attention. The step-parent needs to tread a careful path of warmth and interest without intruding on the child's relationship with both or one of the natural parents.

The Role of Step-parent

Step-parents can make enormous successes of their new role, but the initial stages may not be easy. Overdiscipline, overindulgence, overanxiety—all may play their part. It is important that the parent and the step-parent talk about discipline, rewards, general treatment, and so on before they marry so that they present a united front. A step-parent with no natural children may be surprised to find just how much time the demands of a young baby take and how much they limit their caregivers' freedom.

Endless patience and tolerance may be called for. The stress signals (page 190) that the child may put out are sometimes enough to try the patience of a saint. If acceptable to all, it might help if the step-parent takes on some of the routine care of the young child—bathing, perhaps, or a weekly outing—so that the child feels she is important to each parent in a different way and is certain of some special period when she has the sole attention of the new adult.

Think carefully before you change the child's name. A name is part of a child, and she may feel that if she loses it she is losing part of herself.

Joining two families is never easy. If a wide difference in ages exists, the older children must have time and attention for themselves and must not be expected to help too much.

When Two Families Join

The situation may be further complicated if two families with children are united. Things sometimes go more smoothly if a gap exists between the two age groups. Although young children can curtail the freedom of the older children as regards holidays, outings, and daily routines, it may be easier to separate the demands of each group and give individual attention in that situation than if the children of the two families are close in age.

If the parents wish to have children of their own, it could be a heavy undertaking for a toddler to have to cope with a new parent *and* a new baby. It would be wiser to wait until the older child is settled into the new situation before embarking on a second family. How long the gap should be is something only the parents themselves can assess through their observations and knowledge of their own child, but the aim must always be to make the first child realize she has a secure place in the family and is valued as a person in her own right.

ADDING TO THE FAMILY

An addition to the family also involves a degree of separation of the parents from the previous children or child, since no longer will they be receiving as much undivided attention.

Having a second or third child when the next youngest is only a year or eighteen months old imposes a physical strain on a mother. Not only must she cope with lifting a heavy toddler while she is pregnant, but after the birth she must face demands from the two that cannot help but clash. What a one-year-old wants, he wants *now*–food, attention, or hauling down from the wobbly stool he has managed to climb while you were starting to change the new baby's diaper. A two- to three-year-old understands a bit more about waiting his turn, is interested in seeing what is going on with the baby, and can be very helpful with fetching and carrying–as long as he is made to feel useful.

A gap of about two years is thought to provide adequate time for the mother to recover from her earlier pregnancy and from the birth of her first child, as well as for the first child to gain enough security to carry him through possible squalls ahead. A longer gap may be your preference and is workable, but it may be difficult for the older child if you add to the family when he is beginning play group or full-time school. These are times of upheaval for him, and he will be disturbed if he thinks he is being pushed off to school and his place at home is being taken by another baby.

Some parents prefer to have their babies close together so that the children can grow as companions and also in order to release themselves from baby care in a shorter time. What parents gain in earlier independence they probably pay for in greater concentration of care and work over the shorter time. Children born close together usually become close emotionally when they grow up if the parents have been able to provide sufficient support to each child.

PREPARING YOUR CHILD FOR A NEW BABY

However well you prepare your child for the arrival of a new brother or sister, it is still a surprise when the promise becomes a reality. The third or fourth child is usually accepted into the family with a kind of resigned stoicism, but the second is a different matter and makes the most difference to the first.

Second and subsequent babies seem easier than the first for parents to manage, but for a few months at least they need as much attention as any new baby. The older child first has to cope with his mother's disappearing for a few days and then reappearing with a new creature. Moreover, this creature remains all day and all night and at times interferes with the previously pleasant routine.

Do not talk too soon about the coming baby. A toddler who cannot understand "today, tomorrow, and yesterday" is not going to understand "nine months." Drop a few hints at around the seventh month, let him feel your stomach, and take notice of babies in strollers you pass on your walks.

It may be a good idea to "borrow" a friend's young baby occasionally so that the toddler gets used to seeing another baby on his parents' laps.

If any changes need to be made in the toddler's routine, make them well in advance. If he is to be moved out of his room or crib, make the change and ensure he is happy with the arrangement before the new baby arrives. If he sleeps in your room, think about whether it would be wise to move him out before the baby arrives; if the idea distresses him, consider putting the baby into another room and keeping the older child with you.

An older child can also become very possessive if he sees some of his outgrown clothes being prepared for the new arrival. If that happens, give them back to him or ask if you may borrow one or two. Never appropriate a toy or piece of favorite equipment for the new baby without the child's permission –and be prepared to give it back if he changes his mind.

Try not to start him at playschool or full-time school around the time the new baby arrives. Either do it well in advance, so the routine is established, or wait until he is used to the baby before sending him away from home for even part of the day. If being away from you is not already part of his experience, plan a few occasions when he can remain without you at his grandparents' or at a childminder's or playschool so that he gets used to the fact that although you go away you do come back.

Some toddlers feel safe only if they can keep an eye on the baby, so if the older child is used to going to a childminder or play-school, he may want to stay home more with the new baby and with you. Give him time and things that are entirely his. Talk or watch television with him while you feed the baby, or read him a story while the baby sleeps. Involve him in as much responsibility as he can cope with–fetching towels, testing bathwater. Most toddlers cannot wait to soap the baby's back in the bath, although the baby never seems so enthusiastic about it.

Let him help with tasks that are clearly beyond the baby's abilities. A toddler is usually very surprised at how helpless a baby is, and it brings out his protectiveness. Helplessness thus has its advantages.

The crawling baby can infuriate a toddler –knocking over his blocks, tearing his draw-ings, and eating his books. Remove potential trouble before it happens; you cannot blame the older child if he is angry at seeing his possessions maltreated.

Do
Give him a special new feeding plate and spoon, so he feels grown up. Take him to the store and let him choose his own.
Let him join in all the routine of baby care, imitating it with a doll or stuffed animal if he wants.

Do Not
Let grandparents, friends, and neighbors coo over the object in the stroller and ignore him, or bring the new baby presents and leave him out.
Worry if he regresses to bedwetting, thumb-sucking, or bottle-feeding.
Forget that parents can cooperate in taking some of the heat off the primary caregiver.

HAVING TWINS
Twins occur about once in every eighty-six births in the United States. Fraternal twins are three times more common than identical ones (see page 201). Fraternal twins tend

A toddler may be surprised at the
helplessness of a young baby. It is
a time of adjustment—and one not
always easy for the older child.

Involve the older child in as much responsibility as she can cope with – but keep in mind that she may feel supplanted.

to run in families, whereas no similar tendency seems to exist with identical twins. In about 80 percent of all cases, the prospective parents know in advance that they will have twins, but that still leaves 20 percent to be amazed at the last moment. There is no doubt, though, that having twins (or triplets, or more!) presents special practical and emotional challenges for parents.

Because twins are often born prematurely, frequently at about the thirty-seventh week, it is not uncommon for the mother to be asked to spend the last few weeks of her pregnancy resting in the hospital. Once mother and babies are home, the balancing act begins. One big advantage is that the arrival of twins usually excites a great deal of interest among family members and friends. Parents should take advantage of that and accept whatever help is offered – or even orchestrate things a bit.

Think carefully before you buy two of everything. It is possible to double up on a lot of equipment. You may need two cribs and two highchairs, for instance, but you can probably get by with fewer than twice the number of stretch suits you would need for one, and you certainly will not need two changing tables and two baby tubs. You will need a double stroller of some sort. Ask advice from other parents you know. Some side-by-side strollers, for instance, do not fit easily through standard doorways; the models that put the babies one in front of the other or facing tend not to fold away for easy portability.

Establishing a daily routine for twins requires a lot of coordination. Two basics: simplify, and involve both parents as actively as possible. The morning feeding, for example, can go quite smoothly if each of you takes one baby. If your choice is to breastfeed – and there is no reason why the mother cannot, so long as she eats more than her normal caloric requirement – the father can

wake and bring the first baby to the mother and half an hour later bring the next one (who will probably have wakened on his own by then). While the mother is nursing the second, the father can top and tail the first and otherwise look to his needs.

Your health care provider is another important figure in your twins' lives. It is a fact that twins make more trips to the health care provider's office in the first few years than do single children, largely because of their tendency to share infections. When one twin sneezes, you can be reasonably sure that the second one will have a cold within a few days.

These and other practical considerations will soon be second nature to you, but what about the psychological aspects of having twins? There are tremendous advantages to being a twin. Mutual support and the shared sense of security can help each through many difficult situations. At the same time, each child has to struggle to maintain his individuality in a world that tends to treat him as part of a set. Twins have to learn not only to separate from their parents but to separate emotionally from each other. That is why, right from the beginning, they must be treated as individuals, not as mirror images. Some specific approaches are worth considering, but in the end your sensitivity to your children as separate selves should govern the approach you take.

There is a strong temptation to give twins matching names: Donald and Ronald, Jane and Joan. Our advice is not to. Nothing is more personal than one's own name; twins have to share so much of their lives that it is unfair to ask them to share their names as well. Dressing twins alike is another common practice. You may find it convenient when they are small, but as soon as they begin to express their own opinions about how they wish to dress, let them be different if that is what they choose.

As your twins grow, try your best not to compare them. One may walk sooner; the other may speak earlier. The fact is they are two different children. No matter how hard you try to be even-handed, remember that the interaction between the twins themselves is an equally strong influence. Developmentally, one child may hold back or push along the other; it all depends on the temperamental response of each individual whether one strives to master the same skills or tends to lose interest in the task.

Support groups for families with twins exist to help parents deal with the day-to-day and long-term adventure of having twins (see page 231 for addresses). Sharing experiences can be a valuable resource, especially when you are feeling that the only thing more tiring

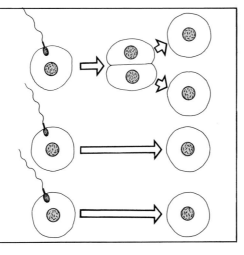

When one egg is fertilized by one sperm and then divides, the result is identical (monozygotic) twins. Usually they share one placenta, but each has its own umbilical cord.

If two eggs are released and then fertilized by two sperm, the result is fraternal or nonidentical (dizygotic) twins, each with its own placenta, amniotic sac, and umbilical cord.

than having a new baby in the house is having two.

FOSTERING

Fostering children demands a very special kind of commitment. By its very nature, you know that you will not be keeping the child or children indefinitely: You are not the parents, although you are being asked to supply a parent's commitment and continuity of affection. If you wish to foster a child, contact your city, county, or state social services department for the rules and procedures in effect in your area.

If you are accepted for fostering, the natural parents will probably be given rights of access to visit the child. A prolonged disruption between an infant and his natural parents should be avoided because it will become increasingly difficult for the child to transfer his attachment back to the parents. Serious questions are being raised by social workers, psychiatrists, and lawyers about the best arrangement for an infant who has been in foster care for more than a year with limited contact with his natural parents. The rights of these parents are more and more being balanced against the rights of the child to a stable home with his foster parents.

Fostering often proves an invaluable temporary solution to a difficult situation, and it can be an opportunity for the foster parents to provide great support to a natural parent who shows by regular visits or by keeping in touch a serious desire to take the child back when circumstances permit.

It is not easy to reconcile children to this divided care. The baby under six months is not likely to show a great deal of reaction but will begin to bond with the foster parents who, in his eyes, become the primary parents. The infant or toddler over six months who goes into foster care reacts usually with sadness and withdrawal and shows the symptoms of stress and regression associated with separation anxiety (see page 190). It may take weeks or months before the child begins to respond to the foster parents. If they are experienced in the stages of this transition period, they will be better able to cope with the child's behavior with understanding and sensitivity. If the child was abused or neglected previously, the period of difficult or withdrawn behavior may be longer. The support of the social worker in initial charge of the placement can be most helpful in such circumstances.

Obviously, the longer the child is in foster care, the more he will become attached to his foster parents. Although frequent visiting by the natural parents helps to keep the original attachment alive, it will–if continued over a long period–also divide the child's loyalties.

It is even more bewildering for a child to go back and forth between his parents' home and his foster parents'. Such a child may become indiscriminately friendly to everyone, an indication that he may become an emotionally impaired adult who is unable to form lasting relationships.

A child needs stability and permanence, and the child who has experienced several changes of home and caregiver in the first three years of his life is at risk for behavioral and emotional problems. He needs to belong to one set of parents who care and are committed to him. Because this need is increasingly being recognized, it is now more frequent for courts to decide to leave a child with his foster parents rather than to return him to the natural parent, particularly when they have had little contact.

ADOPTION

Giving a child for fostering is a less irrevocable act than giving him for adoption. Although fewer babies are available for adoption now that single parenthood carries somewhat less of a social stigma and abortion is available as an alternative in the case of unwanted pregnancy, babies and children from other countries, foster children whose natural parents have consented to adoption, handicapped babies, and older children constitute a significant number of adoptive children.

Before approving an adoption, social workers, doctors, and psychologists study the child carefully for any handicaps that may become apparent only later in life. It is particularly important to be honest about these matters because the parent who knowingly adopts a child with a handicap or possible handicap is more likely to maintain a strong relationship than the parent who finds out later.

Babies under six months usually appear to adapt readily to their new adoptive homes, but if a child has had an attachment to one or both birth parents–which will certainly be the case with older children–it will be more difficult for him to transfer his affection to the new parents. He may go through a period of aloofness or hostility that requires a lot of patience and possibly professional guidance to overcome.

Today many older adopted children are seeking to learn about their birth parents. Regulations on the opening of adoption records vary from state to state, and expert as well as public opinion is divided. It is clearly a highly emotional subject–the rights and feelings of the adopted child must be balanced against those of the birth and adoptive parents; often the conflict is painfully unresolvable.

Twins mean a lot more work, particularly in the early days when the father's help is doubly valuable.

A CHILD'S HEALTH A-Z

Few children escape their early years without an occasional setback in health–from bumps and bruises to minor ailments. But however slight an injury or illness may be, it can still cause distress to the child and concern to the parents, especially if they are not sure what action to take.

This section details ailments and conditions that may be encountered during the childhood years. Most likely you will be faced with only a few of them–some are more serious than others, and some more unusual than others. To help you quickly find the one you are looking for, entries are listed alphabetically, with cross references where necessary. As often as possible, the illness or condition is described first, then its cause, then its symptoms, and finally its treatment.

Emergencies and accidents invariably demand calmness and speed–two essentials difficult to achieve when you are upset and perhaps distracted by a tearful, frightened, and injured child. For swift reference, entries advising about situations that require immediate action have been printed in boldface type. Read through these entries *before* you are faced with an emergency. Then, if in spite of all precautions an emergency does arise–and even if you do not remember the exact treatment–knowing where to find the directions will help you keep control of the situation. "But what *is* an emergency?" you may ask, "Without medical training, how can I recognize a potentially dangerous situation? I don't want to panic and call for medical help unnecessarily, but I also don't want to fail to get help if the occasion demands it." Use the following list to guide you. If you observe any of the following, get immediate help:

1. If the child does not recognize you
2. If the child's skin color changes markedly
3. If the child experiences difficulty in breathing
4. If you suspect that the child has taken poison
5. If the child exhibits a marked change in appetite
6. If the child has a temperature above 104°F (40°C)
7. If the child suffers a temporary loss of consciousness
8. If the child exhibits behavior or symptoms unusual for him

Abrasion

An abrasion is a scrape of the skin from which blood or clear fluid oozes, eventually forming a scab. Wash well with soap and cool water, cleaning from the wound outward. Pat dry and apply an appropriate-size bandage. After 1 day, open it to the air. If the oozing has stopped and a scab has begun to form, do not wash, as this encourages infection. No bandage is necessary once a scab forms unless the abrasion is in a vulnerable place–on a knee, for instance.

Accident to the Teeth

Most injuries to primary teeth are sustained between the ages of 1½ and 2½. The upper central incisors are often the teeth injured because they are most prominent. The most common type of injury, a small fracture of a corner of a tooth, sometimes goes unnoticed. Occasionally, however, a blow causes the nerves and blood vessels at the center of a tooth to rupture. If bleeding occurs within the tooth, the blood trapped in the dentin will, within 3 weeks, discolor the tooth permanently.

Usually a dentist will not treat a traumatized primary tooth unless it develops an abscess, a pus-filled pimple on the gum caused by an infection at the root of an injured tooth. This infection can damage the developing permanent tooth, so it must be treated.

More severe injuries to teeth can produce fractures large enough to expose the chamber containing the nerves and blood vessels. A tooth pushed into the gum or completely knocked out is an emergency requiring immediate dental attention.

If a tooth is knocked out, it should be cleaned under cold running water and immediately pushed back into the socket. If you do not want to perform this procedure yourself, wash the tooth, wrap it in a clean damp cloth, and bring it and your child to a dentist as soon as possible.

Acute Herpetic Gingivostomatitis

This disease is caused by the herpes simplex virus (not the one that causes genital herpes). It is characterized by painful cold sores (or fever blisters) on the lips and in the mouth, and it occurs mostly in 2- to 5-year-olds.

Early symptoms include fatigue, irritability, headache, and fever. Within 2 days, the mouth becomes painful. Swelling and soreness may develop under the chin and at the sides of the neck. Blisters soon appear on the lips and in the mouth. The blisters burst, those on the lips becoming encrusted with blood. Some children run a fever as high as 104°F (40°C). The symptoms and fever subside in about a week, the ulcers that form when the blisters burst heal without scarring, and the whole episode is over in about 2 weeks.

A health care provider will recommend ways to make the child comfortable, reduce the fever, and keep the blisters from becoming infected. Herpes is highly contagious, so the child must be isolated from others in the family.

Adenoids

Two small collections of lymphatic tissues lying between the back of the nose and the throat. Upper respiratory tract infections may cause the adenoids to enlarge, which in turn fairly frequently interferes with hearing, and more rarely hinders breathing. When ear symptoms are troublesome the adenoids may be removed, but the value of the operation is disputed.

Allergy

An allergy is an overreaction of the body to contact–by eating, inhaling, or touching–with a substance that in other individuals produces no symptoms. Allergies are likely to run in families but may take different forms. Allergies cannot be cured, but symptoms frequently improve as the child gets older, and they can be reduced by the use of antiallergic drugs such as antihistamines and aspirin. In this case, acetaminophen is not an effective aspirin substitute.

A health care provider may be able to determine which substance (allergen) is causing the reaction. If it can be eliminated from the child's surroundings, no further treatment is needed. If not, small amounts of the identified substance injected over a period of time will decrease the child's sensitivity to it. Such methods are not usually employed for young children, and the effects may not last for life. Although tracking down the cause of an allergy can be easy–cats may bring on asthma, pollen may result in hay fever–a prolonged series of tests for a less obvious allergen can cause the child more worry than the allergy itself.

Hives are usually caused by food, respiratory infection, or insect bite. Asthma and allergic rhinitis (itchy runny nose) are likely to be caused by something in the air–hair, feathers, dust, mites. Additives in food can also cause allergies, as can environmental pollutants, such as lead from gasoline fumes, and some laundry detergents.

Amblyopia

Commonly but misleadingly called lazy eye, amblyopia signifies a deficient visual acuity in one eye. If the problem is not corrected in early childhood, the affected eye can progress to blindness. Underlying causes of

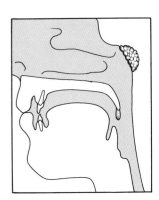

This cross section of the mouth, throat, and nasal cavities shows the position of one of a pair of enlarged adenoids.

amblyopia include STRABISMUS; dramatically different visual acuities in the two eyes so that one sees much less well than the other; and blockage of one eye due, perhaps, to a CATARACT or drooping lid (ptosis). The vision in one eye does not develop as well as in the other, and lack of stimulation causes the vision in that eye to get progressively worse.

This condition must be discovered by a health care provider as soon as possible so that it can be corrected. Usually, if amblyopia is discovered before age 6, improvement can occur. In infants, amblyopia can be corrected in a matter of days after the underlying cause is removed; in older children with long-standing amblyopia, months or years of treatment may be necessary.

Ammonia Dermatitis (diaper rash)

This inflammation of the skin is caused by prolonged contact with the breakdown products of urine. Even when diapers are changed frequently, a baby's bottom cannot be kept dry all the time. The skin may become red and spotty and may then wrinkle and look thick. The rash may spread to the tops of the legs and the lower abdomen.

Keeping the area as clean and dry as possible is often enough. When convenient, let the baby go without diapers. When diapering is unavoidable, any cream or ointment that forms a barrier between the skin and a wet diaper will help. If cloth diapers are used, they must be washed and rinsed well in hot water; disposables should be changed frequently and fastened loosely to allow air to get to the baby's skin.

Even though the rash sometimes looks alarming, it rarely causes discomfort. If it appears to be bothering the child or if it persists despite the measures described, a health care provider should be consulted. A fungal infection may be present, for which medication can be prescribed.

Anemia

Anemia is a general name for various conditions involving an insufficient number of red blood cells or an insufficient amount of the iron-containing pigment that makes the cells red and enables them to carry oxygen. Although children with anemia often appear normal, sometimes pallor, sluggishness, learning difficulties, and even behavior problems can result. Among the possible causes are blood loss, lowered production of red blood cells, and excessive breakdown of the cells. The most common cause of anemia in children is iron deficiency; it is usually seen in children 9 months to 2 years of age whose diets do not include enough iron. A breast-fed baby (particularly one whose mother is

herself low in iron or follows a vegetarian diet) may have less iron in his blood than a baby who is fed an iron-fortified formula.

Treatment is to give iron and to alter the child's diet: meat, whole-grain bread, flour, cereals, vegetables, and apricots all contain iron. It may be advisable to avoid giving the child large amounts of milk because such amounts reduce the child's appetite for iron-rich foods and because milk occasionally impedes the ability of the intestines to absorb iron.

Animal Bites

The most common bites a child is likely to suffer are from dogs, cats, and other domestic pets and–more rarely–from snakes. Rabies from dog bites is not usually a risk in this country. Often, if the child's tetanus injections are up to date (see page 64), bites need only be washed and then dressed with a sterile dressing as for cuts; a health care provider should be consulted to make sure. If the wound is jagged, it may need stitching.

An animal bite or scratch that turns yellow or does not heal should be examined by a health care provider. So should any bite inflicted by a wild or feral animal, since the danger of rabies is considerable. In the case of venomous snake bite, wash, if possible, but do *not* suck out the venom. Take the child to the nearest hospital emergency room. *See also* STINGS.

APPENDICITIS

Appendicitis results when the appendix (which is attached to the large intestine) becomes clogged and subsequently inflamed. The first symptoms are poor appetite and mild to moderate pain around the navel. Nausea is a frequent symptom, although vomiting is not usual. There may be a normal bowel movement. After 6 to 12 hours, the pain migrates and usually becomes definitely right-sided. The child may limp because of inflammation over some of the muscles used for walking. If perforation of the appendix occurs, infected material is spilled through the abdomen, the pain worsens considerably, and the need for surgery is urgent. Vomiting and frequent bowel movements are late signs of infection in the abdominal cavity. The whole course usually takes less than 24 hours.

Artificial Respiration, Resuscitation

Many local Red Cross programs, as well as Ys and Boys Clubs, give courses in lifesaving techniques, and some of them emphasize infants and young children. You might find it comforting and helpful to take one so that you can carry out (or at least begin) resuscitation if needed. No one should attempt CPR or artificial respiration without having undergone such a training course. For the inexperienced, the best approach is prevention and keeping a clear head in order to get trained emergency medical assistance as quickly as possible.

Asthma

Asthma is caused by sudden narrowing of the small air passages (bronchia) in the lungs, resulting in breathing difficulty. Causes of asthma include allergies, exercise, cold air, and respiratory infections (sometimes called wheezing-associated respiratory infections). Treatment is mostly by antispasmodic drugs. Admission to the hospital may be necessary if such medication does not succeed in relieving an attack. *See also* ALLERGY.

Autism

Autism is an extremely rare condition. Usually, the child does not respond to affection and seems indifferent to surroundings and people, as though she lives in a world of her own. Often the condition is noticed only when the child fails to learn to speak and to respond appropriately during the second year of life. Unable to communicate, autistic children may say one or two words over and over again. They likewise exhibit obsessive patterns of behavior–doing the same thing repeatedly. They do learn to walk, and some can care for themselves.

The cause of autism is not yet understood, although several factors are thought to contribute, including prematurity and retardation. Autistic children sometimes have a special gift–for example, for drawing, mathematics, or music. They need long-term care from developmental specialists, as well as regular child care. Further information can be obtained from the National Society for Autistic Children, 1234 Massachusetts Avenue NW, Washington, DC 20005.

Black Eye

A black eye consists of a bruise and sometimes swelling of the tissues surrounding the eye. Usually it is caused by a blow and may be due to a fracture at the base of the skull. It is a good idea to have any bruise around the eye examined by a health care provider. If he or she is not worried about the severity of the injury, cold water compresses may be applied to help ease discomfort during the first day after the injury. The swelling will subside in a few days, and the bruise will disappear within 2 weeks.

BLEEDING

Bleeding from a cut or scrape can usually be controlled by several minutes of direct pressure. (See drawing at right.) If an artery is damaged, the blood will spurt dramatically and must be stopped at once. Put your fingers on the spot where the blood is coming from and press hard. If this does not stop it, press near the spot but a bit closer to the child's heart. If the bleeding stops, put a firm dressing on; but if the dressing does not keep the bleeding stopped, reposition your fingers on the spot, and rush the child to the hospital.

Boil

A boil is a small red spot that feels tender, comes to a head, and then bursts, discharging yellow pus. A health care provider may lance the boil if it does not burst of its own accord.

Never attempt to lance or squeeze a boil at home, as it risks spreading the infection. Instead, treat the boil before it bursts and afterwards, until the skin heals, with hot water soaks or hot compresses. Red streaks running under the skin from the boil indicate that the infection is spreading; a health care provider should be called.

Breath-holding

Breath-holding is a distressing but not necessarily serious form of behavior in children under 3. The child may begin to cry out or may take a deep breath as if about to yell, but no sound comes. The child turns red, blue, or purple, and usually loses consciousness. Once unconscious, he will begin breathing again. The only major danger arises if he holds his breath so long that the brain is momentarily deprived of oxygen, which sometimes causes a convulsion. The cause is usually uncontrolled frustration or anger; attacks almost always decrease after age 3.

A child is unlikely to have an attack when he is alone, but the reaction is nevertheless genuine. Slapping or throwing cold water over the child does not usually help; soothing frequently does. Once he takes a breath, the attack stops. Usually there are no ill effects later in life, but occasionally fainting spells do develop.

Bronchitis

Bronchitis is an inflammation of the lining of the bronchial tubes that lead into the lungs. Children with bronchitis make a characteristic wheezing noise as they breathe. Nurse as for viral PNEUMONIA. The child's health care provider may prescribe medication to clear the tubes of mucus or may offer exercises to

In the case of severe bleeding from a large wound, it is important to restrict blood flow to encourage clotting. Give continual reassurance as you attend to the bleeding. A lot of blood can be frightening to a young child.

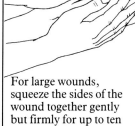

For large wounds, squeeze the sides of the wound together gently but firmly for up to ten minutes. If bleeding continues for longer than that, rush child to an emergency room.

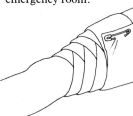

Or if the wound is deep, cover with clean cloth and apply pressure for up to ten minutes. In either case, if bleeding continues, rush child to a hospital emergency room.

Once bleeding has ceased, apply a sterile dressing and secure with a gauze bandage wrapped firmly and pinned. If bleeding begins again, apply a second dressing and bandage on top of the first.

help the child breathe properly. Often children with chronic bronchitis later become asthmatic. *See also* ASTHMA.

Bruise

A bruise is a blue-black mark on the skin indicating that blood has been released into the tissues below the skin following an injury to them. Skin color returns to normal as the blood is absorbed by the tissues and carried away, usually within a week to ten days. If the blow was severe, a bone may be broken, and an x-ray should be taken (*see* FRACTURE). A child who frequently bruises without any obvious cause should be examined by a health care provider for a possible underlying illness.

BURNS

The larger the area of skin burned, the more serious the injury. Burns of more than half the skin area are often fatal.

DO NOT put a dressing on serious burns; tissue damage may result when it is removed at the hospital. Get to the hospital by the quickest route possible.
Trivial burns: **Burns less than 1 inch in diameter can be treated at home. Do not touch the burn, but immediately immerse it in cold water. This cools the skin, thereby limiting the amount of injury to it, and reduces pain. Leave the burn open to the air unless a blister forms.**
If a blister forms: **Do not prick it but apply a medicated ointment recommended by a health care provider. Cover with a sterile dressing and keep it dry. Give aspirin to lessen pain. Aspirin is more effective than acetaminophen in this situation.**
Larger burns: **Cool them immediately in water, and take the child to the hospital.**
Clothes on fire: **Roll the child in a rug or blanket. When fire is quenched, do not attempt to remove clothes. Instead, cover the child with a clean sheet, and go to the hospital immediately.**
Clothes drenched in scalding water: **Remove the clothes quickly–cut them off if necessary–cover the child in a sheet, and rush to the hospital.**
Burns from acids and alkalis: **Flood the skin immediately with plenty of cold water; then deal with the burned skin as above. If possible, identify the liquid that caused the burn, or take the container to the hospital with you.**
Burns from electricity: **Such burns may be deep, although they appear small. If they persist and seem slow to heal, take the child to a health care provider.**

BURN PREVENTION MEASURES
- Do not leave matches within your child's reach.
- Be sure all sleepwear is flameproof.
- Install firescreens or child-guard gates around fireplaces, hot water pipes, and radiators.
- Cover electrical outlets.
- Remove cooking utensils to a safe height and always turn pot handles in so that they do not overhang edges; when possible, use back burners only.
- Never leave your child alone with hot

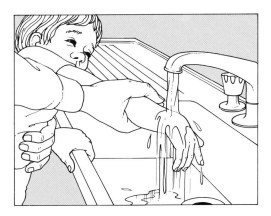

For both minor and severe burns, quickly cool the burn in cold water. This gives instant relief and prevents further damage to underlying tissues.

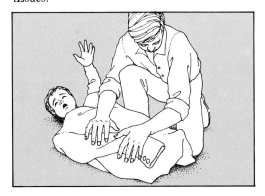

If the child's clothing is on fire, roll him in a rug or blanket or smother the flames with your own body. Do not try to douse him with water and never use a fire extinguisher on any person.

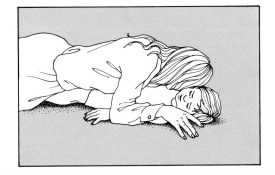

kettles and pots, toasters, irons, cups of coffee, or bath water.
- Do not permit electrical appliance cords to hang within your child's reach.
- Lock away corrosive substances.
  (See also pages 34-39).

Candida Albicans (thrush)

This nonserious fungus infection appears as white patches on the inside of the cheeks and sometimes on the tongue and palate. It may be contracted at birth if the mother has vaginal thrush, through an incompletely sterilized rubber nipple, or as a complication of antibiotic treatment. The patches can make feeding painful–an infant may stop sucking to cry, and an older child may complain of mouth discomfort. A health care provider will treat it by painting the affected areas with gentian violet or will prescribe an oral antifungal medication.

Cardiopulmonary Resuscitation, CPR. *See* ARTIFICIAL RESPIRATION, RESUSCITATION

Cataracts (congenital type)

Cataracts are opaque patches on the lens of the eye. If small, they cause little or no problem, but larger ones appreciably impair vision. Although cataracts are most commonly associated with old age, congenital cataracts (those a child is born with) may be hereditary or caused by pre-natal infection, most notably rubella in the mother.

The lens of the eye can be surgically removed, but special glasses or contact lenses are then usually required to serve as an artificial lens. An untreated cataract in one eye can lead, in a child, to blindness through disuse. *See also* AMBLYOPIA.

Celiac Disease

This is a relatively rare condition in which gluten, the protein in many breads and cereals, damages the small intestine, resulting in excessively bulky, foul-smelling stools containing much fat. This condition is often not apparent until the child begins to eat foods containing fairly large amounts of gluten; it can be ameliorated considerably by a gluten-free diet. Often some gluten can eventually be returned to the diet.

Cerebral Palsy

Cerebral palsy is the result of damage to the part of the brain that controls movement and muscles. It may be caused during early pregnancy, by an infection (such as rubella) in the mother; in later pregnancy, by severe malnutrition either in the mother or in the fetus because of an inadequate placenta; or at birth, usually through lack of oxygen. Severe jaundice in the newborn period may also be a cause. The child has decreased control over movement (either being "floppy" or too stiff) and may also have delayed mental development and defects of hearing or sight.

A child suffering from cerebral palsy is often of normal intelligence; however, the characteristic uncontrolled movements led to the mistaken belief that mental damage inevitably accompanied it. Help for children with cerebral palsy is widely available, often at specialized developmental centers. More information is available from United Cerebral Palsy Association (see page 230).

Chicken Pox (varicella)

The disease begins with mild fever and an itchy rash of red pimples that become fluid-filled blisters and finally scabs. The rash may come in several crops. Discourage scratching, which can cause permanent scarring. Try soothing with cool baths.

The incubation period is usually 14 to 16 days; contagiousness begins 1 to 2 days before the rash appears and ends 7 days after (usually when lesions are all scabbed). Infection is by droplets or by contact with open sores.

Complications are rare. They include bacterial superinfection, causing pus to drain from the rash; inflammation of the brain, joints, or kidney; and Reye's syndrome, an inflammation of the brain and liver causing lethargy or unconsciousness and severe vomiting. Children with chicken pox should not take aspirin, which has been linked with development of Reye's syndrome. Acetaminophen does not present this risk.

CHOKING

An obstruction in the throat or windpipe that makes breathing difficult should be dealt with immediately. Try to hook the object out with your finger; if you cannot, turn the child upside down and slap her between the shoulder blades to dislodge the object and allow the child to cough it out. If this does not succeed–or even if it does, but the child appears different after the episode–take her directly to a health care facility. DO NOT attempt the "Heimlich Maneuver" on a small child: its forceful pushes on the abdomen might break ribs or tear the liver or spleen.

The sudden appearance of a croupy cough in a child who has no other cold symptoms should suggest that an object has been inhaled without anyone's noticing it. The cough itself may dislodge the object; otherwise, the measures outlined above should be taken. Sometimes, however, an object will not cause complete

obstruction but will be wedged in the windpipe. The child will seem to have stopped choking only to have a cough (sometimes croupy) persist or develop over the next day or two. In such a case, suspect a foreign object in the windpipe and call your health care provider. An x-ray may be required to confirm the diagnosis, and if the child cannot be made to cough up or swallow the object, it will have to be removed in an operating room.

Never leave a baby to feed from a propped bottle whose liquid could go down the windpipe instead of into the esophagus, as this could cause choking and vomiting. A child just beginning to eat solids should not be given small hard pieces of food. Never give peanuts – they can lodge in the airway, and the oil in them is irritating if inhaled into the lungs. Frankfurters have also been reported in cases of choking; if given at all, they should be cut into quite small pieces. *See* EPIGLOTTITIS.

Circumcision

Circumcision is the surgical removal of the skin that covers the tip of the penis (glans). Once believed necessary to keep the area between foreskin and glans clean, this operation has, over the past 15 years, become less frequently performed. The foreskin is now thought to be joined naturally to the glans at birth and may provide protection for a sensitive area.

The operation is best performed during the newborn period. The area of surgery will be covered with a dressing for several days, but it soon heals enough to be ignored. If the penis continues to bleed for more than a day or if the area appears more swollen or red, a health care provider should be consulted.

Cleft Lip (hare lip)

This is a condition present at birth in which the sides of the upper lip have not fused together. This failure to fuse occurs in the first trimester of pregnancy. The exact cause is frequently unknown; the cleft may be a completely genetic problem or may be the result of genetic factors influenced by the environment.

If the cleft is of the lip only, no problems in feeding or subsequent language and speech development should arise once the lip is repaired. (This is usually done within a few days of birth, whether or not the palate is also cleft.) If the cleft lip is coupled with a cleft palate, immediate problems in feeding and later problems in speech and language development may result. Medical and speech and language therapeutic programs are widely available.

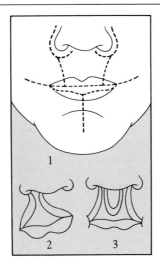

During the development of the fetus, the two sides of the face form separately and then join along the lines shown (1). Sometimes fusion is incomplete on one side (2), and sometimes on both (3). The result is a cleft lip.

The slit of a cleft lip sometimes extends to the palate (1). It is repaired as shown (2).

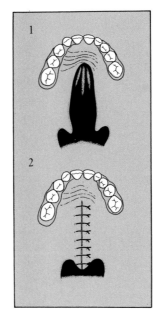

Cleft Palate

This is a condition present at birth in which the opening in the lip extends through the gum ridge and/or roof of the mouth. The condition involves an interruption in the process of fusion during the first trimester of pregnancy and may be caused by genetic factors or influenced by drugs, illness, or radiation. Until the cleft is repaired, the child will not be able to produce the suction required to drink from a conventional bottle or from his mother's breast. Special feeding techniques can overcome this problem.

Cleft palates are usually repaired at about age 2 because much of the mouth's growth has occurred by then. (The exact timing depends on the advice of the plastic surgeons.) The aim is to close the opening, allowing the soft palate to close off the passage between throat and nose so that air does not escape into the nose during speech.

A child with a cleft palate should receive special speech training to prevent distortion of the voice. Frequent ear infections are possible, and these sometimes result in hearing loss, but communication specialists will monitor the child in an attempt to minimize complications. For more information, write to the American Cleft Palate Association, Administrative Office, 331 Salk Hall, University of Pittsburgh, Pittsburgh, PA 15261.

Club Foot (talipes)

Club foot is a condition most often caused by the position of the baby's feet in the uterus. One foot is usually turned in at the ankle, with the heel unable to touch the ground when the child walks. Splints (sometimes) and surgery (usually) correct the condition; recovery can be complete.

Colds

Common cold symptoms include runny nose, runny eyes, cough, fever, muscle aches, sore throat, and occasionally earache. The incubation period of the viruses responsible is 2 to 4 days. Symptoms usually peak by the fourth day, and treatment is directed at these: a suction bulb to clear the nose of a child too young to use tissues; a humidifier or vaporizer to moisten room air; more attention and extra napping for crankiness; and aspirin or acetaminophen for aches. Sufficient fluid must be consumed to prevent dehydration, but poor appetite is unimportant. Antibiotics may be prescribed for complications. Nasal discharge is typically clear and watery; yellow or greenish discharge lasting more than 3 days and accompanied by fever or a strange odor may indicate sinus infection. Consult a health care provider.

Allergies can mimic common colds. A child who seems to have a cold all the time or repeatedly at certain times of year or in certain environments may be suffering from allergies instead. *See also* ALLERGY, FOREIGN BODY IN THE NOSE.

Colic

The cause and exact nature of this syndrome, which occurs exclusively in babies under 3 months, is unknown. Some sort of digestive difficulty causes extreme discomfort, and the baby reacts with intense crying. Parents can do little to relieve the baby's distress, and their helplessness tends only to increase their own distress. Although everything from gas to intolerance to formula or mother's milk has been put forward as a possible cause, none seems to explain the peculiar nature of the problem. It usually occurs at the same time each day and happens every day; it sometimes lasts several hours.

Babies who are colicky do not fit any observable psychological or physical pattern, nor do they tend to be sickly as a result. In fact, they are often particularly active, particularly thriving infants. Colic rarely lasts more than 6 to 8 weeks. Although it is true that time may seem an eternity to anxious and fatigued new parents, the support of the child's health care provider (who will be able to rule out other causes for the bouts of crying) and a chance for both parents to spend some time each day away from the baby will help make the experience bearable.

Color Blindness

More usual in boys than in girls (8 percent versus 0.4 percent), the condition may not be noticed under age 3 because a young child may not be able to name colors accurately. Because of poor color recognition (especially of red and green), the child may appear to be delayed developmentally. Later problems may arise when the child begins school, especially if he is expected to use color-coded equipment, but he will learn to adjust.

Tests have been devised to check for color blindness in young children. A health care provider can obtain these if the condition is suspected.

CONCUSSION

A concussion is a significant jarring of the brain resulting from a fall or a blow to the head. It is signaled by loss of consciousness and, perhaps, by vomiting, dizziness, and headache.

Even if the period of unconsciousness is brief, a health care provider should be called. In the meantime, lay the child on his stomach or side, with head turned to one side; this will ensure that, if vomiting occurs, the matter will not be inhaled. Check for breathing and heartbeat and, if necessary and you know how to do it, begin CARDIOPULMONARY RESUSCITATION. **If you do not know how, call for trained medical assistance. Do not give anything to drink. When the child regains consciousness, seek medical attention even if breathing and heartbeat are normal.**

Congenital Dislocation of the Hip

This term refers to hips that slip in and out of joint too easily. Babies usually are checked for this condition a few days after birth. Treatment consists of holding the hips firmly in joint, often with supporting splints for some months so that the hips develop normally. Complete cures follow early treatment; untreated, the condition may lead to a painful, abnormal walk and sometimes to a permanently dislocated hip.

Conjunctivitis (pink eye)

Conjunctivitis is an inflammation of the lining of the eyelids and of the clear covering of the eye that manifests itself as red, bloodshot, watery eyes, frequently accompanied by discharge. The cause may be a virus (as minor as a cold; as serious as herpes – which if untreated may result in blindness), bacteria (the most serious of which, gonorrheal bacteria, has been successfully avoided by routinely administering silver nitrate and other drops to newborns), or an allergic reaction.

Conjunctivitis usually clears up on its own within a few days. Parents should discourage rubbing of the eyes, particularly with unwashed hands; towels and washcloths should not be shared while the condition is evident. Dried discharge may be gently cleaned away with a moistened cloth or tissue, but drops, eyewashes, or ointments should be limited to those prescribed by a health care provider.

A health care provider should be consulted in any case involving pain, difficulty in seeing, pronounced swelling, fever, worsening discharge and inflammation, or a child under 3 months old, since a more serious infection may be present. *See also* TEAR DUCT OBSTRUCTION.

Constipation

Constipation is the passing of hard stools, usually at infrequent intervals (see page 101). Some children may have a bowel movement every day, others twice a day, others as rarely as once every 3 or 4 days. Normally bowels move when the rectum is full.

A child whose parents worry excessively about the frequency and regularity of bowel movements may well pick up their anxiety and respond by withholding the movements. It is best to pay as little attention to the issue as possible, and if extra fruits and drinks are given, not to continue this for more than a week. If the child's bowel movements seem to cause pain or if small cracks have developed in the skin around the rectum, consult a health care provider, particularly before administering laxatives of any sort.

Convulsions. *See* SEIZURES.

Cradle Cap. *See* SEBORRHEA.

Crib Death. *See* SUDDEN INFANT DEATH SYNDROME.

Crossed Eyes. *See* STRABISMUS.

Croup

Croup is the common name for an illness that occurs frequently in children under 4. Its characteristic sound is similar to the bark of a seal; it is caused by inflammation and narrowing of the windpipe just below the larynx (voice box). Sometimes the voice box is inflamed too.

Croup usually begins as a mild cold, with a cough that becomes croupy and causes difficulty in breathing during the night. Because it commonly awakens the child (and parents), it can be a frightening experience for all concerned. A health care provider should be called, and if he or she recommends it or cannot be reached, the child should be taken to the nearest emergency room. Croup can progress to a life-threatening obstruction of the windpipe and should not be taken lightly, but most episodes are mild and last only 2 or 3 days.

Parents accustomed to croup (it may recur in the same child and in other children in the family as well) become practiced at filling a bathroom with steam (closing all doors and windows, and then running a hot shower), and staying there with the child until breathing improves. This procedure should be repeated several times a day; a vaporizer or humidifier may also be used in the child's room. *See also* EPIGLOTTITIS.

Cuts

The first step in treating any cut is to stop the bleeding. Do so by applying pressure with a clean cloth or gauze pad for 3 to 5 minutes, depending on severity. Then wash the cut well with soap and water, gently pat dry, and cover with an appropriate-size bandage.

Most cuts do not require further treatment. If, however, the cut is deep and happens outdoors, a tetanus injection may be necessary if the child's immunizations are not up to date (see page 64). If the cut is deep or extensive or has edges that do not meet, stitches may be required. If the cut is surrounded by reddened skin and is painful to the touch, an infection may have developed. In any of these circumstances, the child should be taken to a health care provider or hospital emergency room. *See also* BLEEDING.

Cystic Fibrosis

Cystic fibrosis is a disease inherited from both parents. In a baby, symptoms include repeated lung infections, failure to thrive, and diarrhea. Although at present incurable, cystic fibrosis can be treated–usually for many years–with antibiotics, pancreatic extracts, and chest therapy, by specially trained health care providers. Write to the Cystic Fibrosis Foundation, 6000 Executive Boulevard, Suite 309, Rockville, MD 20852, for further information. *See also* GENETIC COUNSELING.

Deafness

Hearing loss may vary from very mild to profound and may go unrecognized in infants and young children until the age at which they are expected to begin to talk. A hearing-impaired infant will begin to make sounds at the same age as a baby with normal hearing, but because she cannot hear her own voice and those of others for encouragement and reinforcement, the sounds gradually disappear and speech fails to develop appropriately. The child usually becomes acutely aware of her parents' facial and body expressions, depending on these for understanding if hearing is severely impaired.

If significant hearing loss exists, an alert parent of a 2- to 3-month-old will notice lack of response to sound. Around 6 to 8 months, the child's failure to respond to her name and to environmental sounds becomes increasingly apparent. As a child grows older, even mild hearing loss becomes noticeable, affecting the youngster's ability to pronounce sounds or causing confusion in understanding directions. If any of these signals is present, a hearing assessment is essential.

Hearing may be evaluated accurately even in infants. If hearing loss is discovered that medical treatment cannot correct, hearing aids and speech and language therapy will help develop the child's communicative abilities. The earlier hearing loss is discovered, the more successful treatment and speech and language therapy will be. Many organizations exist to aid the deaf and hearing-impaired; one of particular interest to parents may be the International Association of Parents of the Deaf, 814 Thayer Avenue, Silver Spring, MD 20910.

Dehydration

Dehydration is a drying out of the body caused by excessive diarrhea, vomiting, urination, or heat. When dehydration is moderate to severe, symptoms may include sunken eyes, listlessness, weight loss, dry lips and mouth, and decreased urine output. A health care provider must be consulted without delay. Treatment involves correcting the fluid loss, usually after analysis of blood and urine. If vomiting poses a problem, fluids may be given intravenously. Dehydration can sometimes be avoided at home by giving fluids and keeping fever down. *See also* SWEATING.

Dental Caries

Cavities occur in teeth when a sticky coating called plaque consisting almost entirely of bacteria, adheres to the teeth and converts sugar from food particles into acid. The acid then bites into the enamel of the teeth.

By the time a baby's first teeth erupt, decay-producing germs are already present, so his teeth (or tooth) must be cleaned every day to remove plaque (see pages 89-90).

Nursing caries (also called "nursing bottle mouth" and "nursing bottle caries") is a dental condition in infants and young children associated with prolonged use of the nursing bottle. It occurs when a bottle of milk or fruit juice is left for the child to suck on as she pleases throughout her nap or sleep period. As the child sleeps and sucks, a pool of liquid collects around the necks of her teeth. Milk and fruit juices both contain natural sugars, and juices are also naturally acidic. As the liquid stagnates around the teeth, the germs produce acid and the teeth decay.

The teeth most affected are the upper incisors; the lower teeth are protected by the tongue from the pool of liquid. A white band develops along the gum line of the upper teeth—usually undetected by the parents—and eventually turns into dark brown or black collars of decay circling the necks of the teeth. In advanced cases, all four upper incisors are reduced to brownish stumps.

Nursing caries is also seen in children who suck pacifiers dipped in a sweetener such as honey, and it has been reported in children who are breastfed to the age of 2 or 3.

The condition can be prevented by weaning the child from breast or bottle when teeth begin to come into her mouth, by not using a bottle as a pacifier when the child is napping (this will also avoid accidental choking), and by never giving a child a pacifier that has been sweetened.

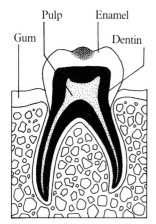

Pulp   Enamel

Gum   Dentin

This cross section through a tooth shows how a cavity forms.

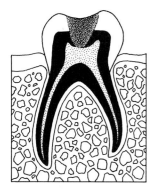

The enamel is eroded until the decay reaches the dentin, where it can spread rapidly, eventually reaching the pulp.

Dental cavities are not inevitable if diet is controlled, if plaque is removed, and if efficient hygiene is observed.

Diabetes

In children this disorder usually stems from failure of part of the pancreas, resulting in a lack of insulin—a hormone that enables the body to use the sugar carried in the blood. Sugar builds up in the blood and passes out in the urine. Usual symptoms are intense thirst and appetite and increased output of urine (often pale). Other, less frequent signs are drowsiness, weight loss or failure to gain weight, abdominal pain, and nausea. Insulin injections are the primary treatment; children can learn the procedure quite young. Diet control may also help. Although it cannot be cured, diabetes usually can be controlled through cooperative effort. Write to Juvenile Diabetes Foundation International, 23 East 26th Street, New York, NY 10010.

Diaper Rash. *See* AMMONIA DERMATITIS.

Diarrhea

In babies, diarrhea (loose, even watery, frequent stools) is usually caused by viral infection. Occasionally diarrhea may be caused by intolerance to certain foods, especially milk, or more rarely to medications. Unformed stools alone (as from a breastfed baby) do not necessarily signify diarrhea, but loose stools produced by a young infant who has previously been producing formed ones is a sign to watch; a health care provider should be called if the child refuses feedings, vomits, and produces an increased frequency and volume of stool over a 24-hour period. A health care provider should also be consulted about any new and persisting diarrhea, since it could lead to DEHYDRATION.

Treatment of diarrhea depends on the cause but usually includes adopting a simplified diet of mild foods and extra fluids. *See also* CELIAC DISEASE, CYSTIC FIBROSIS.

Diphtheria

Diphtheria is a serious bacterial disease that causes infection in the nose and throat, interfering with breathing. In rare cases it may cause heart failure or paralysis. The incubation period is 2 to 5 days after exposure; symptoms are fever, sore throat, and hoarseness.

Immunization has practically eliminated diphtheria in the United States. An immunized child is fully protected, but periodic booster doses are needed (see page 60).

Down's Syndrome (mongolism)

Often obvious at birth, Down's syndrome is a product of genetic error. Down's syndrome babies are characterized by narrow and slanted eyes, a small head with flattened brow, and mental retardation; they often suffer more frequent colds and ear and chest infections than other infants.

Children with this condition are affectionate and active. Although retarded, they can achieve certain skills and are usually able to live with their families.

The chance that Down's syndrome will occur increases with the mother's age. Its existence can be determined before birth by amniocentesis, which is one reason the procedure is commonly recommended for pregnant women over 35.

DROWNING

A baby or toddler can drown in a few inches of water; it does not take submersion in deep water, only inhalation of a sufficient quantity to block the airway. Prevention is the best remedy: Constant vigilance at bath time and when unfenced pools are a temptation to a curious toddler. A child who has inhaled water may cough violently and even vomit. If vomiting seems imminent, keep the child upright to avoid her inhaling the vomitus and choking on that. If the child is not breathing, begin ARTIFICIAL RESPIRATION **at once if you know how. Call for help, either asking someone with you to summon emergency medical assistance or telephoning yourself.**

Dyslexia

Dyslexia involves an inability to sort out the order of words or letters. It is unlikely to be recognized before a child reaches reading age. Distinguishing a dyslexic child from a slow-to-read child can be difficult. Dyslexic children are of normal intelligence and have normal vision, but for reasons not completely understood, they see letters and words as a jumble and are unable to translate sound into correct spelling. Treatment, consisting of individual lessons from a remedial teacher (often available through the school) can help a great deal. Write to the Orton Society, 8415 Bellina Lane, Towson, MD 21204, for more information.

Ears. *See* OTITIS EXTERNA, OTITIS MEDIA, OTITIS MEDIA WITH EFFUSION, RUNNY EAR, WATER IN THE EARS, WAX IN THE EARS.

Eczema

An allergic skin reaction more common in boys than in girls, infantile eczema usually begins as red patches on cheeks and forehead. The skin is dry and may show white flakes. The discomfort can be enormous, and it worsens if the child becomes upset. Because scratching can lead to infection, keep the child's fingernails clipped short.

Eczema tends to run in families, especially those with a history of the associated allergies asthma and hay fever. It is more common in babies fed cow's milk than in those fed breast milk, and if it first appears when cow's milk is introduced to a previously breast-fed baby, a health care provider may recommend changing to another type of milk. The condition can be aggravated by soap and water (clean with oil instead), wool against the skin, and certain foods.

Eczema usually leaves no scars, and although it has no cure, most children grow out of the tendency in 2 to 3 years. Hydrocortisone ointments can be prescribed to control the inflammation; in severe cases, a sedative may be prescribed in the early stages to lessen the irritation.

EEG (electroencephalogram)

An EEG records brain waves and may help to diagnose seizures. The test takes 1 or 2 hours, since usually the child is recorded both asleep and awake, but it rarely involves a hospital stay. Electrical wires are stuck to the scalp with a special glue and connected to a brain wave recorder. The test is usually painless, although the wires and equipment may look frightening. If the child knows the procedure in advance, cooperation during the test will be easier to obtain; sometimes it helps to have the child practice on a doll or stuffed animal at home.

ELECTRICAL SHOCK

If a shock is so severe that the child cannot pull away from the source of electricity, touching the child will only connect you to the circuit. Instead, switch off the power or, if this is not possible, move the child away, by dragging at his clothes, kicking him away, or pushing him with a broom or other nonmetallic object. Once the child is free, attempt CARDIOPULMONARY RESUSCITATION, **if the child is not breathing adequately and if you know how. Treat burns as detailed for** BURNS **from electricity, and then contact a health care provider or seek emergency medical help.**

EPIGLOTTITIS

Epiglottitis is a life-threatening bacterial infection that can dangerously swell the

If you cannot quickly switch off the power supply, kick or push the child away from the cable with anything that will not conduct electricity. In this case, the broom end is preferable to the handle.

epiglottis, the flap that covers the windpipe during swallowing. Children from the ages of 1 to 5 are most susceptible. First symptoms are high fever and mildly noisy breathing, which rapidly becomes loud inhalation (stridor). Because swallowing is painful, the child will drool and will refuse food and drink.

This is a true emergency. Keep the child from crying and becoming agitated (which may increase swelling), and rush him to a hospital emergency room. Treatment may involve inserting a tube into the trachea or making a surgical opening through the front of the neck into the trachea to assist breathing; the infection is treated with antibiotics. The child is usually able to breathe unaided in 2 or 3 days.

A vaccine has recently been released for the prevention of *Hemophilus influenzae* disease in children over 2 years of age. It is hoped that many cases of epiglottitis, which can occur as a secondary infection of *H. influenzae*, will be prevented once this vaccine is widely used.

Epilepsy

Epilepsy, also referred to as fits, seizures, or convulsions, may take different forms.

In what is called petit mal, the child may have a vacant look for a few seconds, may momentarily lose consciousness, but then will continue her activity as though nothing had happened. This should not be confused with daydreaming from which the child can quite easily be returned to his surroundings.

Epilepsy is sometimes manifested as startling spells or jerky movements during sleep. Other indications are sudden pallor, chewing or smacking movements, eye flutter, and changes in color. Deep sleep often follows these attacks.

Grand mal epilepsy usually consists of rhythmic movements of the arms and legs, accompanied by loss of consciousness and sometimes by incontinence. Seizures are the result of abnormal electrical discharges in the brain, which could be due to a tumor, bleeding, a chemical imbalance, structural anomalies, flashing lights, or trauma; quite often, no specific cause is found.

Much of the fear of epilepsy is rooted in misguided social attitudes. For the most part, children with epilepsy do not need special attention, although they do need supervision in certain things—bathing, swimming, and cycling, for instance. They can be encouraged to play games and enter into ordinary activities. Treatment with drugs often eliminates a tendency toward epileptic fits. Further information is available from the Epilepsy Foundation of America, 4351 Garden City Drive, Landover, MD 20781.

Eustachian Tubes. *See* OTITIS MEDIA, OTITIS MEDIA WITH EFFUSION.

Eyes. *See* AMBLYOPIA, BLACK EYE, CATARACTS, COLOR BLINDNESS, CONJUNCTIVITIS, FOREIGN BODY IN THE EYE, GLAUCOMA, STRABISMUS, STYE.

Fainting

Fainting, a temporary loss of consciousness due to insufficient blood reaching the brain, is rare in children under 3. Although fainting can occur after exertion or during times of stress, what appears to be a simple case of fainting might actually mark a seizure disorder or a heart problem. A health care provider should be seen promptly. Simple fainting is often preceded by a feeling of dizziness, nausea, or nonspecific malaise, but seizures may also start this way. *See* SEIZURES.

Farsightedness. *See* HYPEROPIA.

Fever

A common sign of illness in children and frequently the first symptom noticed, fever is a double threat: The cause must be determined, and ill effects of the fever itself must be prevented.

A baby's normal body temperature varies during the day from 98° to 100°F (36.6°–37.7°C); in older children the range is 97° to 100°F (36.1°–37.7°C), the lowest usually occurring in the morning, the highest in the late afternoon. Some children tolerate temperatures of 101° to 103°F (38.3°–39.5°C) extremely well and may require no treatment of the fever itself; other children become irritable and sleepy and feel better at a lower temperature. Nonetheless, fever usually means a temperature over 100°F taken rectally.

Potential causes of fever are numerous:

Infections: These, especially respiratory infections, are the most common cause of fever in children.

Dehydration: This usually results from vomiting and/or diarrhea, but occasionally from drinking too little or voiding too much.

Environmental effects: Overdressing, over-exercising, or being in an excessively hot room or car are typical of these effects.

Immunizations: DPT immunization may cause fever the day it is given; measles vaccine may cause fever 7 to 10 days after it is given.

Medications: Antibiotics and overuse of aspirin to lower fever may occasionally cause fever as a side effect.

To help the child's body control its own heat production, promote sweating by encouraging a good intake of fluids, providing loose clothing, and maintaining a comfortable room temperature (68°–70°F/20°–21°C); encourage quiet activities rather than exercise (protracted crying is similar for a baby to exercise for an older child and may increase fever).

Temperatures over 103° or 104°F (39.4° or 40°C) require other treatments. Cool the skin quickly by bathing the child in a few inches of tepid water. Wet the skin all over and allow the child to play while the water evaporates from his skin. When the skin is dry, repeat the process until the child feels cooler; then recheck his temperature. The evaporating water cools the body; sitting a feverish child waist-deep in warm water will not help. Shivering causes body temperature to rise, so if the child starts to shiver, take him out, dry him off, and try again later. Do not add alcohol to the water: It promotes shivering, and inhaling the fumes may be harmful. Supplement surface cooling with aspirin or acetaminophen.

Fits. *See* SEIZURES.

Flu. *See* INFLUENZA.

Foreign Body in the Eye

A speck of dust or other foreign body in the eye causes watering, and in most cases the offender is quickly floated out. Rubbing the eye may further irritate it, so encourage blinking rather than rubbing. If the object stays in, do not attempt to remove it by hand. Instead, flush the eye: Holding the child's head back so that the face is toward the ceiling and slightly turned to the affected side to allow runoff, pour water from the nose side of the eye and allow it to run out toward the ear. If a corrosive liquid has splashed into the eye, dilute it immediately by pouring water on the eye for at least 5 minutes; ignore the child's objections and the mess. Telephone a health care provider as soon as possible for further advice.

If you are unable to remove the object or if it seems to be causing injury, cover the eye lightly with a gauze pad and take the child to the hospital.

Foreign Body in the Nose

A foreign body in the nose can cause a runny nose, leading parents to suspect a cold. When a foreign body is responsible, the discharge is usually from just one nostril, no other cold symptoms are present, and a very offensive odor may develop. Parents should not attempt to remove the object; a health care provider can do so safely and, usually, easily.

Fracture

A fracture, or broken bone, can be one of four types: "green stick" (the bone bends but does not break all the way through); simple (the bone breaks cleanly); compound (the bone pierces the skin); or comminuted (the bone is shattered). A fracture may be evident to the naked eye or may defy diagnosis except by x-ray. Furthermore, distinguishing between a fracture and a bad sprain (bruised tendons and ligaments) may be difficult because both are painful and cause swelling. In general, it is possible to put some weight on a sprain, but not on a fracture. Food and drink should be withheld from a child who may have a fracture, since a general anesthetic may be necessary.

Children's bones are supple and heal quickly. A fractured bone generally must be set and fixed in place, usually with a plaster cast to support the bone as it heals. Complete healing may take from 6 to 10 weeks.

Skull injuries must be taken seriously and need immediate medical attention. If a child hits her head and loses consciousness, take her to the emergency room of the nearest hospital. If, after a fall, the child becomes drowsy, vomits frequently, or is bleeding from the nose or ears, get medical help at once.

Bones can fracture in a variety of ways. Children tend to suffer partial or "green stick" fractures (1). In a simple fracture (2), the break is complete, but the skin is not punctured; in a compound fracture (3), the skin is punctured by the broken bone; and in a comminuted fracture (4), the bone is broken in several places.

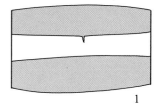

1

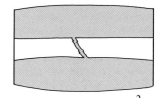

2

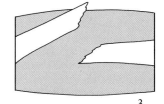

3

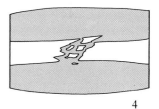

4

If the child's eye or eyes have been splashed with corrosive fluid, flush with copious amounts of clear, cool water. This procedure can be tried if the child complains of a foreign body in the eye that is not washed away by his own blinking and tears (a handful of sand from the sandbox, for example).

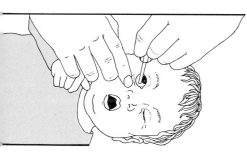

Put drops in the eye of a cooperative child, who may either sit up or lie down, by pulling down the lower lid with the pad of your index finger and squeezing a drop in the resultant pouch. A child who protests will have to be restrained while lying down by a second person.

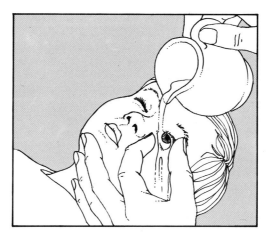

Frostbite

Prolonged exposure to intense cold may cause blood vessels under the skin to contract, cutting off blood supply to the surface. The skin turns hard and pale and, if untreated, can suffer permanent damage. Intense pain is felt in the areas affected–usually hands, feet, nose, and ears.

Immerse affected areas in warm, not hot, water and gently massage them to stimulate blood flow. If the areas cannot be immersed, place towels or sponges dampened with warm water over them. Treated promptly, frostbite is unlikely to cause permanent damage. Nonetheless, a health care provider should be consulted.

Gastroenteritis

Gastroenteritis is an infection of stomach and intestines usually caused by virus or bacteria spread through feces to food. The symptoms are vomiting and diarrhea. Because gastroenteritis is highly infectious, hands must be washed after handling the ill baby. In a young baby, dehydration can be an added complication.

Vomiting and diarrhea could be symptoms of a problem other than gastroenteritis; a health care provider should make the diagnosis.

Genetic Counseling

Certain illnesses or conditions can be inherited from one or both parents and passed down in families, especially through the female line. Genetic counselors will discuss with prospective parents the possibility that their children might suffer from such diseases. In some cases, prenatal testing or testing of the prospective parents can reveal risks or the actual presence of inheritable conditions.

German Measles. *See* RUBELLA.

Glaucoma (congenital type)

Glaucoma is a condition in which the pressure of the fluid inside the eye is higher than normal because the channel between the back and front of the lens is blocked or because more fluid is produced in the eye than is absorbed. A hard, painful, cloudy eyeball results, and vision may be disturbed. Congenital glaucoma is relatively rare; it is more painful than the noncongenital type and more likely to result in permanent blindness if not treated. Treatment is with eyedrops, other drugs, or surgery to lower pressure within the eye.

Hare Lip. *See* CLEFT LIP.

Hay Fever. *See* ALLERGY.

Heat Rash

Hot weather or being overdressed in any weather causes sweating, which in turn can cause heat rash on face, neck, shoulders, and chest and in the folds of the skin. Although rarely uncomfortable to the child, it can be relieved somewhat by cooling the child and bathing him with tepid water to which baking soda or cornstarch has been added. Applying calamine lotion and dusting lightly with cornstarch or baby powder may also help.

HEAT STROKE

Heat stroke occurs when the body is unable to sweat enough to cool itself adequately. This usually occurs when the body has already lost so much fluid that it turns off the sweating mechanism. If the body is not cooled in another manner–such as by loosening or removing clothes, moving to a cooler place, or bathing in cool water – the body temperature may continue to rise.

Signs of heat stroke are a very flushed appearance, lack of sweating, a rapid heart beat, a change in mental state ranging from dizziness or confusion to unconsciousness, and a body temperature above 106°F (41°C). This is an emergency situation that needs to be treated immediately by cooling the body and administering fluids. A child with heat stroke should be taken to the hospital.

Hemophilia

This condition involves the inability of the blood to clot because it lacks a blood-clotting protein. Almost all sufferers are male, but the disease is transmitted through the mother. Even small cuts and scratches can provoke prolonged bleeding. Spontaneous bleeding may occasionally occur.

Sufferers from the disease should carry a card or wear a tag identifying them as hemophiliacs; in case of an accident, hospital treatment is likely to be necessary to stem the bleeding. Injections of the missing protein or transfusions of plasma usually control bleeding in hemophiliacs, and sometimes they are given routinely to keep clotting normal. Although those receiving these treatments have been at somewhat increased risk for Acquired Immune Deficiency Syndrome, they are usually quite safe and advances in testing donated plasma have now eliminated the risk. Further information is available from the National Hemophilia Foundation, 19 West 34th Street, Room 1204, New York, NY 10001.

Hepatitis

Hepatitis is an inflammation of the liver, commonly caused by viral infection such as Hepatitis A and B and the virus of infectious mononucleosis (E.B. virus).

Symptoms are nausea, occasional vomiting, loose stools, fatigue, and decreased appetite. The well-known symptom of jaundice (yellowish discoloration of eyeballs and skin) is not always present in children. Symptoms are generally so mild and short-lived that the illness may be unnoticed until another member of the family becomes ill.

If the illness is more serious, liver injury may occur and (rarely) may result in liver failure and coma; long-lasting problems are unusual, however, because the liver has great recuperative capacity.

Treatment is rest; no medication should be given without a prescription, since hepatitis can alter the body's reaction to drugs. The spread of the illness may be prevented by administration of gamma globulin to those who have had contact with the ill person. If a member of the household has hepatitis, extra precautions should be taken in not sharing dishes, glasses, or bottles and in handwashing.

Hives. *See* URTICARIA.

Hydrocephalus (water on the brain)

A birth defect that occurs when fluid in hollow spaces (ventricles) in the brain overaccumulate, press on the brain, and ultimately enlarge the head, leading to mental retardation or seizures if untreated. Hydrocephalus can result from bleeding inside the brain and can be accompanied by SPINA BIFIDA. Treatment is by specific medications or more often by inserting a plasic tube (shunt) into a ventricle to drain excess fluid into the abdomen.

Hyperactivity

Hyperactivity is a behavioral condition also called *attentional deficit disorder*. Signs of it are overactiveness, inability to pay attention or focus on a task for any length of time, impulsiveness, and distractibility. Some medicines may help, but special diets, exercises, and vitamin supplements have no proven value. Often the child's behavior improves with age. A health care provider may offer treatment or may refer the child to a specialist.

Hyperopia (farsightedness)

When the lens of the eye has too little focusing power, close objects will appear blurred. Squinting, eye rubbing, lid inflammation, and a lack of interest in looking at picture books are the most frequent manifestations of farsightedness in a young child. The child may complain of eye strain, headaches, and fatigue. An eye doctor can examine the child's eyes to determine if hyperopia is present. Prescription glasses will enable the child to see correctly. *See also* MYOPIA.

Hypothermia

Hypothermia is not particularly worrisome until the temperature falls below about 95°F (35°C). Such a low body temperature suggests a severe infection, some major difficulty in the brain, or recent exposure to very cold air or water without adequately protective clothing. Prompt medical care is required both to treat the hypothermia slowly (so that the heart does not begin beating abnormally) as well as to investigate a possible infectious or neurologic cause.

Impetigo

Impetigo, a contagious bacterial skin infection, may be a complication of another condition or may occur on its own. Small red spots appear, mostly on face, hands, and scalp, turning into watery blisters and then yellow crusts. The sores may itch; soak in water with baking soda. Treatment is by oral antibiotics.

Incubation Period

The incubation period is the period between time of exposure to a disease and the time symptoms begin to show.

Influenza (flu)

Any one of several viral infections, the symptoms of which are chills, feverishness, and pains in the legs, arms, and abdomen. Nausea and even nosebleeds may also be present. Treatment is as for COLDS. Flu is not nearly as apt to be severe in previously healthy children as in adults.

Intestinal Infections

Intestinal infections are most commonly caused by viruses. Symptoms may include vomiting, diarrhea, or both, accompanied by decreased appetite. Fever, if any, will be low. The symptoms are mild, with a few episodes of vomiting and perhaps 2 or 3 days of looser bowel movements; occasionally a child will have stomach cramps. In summer, the virus may cause a rash, with MENINGITIS as a potential complication; in winter, the virus is more likely to produce upper respiratory symptoms as well as intestinal ones. The intestines can also be infected by bacteria, the best known of which is salmonella. Symptoms include fever, stomach cramps, and frequent watery stools (occasionally bloody).

Vomiting and diarrhea that persist beyond 24 hours or seem to interfere with adequate fluid intake should be promptly discussed with your health care provider, as dehydration can occur rapidly. Adequate fluid intake can be checked by noting urine output: if the child has fewer than 3 wet diapers a day or if the urine seems very concentrated–deep yellow and strong smelling–the child should be examined by a health care provider. A diet of decreased solids, with clear liquids (no milk) for a day or so will often help alleviate diarrhea.

Jaundice in the Newborn

A yellow skin color due to accumulated bilirubin (a yellow pigment) is usually transient and harmless in newborn babies. When it is first produced by the conversion of hemoglobin from red blood cells, bilirubin is insoluble and so cannot be excreted. In newborns, the enzymes that dissolve and remove bilirubin are fairly inactive for a few days, and jaundice may develop on about the third day. This is called physiological jaundice, signifying that no underlying disease has caused it.

Jaundice is more usual in preterm babies. In rare cases, it may be due to a compound in breast milk or to some obstruction of the tract that conveys soluble bilirubin from the liver to the intestines for elimination.

Any jaundice that develops in the first 24 hours of life should be investigated promptly, with a precise laboratory diagnosis. Babies with jaundice sometimes are placed under lights (phototherapy) or more rarely have their blood exchanged to help remove excess bilirubin; often they are merely observed and their bilirubin level is checked once or twice a day until it declines.

Lazy Eye. *See* AMBLYOPIA.

Lice

Three types of lice affect humans: crab lice, which tend to nest in pubic hair; body lice, which tend to nest in clothing and feed on the torso; and head lice, which nest in the hair and feed on the scalp.

Head lice occur frequently among school-age children. They lay gray-white eggs, called nits, which stick firmly to the hair and may be visible as tiny specks along the hair shaft. The first sign of louse infestation is usually intense itching as the hatched lice feed on the skin. Scratching should be discouraged, as the resulting irritation can lead to IMPETIGO.

Once spotted, lice are relatively easy to eradicate. Treatment involves two applications of a special pediculicide shampoo, lotion, or powder (at an interval of 7-10 days)

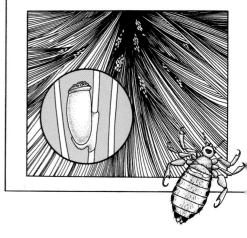

Nits, the tiny, cylindrical eggs of the head louse, are cemented to hairs in clumps near the scalp. The inset left shows a magnified egg; the inset right shows an adult louse.

and thorough removal of nits attached to the hair using a fine comb. Clothes, towels, and bedding should be washed thoroughly in hot water, and other members of the household should be observed over several weeks for signs of infestation.

An infestation of lice is a sign not of poor hygiene but of the highly communicable nature of the condition within an affected population. A health care provider's advice should be sought quickly and without embarrassment.

Lisp

A frontal lisp ("th" for "s," as in "thoup" for "soup") in a child under 3 should not cause alarm. Loss of front teeth, faulty tongue placement, or inappropriate articulation skills often contribute to the pronunciation problem, and these are largely resolved in time. If the child is unable to make an appropriate "s" sound by age 5 or to use it and all other sounds without error by age 6, a health care provider, a speech and language clinician, or both should be consulted.

Lumbar Puncture. *See* MENINGITIS.

Measles

The incubation period of this highly contagious virus is 9 to 12 days; contagiousness lasts from 5 days after exposure until 4 days after the rash begins. First symptoms are runny nose, cough, and red eyes. Fever, vomiting, or diarrhea may precede the rash of small red spots that appears 3 or 4 days later. The fever may become so high that delirium results; try giving tepid-water sponge baths and acetaminophen or aspirin (see FEVER). Small white spots on the inside of the cheeks, visible during the first several days, are a positive confirmation of the development of measles.

When the rash appears, the child often begins to feel better and need not be confined to bed. Watch the child closely for symptoms of complications–earache, increasing cough, changes in alertness–and report them immediately to a health care provider. Immunization against measles is now routine (see page 62).

Meatal Ulcer

This is a small sore that forms at the tip of a circumcised penis. Caused by the rubbing of wet diapers, it can be very painful, particularly when urine passes over it. An antibiotic or hydrocortisone ointment, prescribed by a health care provider, keeps urine from touching the ulcer and helps it to heal. In uncircumcised babies, the foreskin protects against this irritation.

Meningitis

Meningitis is a general term for infections of the lining of the brain and spinal cord, whether caused by bacteria, a virus, certain parasites, a brain abscess, or head injuries. Symptoms include fever, sleepiness, irritability, shrill crying, stiff neck (an unreliable sign in babies), vomiting, headache, seizures, and weakness. Any infant or young child who gets worse with an illness that includes fever and irritability should be given diagnostic tests, including blood tests, a spinal tap (lumbar puncture), and possibly a CAT scan of the head.

Bacterial meningitis can be life-threatening, particularly if prolonged seizures, coma, or shock occur before treatment is started. It is treated with antibiotics; a hospital stay of 10 to 14 days is generally required. Family members and day-care or nursery school contacts should be observed for symptoms of this contagious illness.

Viral meningitis cannot be treated with antibiotics, but the symptoms are generally milder and the infection self-limiting. Frequently, the spinal tap itself brings relief. A brief hospital stay may be required. Some types of viral meningitis are very serious; one is polio, now virtually eliminated through immunization.

Although many cases of meningitis due to *Hemophilus influenzae* occur in children younger than 2 years, a vaccine effective in preventing most such infections in children over 2 years of age has recently been released. It is hoped that a vaccine will soon be developed for younger children.

Middle Ear Fluid. *See* OTITIS MEDIA WITH EFFUSION.

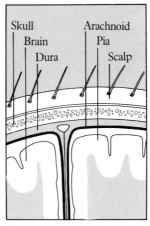

This cross section through the skull shows the dura, arachnoid, and pia–the three coverings (meninges) that protect the brain and spinal cord.

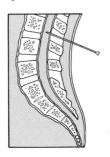

A lumbar puncture draws fluid from the space in the spinal column to test for meningitis.

Migraine

Migraines are severe recurring headaches, often confined to one side of the head but in children frequently on both sides. Nausea, distortion of sight–spots and shapes before the eyes–vertigo, or a general feeling of worry may occur before the headache worsens. The condition tends to be hereditary; attacks may be as frequent as once or twice a week or as infrequent as once or twice a year. The attacks are probably caused by narrowing of blood vessels in the head, which then widen and stretch the nerve endings in the vessels' walls. Sleep usually follows an attack, and between attacks there are no symptoms. Medicines are available to decrease the frequency and severity of migraines.

Mongolism. *See* DOWN'S SYNDROME.

Motion Sickness

Some children are upset by the motion of a car, bus, or boat, less often airplanes or trains. A partial cause is often excitement. Give a light meal without too much to drink an hour or so before setting out, and take a plastic bag just in case. If the child begins to complain of nausea or appears pale and uncomfortable, encourage her to look straight ahead out of the window or at the horizon. If the child is frequently troubled by motion sickness, ask your health care provider to recommend an appropriate dosage of over-the-counter medication.

Mumps

Mumps is a viral illness. Symptoms are fever, headache, and inflammation of the salivary glands on one side or both sides of the face, causing the cheeks to appear swollen. The incubation period is 16 to 18 days; contagiousness ends 9 days after the disappearance of the swelling. The disease is often very mild and may even lack symptoms. If the child is in pain, aspirin or acetaminophen may give some relief. Because the child may find that swallowing is difficult, liquid nourishment rather than solid foods are preferable.

One complication is mumps MENINGITIS, which causes fever, stiff neck, sore throat, and, in rare cases, brain inflammation; recovery is usually complete. Mumps can also cause deafness. In adolescent or adult males, mumps is more painful and may lead to temporarily swollen testicles. Sterility rarely results, but men who have not already had the disease should be immunized or should avoid contact with patients who have mumps. Immunization is routinely available (see page 63).

Myopia (nearsightedness)

When the lens of the eye has too much focusing power, distant objects will appear blurred. A child who holds books or objects close to her eyes, who sits close to the television, or who appears uninterested in distant activities may have myopia. The diagnosis can be confirmed only by examination by an eye doctor. Prescription glasses will enable the child to see correctly. *See also* HYPEROPIA.

Nightmares

Nightmares start occurring normally in children around age 2. They take place during the REM (rapid eye movement) sleeping phase, which begins an hour or so after a person falls asleep and constitutes about half of a young child's total sleep time.

Worry, fear, or even medication may lie behind a child's "bad dream." A child who has frequent nightmares may be worried about something specific; gentle questioning often reveals his concerns. Trying to avoid stressful or overstimulating situations near bedtime may also help. The child's health care provider is a good source of advice.

If a child wakes up crying out in fear, his parent should go to him, remaining calm while comforting and reassuring him that the experience was only a dream. Most frequently, he will return to stable sleep after brief cuddling. Leaving the child to "cry it out" is not recommended. *See also* NIGHT TERRORS.

Night Terrors

A child who wakes up screaming and (often) perspiring, who does not seem aware of you, and who cannot be comforted has probably had a night terror. She will not be able to say what has frightened her; gentle consoling and cuddling will help her calm down (usually within 5 minutes) and go to sleep again. Night terrors usually happen during a non-REM phase of sleep and tend not to be remembered. They are sometimes accompanied by sleepwalking, but this is rare in children under 5. Night terrors occur more frequently in boys than girls, are most common from age 5 to age 7, and are usually outgrown by adolescence. Frequently other family members have also experienced them. *See also* NIGHTMARES.

Nits. *See* LICE.

Nosebleeds

Nosebleeds are common in childhood and are most often caused by "picking" the nose, a habit developed by children with colds or allergies that produce a chronic drippy nose. Injuries to the nose after a fall or a blow may also result in bleeding.

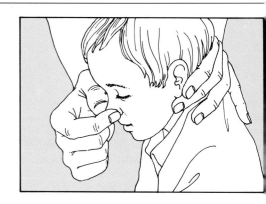

If a nosebleed occurs, pinch the child's nose gently to stem the flow. It will probably stop in several minutes.

To treat, place firm pressure against the sides of the nose to close the nasal air passages. Pressure should be maintained for five minutes to allow a good clot to form. The position of the head is not critical: Some prefer the head tipped backwards, while others prefer the head bent forward. The latter has the advantage of preventing blood from being swallowed. Repeated or prolonged (longer than 10 minutes) nosebleeds should be evaluated by a health care provider.

Otitis Externa (earache)

This term identifies inflammation of the ear canal; it is sometimes caused by poking things into the ear, but more often it results from irritating substances encountered in the water while swimming or from a generalized skin rash. Moving the ear hurts, and a discharge may be present. A health care provider should be consulted whenever a child complains of ear pain or, in the case of a child who cannot yet speak, pulls at or rubs the ear repeatedly. Otitis externa is usually a bacterial infection treated with antibiotic ear drops.

Otitis Media (earache)

This term identifies infection of the middle ear, caused by bacteria from the throat or nose. Children more frequently contract this than adults because their eustachian tubes, which connect the throat and middle ears and serve to equalize air pressure on either side of the eardrum, are shorter and usually less well coordinated. Otitis media can follow another infection such as a cold. A child of 3 may complain of pain; younger children and babies may pull at their ears. If the child seems not to hear well when he has a cold, especially if he has fever, a health care provider should check his ears. Treatment is usually with an antibiotic. *See also* OTITIS MEDIA WITH EFFUSION.

Otitis Media with Effusion (middle ear fluid)

Often a child seems to hear poorly even though he does not complain of an earache or show any signs of having one. Examination by a health care provider may reveal that a liquid (often a gluelike substance) has formed in the middle ear, preventing the eardrum from moving as it should.

If antibiotics do not clear the trouble, which is often at least partly due to a bacterial infection, small plastic or metal tubes may be inserted into the eardrum (under anesthesia) to provide air passages to equalize pressure on either side of the drum, and thus to decrease irritation within the ear that often results in the fluid condition. After a few months the tubes usually drop out on their own, after which recurrences are rare. The procedure is favored by many ear specialists, although others question its value. You may wish to obtain a second opinion if ear tubes are suggested for your child. A health care provider may also recommend ear plugs for the child to prevent ear infections during swimming or bathing.

Pertussis (whooping cough)

Pertussis is a serious bacterial disease that may last for weeks or even months. The first symptoms are usually a runny nose and a cough. After a few days, paroxysms of coughing begin. The coughs occur in rapid succession; when a breath is finally taken, the air rushing through the windpipe causes the characteristic "whoop." Vomiting some-

This cross section shows the major divisions of the ear.

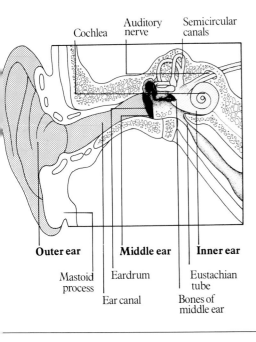

Cochlea · Auditory nerve · Semicircular canals

Outer ear · **Middle ear** · **Inner ear**

Mastoid process · Eardrum · Eustachian tube

Ear canal · Bones of middle ear

times follows a coughing paroxysm. Complications include ear infections and pneumonia; convulsions, brain damage, and death can occur in infants. The incubation period is from 7 to 10 days; the illness is contagious for 3 weeks from the onset of the paroxysms.

Treatment is by antibiotics, but although these kill the bacteria that caused the cough initially, the cough usually continues for some time. Frequent small meals in place of periodic large ones will reduce the chance of vomiting.

Because pertussis is especially dangerous in babies under age 1, immunization should be started when the baby is 2 months old (see page 60). Sometimes children who have been immunized catch the illness anyway, though usually only a mild case of it.

Pink Eye. *See* CONJUNCTIVITIS.

Pinworms

Pinworms are quite common in young children and often run in families. They may be visible in the stool as small, white, threadlike forms. They are a frequent cause of anal-area itching, especially at night, when the worms may migrate from the intestines to lay their eggs outside the body, but they rarely cause more worrisome problems. They are easily treated with oral medication prescribed by a health care provider.

Pneumonia

An infection of the lung caused by virus or bacteria. The viral form is generally not serious; it begins as a head cold with low-grade fever and a lot of nasal discharge, which results in coughing and some breathing difficulty. If the influenza virus is the cause, the child will often feel sicker than with other viruses. Since viral illnesses are self-limiting, treatment is for the symptoms: aspirin or acetaminophen to lower temperature, room humidification, lots of liquids, and, if a health care provider recommends it, decongestants to ease breathing difficulties. Poor appetite is to be expected and should not cause concern.

Bacterial pneumonia develops as a complication of an upper respiratory viral infection and usually begins with a very high fever (103°F/39.4°C or more). Breathing may be painful. Positive diagnosis must be made by a health care provider, who may order x-rays and blood tests to confirm that pneumonia is present. Treatment for bacterial pneumonia is as for the viral form, with the addition of antibiotics. Hospitalization is infrequently necessary, and recovery, once the illness is diagnosed and treatment begun, is usually smooth.

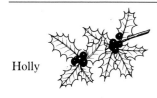

Holly

Poinsettia

Lily of the Valley

Children are attracted to the bright berries and leaves of many poisonous plants. Be aware of potentially dangerous plants in your home and garden. Three common species are shown here; others include lantana, morning glory, oleander, rhododendron, yew, privet, laurel, sweet pea, daffodil, iris, and jonquil. See page 38.

POISONING

Every household should have a bottle of syrup of ipecac, available without prescription, in the medicine cabinet. The number of the poison control center should be posted prominently at each telephone. If a child ingests a suspected poison, *call the poison control center immediately*. Do not waste time calling the family health care provider or an ambulance, as neither will respond as quickly, knowledgeably, and helpfully as the poison control center. Be prepared to tell: WHAT was taken, WHEN it was taken, and HOW MUCH was taken. *Do nothing without medical advice*. Inducing vomiting with syrup of ipecac may not be appropriate, depending on the poison taken. For example, if the ingested substance is caustic, vomiting may damage the lungs if the vomitus is inhaled.

The best course, however, is prevention.

POISON PREVENTION MEASURES
- Keep pills, household cleaners, and all toxic substances locked away—out of sight and out of reach.
- Never refer to medication as candy, and do not take medication in the presence of a child during this "copy cat" stage of life.
- Do not let a child play where substances used for hobbies, repair and maintenance, or gardening are stored.
- Never put acids, cleaning fluids, or any nonfood liquid into a soft drink or fruit juice bottle, as a child may mistake the contents and take a drink.

It bears repeating: the best treatment is *prevention* accomplished by following the above recommendations and *prompt treatment* accomplished by having syrup of ipecac on hand, by calling the poison control center, and by following the procedures the person there advises.

Poliomyelitis (polio)

Poliomyelitis is a viral disease that affects the spinal cord and is spread by droplets or through the stools. The incubation period is 3 to 14 days. Symptoms in children are often the same as for influenza and similar illnesses: fever, irritability, and sleepiness. Rarely, MENINGITIS or paralysis (temporary or permanent) develops. Once a cause of paralysis and even death to many children, poliomyelitis has largely been eliminated in the United States through routine immunization (see page 62).

Projectile Vomiting. *See* PYLORIC STENOSIS.

Pyloric Stenosis

More common among boys than girls, the condition is caused by a thickening or spasm of the pyloric muscle at the end of the stomach, which narrows the channel into the duodenum. Typically, at 2 to 3 weeks of age, the baby begins to vomit with such force that a whole feeding can be shot across the room. Appetite continues to be good, and no other signs of illness—fever, for example—are present. The condition rarely develops after 6 weeks of age. Treatment is by surgery, and the cure is generally complete.

Rash

A skin rash is not a disease in itself but a sign of any of a number of conditions, including viral, fungal, and bacterial infections, allergic reactions, insect bites, and parasitic infestations. The underlying cause must be determined and treated, although in many cases the cause cannot be discovered and the child simply outgrows the sensitivity that caused the rash. If the rash causes discomfort, calamine lotion, a tepid bath into which cornstarch or baking soda has been mixed, and various over-the-counter anti-itch creams and lotions may supply relief. *See* ALLERGY, AMMONIA DERMATITIS, CHICKEN POX, ECZEMA, HEAT RASH, IMPETIGO, MEASLES, OTITIS EXTERNA, RINGWORM, ROSEOLA INFANTUM, RUBELLA, SCABIES, SCARLET FEVER, SEBORRHEA, SEBORRHEIC DERMATITIS, URTICARIA.

Regurgitation

Regurgitation is the dribbling back of milk or formula that often occurs in young babies after a feeding or burping. It is usually more of a nuisance than a problem. Rarely will a baby lose significant nourishment. Burping the baby frequently or sitting her up for a while after a feeding may stop the tendency. Overfeeding may be a cause; smaller amounts of milk or formula may be in order. When the baby appears to lose interest in the breast or bottle, that feeding should be stopped. *See also* VOMITING.

Ringworm (tinea)

Ringworm is a fungal infection of the skin that appears as a circular rash with small bumps at its outer edges. It is not caused by a worm. Ringworm on the scalp produces bald patches covered with scales. A health care provider should be consulted at once, as ringworm is highly infectious; the affected person's brushes, combs, and towels must not be used by other members of the family. Antifungal medication will be prescribed, and as the ringworm disappears, new hair will grow. The health care provider may recommend that the child be kept isolated.

Roseola Infantum
This is a noncontagious infection, probably viral, that affects infants. The first symptom is a high fever lasting 2 to 4 days. A convulsion may occur. When the fever breaks, a rash of small pink spots appears; the child otherwise appears (and is) quite well. The fever may be treated with aspirin or acetominophen. *See also* SEIZURES, FEVER.

Roundworms (ascariasis)
Roundworms are a parasitic infestation of dogs and cats. The stools of an affected dog or cat contain the eggs of the worm. If a child's hands become contaminated and he then puts them to his mouth, the eggs enter his body, hatching in the child's intestines, and the worms may pass to organs of the body, such as the liver, brain, spleen, and eyes.

The danger is not from the child's own pet, which is presumably kept free of worms, but from animal feces in open spaces and parks. Children should be taught to wash their hands with soap and warm water when they come in from playing outdoors. The worms may be visible in the stool, but they rarely cause any symptoms. They can be treated by a health care provider.

Rubella (German measles)
A milder complaint than measles, rubella lasts only 1 or 2 days. Symptoms are a rash that begins on the head and spreads to the rest of the body, mild fever, and swollen glands at the back of the neck. Rubella is spread by droplet infection; the incubation period is 14 to 21 days, and contagiousness lasts 5 days after the rash appears. The child should be isolated to avoid spreading the infection; rest and plenty of liquids will alleviate discomfort to a degree.

Complications of rubella are rare. The great danger of the illness lies in the harmful effects it can have on a developing fetus–deafness, blindness, heart problems, physical deformity, or mental retardation can afflict a baby whose mother contracted rubella early in her pregnancy. Any pregnant woman who has not been immunized (or is uncertain that she has been) and who is exposed to rubella should inform her health care provider immediately. A test will reveal if she has the needed antibodies (either from immunization or previous exposure): If so, the fetus will not be affected; if not, the fetus is at risk. Immunization against rubella is available (see page 63) and is routinely given. *See also* ROSEOLA INFANTUM.

Runny Ear
A discharging ear should always be taken seriously; delaying treatment could lead to serious medical problems and deafness. *See* OTITIS MEDIA, OTITIS MEDIA WITH EFFUSION.

Scabies
Scabies is an infectious skin disease caused by a mite that burrows into the skin and lays eggs; the mites then return to the surface, mate, and renew the cycle. Symptoms are intense itching–especially at night and mainly between the fingers, in the armpits, around the waist–and a rash of little blisters. Extremely contagious, it can be transmitted by person-to-person contact or from infested bedding, clothing, or towels. A health care provider will prescribe a chemical solution to eradicate the mites. Infected bedding and clothing must be washed in hot water and dried at high heat.

Scarlet Fever
Scarlet fever is a streptococcal infection that produces a sore throat and a red rash. It can be transmitted from streptococcal infections elsewhere in the body–on the skin (as with IMPETIGO or an infected BURN) or in an abscess, for example. Treatment is with antibiotics, as for STREP THROAT.

Scrape. *See* ABRASION.

Seborrhea (cradle cap)
Seborrhea, a layer of brown or yellowish crusts on the scalp, is caused by somewhat oily skin too gently washed. If the trouble spreads, it can cause a red scaly inflammation with cracks above the ears. In its early stages, cradle cap can be treated by soaking with baby oil until it softens, then lifting the crusts gently off with a comb, and rubbing in a mild shampoo with a washcloth. If the skin underneath is red, ask a health care provider for advice. Medicated baby shampoos are available. *See also* SEBORRHEIC DERMATITIS.

Seborrheic Dermatitis
This condition is characterized by thick scaly flaking and redness of the skin. When it occurs on the scalp (particularly of newborns), it is commonly called cradle cap. It may also appear on other parts of the body, especially at skin folds and where oil glands are most active. The affected areas may be irritated and itchy.

Treatment is with compresses of warm mineral oil applied for thirty minutes to soften the crusts, followed by washing with mild soap (shampoo for cradle cap) and thorough rinsing with clear water. Pat dry. If this treatment is carried out daily for three days and if careful bathing and shampooing is continued thereafter daily or every other day, the condition should be controllable without medical treatment. In stubborn or persistent cases, a health care provider may prescribe steroid or other preparations, but none should be tried without specific medical advice.

Seizures

Seizures or convulsions can be caused by fever or disease, epilepsy, or severe head trauma. They are marked by uncontrollable jerking of arms and legs. The child's eyes may turn to one side or roll back in her head. She may lose control of bowels and bladder. Nothing can be done to stop a seizure, but the possibility of the child's injuring herself during the seizure can be minimized.

Lay her on the floor, on her side or stomach, and turn her head to one side to ensure that she will not choke on her secretions. Make certain her breathing passages are clear; if she appears to have difficulty breathing or begins to turn blue, begin rescue breathing if you know how (see ARTIFICIAL RESPIRATION); otherwise, call for help. Do not leave the child until the convulsion stops, generally within 10 minutes. When it does, or if it continues beyond 10 minutes, seek emergency help.

SHOCK

A child in shock may show few or many symptoms: paleness, rapid breathing, sweating, vomiting, and even unconsciousness. Shock may follow an accident or a severe emotional upset. Deal first with the cause, and then with the condition. Keep calm yourself; lay the child down on his stomach or side, loosen his clothing, and cover him with a blanket. Give him nothing to drink if you think an anesthetic may be needed to treat any injury. Do not attempt

to warm him with a hot water bottle or heating pad. (The purpose of the blanket is to maintain body temperature, not to increase it.) Simply keep him still and warm. If these measures do not result in some improvement within fifteen minutes (less sweating, a more normal breathing pattern, return to consciousness), the child should be taken to the hospital. Failure to improve with these measures in this period of time indicates that the problem is serious and requires prompt treatment to prevent possible life-threatening complications.

The underlying cause *must* be treated first: if the child is bleeding, do what you can to stop it; if the child is suffering heat stroke, treat it appropriately with cooling, and do not cover him with the blanket. *See also* BLEEDING, HEAT STROKE.

Smallpox

Smallpox is a very serious viral disease that was often fatal. It has been eradicated throughout the world. In the unlikely event of a future outbreak, vaccination would provide immediate protection.

Sore Throat

Sore throats are a symptom of various illnesses, including tonsilitis, viral infections resulting in colds or flu, and bacterial infections such as strep throat. The underlying condition should be treated. Relief of symptomatic throat discomfort may be accomplished by giving liquids and soft, cool foods such as ice cream, fruit ices, yogurt, gelatin, pudding, and applesauce. A child may temporarily refuse other solids without harm. *See* COLDS, INFLUENZA, SCARLET FEVER, STREP THROAT, TONSILITIS.

Spina Bifida

Spina bifida is a congenital defect of the spine and spinal cord that develops in the embryo. At birth, a portion of the spinal cord is exposed or covered only by a sac of fluid. Nerve damage usually where the spinal cord protrudes results in some degree of permanent numbness and paralysis of the buttocks, legs, and feet. Paralysis of bladder and rectum often causes incontinence. Recurrent urinary tract infections require prompt treatment. Surgery can close the skin but cannot correct the damaged spinal cord. The child's intelligence may be normal, even if the spina bifida is accompanied by HYDROCEPHALUS. The condition can be discovered by amniocentesis before birth.

Spinal Tap. *See* MENINGITIS.

Sprain

Sprains and strains (which are somewhat less

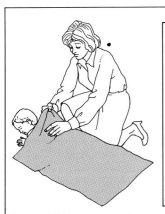

Lay a child in shock on his side or stomach with head turned and keep him warm.

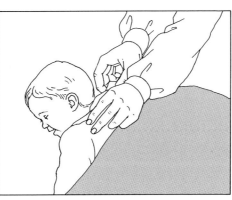

To help circulation and assist his breathing, loosen any tight clothing around his neck.

serious) are externally induced injuries to muscles, tendons, and ligaments. Distinguishing between a sprain or strain and a fracture may be difficult if the injury is accompanied by pain, swelling, and redness. The safest course is to consult a health care provider, who may obtain x-rays to determine if a bone is broken and (if it is not) can advise treatment for the sprain–the use of ice or warm soaks, wrapping or splinting, and any special positioning of the injured area to reduce discomfort and hasten healing.

Squint. *See* STRABISMUS.

Stings

Most insect stings need only washing with cool water and soothing with calamine lotion or an anti-itch spray or cream. If the stinger is visible, try teasing it out gently with a fingernail. Using two fingers or tweezers can compress the stinger, injecting more venom (*see* drawing).

If a child is stung on or inside the mouth, swelling may hinder breathing; have the child suck an ice cube to limit absorption of venom, and go to a health care provider. A wasp or bee sting occasionally causes allergic reaction–paleness, severe pain, and inflammation. If this occurs, obtain medical attention. Very rarely, a reaction is so severe that it results in shock; keep the child warm and lying on his stomach or side, with head turned. Seek immediate medical help. *See* SHOCK.

Strabismus (crossed eyes, squint)

The relatively large amount of skin at the inner corners of their eyes (called epicanthal folds) frequently causes new babies to look cross-eyed. If a baby over 3 months old always looks cross-eyed, consult a health care provider, who may recommend an eye specialist. True strabismus is an eye muscle imbalance, early treatment of which is essential to prevent AMBLYOPIA.

Treatment may involve surgery or patching one eye for a while. Surgery to correct strabismus can be done any time in the first 3 years of life (after that, repair will be cosmetic only as it is probably too late to correct the amblyopia); usually it is done around age 2. The procedure generally requires, at most, an overnight stay in the hospital. Sometimes more than one operation is needed to achieve optimal results. *See also* AMBLYOPIA.

Strain. *See* SPRAIN.

Strep Throat

Strep throat is a sore throat caused by streptococcus bacteria. It is diagnosed by

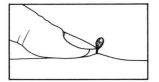

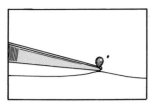

Try to tease out an insect sting with your fingernail (1). If this fails, grip the sting below the poison sac with a pair of tweezers (2) and remove. Using your fingers risks squeezing the poison into the wound.

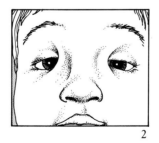

Six muscles control the movement of each eyeball. Strabismus (1) occurs when an imbalance in their strength results in a failure of the six to hold the eyes in alignment. The appearance of strabismus may be falsely given by wide skin folds (common in young babies) in the epicanthus at the inner corner of the eyes (2).

wiping a swab across the back of the throat and then analyzing the specimen in a laboratory for the presence of streptococcus. Treatment is with antibiotics. Discomfort can be relieved as for any sore throat. *See also* SCARLET FEVER, SORE THROAT.

Stye

A stye is an infection of a hair follicle in an eyelash, causing a small boil on the eyelid. Applying moist heat–a clean handkerchief or washcloth dipped in warm water–often helps to clear the infection. A health care provider should be consulted if the swelling persists for more than 2 days or if it spreads or otherwise worsens. A child who has recurring styes should be examined for a chronic skin problem that might be causing difficulties elsewhere.

Styes can be transferred from one eye to the other, so eye-rubbing should be discouraged. The child's facecloth and towels should be kept separate to avoid spreading the infection to other family members.

Sudden Infant Death Syndrome (crib death)

The sudden infant death syndrome or crib death are terms given to the sudden unexplained death of an apparently healthy baby. It is most common between the ages of 2 and 6 months. It occurs more frequently in winter, in babies who are bottle-fed, in economically disadvantaged families, and in areas where there are reports of chest infections. It has occurred in hospitals to otherwise apparently healthy babies. Among the contributory factors put forward are allergies, suffocations, overheating, or that the baby quite literally forgets to breathe. Although research continues into its cause, no single factor has been isolated.

Because the tragedy is so devastating and so mysterious, a crib death usually attracts publicity, so that it may seem more common than it really is.

Parents who have suffered such a sorrow must be helped not only by the support of friends and relations, but by expert counseling. To the parents' overwhelming distress is added the trauma of the legal process because it is necessary to establish that the baby died from natural causes. Happily a more enlightened and sympathetic attitude is now usual from those responsible for administering the law as knowledge of the disease becomes more widespread, but great suffering has been caused by the occasional suggestion that the parents were in some way to blame for the death. "Could I have prevented this?" must always be in the parents' minds without the inference of others, and so guilt and responsibility are often added to sorrow.

It is not only the parents who have suffered: Other children, grandparents, and relations are also affected. Older children in the family may also need extra love and comfort just at the time when the parents, needing it most themselves, find it difficult to give. It is important for parents not to shut themselves away at such times, mentally, emotionally, or physically. Mutual support and understanding between the parents can help to deepen the ties between them.

Counseling and advice is available through professionals–doctors, clergy, counselors– and support groups (see page 230 for addresses). A period of grieving is essential; the sorrow should not lead to the birth of a second child as a "replacement" before the first has been fully mourned. Nor should fear of another such catastrophe dissuade parents from having another child.

Sunburn

Sunburn is painful reddening and, possibly, blistering of the skin caused by the sun. Discomfort develops some time after the skin has been burned. Fair-skinned children burn more easily than darker children, but no child should be exposed to steady sun for longer than ½ hour for the first 2 or 3 days of sunny weather. Repeated overexposure to sunlight has been shown to have a strong relationship to skin cancers later in life. The shoulders and back of the neck and legs are particularly vulnerable. At the beach or pool, use a sunscreen lotion that gives maximum protection and provide a hat and loose shirt for wear over the bathing suit.

Calamine lotion will soothe sunburned skin, and children's aspirin will reduce the pain (in this case, acetaminophen is not effective). The burns may blister, but then they fade and peel.

Sun Stroke

Sun stroke is a particular form of HEAT STROKE caused by exposure to the heat of the sun.

Sweating

Sweating is the body's way of bringing down its temperature. The evaporation of sweat helps the body lose heat and results in a cool feeling. If the surrounding air is warmer than the body, however, the body can pick up heat and become even warmer. Thus, over-dressing a child or keeping her in an overheated room can interfere with the sweating mechanism. Most children will slow down of their own accord if an activity– running around, for instance–makes them uncomfortably hot. If your child does not and appears very flushed, calm her down and loosen her clothing. *See also* HEAT STROKE.

Talipes. *See* CLUB FOOT.

Tear Duct Obstruction

Discharge from an eye that is not inflamed (as with conjunctivitis) may be caused by a blocked tear duct. Located at the inner corner of each eye, these ducts allow tears to drain out of the eye and into the nose. If the duct is blocked during infancy, the baby's eye looks constantly wet and is often covered by a mucuslike material.

The blockage usually disappears on its own within the first 2 months of life, and by 8 months most cases have cleared. In rare cases, a health care provider must probe the duct to open it. This is done under general anesthesia in a clinic or doctor's office and does not require a hospital stay.

Teeth. *See* ACCIDENT TO THE TEETH, DENTAL CARIES.

Tetanus

This painful and potentially fatal disease is caused by toxins produced in deep puncture wounds infected by tetanus bacteria. The first sign is a stiff jaw, from which the common name lockjaw derives. Severe and painful muscle spasms develop throughout the body as the poison spreads through the bloodstream. In fatal cases, the muscle spasms interfere with breathing. Immuniza-tion against tetanus with periodic boosters (see page 62) provides protection in the event of a deep puncture wound, but any such wound should receive medical attention, which may include an additional booster shot if none has been given in the past 5 years.

Thrush. *See* CANDIDA ALBICANS.

Tinea. *See* RINGWORM.

Tonsilitis

Tonsilitis is an inflammation of the tonsils. It is rare in a child under 3. Symptoms are a sore and inflamed throat, general aches and pains, and fever. Tonsils in a young baby are quite small, but they grow larger after the first year.

Tonsilitis is infectious for the first 2 days, so the ill child should be kept away from others. Treatment for a child under 3 is usually with aspirin or acetaminophen for discomfort and fever (if any), and with cool liquids. Surgical removal of tonsils is rarely necessary, even for a child who has had repeated episodes of tonsilitis.

Umbilical Hernia

Common in babies. When the gap in the navel through which the umbilical cord has passed does not immediately close, a small piece of intestine shows through in a lump. Left untreated, it will almost always disappear. It is not painful.

Urinary Infection

Urinary infections are fairly uncommon in young children, but because some of the symptoms–poor appetite, fever, vomiting, failure to thrive–are common to other conditions, a health care provider may not discover the cause until all other explanations have been eliminated and a urine test is finally done. A child who has difficulty or pain when passing urine, does so very frequently, or has bloodstained urine should be given a urine test. X-rays of the child's kidneys and bladder may be needed to confirm the diagnosis. Once the infection is diagnosed, antibiotics usually clear it up rapidly.

Urticaria (hives)

These round raised patches and reddened skin itch intensely. Possible causes are allergies to drugs, foods, or insect bites. Emotional stress can also produce the symptoms. Apply calamine lotion on the spots to soothe the itching or add two tablespoons of sodium bicarbonate to bath water. A health care provider may also recommend an oral antihistamine.

Not usually a dangerous problem, the hives should disappear in a few hours. Sometimes others appear soon after–or over the course of several weeks–but this is uncommon. *See also* ALLERGY.

Varicella. *See* CHICKEN POX.

Verrucae (warts)

Caused by a virus, warts are infectious skin growths that most commonly appear on hands and feet. They do not lead to cancer and are generally painless unless subjected to external pressure.

Warts usually disappear without treatment, but a health care provider may prescribe an ointment or remove a wart by chemical or surgical means if it is painful or bothersome.

Vomiting

Vomiting is the forceful emptying of the stomach when the stomach or bowel is unable to move its contents along as quickly as usual; a back-up of liquids and food ensues, followed by vomiting. This is not the same as regurgitation. Occasional vomiting needs no specific treatment, although the underlying cause should be determined and treated. Causes include moderate to severe pain (such as earaches and fractures), head injuries, excessive crying, excessive coughing, tonsilitis, fear, motion sickness, and certain medicines (especially codeine, erythromycin, and theophylline).

Repeated vomiting in a young baby should be brought to the attention of a health care provider. It may lead to dehydration, and the underlying cause must be determined. The commonest causes are intestinal infections and milk or formula intolerance. Diarrhea may be an associated symptom.

An older, previously healthy child who vomits a few times usually has an intestinal infection. Allow the child free access to liquids other than milk, but limit the amount to one or two ounces at a time, which may help the child to hold it down. Vomiting may also come with infections of the ear, lungs, or kidneys. *See also* DEHYDRATION, DIARRHEA, INTESTINAL INFECTIONS, PYLORIC STENOSIS, REGURGITATION.

Warts. *See* VERRUCAE.

Water in the Ears

Water that gets in the ears during bathing or swimming will not cause a problem unless the child already has an ear infection. The water will not go beyond the ear drum and will drain out again; there is no need to try to clean inside the ear canals.

Water on the Brain. *See* HYDROCEPHALUS.

Wax in the Ears

Wax serves the natural role of protecting the ear from dust; it should not, therefore, be wiped away until it reaches the outer edge of the ear canal. Do not attempt to clean a child's ears with cotton swabs: It is unnecessary and may cause damage.

Whooping Cough. *See* PERTUSSIS.

NATIONAL INFORMATION AND SUPPORT ORGANIZATIONS

arthritis
National Foundation for Childhood Arthritis
2424 Pennsylvania Avenue NW, Washington, DC 20037
Arthritis Foundation
3400 Peachtree Road, NE, Atlanta GA 30326

asthma
Asthma and Allergy Association
1302 18th Street NW, Washington, DC 20036

autism
National Society for Autistic Children
1234 Massachusetts Avenue NW,
Suite 1017, Washington, DC 20005 (202) 783-0125

bereavement
Compassionate Friends, Inc.
Box 1347, Oak Brook, IL 60521 (312) 323-5010
SHARE
St. John's Hospital, 800 E. Carpenter St., Springfield, IL 62702 (217) 544-6464

blindness
American Foundation for the Blind
15 West 16th Street, New York, NY 10011

bone formation
Osteogenesis Imperfecta Foundation
Box 838, Manchester, NH 03105

breastfeeding
La Leche International
9616 Minneapolis Avenue, Franklin Park, IL 60131
Nursing Mothers Counsel, Inc.
Box 50063, Palo Alto, CA 94303

Caesarean birth
CSEC, Inc.
22 Forest Road, Framingham, MA 01701

cancer in childhood
The Candlelighters Foundation
2025 I Street NW, Suite 1011, Washington, DC 20003

cerebral palsy
United Cerebral Palsy Association
66 East 34th Street, New York, NY 10016 (212) 481-6300

child abuse
Child Welfare League of America
67 Irving Place, New York, NY 10003
Parents Anonymous, National Office
2810 Artesia Boulevard, Redondo Beach, CA 90278

childbirth associations
American Academy of Husband-Coached Childbirth
    Box 5224, Sherman Oaks, CA 91413 (Bradley method)
American Society for Psychoprophylaxis in Obstetrics

33429 Farragut Station, Washington, DC 20033 (Lamaze method)
Cooperative Birth Center Network
Box 1, Route 1, Perkiomenville, PA 18074 (alternative birth center information)
International Childbirth Education Association
Box 20048, Minneapolis, MN 55420 (family-centered maternity care, and combined Bradley, Lamaze, and other methods)

cleft palate
American Cleft Palate Association
Administrative Office, 331 Salk Hall, University of Pittsburgh, Pittsburgh, PA 15261 (412) 681-9620

cystic fibrosis
Cystic Fibrosis Foundation
6000 Executive Boulevard, Suite 309, Rockville, MD 20852 (301) 881-9130

day care
Day Care Division
Administration for Children, Youth and Families, U.S. Department of Health and Human Services, Washington, DC 20013

diabetes
Juvenile Diabetes Foundation International
23 East 26th Street, New York, NY 10010 (212) 889-7575

Down's syndrome
Caring
Box 400, Milton, WI 98354

dyslexia
The Orton Society
8415 Bellina Lane, Towson, MD 21204

epilepsy
Epilepsy Foundation of America
4351 Garden City Drive, Landover, MD 20781 (301) 459-3700

family counseling
American Association for Marriage and Family Therapy
1710 K Street, NW, Suite 407, Washington, DC 20006

family planning
Planned Parenthood Federation
810 Seventh Avenue, New York, NY 10019

handicapped
National Information Center for Handicapped Children and Youth
Closer Look, Box 1492, Washington, DC 20003

health care
Association for the Care of Children's Health
3615 Wisconsin Avenue, Washington, DC 20016 (202) 244-1801

hearing-impaired
American Speech-Language-Hearing Association

10801 Rockville Pike, Rockville MD 20852 (301) 897-5700

International Association of Parents of the Deaf
814 Thayer Avenue, Silver Spring, MD 20910 (301) 585-5400

hemophilia
National Hemophilia Foundation
19 West 34th Street, Room 1204, New York, NY 10001 (212) 563-0211

hospital stays
Children in Hospital, Inc.
31 Wilshire Park, Needham, MA 02192

language disabilities
Foundation for Children with Language Disabilities
99 Park Avenue, New York, NY 10016

American Speech-Language-Hearing Association
10801 Rockville Pike, Rockville, MD 20852 (301) 897-5700

learning disabilities
Association for Children with Learning Disabilities
2200 Brownsville Road, Pittsburgh, PA 15210

motor disabilities
National Information Center for Handicapped Children and Youth
Closer Look, Box 1492, Washington, DC 20013

National Easter Seal Society for Crippled Children and Adults
2023 West Ogden Avenue, Chicago, IL 60612

muscular dystrophy
Muscular Dystrophy Association
810 Seventh Avenue, New York, NY 10019

poison control
American Association of Poison Control Centers
2025 I Street NW, Washington, DC 20006

postpartum support
Mothers Are People Too
Box 9956, Asheville, NC 28805

prematurity
Parents of Premature and High Risk Infants International
c/o C.A.S.E., 33 West 42nd Street, New York, NY 10036

retardation
Council for Exceptional Children
1920 Association Drive, Reston, VA 22091
National Association of Retarded Citizens
2501 Avenue J, Arlington, TX 76011

safety
Consumer Product Safety Commission
Washington, DC 20207 (800) 638-2772 (in

Maryland, (800) 492-8363; Alaska, Hawaii, Puerto Rico, Virgin Islands, (800) 638-8333

National Highway Traffic Safety Commission
Washington, DC 20590 (800) 424-9393

Consumers Union
256 Washington Street, Mount Vernon, NY 10553

sickle cell
National Association for Sickle Cell Disease
3460 Wilshire Boulevard, Suite 1012, Los Angeles, CA 90010

single-parent families
Parents Without Partners
7910 Woodmont Avenue, Bethesda, MD 20814

speech-impaired
Speech Foundation of America
152 Lombardy Road, Memphis, TN 38111

American Speech-Language-Hearing Association
10801 Rockville Pike, Rockville, MD 20852 (301) 897-5700

spina bifida
Spina Bifida Association of America
343 South Dearborn Street, Suite 319, Chicago, IL 60604

sudden infant death syndrome
National SIDS Foundation
2 Metro Plaza, Suite 205, 8240 Professional Place, Landover, MD 20785 (301) 459-3388

twins
National Organization of Mothers of Twins Clubs, Inc.
5402 Amberwood Lane, Rockville, MD 20853

International Twins Association
c/o Elspeth Corley, Box 77386, Station C, Atlanta, GA 30357

FURTHER READING

BECOMING A PARENT

pregnancy and childbirth
Bean, Constance A. *Methods of Childbirth*. Garden City, New York: Doubleday, 1982.

Bradley, Robert A. *Husband-Coached Childbirth*. 3d ed. New York: Harper & Row, 1981.

Curto, Josephine L. *How to Become a Single Parent*. Englewood Cliffs, New Jersey: Prentice-Hall, 1983.

Hotchner, Tracy. *Pregnancy and Childbirth*. New York: Avon, 1984.

Kitzinger, Sheila. *The Complete Book of Pregnancy and Childbirth*. New York: Knopf, 1980.

Queenan, John T. *A New Life*. Rev. ed. Boston: Little, Brown, 1986.

buying for the baby
Bundy, Darcie. *The Affordable Baby*. New York: Harper & Row, 1985.

safety
Brown, Jean. *Keeping Your Kids Safe*. New York: Monarch, 1985.

Stewart, Arlene. *Childproofing Your Home*. Reading, Massachusetts: Addison-Wesley, 1984.

bereavement
Tengbom, Mildred. *Help for Bereaved Parents*. St. Louis: Concordia, 1981.

DAILY CARE

early adjustment
Brazelton, T. Berry. *Infants and Mothers*. New York: Dell, 1986.

Eheart, Brenda K., and Martel, Susan K. *The Fourth Trimester*. New York: Ballantine, 1984.

Henig, Robin M., and Fletcher, Anne B. *Your Premature Baby*. New York: Ballantine, 1984.

Panter, Gideon G., and Linde, Shirley M. *Now That You've Had Your Baby: How to Feel Better and Happier Than Ever, After Childbirth*. Englewood Cliffs, New Jersey. Prentice-Hall, 1977.

Verrilli, George, and Mueser, Anne M. *Welcome Baby: A Guide to the First Six Weeks*. New York: St. Martin's, 1982.

children with special needs
Blacher, J. *Severely Handicapped Young Children and Their Families*. Orlando, Florida: Harcourt, Brace, 1984.

Cunningham, C. *Helping Your Exceptional Baby: A Practical and Honest Approach to Raising a Mentally Handicapped Baby*. New York: Pantheon, 1981.

Featherstone, H. *A Difference in the Family: Living with a Disabled Child*. New York: Penguin, 1981.

Jones, Monica L. *Home Care for the Chronically Ill or Disabled Child*. New York: Harper & Row, 1985.

Murray, J.B., and Murray, E. *And Say What He Is: The Life of a Special Child*. Boston: M.I.T. Press, 1975.

Ross, B. *Our Special Child: A Guide to Successful Parenting of Handicapped Children*. Old Tappan, New Jersey: Revell, 1984

Thompson, Charlotte. *Raising Handicapped Children*. New York: William Morrow, 1986.

for children
Exley, H. *What It's Like to Be Me*. New York: Friendship, 1984.

Lasker, J. *He's My Brother*. New York: Albert Whitman, 1974.

feeding and nutrition
Castle, Sue. *The Complete New Guide to Preparing Baby Foods*. New York: Bantam, 1983.

Castle, Sue. *Nutrition for Your Child's Most Important Years*. New York: Simon & Schuster, 1984.

Kitzinger, Sheila. *The Experience of Breastfeeding*. New York: Penguin, 1980.

La Leche League International. *The Womanly Art of Breastfeeding*. New York: New American Library, 1983.

Lauwers, J. *Breastfeeding Today*. Garden City, New York: Avery, 1986.

Lawrence, R. A. *Breastfeeding*. St. Louis: C. B. Mosby, 1985.

White, A. *The Complete Nutrition Guide for You and Your Baby*. New York: Ballantine, 1983.

sleep and bedtime
Cuthbertson, Joane, and Schevill, Susie. *Helping Your Child Sleep Through the Night*. Garden City, New York: Doubleday, 1985.

Dement, W. C. *Some Must Watch While Some Must Sleep*. New York: Norton, 1978.

Ferber, Richard. *Solve Your Child's Sleep Problems*. New York: Simon & Schuster, 1986.

HOME MEDICAL CARE

Bevan, James. *The Family First Aid and Medical Guide*. New York: Simon & Schuster, 1984.

Brace, Edward R., and Pacanowski, John P. *Childhood Symptoms*. New York: Harper & Row, 1985.

Brazelton, T. Berry. *Doctor and Child*. New York: Dell, 1986.

Pantell, Robert H., Fries, James F., and Vickery, Donald M. *Taking Care of Your Child: A Parent's Guide to Medical Care*. Reading, Massachusetts: Addison-Wesley, 1984.

Samuels, Mike, and Samuels, Nancy. *The Well Baby Book*. New York: Summit, 1979.

Simon, Gilbert, and Cohen, Marcia. *The Parent's Pediatric Companion*. New York: William Morrow, 1985.

for children:
Odor, R. *What's A Body to Do?* Elgin, Illinois: Childs World, 1981.

Roberts, S. *Nobody Cares About Me!* New York: Random House, 1982.

Rockwell, H. *My Doctor*. New York: Macmillan, 1973.

Scarry, R. *Richard Scarry's Nicky Goes to the Doctor*. Racine, Wisconsin: Western Publishing, 1978.

HOSPITAL STAYS

Hardgrove, C., and Dawson, R. *Parents and Children in the Hospital*. Boston: Little, Brown, 1972.

Howe, J. *The Hospital Book*. New York: Crown, 1981.

for children:
Bemelmans, Ludwig. *Madeline*. New York: Penguin, 1977.

Cilotta, C., and Livingston, C. *"Why Am I Going to the Hospital?"* Secaucus, New Jersey: Lyle Stuart, 1981.

Coleman, W. *My Hospital Book*. Minneapolis: Bethany, 1981.

Rey, H. A., and Rey, M. *Curious George Goes to the Hospital*. Boston: Houghton Mifflin, 1966.

Stein, S. *A Hospital Story*. New York: Walker, 1984.

GROWING CHILD

physical development
Brazelton, T. Berry. *Toddlers and Par-*

ents. New York: Dell, 1986.

Caplan, Frank. *The First Twelve Months of Life*. New York: Bantam, 1978.

Caplan, F., and Caplan, T. *The Second Twelve Months of Life*. New York: Bantam, 1980.

Fraiberg, Selma H. *The Magic Years*. New York: Charles Scribner's, 1984.

White, Burton L. *The First Three Years of Life*. New York: Avon, 1984.

communication

Berko-Gleason, J. *The Development of Language*. Columbus, Ohio: Merrill, 1985.

Hersor, L.A. *Language and Language Disorders in Children*. Elmsford, New York: Pergamon, 1980.

Speech Foundation of America. *If Your Child Stutters: A Guide for Parents*. Memphis: SFA, 1981.

thinking, learning, and playing

Ault, R. L. *Children's Cognitive Development*. 2d ed. New York: Oxford, 1983.

Azarnoff, P., and Flegal, S. *A Pediatric Play Program*. Springfield, Illinois: CC Thomas, 1980.

Bower, T.G.R. *Development in Infancy*. San Francisco: W. H. Freeman, 1974.

Burtt, K., and Kalkstein, K. *Smart Toys*. New York: Harper & Row, 1981.

Flavell, J. H. *Cognitive Development*. Englewood Cliffs, New Jersey: Prentice-Hall, 1985.

Pulaski, Mary Ann. *Understanding Piaget*. New York: Harper & Row, 1980.

White, Burton L., Kaban, Barbara T., and Attanucci, Jane S. *The Origins of Human Competence: The Final Report of the Harvard Preschool Project*. Lexington, Massachusetts: D. C. Heath, 1979.

personality development

Gesell, Arnold. *Infant and Child in the Culture of Today*. New York: Harper & Row, 1974.

Ginsburg, H., and Opper, S. *Piaget's Theory of Intellectual Development*. Englewood Cliffs, New Jersey: Prentice-Hall, 1979.

Ilg, Frances L., and Ames, Louise B. *Child Behavior*. New York: Harper

& Row, 1982.

Piaget, Jean. *The Child's Conception of the World*. Totowa, New Jersey: Littlefield, Adams, 1975.

Sants, J., and Butcher, H. J., eds. *Developmental Psychology and Society*. New York: St. Martin's, 1980.

Zimbardo, Philip G., and Radl, Shirley L. *The Shy Child*. New York: McGraw-Hill, 1982.

FAMILY MATTERS

working parents and child care

Dreskin, William, and Dreskin, Wendy. *The Day Care Decision*. New York: M. Evans, 1983.

Glickman, Beatrice M., and Springer, Nesha B. *Who Cares for the Baby? Choices in Child Care*. New York: Schocken, 1979.

Norris, Gloria, and Miller, Jo Ann. *The Working Mother's Complete Handbook*. New York: New American Library, 1984.

stress and separation

Fassler, J. *Helping Children Cope: Managing Stress Through Books and Stories*. New York: Free Press, 1978.

Jewett, C. *Helping Children Cope with Separation and Loss*. Washington: ACCH Clearinghouse, 1982.

adding to family

Friedrich, Elizabeth, and Rowland, Cherry. *The Parent's Guide to Raising Twins*. New York: St. Martin's, 1984.

McNamara, Joan. *The Adoption Adviser*. New York: Hawthorn, 1975.

Paris, Erna. *Step-Families: Making Them Work*. New York: Avon, 1985.

CHILD'S HEALTH ENCYCLOPEDIAS

Boston Children's Medical Center. *Child Health Encyclopedia*. New York: Dell, 1986.

Pomerantz, Virginia, and Schultz, Dodi. *The Mothers' and Fathers' Medical Encyclopedia*. New York: New American Library, 1978.

GENERAL INFORMATION

Boston Women's Health Book Collec

tive. *Ourselves and Our Children*. New York: Random House, 1978.

Burck, Frances W. *Babysense*. New York: St. Martin's, 1979.

Eden, Alvin N. *Positive Parenting: How to Raise a Healthier and Happier Child*. New York: New American Library, 1982.

Gordon, Thomas. *P.E.T.: Parent Effectiveness Training*. New York: New American Library, 1975.

Leach, Penelope. *Your Baby and Child*. New York: Alfred A. Knopf, 1981.

Neville, Helen, and Hallaby, Mona. *No-Fault Parenting*. New York: Facts on File, 1984.

Pogrebin, Letty C. *Growing Up Free*. New York: Bantam, 1981.

Spock, Benjamin, and Rothenberg, Michael Ь. *Baby and Child Care*. Rev. ed. New York: Pocket Books, 1985.

Baby records

Use this page to plot your baby's weight and height and to record the dates on which immunizations were given. The tinted areas on the graphs show the range between "large" and "small" babies. Don't expect your baby to follow the curves exactly. Space has been provided for the immunization records for two children. Using different colored pencils on the growth charts will distinguish between children there.

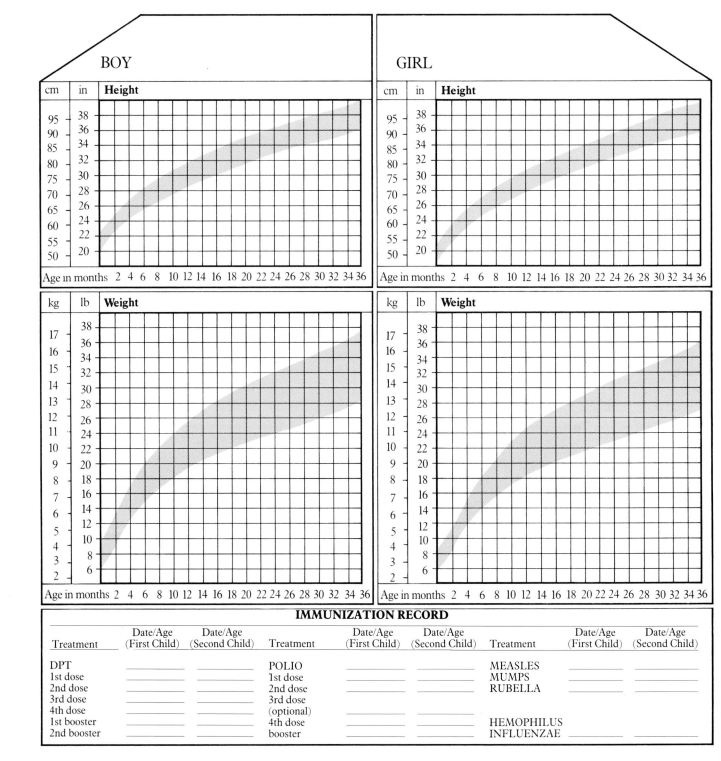

IMMUNIZATION RECORD

Treatment	Date/Age (First Child)	Date/Age (Second Child)	Treatment	Date/Age (First Child)	Date/Age (Second Child)	Treatment	Date/Age (First Child)	Date/Age (Second Child)
DPT			POLIO			MEASLES		
1st dose			1st dose			MUMPS		
2nd dose			2nd dose			RUBELLA		
3rd dose			3rd dose					
4th dose			(optional)					
1st booster			4th dose			HEMOPHILUS		
2nd booster			booster			INFLUENZAE		

234

ACKNOWLEDGMENTS

The publisher extends special thanks to the following individuals for their endless patience and assistance with photographs: Sally Connelly, Adam and Charlotte; Maud da Rocha and Rowena; Sue and Bruce Degnam, Josie and Oliver; Siobhan Haley and Vivienne; Julia Nicholson, Becky and Hannah; the Pinner Parkside Playgroup; Georgina Steeds and Tony Armolea; Clare Walker; and especially to Sam and Edward Eddison

ARTISTS

T=Top B=Bottom M=Middle L=Left R=Right

David Ashby 14T, 14B, 29TL, 29LM, 35T, 52BL, 56L, 56-7T, 56-7B, 58-9, 72T, 75, 82, 90T, 121, 130, 131, 141, 165, 173, 208, 214, 217BL, 226; Brian Bull (retouching) 23B, 50-1M, 115, 188, 197; Chris Chapman (Spectron Artists) 13, 27, 28, 184-5; Claire Davies 34-5B; Anthony Duke 31MR, 232; Andrew Farmer 17, 46-7, 50T, 51TR, 83B, 124, 133, 149, 166-7, 186; Industrial Art Studio (David Lewis Artists) 30, 31TR, 31BR, 34T, 36-7T, 39B, 49; Dee McLean and Clive Spong (Linden Artists) 20B, 50B, 51TL, BL, BR, 52BR, 86B, 88L, 90T, 102B, 112, 201, 206, 209, 211, 217BR, 217MR, 220, 221, 222, 223, 224, 227

PHOTOGRAPHIC CREDITS

T=Top B=Bottom M=Middle L=Left R=Right

Malcolm Aird prelims and section openers, 179, 198; Art Directors Photo Library 123, 146B, 177, 200; Daily Telegraph Colour Library: William Strode 22T; Nick Eddison 188; Mary Evans Picture Library 184T; Sally and Richard Greenhill Photo Library 44, 48, 61, 68 (SENSE), 70, 98, 126B, 163B, 164R, 175, 187; Susan Griggs Agency Ltd: Sandra Lousada 132, 135T, 203, Dick Rowan 195, Patrick Ward 142; Jessop Acoustics 152; King's College Hospital 22B; Trannies: Liz Eddison 89, 91, 103, 107, 116, 118, 119, 120, 122, 124, 125T, 125B, 127, 129T, 129B, 137B, 139, 146T, 148, 151, 153, 156, 157, 158, 160, 161, 163T, 174L, 174R, 176, 182, 193, 196; Vision International 144: S. Cunningham 169, Anthea Sieveking 10, 21, 23, 42, 50, 52, 53, 56, 65, 69, 71, 72, 73, 79, 86, 92, 94, 96, 104, 109, 126T, 133, 135BL, 135BR, 137T, 140, 145, 154, 164L, 171L, 171R

The chart on page 150, originally entitled "How Does Your Child Hear and Talk," was developed by Psi Iota Xi Sorority, Indianapolis, Indiana, and the American Speech-Language-Hearing Foundation, Rockville, Maryland, and was adapted herein with permission of the National Association for Hearing and Speech Action, Rockville, Maryland, © copyright 1983.